A Soldier Gone to Sea

A Soldier Gone to Sea
Memoir of a Royal Marine in Both World Wars

CHARLES FREDERIC JERRAM

Edited by Donald F. Bittner

McFarland & Company, Inc., Publishers
Jefferson, North Carolina

LIBRARY OF CONGRESS CATALOGUING-IN-PUBLICATION DATA

Names: Jerram, Charles Frederic, 1882–1969, author. | Bittner, Donald F., editor.
Title: A soldier gone to sea : memoir of a Royal Marine in both world wars / Charles Frederic Jerram ; edited by Donald F. Bittner.
Description: Jefferson, North Carolina : McFarland & Company, Inc., Publishers, 2016. | Includes bibliographical references and index.
Identifiers: LCCN 2016014243 | ISBN 9780786446186 (softcover : acid free paper) ∞
Subjects: LCSH: Jerram, Charles Frederic, 1882–1969. | World War, 1914–1918—Personal narratives, British. | World War, 1939–1945—Personal narratives, British. | Great Britain. Royal Marines—Biography. | Marines—Great Britain—Biography.
Classification: LCC D640 .J46 2016 | DDC 359.9/6092—dc23
LC record available at http://lccn.loc.gov/2016014243

BRITISH LIBRARY CATALOGUING DATA ARE AVAILABLE

ISBN (print) 978-0-7864-4618-6
ISBN (ebook) 978-1-4766-2406-8

© 2016 Donald F. Bittner. All rights reserved

No part of this book may be reproduced or transmitted in any form or by any means, electronic or mechanical, including photocopying or recording, or by any information storage and retrieval system, without permission in writing from the publisher.

Front cover: Lieutenant Colonel Charles Frederic Jerram, CMG, DSO Royal Marines; photo circa First World War (© Trustees RMM); "Royal Marine Battalion" on parade in white uniforms, helmets, and with rifles, composed of detachments from ships on the China Station at Wei-Hai-Wei, 1909 (© Trustees RMM)

Printed in the United States of America

McFarland & Company, Inc., Publishers
Box 611, Jefferson, North Carolina 28640
www.mcfarlandpub.com

This work is dedicated
to my wife, Jean, and daughter, Sharon Lynne,
who have seen it evolve over the years,
and supported the endeavors to bring
Lieutenant Colonel Jerram's life
to later generations.

Contents

Acknowledgments (Donald F. Bittner) ix
A Note on Illustrations (Donald F. Bittner) xi
Preface by Donald F. Bittner 1

1. Prologue—Early Life 9
   Early Days 9
   We Move to Cornwall 11
   A Brief Description of Talland 12
   The Road to Looe 13
   "Doddites" (Hillside) 14
   Excursions and Discoveries 16

2. Joining the Royal Marines, 1901–04 20

3. The Mediterranean Fleet, 1904–06 33

4. China Station, 1907–10 43
   To China, 1907 43
   Shanghai, 1907–10 54

5. Marking Time, 1910–14 68

6. War at Sea, 1914 78

7. Gallipoli, 1915 87

8. The Western Front, I—1915–18 97
   With the Marines in France, 1915–16 97
   With the Army: The 31st Division, 1917 100
   With the Army: XIII Corps, 1917–18 104

9. The Western Front, II—1918 109
   With the 46th (North Midland) Division 109
   Open Warfare, 1918 119

10. Between the Wars, 1919–40 125
Staff College, Camberley 125
Back to the Sea 130
Between the Wars, 1922–40 137
Pensioned Off 142

11. Epilogue—World War II and Beyond, 1940–69 144
Back to the Regiment: World War II 144
The End 149

APPENDICES

*I. Lieutenant Colonel Jerram: An Historian's Assessment of an Officer
    and His Career (Donald F. Bittner)* 153
II. Career Chronology 170
*III. Service Career of Lieutenant Colonel Charles Frederic Jerram,
    CMG, DSO, RM, as Drafted by Him* 174
IV. War and Other Services of My Family 176
V. [World] War [II] Services of My Wife's and My Own Family 177
VI. Abbreviations 178
VII. Royal Marine Light Infantry Batch, 1 September 1901 180
VIII. Status of Divisions on the Western Front, 11 November 1918 182
IX. King George V Prize Recipients, 1914 to 1923 183
X. British Armoured Divisions of World War II 184

Notes 187
Essay on Sources 213
Index 219

Acknowledgments

Preparing the Jerram memoir for publication is an achievement I could not have accomplished alone. Six individuals must be cited for their support, counsel, and help which ensured the project's completion: The late Major General James L. Moulton, CB, DSO, OBE, a friend of Lieutenant Colonel Jerram who initially saw the value in publishing this memoir and passed the task to me; Major Alastair Donald, RM, recently deceased, and Captain Derek Oakley, MBE, RM; Bridget E. J. Spiers and Matthew Little, both formerly the librarians and archivists at the Royal Marines Museum; and the late Alan J. Francis of the Royal Navy's Naval Historical Branch.

Essential to bringing the memoir to "life" has been the support over the years of the Royal Marines Museum, Eastney. Its staff ensured that I had full access to its archives and library, plus responded to many inquiries: Major Robert Bruce, OBE, the current director, and his two predecessors, Chris Newberry and Colonel Keith Wilkins, OBE; the aforementioned Bridget Spiers and Matthew Little, librarians and archivists, and their successor, Amy Adams; three photo archivists, Eddie Bartholomew, John Ambler, and Alison Firth; and Susan Lindsay, former curator of artifacts and now curator of the Museum of Army Flying at Middle Wallop. Also, two editors of *The Globe and Laurel*, the journal of the Corps, Captain Oakley and then his successor, Captain A. G. Newing, Royal Marines, were most generous in discussions on the Corps and its history and sub-culture.

In Britain, the staffs of other archives and libraries provided assistance so necessary to completing this work: the National Archives (formerly the Public Record Office); the National Maritime Museum, Greenwich; the libraries of the former Royal Naval College, Greenwich, and Army Staff College, Camberley; the School of Infantry, Warminster; the Royal Military Academy Sandhurst; the Britannia Royal Naval College, Dartmouth; the Royal United Services Institute; and the Army and Navy Club ("The Rag") and the Naval and Military Club (the "In and Out"), both in London. Specific individuals must also be mentioned: Dr. Geoffrey Till and Stuart Thomson, MBE, of the British Joint Services Command and Staff College, Shrevenham; the late Dr. David Chandler, former head of the Department of War Studies, the Royal Military Academy Sandhurst; and, in the United States, the staff of the Alfred M. Gray Research Center of the Marine Corps University, Quantico, Virginia, especially David Brown, Mary Porter, and Patricia Lane;

Lieutenant Colonel Humphrey M. Wilson, MC, Royal Norfolk Regiment (retired); Lieutenant Colonel Bert Couetdic, French Army; and Royal Marine Exchange Officers on the staff of the Marine Corps University: Lieutenant Colonels John Weston, Michael Phillips, Nick Vaux, Pat Howgill, Jake Hensman, Mark Gosling, Peter Ward, Roger Lane, Henk DeJager, Paddy George, Colin Beadon, John Herring, and Edward Musto.

Over the years, five individuals have provided both counsel and candid opinions on various versions of the manuscript and their support is very much appreciated: Dr. Dennis Showalter, Colorado College; Dr. Raymond Callahan, University of Delaware; Dr. Anne Cipriano Venzon, independent scholar; A. Kerry Strong, archives director (retired), Alfred M. Gray Research Center; and Mrs. Linda Rohler, operations officer (retired), Marine Corps College and Staff College. Colonel G.E. "Ed" Smith, USMC (retired), has over time consistently provided professional and personal encouragement in many ways too numerous to mention.

Also, a special note of appreciation to Major General Julian Thompson, CB, OBE, of the Royal Marines. During one of several meetings at the Army and Navy Club, in a discussion over tea, he suggested a solution to the challenge of a title for the edited memoir. This became "A Soldier Gone to Sea"—which succinctly and accurately captured the essence of the Corps during Lieutenant Colonel Jerram's active service.

Research support from two sources has helped ensure the completion of this project. The American Philosophical Society provided two research grants, through which the memoir was discovered and work commenced. Research grants from the Marine Corps University Foundation funded subsequent research trips to Britain, without which this endeavor could never have been completed.

Finally, I must mention the silent support of my wife, Jean, and our daughter, Sharon Lynne, given to me as I worked on "Colonel Jerram." They remained at their homes in the United States and Great Britain while research trips were made to and within England, or in other rooms of their houses while I was typing, editing, revising, and proofreading. They never uttered a word of complaint, and tolerantly listened to comments or watched me depart and return as the task consumed time and energy. Without their understanding, Lieutenant Colonel Jerram would never have been able to "speak" to us today.—Donald F. Bittner

A Note on Illustrations

Most of the photographs accompanying the text are, unless otherwise noted, from the Jerram personal papers and photo albums held in the archives of the Royal Marines Museum, Eastney, Southsea, Portsmouth, Hampshire, England; the several photographs of officers with whom Jerram served are from the museum's photographic collections. The Royal Marines Museum retains the copyright to these pictures. These images have been reproduced with the kind permission of the trustees of the Royal Marines Museum and are identified by © Trustees RMM in brackets after appropriate captions.

These photographs are from before and after the First World War, as Lieutenant Colonel Jerrams's personal papers, although quite voluminous, contained no photographs from that conflict. However, his commentaries, reflections, and descriptions for 1914 to 1918 vividly describe where and what he experienced during the Great War—and his reactions thereto. Since I opted not to use photographs from other sources for those years, I mention the following published volumes (each in a series) from the years of the First World War. They have extensive photographs, illustrations, and maps (as well as contemporary accompanying commentary reflecting when published) pertaining to the operations and localities of that conflict in which Jerram served. The point in citing these are the photographs and illustrations in each volume.

(1) The Times, *The Times History of the Great War* (London: The Times, 1914–1921), Volumes I to XXII.

(2) J.A. Hammerton, ed., *The War Illustrated: A Pictorial Record of the Conflict of Nations* (London: The Amalgamated Press Ltd., 1914–1919), Volumes I to VIII.

(3) H.W. Wilson and J.A. Hammerton, eds., *The Great War: The Standard History of the All European Conflict* (London: The Amalgamated Press Ltd., 1914–1919), Volumes I to XIII.

(4) Sir J.A. Hammerton, ed., *A Popular History of the Great War* (London: The Fleetwood House, 1933), Volumes I to VI.

With regard to the areas which Jerram considered "home" before and after the Great War, a published four-volume series on the counties of Britain appeared during his period of active service. This provides commentary with many supporting photographs of where most of his time ashore was spent: Walter Hutchinson, ed., *Hutchinson's Britain Beautiful*, Vol. I (London, circa 1920), notably

(a) "Cornwall," pp. 425–476; and
(b) "Devonshire," pp. 517–552.

For Royal Marine officers mentioned by name or in a general reference who can be identified, basic career information has been provided. However, photographs of these officers are limited due to one basic reason: The archives of the Royal Marines Museum have few in their possession. The journal of the Corps, *The Globe and Laurel*, transferred its collection of photographs to the museum many years ago. Although that journal printed obituaries of most of the officers of the Corps with whom Jerram served, some brief and others lengthy, few of these included an accompanying photograph. Where available, these have been included.

A limited number of photographs from other sources have also been used. The sources for these photographs are also included in brackets after the captions.

—Donald F. Bittner

Preface
by Donald F. Bittner

Why Another Memoir?

Why another memoir about the late Victorian to World War II eras? Are there not enough either already in print or appearing during the centennial of the First World War? Indeed, there are many memoirs of the famous and powerful, the decision makers and celebrities; also, in recent and coming years, especially with the centennial of the First World War, there have been and will be those of troops in the ranks, preceded by and since the interwar era of junior officers who served for the duration of that seminal event of the 20th century: The Great War.[1] How to understand what occurred during that conflict? For decades down to the spring of 2016, much of the view of that war has been dominated by the young, well-educated company grade officers—especially the "young poets." These have also been augmented by various diaries and memoirs that have appeared of men serving in the ranks, and books by historians who have adopted the "bottom up" approach to what occurred. Then, of course, there were the memoirs of the major military and political leaders which began to appear shortly after the war.

All such writings are valuable in various ways, especially as the decades have passed and all of the veterans of the First World War are now deceased. Conscious memories have passed with them, and we are now within the centennial of that cataclysmic event of the early 20th century. How are succeeding generations to understand what happened to both professional and "for the duration of the war" military personnel before, during, and after their service? Historian Gordon Corrigon succinctly addressed this issue in his insightful introduction to his *Mud, Blood and Poppycock: Britain and the First World War* (2003):

> As experience of war recedes—and anyone who was old enough to take part in the Second World War is in their seventies now—and when no one under the age of sixty has any experiences of National Service, it cannot be surprising that the great majority of the British people [and other nationalities] have no understanding of war or any insight into what an army [or navy or air force] does and how it operates.[2]

Even with recent combat operations in the Balkans, Iraq, and Afghanistan, Corrigon's comment is valid as fewer and fewer citizens serve in most nations' armed forces. Note also Corrigon's use of the phrase National Service (or, in the terminology of the United States, conscription or the draft), and his point becomes even a more valid one.

However, there is another type of memoir penned by another type of individual: That of the observant and insightful professional field grade officer who, at a mature and reflective stage of his life, decided to write about his experiences—officers whose careers and assignments placed them in positions to participate, observe, reflect, and then produce such commentaries. Such voices add different perspectives and perceptions to our understanding of conflict and the context of an era. Or, as noted in a recent bulletin of the Napoleonic Society, "Soldiers' memoirs are particularly fertile ground for new analysis. Not only do they provide us with the unrivalled accounts of experience of battle and campaign, they also shed key light on thematic questions regarding concepts such as fear, honour, masculinity, nationality etc."[3]

Lieutenant Colonel Charles Frederic Jerram, CMG, DSO, RM, was one such officer—who during his career in peace and war participated in diverse events and associated with significant personages. However, he was not of such a high rank, i.e., general or flag officer, to defend controversial decisions, nor to say, "If you had only followed my counsel, the outcome would have been different." His memoir is thus a candid and personal account of his life and military career, privately written with no goal of publication but with forthright observations and opinions.

Jerram's account begins with an interesting backward glance into a middle- to upper-middle-class childhood in the late Victorian era. What he did as a young boy, linked to the assumptions of his parents on such matters as safety and responsibility, are in stark contrast to the dangers and pressures, imagined or real, of childhood of the late 20th and early 21st centuries. His early boyhood is also significant for another reason: A military leader, especially one who makes the profession of arms his lifelong calling, must have confidence in himself and his abilities. Jerram's youthful experiences can be seen as the foundation for his subsequent military career success as a commander and staff officer, in war and peace, on land and at sea, and as a leader and trainer of men. His upbringing nurtured the traits of independence, self-reliance, confidence, judgment, and a love of the outdoor life. All of these were (and are) essential for a successful Marine officer, especially a "soldier gone to sea"—a calling that required two types of professional approaches, skills, expertise, and understanding merged into one person with extensive service both afloat and ashore, within one's own service, the Army, and allies.

In 1901, the Royal Marines thus accessioned a young man with the personality traits for a military career; training, education, and opportunity developed him into a professional officer who succeeded in his many diverse assignments. This memoir of Lieutenant Colonel Jerram thus provides insight into Royal Marines officer training, duties, and mess life of the early 20th century. Although records can give school names, course titles, class listings, instructor names, and hours taught, he conveys in his own words exactly what a young officer really encountered in his entry into "The Service," followed by his early postings once initial training and education had been completed. Stated another way, this is a record of how he reacted to the military life in Britain's pre–First World War Royal Marines and service with the Royal Navy, for the Corps was indeed part of Britain's naval establishment and since 1755 has been viewed as such.

Jerram thus provides interesting insight into the Royal Navy of the early 20th century. His perspective is that of a Royal Marine devoted to both of Britain's maritime services. He describes the last vestiges of the Victorian navy, still with some age of sail traditions but becoming technologically modern with its new, but often unreliable, equipment and machinery. Amid this, he addresses the perpetual issue associated with Marines in the early 20th century: What was their role in a service still tied to attitudes and traditions of the late 19th century? What were they to do when afloat? What were the specific duties of Marine officers and troops aboard ship and when ashore? Should they even be aboard ship?

The imperial focus of *Pax Britannia* is also seen, as is the rising specter of the naval and colonial challenge of Imperial Germany (and, in the background, Japan). Jerram thus takes us into the early 20th century "China Station"—a world which disappeared decades ago with the passage of time and through the changes associated with political, social, economic, and ideological revolutions, coupled with the consequences of major national and civil wars. Whether it is the life of Europeans, especially the British, in the Far East, acquiring intelligence information on German military positions at Tsingtao on the Shantung peninsula, the changing Imperial Chinese Navy, or his stark assessments of the Japanese in Korea, this imperial age lives again through his own words.

However, the heart of this memoir is the First World War. With regard to that conflict, David Lloyd George in his insightful memoir of the Great War significantly commented that of all the prominent ministers of the warring powers involved in that catastrophic event, he was the only one to hold significant decision making government positions from before its beginning through the conflict and to Armistice Day.[4] At the tactical level of war, Lieutenant Colonel Jerram, like many others, could likewise have said something similar with respect to his service at sea and on land, in Europe and Asia, in many and increasing positions of responsibility under fire. From his individual perspective, Jerram writes a personal and professional account about what occurred—while sparing the reader many of the descriptive horrific details of combat at sea and on land—but conveying the stress and pressures attendant to a person in combat on the individual level as well as in command or significant staff positions responsible for both operations and the lives of men.

Thus, Jerram approaches his service in the Great War from three perspectives: The war at sea in 1914, followed by Gallipoli in 1915, and then into the Western Front between 1915 and 1918. He served at sea with the Royal Navy, with the Royal Naval Division in the Dardanelles and in France, and finally with the British Army on the Western Front. In succinct and gripping prose, he recounts the war in its many manifestations: good and bad, honorable and dishonorable, successful and calamitous, victory and defeat. He describes himself and his men, peers, seniors, and subordinates in diverse situations and environments. Jerram recounts and depicts the vast array of human experience and emotion of combat and how a person is affected by the role of chance and luck, good and bad leadership, exemplary and inadequate staff functioning, aptitude and bungling, with all of this linked to the changing character of war at sea and on the ground between 1914 and 1918. In the midst of these great evolutions, British service relations and poignant evaluations of allies (both individual and national), both positive and negative, are articulated. His writing is such that just enough detail is provided for understanding, but without excessive particulars which would obscure comprehension.

Insight into the transitional character of World War I is thus clearly delineated, from changes in combat at sea and tactical command and communication problems ashore to the increased lethality of weapons on the battlefield and problems attendant to hastily raised and committed ground forces. Amid this, universal lessons appear which all military leaders are taught from initial entry into the armed forces which Jerram continually stressed in his accounts of combat in the "war to end all wars." These range from not "bunching up" when in combat to "looking after your men." These observations are textbook examples for young leaders and scholars; as with all principles, these must be constantly reiterated as they are too often forgotten.

Finally, Jerram discusses his postwar career and life. With respect to the Royal Marines, the central question of their role (or of Marines of any nation) is raised both directly and indirectly. If the traditional tasks and organization of Britain's "Soldiers of the Sea" were outmoded, what was the Corps' place in Britain's defence establishment? How was it to be reformed and modernized? He addresses these crucial questions in two ways: Indirectly through his postwar postings which reflected a return to pre-war ways, and directly in his views via a paper on proposed changes to his Corps submitted in 1924 to the Madden Committee studying the mission and function of the Royal Marines. Jerram then briefly wrote of his initial retirement and recall to active service during World War II. Here, he notes the differences between the Great War and the Second World War. Lastly, he succinctly comments on the post–1945 era, providing a glimpse of a Britain undergoing major changes which he obviously disliked. However, as a veteran of both World Wars I and II, and a defender of Great Britain's interests, had he not earned the right to assess, critique, and articulate his disapproval? Notably, with the passage of time his commentary is now more than a half a century old—hence his remarks reflect both his personal values and a Britain of the initial two post-war decades—all now part of history.

A century ago as today, acquiring the skills and understanding to comprehend and work within and outside of an officer's own service is more easily said than done. In a pre-war article published in 1915, a Royal Navy contemporary of Jerram's adroitly commented on this issue when he wrote in *The Naval Review* about potential friction between officers of ground and maritime forces when they operate together, especially under the stress of war:

> The difference between the officers of the two services is really slight, and exists mainly in external details, but these details may very easily give rise to misconceptions on either side. The main point to remember is that the difference exists, and that it has often in the past caused the two services some little difficulty in understanding one another. In any place where they have opportunities for mixing, a clear and cordial mutual understanding is soon arrived

at. But superficially, when brought suddenly into contact as they might be in war, I believe that each service is seriously hampered at the outset by lack of knowledge of the other.[5]

For Jerram, these issues would arise more within his own naval service and Corps than when he served with the Army. Regardless, he was a consummate professional at sea and on land, excelling in the attributes and understanding of both ground and naval duty and arms at the tactical level of war.

A final note. Lieutenant Colonel Jerram came from a family of extensive service, direct and indirect, to Britain. Of these many talented and dedicated members of his family over several generations, only three have been included in the *Oxford Dictionary of National Biography* (2004): His grandfather, a noted Church of England cleric, Charles Jerram (1770–1853); his uncle, Admiral Sir (Thomas Henry) Martyn Jerram (1858–1933), who commanded the 2nd Battle Squadron at Jutland; and Jerram himself, Lieutenant Colonel Charles Frederic Jerram, RM (1882–1969).[6] As his entry in that seminal reference work concluded, "His own professionalism, courage, and abilities enabled him to function well not only in the marines, but working alongside the army and navy as well. He personified the best traditions of Britain's armed forces."[7]

Jerram's Manuscript

Lieutenant Colonel Jerram wrote his memoir in the 1960s. He titled it simply "The Life of Lt.-Colonel Charles Frederic Jerram, CMG, DSO, Royal Marines." The manuscript is retained in the archives of the Royal Marines Museum, Eastney, Southsea, Portsmouth, Hampshire, England (ARCHIVES 11/13/206). In the original draft, it consists of 313 numbered and single-spaced pages, with three short appendices. The initial 30 are typed, the remainder handwritten with a fountain pen. Significantly, Jerram wrote candidly and from the heart. He is both critical and laudatory of statesmen, institutions, officers, men, ships, units, nationalities, and trends. When warranted in his opinion, his negative critiques are candid, if not harsh and judgmental, but where merit is deserved, equally praiseworthy and why.

This approach only adds to the value of his observations and assessments. Readers may disagree with what Jerram says, but there is no doubt about his views on any issue. Some readers may be surprised at what Jerram has to say; for example, Churchill was not one of his favorites and he explicitly says why. He had caustic opinions about what he saw of the Japanese in the Far East. His commentaries on leadership and courage are blunt, and military professionals, scholars, students, and the general reader can comprehend and learn from the positive and negative examples he cites. Equally important is Jerram's enlightened commentary on proper or poor functioning of headquarters and individual officers who served in them. Candor abounds in his text, as does the obvious mixture of traditional military values and customs coupled with changes in society and the forces which effected the profession of arms and war in the "modern" era … or throughout his life and career.

After the memoir there is a general overview of Jerram's life written by an historian, i.e., the editor. *No material from the memoir was used in preparing this*. Rather, it is based on documentation from other sources written by Jerram or about him. It is important for providing context, further background to events or views mentioned by him in his memoir, or more details on various subjects or issues. Other appendices are included to provide contextual and factual information to the memoir on matters directly or indirectly raised by Jerram—the details or specifics of which he did not provide himself.

Editing the Jerram Memoir

The approach to editing the memoir can be simply stated: Essentially, Jerram would speak for himself, so the memoir is presented as he wrote it. However, several caveats must be noted. His manuscript was a rough draft. Punctuation and capitalization had to be standardized; this has been done without changing the meaning, detracting from theme and ambience, or affecting Jerram's communication with the reader. Material then had to be divided into paragraphs and, in some instances, shifted to ensure a more logical sequence and better comprehension of what was intended. Where words have been added or a change was necessary for clarity, these are indicated by brackets. Jerram also divided his manuscript into 23 chapters. These have been reduced to 11 with his titles; however, his organization has been retained through the use of sub-chapters with their—i.e., his—titles, as appropriate. Where material has been edited out, this is mentioned in a note and the reason given; this is

Handwritten title page of Jerram's memoir, with his original title, chapter numbers and titles, and page numbering. Note the title of Chapter XXIII; he often referred to the Corps as a "regiment" [© Trustees RMM].

especially true of his life before entering the Royal Marines, as excessive local detail has been pruned although the essence of these key formative years has been retained. None of this alters the memoir in any meaningful way; significantly, the original manuscript is available in the archives of the library at the Royal Marines Museum, Eastney, Southsea, Hampshire, England.

The events portrayed and the factual data presented in the text, as well as the views, opinions, commentary, perspectives, and analyses, are those of Lieutenant Colonel Jerram. Factual statements are as written by him, but if an error has occurred a correction is made in the notes; however, such are rare as Jerram used reference material retained from his long years of service. Other primary and secondary sources consulted in the editing and for the editor's notes confirmed his accuracy.

I have provided notes for each chapter, and accept responsibility for their content and accuracy. Jerram included none in his memoir. However, in editing the manuscript, certain commentary and citation notes were deemed necessary. These include the definitions of Marine, naval, military, sailing, and other terms encompassing the military subculture of the past and current eras; the location of sites, and elaboration on events, personages, books, and trends mentioned by Jerram; details on specific ships and their classes; identification of military units noted in the account of World War I; and literature on some events pertinent to his life or in which Jerram participated which the reader might find of interest. Generally, all persons mentioned by Jerram, either by name or billet, have been identified—with more information provided for Royal Marines since the Corps was Jerram's parent "regiment" (as he often called it). Except for an obviously known personage, if no identification was possible no notation is made—but such instances are rare. Generally, reference citations have been avoided except in the instances where such were deemed appropriate to place matters in context and, as deemed appropriate, to refer the reader to publications which address an issue or subject raised in the work. *Ultimately, the memoir is Lieutenant Colonel Jerram speaking to us, candidly and clearly, about his personal and professional life, career, and events, major and minor, in which he had a part.* As such, it reflects his life, his service, his time—and that is its value. The reader can determine for himself or herself the relevance of this to both an understanding of the past or the 21st century.

Chapter 1

Prologue—Early Life

Early Days

A world nearer akin to medieval times than to the present. A world without aircraft, motors, telephones or wireless. A world of horses and carriages; houses great and houses small. And a world, so far as the English countryside was concerned, of happiness and content, whether squire, servant, farmer or labourer, shopkeeper or fisherman. Into this world I was born on the 13th of November 1882, at Frith Hill Cottage, Godalming [near Guildford], in Surrey.

My father was the eldest son of the Reverend Charles Samuel Jerram, Vicar of Chobham,[1] and my mother [Maria Florence], the elder daughter of Edward Knight of Papcastle in Cumberland. She had spent much of her childhood on Exmoor, then owned by her cousin Sir Frederic Knight.[2] On the verge of the great school of Charterhouse[3] was a preparatory school, Hillside. Or, to give it its unofficial name, "Doddites." At this time it was owned by a Mr. Curtiss, and for some years my father joined him. Later, however, he started a school of his own, called "Uskites" up the Peper Harrow Road, with a few boys. It is of this house that my memory begins. And that, only of a pram: My eldest sister [Posy] and I being wheeled down the road by our nurse, in a wooden three-wheeled pram, with wooden wheels and iron tyres.

But it is of our next house that my memories really commence. For Charterhouse bought "Uskites" over our heads for assistant masters, and we moved down the road to two semi-detached houses, which my father converted into one, and called it "Sunnyside." In general one side was occupied by our rapidly increasing family and the other by the boys. My father was assisted by a Mr. Jacques for mathematics, my father being a Classical M.A. of Oxford. By 1889 our household consisted of my parents, three boys and three girls, [and] a governess, nurse and nursemaid, cook, two servants, and a boot boy. A rough gardener came in three or four days a week. And there were six or seven pupils. Of these the governess stayed with the family until the last of us went to boarding school, one maid for many years, and the nurse till she was married in Cornwall. She remained a friend of the family till she died in 1960.

In addition to our garden, we also had the field opposite, which was used in a general way for games and hay. It ran down to the River Wey and is still unbuilt over [in

1961] except for the electricity poles which run up the valley. This field is bordered by a group of Pollard Willows, and these the boys turned into a continuous bridge by bending over and interlacing the branches. It is in this, I think, that I first appreciate[d] the amount of freedom we enjoyed. Neither of my parents seem to have suffered from a tendency to nerves, so common in modern parents. The boys—then and we later—were allowed to do all sorts of things which would have horrified most parents I now know. This bridge even we children used daily, when a fall would have meant broken bones at least. The reason is probably to be found in their own upbringing. My father was one of eight and had been brought up mainly in France during the Franco-Prussian War, and had later joined my mother's brother in his early canoeing expeditions around the north of France. This brother of my mother, E. F. Knight[4] was, by the time I was born, an explorer and navigator and was to become a great war correspondent for *The Times* and *Morning Post*. My mother also had run pretty wild on Exmoor and certainly never put anything in our way to being independent. At the same time, neither ever suggested anything, but left it to us to form our own character.

[Mother] was quite fearless and did all sorts of things in a perfectly natural way, which must have necessitated a good deal of courage. Old Mares, our jobbing handy man, spent most of his money on beer, and on one occasion he was cutting hay with a scythe. [She] took him some tea to find him just going to commence on a bottle of beer. She seized the bottle and broke it. Old Mares just looked sorrowfully at her and took the tea instead. I could not help feeling sorry for him. He was very fond of and good to us children, and worshipped my sister Winnie.

Then there was the tramps' lodging house in Godalming. At a time when labourers all drank more than enough, tramps, as can be imagined, were very rough indeed. My mother conceived the idea of reading to them once a week and chose "Black Beauty." How she started I cannot imagine, but it was not long before these evenings became famous and [the] tramps used to make a point of collecting there. On one occasion a newcomer, known as "Bloody Bill," arrived and started throwing his weight about, with a good deal of bad language. He was promptly suppressed by the remainder and, when order had been restored, my mother was begged to [go] on and "tell what 'appened to the little 'orse."

In those days Godalming parish church[5] was full at morning service and we sat in pews in the chancel, east of the choir. These seats have now been removed, being no longer required for a congregation loosely scattered over the nave. The bridge to the ringing chamber in the central tower used to intrigue me. When the bells stopped, eight to ten men in black Sunday suits used to, and still do, walk out over this bridge. They probably reentered by another door, but I never could think why they were being turned out. In 1960, I achieved my ambition to ring on those bells and walk out over the same bridge. My other memory is of the death of General [Charles George "Chinese"] Gordon [at Khartoum in 1885], as I discovered later. At the time I remember standing with the huge congregation listening in terror to a terrific thunderstorm as I conceived it, with intervals of soft music carrying our prayers for deliverance. It was the then famous organist, Mr. Mackintosh, playing the Dead March.

My father rode a "penny-farthing" bicycle, one of the old high wheelers, as did the postman. There was a letter box at the bottom of Charterhouse Hill and we used to run down there to meet the postman and beg a ride. One day we went to the Charterhouse sports and saw our first "safety" bicycles and one cushion tyre, very modern. My brother and I had an argument as to the purpose it served, and eventually came to the conclusion that it must be easier to balance. One other friend was the milkman, who let us ride on the milk float to the end of the road. These floats were two-wheeled carts, low on the ground, with high front and sides and no back. They normally carried two churns and had a small seat in the back for the driver, who, however, usually stood. The cob or pony had to be a steady one and always knew exactly at which houses they had to stop. As the milkman appeared from the back door of the house, the horse would move quietly on to the next without orders.

A boat on the River Wey, fun on the ice at Broadwater, and picnics by donkey cart to Cutmill and Forkey ponds about sum up my memories of Godalming other than a vivid memory of my first "school." Old Miss Quecy and her brother took [in] four or five children [as pupils]. She had long ringlets down each side of her face and we were desperately afraid of her. I believe she was really a very kindly old dame. He was a musician and composed hymn tunes, which my mother used to play on Sunday evenings.

We Move to Cornwall[6]

My mother's family owned several large houses in the North West of England. Among these was Downton Castle near Ludlow. Andrew Knight's heiress was a daughter, Charlotte, who married Rouse-Boughton of Downton Hall. He immediately annexed the Castle and took the name of Knight. This led to a law suit, to which all the Knights subscribed. After a long and tedious hearing, Rouse-Boughton won his case, though the judge kept back in Chancery 5,000 pounds in case of an appeal. One supposes that this 5,000 pounds still exists.

However, the case largely impoverished the family, and I think my mother must have been involved, as was her brother. As a consequence my parents looked for somewhere cheaper to live, and a more healthy upbringing for their family. They found the ideal in Talland Vicarage between Looe and Polperro on the southeast coast of Cornwall. The pupils, governess, nurse, and housemaid moved with us—this in the year 1890, when I was seven years old.

This seems a good place to introduce my brother Ralph.[7] Though eighteen months younger than I was, he was always the leader and adventurer, and this became characteristic of his whole life. It was he who organized the early morning "wrecking"[8] parties. He invented the first slings for rabbits and starlings. He, who skinned and cooked them; made our gunpowder; led the way up the cliffs and he who every so often challenged me to fight. For that I required a great deal of "Dutch courage," which I obtained by tightly lacing up my boots. To anticipate some twenty years on, when coming under fire for the first time, this is what I automatically did: Tighten up my boots.

The rest of the family [and household] consisted of three girls, Kitty (Posy), Winnie, and Muriel, and the youngest boy, Rowland. Another boy, Bertrand, was to be born the next year. For the rest we had those who had come with us from Surrey, and a new cook and tweeny maid, a gardener, and a boy. In addition, we had six resident pupils. How we all fitted in I've no idea. It's puzzled me ever since.

The house was fairly large, consisting of the main block and kitchen wing. One downstairs room became the governess' schoolroom and one upstairs the nursery. Exclusive of kitchens, large offices, and cellars, this left [the] drawing room, dining room, and my father's study downstairs, and six bedrooms up[stairs], in addition to two servants' rooms, which seemed to necessitate a jigsaw puzzle. Beyond this down the entrance drive was a large coach house, stable for two horses with [a] loft over, [a] coal house and tool house, and a yard with two pig sheds. The loft was given an outside staircase and converted to the pupils' classroom [with] the pighouses given to the donkey, later joined by another.

Ralph and I shared a small room at the back, facing north and some great elms. I don't think we were ever dry, night or day, but seem to have survived. There was, of course, no bathroom. Saturday was bath night when round tin baths were laid out on the floor and water brought up in great cans. Naturally, as many as possible shared one bath. The outside grounds were good, consisting of a field of two or three acres with a tennis lawn, plenty of garden, and very good supply of fruit trees. In effect, a quite ideal spot.

A Brief Description of Talland[9]

The Parish of Talland originally included the west side of Looe and east side of Polperro. But a few years previous to our arrival, West Looe had been incorporated in the new Parish of Looe, and [the] Lansallos side of Polperro into Talland. This gave the whole of Polperro to the Vicar of Talland, [who then] decided to live there and let the Vicarage. Below us the field descended steeply to the cliffs and a sandy bay, "Stinkard," which we renamed "Our Bay." Here there is an inlet in the rocks into which steps are cut to a rough path which [wound] up past our house, through the barton [farm-yard], and on into the country. There are, or were, holes in the rock for mooring boats and a small flat landing.

This is the old smugglers' landing and pack horse route, and the Talland ghost may well be the invention of the smugglers, though my brother Ralph was quite sure he once saw him. The ghost was that of Parson Doidge, a famous ghost layer in his day. He comes from one of the bedrooms, goes out to the stables for his horse, and drives devils down the cliff from 11 p.m. till midnight on stormy Sunday nights. He was firmly believed in by the people of Polperro and Looe, who would not dream of passing the house unaccompanied at night and who thought we were very brave people to live there. Rooting round the upper churchyard one day, Ralph and I found Parson Doidge's grave: A built-up grave with a slab on top. [But] it was very much broken and, as we found an adder's nest mixed up with it, we left it alone. However, we clearly made out the name and part of the inscription. Some years ago I looked for it, [but] in vain.

Polperro was as different as it could possibly be to its present state, a picnic ground for the North. It was inhabited almost entirely by fishermen and those on whom they were dependent, or who were dependent on them. There were no foreigners and, other than the Parson, no gentry. The few upper classes consisted of retired sailing ship captains and their dependents. But everyone in Polperro was related, and there were few surnames. As there were about 1,000 inhabitants, most of them were known by nicknames. The most famous house in Polperro was Couch's House, home of the famous Doctor Thomas Quiller Couch, Polperro's historian. This house also had a smuggler's hole under the post office counter in those days.

In the harbor there were some fifty or more boats, well worth a story of their own. The story of the pilchard industry is told in every book on Cornwall and needs no repetition. Suffice to say that there were two pilchard factories in Polperro, catering for the Italian market and that they were kept pretty busy, [and] the boats, or their rig, were unique.

The Road to Looe[10]

Across the road to Talland is the Barton, or old manor house. Here we were always welcome, and when going down for milk invariably received a big bright red apple. On the other side was the farm pond where we sailed our boats. There is a clockwork [wind-up] steamer of mine still at the bottom of this pond somewhere—for as we got older, Ralph and I had great battles between my lugger and his schooner, which involved a collision with the steamer in which she was sunk. This was later, after we went to school and acquired a liking for cannon and gunpowder. Making our own gunpowder, we would load our broadside guns. Then, with a homemade fuse, we would try and arrange [it] so that the guns would fire as the boats crossed each other on opposite tacks. My lugger to the end of her days had several shot holes in her hull.

[At] Looe, on the south side of the bridge one could see, beyond the schooners, a solid mass of luggers. There were about 120 belonging to the port, mackerel and pilchard boats. The big mackerel boats were always the cleanest fishing boats in the country, and the two or three now remaining still pride themselves on being so.

Over the bridge on the left hand side you['d] come to the Mastin's Coach office. We didn't have much to do with the coach until we went to school at about ten years of age. Until then we were taught at home, first by the governess and then joined my father's pupils. [The] return to school at Hillside, "Doddites," at Godalming in Surrey meant a pretty long day. Up by 6 a.m., we caught, groomed and harnessed the pony, and when there were two of us, the donkey as well. Then to dress and get breakfast and drive to Looe to catch the 8 a.m. bus. I hardly know what to call this vehicle. It was always known as "the bus," but it had room for three people alongside the driver, and a seat behind that holding five more. Behind that came the boxes and mail. And on the step the bugle boy. Inside were two seats [along] the whole length.

At 7:50 a.m. Robert, the coachman, appeared whip in hand, mounted the box, fastened his apron, slipped the brake and, with flourishes on the bugle, drove off downtown to the sea front, with a halt at the Looe Hotel. Having thoroughly wakened everyone up, we'd halt again at the post office to collect [the] mail, and were then really off. At Plymouth we changed to the London and South Western Railway to Woking, where we were always met by an old one-armed porter. Called Wright, an old friend of my mother, [he] saw us in to the Godalming train. Here were usually several other boys from London and the North, [and] at Godalming['s] new [station], we took hansom-cabs[11] to school.

Normally on the holidays we were left, boys and girls, to look after ourselves. Wrecking was always our chief pastime in the winter and, for me, still is. I simply cannot resist going round after a gale and picking up anything that might come in useful. As we got older we took possession of my father's muzzle loading gun, made our own powder, spent a few pence on shot and caps, and [then] went out after starlings and pigeons. [And then] there were parties. In the winter, children's parties at various country houses and vicarages, and in the summer tennis parties. The nearest we got to the tennis or tea was rolling the lawn, marking it, and retrieving balls. I've never managed to raise much enthusiasm for the game since. Finding room for all the horses and carriages was a problem, but the farm always helped us out.

"Doddites" (Hillside)

[This was] the preparatory school to which we all eventually went, of about 50 boarders [and] was on the Farmcoombe side of Godalming, close to the great public school of Charterhouse. Our playing field was surrounded on two sides by two of their houses, Robinsonites and Pageites. Officially we were "Hillside," but as Charterhouse houses were all named after their first house masters, so we called ourselves "Doddites" after a Mr. Dodd.

At the time I joined, it was kept by Mr. Curtiss, an old family friend, soon to retire, and Mr. Robinson. I suppose it was as different to a modern prep school as anything could be. I still look upon it as a fine man-making and character-building place, unlike the present rather namby-pamby affairs to which my sons and, still more, grandson went. For one thing, we were older. There was no boy under nine and the first eight year old came in my last term. We all thought him a baby, and I doubt if he would have survived my first term. But one has to remember that it was all much what we were used to. Hard beds, but [then] we had them at home. A fire only in the big schoolroom, but we only had one at home. There was, of course, no heating in the dormitories and no hot baths.

Meals were all taken in the big dining room at four long tables, with a horseshoe table on a dais at one end for the masters. The Headmaster only appeared at dinner. For those days the food was good and plentiful; but the boys [now] would probably go on strike if they got now what we did. Breakfast at 8 a.m.: Porridge, tea, bread, scrape [i.e., leftover remnants from previous meals] and, invariably, either cold beef or cold bacon. In summer we had an hour's work before it. It was some years before a boy came who had to have hot meals; and it wasn't long before it was found necessary to give them to us, too, in order to save his life! Dinner at 1 p.m., a good meat and pudding meal. A few boys even at this late period had beer.

Tea at 4 p.m. was tea, bread, and scrape only, unless you were lucky in your "Tuck Box." The tuck box was a great money saver for the Head. Every boy brought one, an oblong wooden box about 2'6" by 1'6" by 1'6", and what it contained depended entirely upon one's mother. They were kept in a basement to which we all had access, but on arrival at school all jams, potted meats, sardines, etc., were collected by "Ma" James, the Matron, and locked up in her room. If you wanted anything for tea you went to "Ma" and asked for a pot of your jam. According to how much had already gone out and how much you had, you got it or you didn't. Everything had to be finished at that meal. So, if you had a pot of jam out, you went round making swaps. The answer really was to induce your mother to pack your tuck box with many small pots rather than a few big ones. But even then, your lot was most often bread and scrape. At 8:30 p.m., we had a bit of bread and cheese, and [then] to bed.

In the morning, dormitory by dormitory, we repaired to the one bathroom, with one long bath filled with cold water, winter or summer, and a few round footbaths for the privileged mothers' darlings who had to have hot water. We did not belong to that class, [hence] had to go into and under the cold water, with Ma James ready with her hard hand to give you a smack on the bottom if you hesitated. Then into your clothes: Long trousers, dark grey coats, hard Eton collars, and round black and red striped capes. On Sundays we wore Eton suits[12] and top hats to church, but exchanged the hat for a cap in winter and straw in summer for the afternoon walk under the Serjeant.

The Serjeant, or "Savvy" as we called him, was a grand chap, and a credit to his late regiment, The East Surreys.[13] He wore a black braided uniform and the peaked cap of the period. He took us in gym, with horse, parallel bars and horizontal bars, dumbbell exercise, and wooden rifle drill. Nowadays much of it would be considered far too strenuous, especially the four pound dumbbells. But it never did any of us any harm. One other fine chap was the Surrey cricket pro, Street, who did his best to teach us the rudiments of the game. The Senior Master, Helmsley, didn't like me, but I never bore him any ill will. I still have a great admiration for him, though he wasn't always fair. I suppose that must be an impossibility in a prep school. One must get pretty fed up at times, but he was an outstanding character as compared with most others I have seen.

Cowie was a sadistic cad. His chief amusement was to make you lay your hand, palm down, on the desk and bring down the edge of a Revised Latin primer on the back of it. He also took to using his gold signet ring for the same purpose, and on one's head! However, he broke it at last and with it a bone in a boy's hand. That led to his undoing and he was replaced by Mr. Taylor, one of the wittiest men that ever lived. He was still at the school, beloved by everybody in 1928, when I was approached to act as Treasurer to a fund to give him a present. I think that it was hoped to raise about 50 pounds.

In the public school, with its Old Boys' Association, this would be a fairly simple task. But a private school merely has, with luck, the original address of the boys. And these addresses went back to 1895 when Mr. Taylor joined. I sent out about 300 original appeals, of which about 250 came back, address not known. However, with various aids I collected 750 pounds in about six months, and we gave the old man a fishing rod and cheque at a great rally of old boys at the school. No serving boy or his parent was allowed to subscribe unless the parent was an old boy himself. It gives a good idea of the feeling of generations of boys towards a great master.

Excursions and Discoveries[14]

For some reason or reasons we sometimes went away in the summer holidays. Whether to give the servants a holiday, or to improve our education, or both, I don't know. But we certainly saw a good deal of different kinds of life. When I was about nine years old, I was sent to stay with cousins, the Landers, who had a farm in Shropshire. The two boys were pupils of my father and, besides them, there were two girls more of my age. One of these, Lucy Landers, eventually was to become music mistress to the Royal Princesses, who nicknamed her "Goosey Gander," rather naturally.

[In the summer of 1893] we let the house and all went off to a house we took in London, Chiswick. Here we three elder ones, my sister Posy, Ralph, and I, aged about twelve, ten, and nine, were treated exactly as we were at home. With a few pence in our pocket, we went out after breakfast with orders to return by tea time, 5 o'clock. Our usual routine was to walk down to Turnham Green, where we caught a tram to the lower end of Kensington High Street. At one point the tram made a right angle turn, and having soon made friends with the driver we urged him to whip up the horses so as to take this turn at a screaming speed. The trip cost us one penny each, a bun at the shop at the top of Kensington High Street, another penny, and a glass of milk next door, another. The rest of the day we spent in Kensington Gardens, and then [we] took the tram back.

When I was 13 and Ralph 12, we all went to Honfleur in Normandy and lodged in the house where my grandfather had been English Chaplain, and where my father and mother had met. It must have been a nightmare move for our parents, with seven children from 14 downwards. Honfleur was my first introduction to the sailing ship at close quarters. There were always one or two British barques unloading timber, and Ralph and I used to clamber all over them. One captain was very good to us when he called us down from aloft and gave us good advice: "Go anywhere you like in this ship," he said, "for I know the gear is all sound. But there are plenty of ships that are not so well found. So test every ratline as you go, or stay down from aloft."

During this holiday, Ralph and I went off alone on a walking tour. The only instructions we had were: (1) We must avoid stopping at low auberges. I still wonder how we were supposed to know? (2) We had to do it on our own money. This was a bit of a teaser, when our school pocket money was six pence a week when not stopped, holiday money nil, and otherwise two shillings and six pence or two shillings from Granny at Christmas. (3) We were to contact the Lethbridges[15] at Ouistreham, near Caen. He was British vice consul, a cousin of sorts, and had an interest in the cross Channel to Caen steamers. At the Lethbridges we were made welcome and found not only the boy and girl of the family, but Bobby Bush and his brother, Tobin,[16] later to become an Admiral and [both] former pupils of my father.

Our expenses worked out at about one franc a day, [or] ten pence. For fifty centimes we always managed to get a bed between us. Then we'd walk about five miles to a convenient stream where we had stream water, half a roll of bread, and a bar of chocolate. The bread cost two sous and the chocolate the same, and three meals made up about the other half franc. We seem to have thrived on it. We went by the coast road through Trouville, and crossed the river and canal by the bridges made famous in World War II when the [British 6th] Airborne Division captured them in the Normandy landing [in 1944].

Just outside the house and along the front ran one of the innumerable miniature railways of France, with open sided carriages filled with fat ladies on their way to market in Caen. Mr. Lethbridge used to get English Vesta matches. French matches were terrible smelly sulphur ones. These matches with the cotton threads split back over the head made grand bombs, as we had discovered at home by hitting them with a hammer. We had the great idea of using the train as a hammer, and made about a dozen bombs and put them on the line just before the train came along. It was a grand show. The Negro driver roared with laughter, all the old ladies screamed, and everyone was pleased till the evening when the Gendarmes paid us a visit. However, even they treated it as a good joke but said we mustn't upset the old ladies again.

After three days we again set off on our travels and returned to Honfleur by way of Caen and Liseux, having been away about a fortnight. As far as Honfleur was concerned, provided that we went to church, we could go where we liked, and there we three elder ones usually preferred to go to the charming old church with the wooden tower. St. Catherine's, I think. We didn't understand much of the Roman Mass, I'm afraid, with its continental pronunciation. The two things I remember chiefly are that they had two sermons, one for children, and apparently two collections. When the wooden boxes came round the first time we put in our half franc, [with] much expostulation by the collector in rapid French. Eventually, when we tried to explain we simply hadn't any more, he held up one sou (halfpenny) and we realized at last that we had paid too much and were being charged one sou each for our seat! The collection came later. A year or two later, Ralph and I were sent to Honfleur again for the Easter holidays to polish up our French for Service Examinations.[17]

Whilst we were all at Chiswick my mother's cousin, Sir Frederic Knight and Lady Knight, had visited us.[18] The only thing I remember about it is that Frederic Knight was just going to show me the great wrestling throw known as the "Flying Mare" when Lady Knight dashed up and said, "you'll break the boy's neck." But a sequel to this was that my mother, Posy, and I went to stay with them at Wolverley House, near Kidderminster, [Worcestershire]. It was all very terrifying and I would much sooner have gone to their Simon's Bath House on Exmoor,[19] for at that time they owned most of the Moor. Just across the valley is Lea Castle, the residence of another Knight cousin; but I cannot remember going there. Downton Castle and Henley Hall were then owned by other branches. With the exception of Eric of Henley, who has descendants, they've all disappeared in that generation. With the early death of Frederic's son, he gave up his Exmoor improvements and sold it to Lord Fortescue. Wolverley is now a school. Lea Castle is a farm and belongs to Kidderminster town council. Henley was sold and Downton passed to the Rouse-Boughtons.

The year after going to Honfleur we all went to stay with our paternal grandmother and aunts in Worcester. Here Ralph and I set off to explore North Wales. Except that francs were shillings, we managed a fortnight at about the same cost as in France. On three successive days we walked 30, 33, and 31 miles, which is not bad for 13 and 14 year old boys. We had a certain amount of difficulty with the language because, as we were warned by a man we met on the road, the older people, even if they could [speak] English, always pretended they couldn't, and we had to wait till some children appeared to interpret.

As we worked up into our early "teens" other interests got hold of us. The slings of earlier days gave way to my father's old muzzle loader gun. Our orders as to guns consisted of—"Fire it off before coming in the house" and, when we reached the breach loader stage,—"unload before coming in, and NEVER point a gun at anyone." In the summer holidays, Ralph and I often went out in one of the Pilchard drifters. On calm nights, it was like a town afloat when pilchard were up East of the Deadman.[20] With about 100 boats from Mevagissey, another 100 from Looe, our 50 odd, and many [more] from Plymouth, it was a fine sight. Often many West Cornwall boats came up too. But this was mainly in the real pilchard seasons. Some boat a mile or so away might start a hymn and this would gradually be taken up by boat after boat, till the whole fleet was singing. The more pious boats always shot their nets with a short grace for a blessing. I'm afraid ours was not in that category, but for all that they were a grand lot and nothing was ever said to hurt the most susceptible ears.

In the meantime, I had left my prep school at 14. I was to have gone to Pageites at Charterhouse, but my father had little faith in a public school preparation for the Navy, into which service he desired to send me, [for] such tradition as we had was naval. My uncle Martyn, later Admiral Sir Martyn Jerram,[21] was then a Commander, and Ralph and I had stayed aboard his ship, a "C" Class corvette, full rigged ship, and had our feet chalked by the captain of the main top as we went over the futtock shroud. And there we had to stay till someone was found to pay our footing for us, 2/6.

To digress for a moment, it may seem strange in these days of self-determination for everyone of two years old and upward and of whatever degree of education, that we never queried our parents' choice of careers. All we were concerned with was getting there. My two youngest brothers [Rowland Christopher and Cecil Bertrand] achieved the flower of knighthood, [and] Ralph, after a most useful life in India and two wars, died recently and left behind him a classic [book] on forestry. [This] shows that my father had summed us up pretty well.[22] We share ten decorations between us, and I have had the life I'd certainly choose again.

So I didn't go to Charterhouse, but to the Hermitage in Bath. The school lay back behind the west end of Lansdowne Crescent, separated from it by a deep dell in which was the laboratory. The only reason for that I can think of is that my mother's brother had been there about "a million years" previously. Mr. and Mrs. Hand were really charming people, but, as my father said later, he was too much of a gentleman to make a successful schoolmaster. I don't think I learned anything there, but nearly blew the lab down one day.

One afternoon, having nothing to do, I thought of our old muzzle loading gun at home and went off to the lab to make some powder on the cheap. Having ground up my charcoal and added the other ingredients, I was quite incapable of turning down a temptation to make a test. The lab's basin drainpipe led outside about three feet from the ground. And one of these seemed likely to make a useful cannon. Having filled it up to the bend, I then made a fuse, or slow match, of string and saltpeter which I jammed in with a paper wad, lit the end, and retired round the corner of the building. Nothing happened for some time until I'd just started to look and see if the fuse had gone out. Then there was a real success of a bang and a bit of lead pipe flew past my ear. In record time the headmaster arrived. But I think he was secretly rather amused, for all that happened was that we were forbidden to use the lab unless the science master was present. It's all gone now and the field built over.

Years later, in 1919, I took my wife to see the place. There was the drive and the dell, but the house was gone. Whilst we were looking round, a lady came out from the back door of the End Crescent house and we found that they now owned the dell. After apologizing for our trespass, I explained why we had come. She then said, "Good gracious, are you the boy that nearly blew up the school, why you were famous," so it must have caused a stir at the time.

[But it was not to be, after] having gone up and failed for the Navy. My father [then] removed me to Clifton House at the top of the Avenue at Eastbourne, where Ralph already was. At Bath I had become captain of the Rugger 15 and I still have the cap; but here I had to return to soccer. Small remote schools had ceased to pay, and my father had given up his. [He] had worked up a lecturing connection with many big schools, but he made his headquarters at Clifton House, where he taught classics, Mr. Windex, the Head, mathematics, and his son, science. The standard of discipline and freedom at Clifton House was more or less that of a "crammer."[23] But the teaching was excellent and we were not crammed. It was a quiet place in some ways. We had very good food, but dinner was limited to one helping of meat and one of pudding, except on Sundays when we could have three helpings of each! Amongst the boarders were four sons of the Prime Minister of the Hizam of Hyderabad,[24] good fellows and one of them a particular pal of mine.

At 17½ I went up for the Woolwich[25] exam for entry into the Royal Marine Artillery. More, I think, to see what I could master of it and where I was weakest than for any hope of passing, for my maths was not nearly good enough to have any hope. I don't think I was actually bottom out of the 600 or 700 candidates, but the ones below me must have been very bad indeed! However, the following year I passed the Sandhurst exam and selected, or it was selected for me, the Royal Marines Light Infantry.[26] That was in the last year [1901] of Queen Victoria. But I did not get her signed commission, as she was in her last illness and died before I actually joined.

Although none of us subsequently did anything very marvelous, we were rather a distinguished batch[27] of 15 (sic) at the time—for we were all within the first 30 on the Sandhurst list, including first, third, and, I think, fifth. Wace,[28] the top dog, got full marks for math and I got nearly full for Latin, thanks to my father, and at least qualified in math and science, my two weakest subjects, thanks to the Windexes. Thus, except for short leave periods, my life at Talland ended. [See Appendix VII for details of the RMLI officers commissioned with Jerram.]

CHAPTER 2

Joining the Royal Marines, 1901–04

Although taking the Woolwich and Sandhurst exams, the Marines went to neither. Nor were we ever cadets, but at once became Probationary Second Lieutenants, with pay at 5/3 a day; the [Royal Marines] Artillery got rather more. It wasn't much, but it did save our parents' pockets quite a bit, for at Sandhurst and Woolwich you not only were not paid but had to pay heavy fees.[1] In fact, the services were looked upon as careers for gentlemen of means rather than a way to make a fortune. If you did not get much in the way of pay, you were not expected to do a great deal of work. But times had begun to change. Our pay never changed at all until well after the 1914–18 War, but the amount of work expected of an officer increased yearly.

At this time, the Corps was divided into two branches: the Royal Marine Artillery with Headquarters at Eastney, Portsmouth; [and] the [Royal Marine Light] Infantry [with] their Depot at Deal [Kent] [and] three "Divisions" at Chatham; Forton, (Gosport), [Portsmouth]; and Stonehouse (Plymouth). These divisions [i.e., barracks] had no resemblance to Army divisions, but were more in the nature of advanced training establishments and drafting depots. A man joining one of these remained attached to it for life and always returned to it and to the same company on returning from [service at sea or] abroad. Officers, however, were on a general list and normally were appointed to a different division upon promotion.

In the first instance we went to the Royal Naval College, Greenwich. Starting at the top was the Admiral Superintendent, [then] the Captain of the College, Captain May. The Commander [was] Commander Nicholas, who later commanded a ship to which I was appointed in China.[2] A large class of naval captains were there for the first War Course ever held.[3] I don't think it was even then taken very seriously by the Admiralty. It was fairly obvious that most of the class were there to keep them off half pay rather than specially selected, for half pay was still a nightmare for a naval officer.[4] As soon as his ship was paid off, he went on half pay until he [received] another appointment. Among senior officers this might be for years or forever. The seamen were better off, for they went to various depot ships. Naval Barracks, still illegal by the way, had not yet been built.

Then there were about 250 Sublieutenants newly promoted from Midshipmen doing courses, about 100 naval engineers and naval constructors doing preliminary

2. Joining the Royal Marines, 1901–04   21

Royal Naval College, Greenwich, Jerram's initial posting (September 1901 to June 1902) after receiving his commission in the Royal Marines. He had high praise for his initial education and training there [editor's collection].

engineering, and ourselves. "We" consisted of two RMA batches and two RMLI, of which we were the junior. [There were] fifteen [*sic*] in our batch and about 40 in all.[5] Our instructors were a Major, RMA, and two Captains, one RMA and one [RMLI].[6] In addition, there were two Sergeants for drills, boxing, fencing, and gym. They were both Army boxing champions, one a middleweight and the other light, and were the salt of the earth. A Frenchman who had been through the siege of Paris in the Franco-German War and a drawing master were extras. The Frenchman told us how they had kept alive in the siege, picking leaves and grass till it was all gone, and ate all the animals in the zoo. Rat was a delicacy, but no one could ever manage dog: however disguised, it always made you sick.

The Navy at this time was undergoing changes, but was still tied down to masts and yards. There had been no naval action for two or three generations, but there had been many small wars and punitive expeditions in most of which sailors fought on land. There had even been occasions when the trained soldiers [i.e., Marines] had been left on board to clean paintwork whilst the sailors took their place on shore. In the Boxer War in China [1900–01], there were hundreds of Marines left in ships whilst the Naval Brigade was doing the fighting![7] One cannot blame the Navy. An officer who landed on active service was certain of immediate promotion. And although there were regrettable incidents owing to the military ignorance of the naval officer, yet once engaged they

Royal Marine probationary lieutenants training at the Royal Naval College, Greenwich: erecting and dismantling a bridge. Depending upon era, probationary Royal Marine Light Infantry officers studied and trained at the College for one year or not at all, Royal Marine Artillery officers for two years [© Trustees RMM].

almost invariably succeeded. For whatever their tactics, there could be no question of their courage. And as most of the actual fighting was hand to hand, courage was about all that was needed.[8]

In a ship, the Marines worked on deck and could tramp away with a halliard or brace as well as a sailor. But for the officers, there was little or nothing to do.[9] He had his hour's drill once a week, if his men were not wanted for something else. A Captain who commanded a company on shore had no control over his men afloat except for offences under guard and clothing, and was junior to naval Lieutenants half his age. Some years later I was in a ship where I was six years senior to the Sublieutenant when he was promoted, and at once [he] became a whole rank senior to me.[10]

All this made for bad feelings and, still worse, to [the] deterioration of Marine officers. It is easy to see that naval officers had no use for us, and that many Marine officers gave up hope and let things slide, or [had] become embittered. Under it all, there were fine officers in both services striving for better things, and they began to arrive soon after I joined. However, for the present, we were destined to come under the command of the best instructor I've ever met in military matters and, at the same time, the most bitter hater of the Navy. None of this, of course, we knew at the time; we only saw the result. In effect, we were soldiers pure and simple, going to sea was a disaster, and we

2. Joining the Royal Marines, 1901–04

Stonehouse Barracks, circa 1900, home of the former Plymouth Division (barracks), the shore "home" of Lieutenant Colonel Jerram throughout his Royal Marine career (except for one short period at Melville Barracks, Chatham, in 1914). Note the troops and band in parade formation before the main entrance to the barracks [© Trustees RMM].

were strongly discouraged from having anything to do with the rest of the College. In a way this is understandable, for our discipline must be entirely different from that of the Navy, even at its best. And no one can imagine that the discipline of 300 youngsters just released from gun rooms all over the world was very high!

But my instincts at the time were purely naval. My uncle was a naval Captain. A cousin was a Sub[lieutenant] at the College, and I had introductions to other naval Captains. Alas, it cost me my Sword of Honour,[11] for I became, with two or three others, fast friends of the May family, son and daughter of the Captain of the College. And a more undisciplined, or charming, family it would be hard to meet. [Alfred] Godfray,[12] an RMA Second Lieutenant, Will May,[13] and I climbed all over the roofs of the College, whilst the May girls bicycled down the steps through the buildings. Mrs. May started a dancing class in her house which three or four of us attended, and Sunday tea was almost a regular [event].

We realized that we were not popular with the Major,[14] but for the life of us we couldn't see why. I for one reveled in our military work, which I took to like a duck to water. And everything I know I learned from those admirable instructors, and it never occurred to me that the Major simply hated all things naval and resented our friendship with the Mays. Things came to a head at the very end of our year. The Mays got chicken pox and we were, quite rightly, forbidden to go near them. One day some weeks later, Godfray and I were sitting on a bench overlooking the river when Elsie May bicycled up and called out, "Hurrah, we are out of quarantine and mother says will you come to tea on Sunday." We told her to go away and we couldn't give an answer till we'd seen the Major and she rode off. Then we heard behind us, "Mr. Godfray and Mr. Jerram go to your quarters, you are under close arrest and will not leave your rooms until ordered." No opportunity was ever given us to explain, and at the end of the term we were still under arrest with an officer in charge of us. The postponed coronation of King Edward VII [due to monarch's serious illness] was to come off in a week's time. We were all told that we could stay up for it, but "Mr. Godfray and Mr. Jerram if they stay will remain under arrest." Needless to say, I went home!

However, Godfray got an invitation to stay with Captain and Mrs. May and later I learned the sequel. One day the Major met Godfray on the grounds, and ordered him to his quarters under arrest. Godfray explained that he hadn't any quarters and was staying with Captain May. That put the lid on it, for Captain May had the Major up before the Admiral where the whole story came out. The Major was made to promise that nothing was to go against us in his report. However, he didn't keep his word, for although I passed out an easy top, I never [received] my Sword of Honour,[15] and I was not only reported to the Marine Office but to my new C.O. at Plymouth, to which Headquarters I was appointed. However, whatever faults there may have been in certain officers, those appointed to command and staff ashore were the salt of the earth. Never so much as by a hint was I allowed to know that I'd come with an adverse report. I was told by the Adjutant when I left for sea that they always gave everyone a clean start. Nearly 40 years later in World War II, I was to remember that when Second Lieutenants came to me with adverse reports. Will May joined the Hampshire Regiment and gained a name for conspicuous gallantry in the 1914–18 War, and his son has followed his footsteps. Ita May, "Aunty" Ita to my children, remained a devoted friend all her life and frequently stayed with us after my retirement. There is a memorial pew to her memory in Manaccan Church [Cornwall].

One of the batch before us, [Robert] Nutt,[16] a friend of Greenwich days, had advised me to join [the Division] early and to have 10 pounds in my pocket for immediate necessities. An officer's quarters in those days consisted of a bare room. Subalterns had a fair sized room with an alcove for a bed; the furniture consisted of a solid iron bedstead, a wooden table and chair, and a set of fire irons, and that was all. So the first thing to do was to get some furniture. Nutt took the four of us who had been sent to Plymouth to a furniture shop in Devonport, patronized on account of its cheapness. Here I bought a mattress, pillow, and blankets; washstand and fittings; a tin bath; a wicker arm chair; and two rugs, one for the bedside and one for the hearth. The rest could wait and be acquired gradually as funds permitted.

I also arranged with a tailor for my servant's mess livery, when I knew who he was. This livery, which stood you in for another 10 pounds, consisted of a blue cloth braided tail coat with silver buttons, a scarlet waist coat, and blue cloth trousers. In addition, he had to have shirts, collars, black bow tie and oxford shoes, three sets of striped jean short jackets and waist coats, and a suit of plain clothes. Needless to say, if and when one changed one's servant, his size was even more important than his ability! He had to be the same size as the last man. Finally, there was the mess entrance fee which had

2. Joining the Royal Marines, 1901–04

The officers' mess at Stonehouse Barracks, Royal Marine Light Infantry Division at Plymouth, circa 1896. Jerram joined that mess in 1902. The Royal Marines still maintain a barracks at Plymouth in the same location [© Trustees RMM].

to be paid at once. Obviously on 5/3 a day, one wasn't going to have much cash to sling about for some time to come! Fortunately, my Uncle Fred had given me 100 pounds for my uniform, so I was able to start fair with my tailor. One now had to get the whole fit out, as up to now we had only to provide blue serge, sword with pipe clayed slings, mess kit, riding breeches, and jack boots.[17]

Which reminds me that I have been so taken up with Major D's misdeeds and my own that I have said nothing of the riding school,[18] which stood me in good stead all my life. We went to the Royal Horse Artillery Riding School at Woolwich one afternoon a week whilst at Greenwich. On the first day, I arrived late, having gone to the wrong Greenwich station, and arrived to see the class seated on their horses watching with awe the Riding Master, Learmont,[19] apparently trying to soothe down a mad horse careening, lurching, and pitching about. In fear and trembling, I went up to report when he slipped off, and [he] said, "Well this is the only horse left, do you know how to mount, well get up!" It sounded a poor show to me, [for] my riding had been confined to our pony and donkey, and an occasional ride on a hireling over the Downs at Eastbourne with my father. However, he was a good horseman and had taught me the rudiments, so up I got. After a preliminary twist or two to test my hand and grip, the mare quieted down; I think Learmont had been touching her up on the blind side with a spur to impress us.

But the outcome was lucky for me, because the horse was quite as new as I was and had not learned the orders. On account of that first day, I was the only one allowed to ride her, and when the others were shifted from one rough going brute to another, I was told to stand fast. We soon got to know each other and riding was a pure joy! One test we had no difficulty with: When the Riding Master said, "Don't obey this next order," when we were cantering round the school and then shouted, "Ride Halt," my horse went gaily on whilst all the others halted dead and the riders pitched over their heads. My mare only threw me once and that was near the end of the course. We had to go down the school one at a time, over two jumps, without stirrups or reins, and with drawn sword. When it came to my turn, just as we were about to take the first jump, [Charles] Risk,[20] who never could ride, came charging after us, dropped his sword point to hold on to the saddle, and stuck my mare in the rump with the point! All the sympathy I got was, "Mr. Jerram, Sir, who the hell told you to dismount?" It was fine to get there early sometimes and watch the rough-riding Corporals breaking in a new horse. I suppose they were the most wonderful riders the world has ever seen. By virtue of my mare, I managed to pass out an easy top. And without further instruction, [I] have ridden on various types of horses all over the world, some good and a few very bad.

To return to Plymouth,[21] our first night was guest night. We all gathered in the Ante Room, we new ones feeling very lost and naturally kept together and would have liked to sit together. But Plymouth was a friendly place and Captain [Eric Hody] Morres,[22] the Adjutant, [was] one of the most friendly, and quickly but fairly we were separated up. My first view of the Mess Room, as we went into dinner with the band playing "Roast Beef of Old England," gave me a thrill which I still have when I see it. Though now divested of most of its glory, the room itself is beautifully proportioned and the lower half of the walls were paneled. Above this were a few fine portraits. On one side hung the colours and opposite them flags captured in the recent China War. And at each end were stands of previous colours precariously held together by fine netting; one set had been carried in the Venezuela Campaign.[23] Right down the centre ran a mahogany table, polished by generations of working parties, and loaded with silver and glass. Most of the silver was historical: From the centrepiece, which came from the old Woolwich Mess,[24] through cups won in many competitions, to menu holders showing models of Marines in uniforms from 1664, the date of our birth. On either side, a row of servants in their picturesque uniforms stood to attention. As we sat down, we could note the various uniforms. Our own scarlet and blue, with the Colonel Commandant [Frederick Baldwin][25] in the last of the still more brilliant tunic type mess jacket of the past, [and] soldiers in every colour, naval officers in blue and gold, plus an occasional black civilian coat, formed our guests.

Used only on great occasions and now on a dais behind the President stood Napoleon's chair, brought from St. Helena by the Marine Officer of the Guard. There were so many treasures that it is impossible to name them all, but two wooden snuff boxes are worth a mention. One of oak, so old that the lines on it seemed impossibly far apart, was made from timber from the White Tower in London. This having been built in the year 1076, one wondered at what date that tree had been an acorn. The other had, inserted in the lid, a silver five franc piece, given by Napoleon to his Royal Marine servant, and presented by him to the officers.

Dinner at that time was a vast meal, and after [toasting] the "King" everyone stayed on listening to the band until about 10 p.m. Naturally, everyone remained in the mess until the last of the guests had left. But subalterns were one degree worse off, for they couldn't leave until the senior subaltern said they could. That might be any time up to five in the morning! As we had to be on parade for drill at 5:45 a.m., guest night was a pretty strenuous affair.

As we came out from dinner to disperse to the billiard room or smoking room piano, we passed through a hall containing relics of every war in which we had been engaged, trophies which were to be added to after 1914–18. Of these, the most interesting to me has always been a picture of the Marine Battalion storming Bunker Hill[26] in the war with America. It shows the colours just reaching the top and [Major] John Pitcairn[27] falling dead. Alongside was a small bit of silk in a frame, all that is left of those colours. It was the fashion, until comparatively recently, when a regiment disbanded or new colours were issued, for the old colours to be torn up and given to the Ensigns who had carried them. This piece had been handed down in the family, the last of whom presented it to the officers' [mess].[28]

Next morning in men's Red Kersey tunics and rifles, we met "First Drill" Chanter, an outstanding NCO even among NCO's all of whom might be said to be outstanding. He was to be responsible for teaching us all there was to know about drill; and Captain Morres, the Adjutant, who was to pass us out. He and Captain Morres were the kindest of people. As Adjutant on Parade, Morres was one of the strictest men I've ever known; on Sunday, at tea in his house, the kindest of hosts.[29] My sisters Winnie and Muriel were now at school in Plymouth, and the Morres' frequently invited them to tea.

After passing in parade drills, the next business was naval gunnery. Some 200 men marched up to the gun drill batteries with drum and fife band, and we joined one of the squads; then musketry at Tregantle, at which fort a few years later I saw the ghost. I had marched out a company for training, to find that I was the sole occupant of the mess, everyone else having gone to a dance. My room was in the keep, down a gloomy passage lit by one candle, and [it] was an old gun casemate with an enclosure for a window. In the middle of the curved ceiling was an iron hook. It was a vile night, raining and blowing. As I walked across the parade [ground] and entered the keep, striking a match, I found my door and in the vague light saw what appeared to be a large yellow wolf with flashing eyes. Slamming the door, I made a bolt for it and looked for another room. However, it was my room, No. 3, so carefully screening the match, I tried again. I then found that the yellow dog or wolf was my polished brass and copper water jug standing in my tin bath. But I admit I was by then quite prepared to see anything, with nothing but a flickering candle for light.

In the middle of the night, I woke up and there, hanging by his neck on the hook, was a man who had also apparently cut his throat, seen by the light of a full moon now shining straight in through the embrasure. Having hidden my head under the bed clothes, there I remained till my servant arrived in the morning. Sitting up, I said "Has it gone?" He looked at me in some bewilderment and I passed it off somehow. But I went to the Adjutant and told him he'd given me the haunted room. He poo-pooed it for a bit, but when I told him what I'd seen and said that nothing would induce me to sleep there again, he admitted that it was the haunted room but hadn't thought there was anything to it. However, since then, it has never been used.

Plymouth at this time was a garrison town in the full sense of the word. [It was] the home of the 8th Infantry Brigade,[30] destined to die so gallantly not many years later at Mons [in 1914]. In addition, there was a large contingent of the Royal Garrison Artillery at the Citadel, a Field Company, Royal Engineers, and Army Service Corps. The Devonport based vessels of the Home Fleet, and many depot and training ships, meant thousands of seamen. Our own barracks were not only full, but overflowed into the Milbay Barracks, now demolished; [we also had] companies under training at two forts. It was a picturesque town with its streets crowded with uniforms of all colours. Scarlets and blue; the dark green of the King's Royal Rifle [Corps] and the white and blue of the Army Service Corps, with their long spurs, whips, and swagger. Under Drake's Island[31] lay four to six man o'war brigs, tenders to HMS *Impregnable*,[32] and these in the summer daily put to sea under sail.

Coronation day was celebrated by a Feu-de-Joie right round the Sound, from Penlee to Bovisand, a double line of rifles wherever it was possible to deploy them. The Navy, with the Marines serving afloat who about made up a battalion, took the right from Penlee to Cremyll. Across the river we took over from Devil's Point to the centre of the Moe. Then came the gunners, and the infantry brigade out to Bovisand. It was, I imagine, the longest Feu-de-Joie ever paraded.

When not on duty, our time was our own and we could do whatever we liked except hang around the Mess in uniform. Unless on duty you were not to be seen in uniform after 2 p.m. As there were no organized games, this was a thoroughly sound rule as it forced us to do something on our own initiative. Of course that might become pub crawling, but it certainly didn't in our case. One of us [Lieutenant Francis Home] made the rest miserable by hanging wires around our quarters and inducing us to test his signalling. But, on the invention of wireless, he[33] later became one of its leading experts. For my part, I took to the Moor [i.e., Dartmoor]. For a few pence you could take a ticket to the north by the London South Western Railway, walk step across Dartmoor, and return by the Great Western Railway. When funds wouldn't permit this, you could cross the Cremyll Ferry for a penny return, with all [of] Cornwall in front of you. And sometimes I could, with a friend, walk home on a Saturday and back the next day. Then too, the Mess had five Thames type boats, one of them a four oar, in which we explored miles of river and coast.

At my sisters' school, there was a girl who used to visit her old nurse, [then] bedridden at Cawsand. One day I walked over there with her, and thereby met another link with the old smuggling days. Cawsand was as famous as Polperro, and as I sat talking to the old lady's husband he told me something of his early days. Caught on a smuggling trip, he was given the option of joining the Navy or prison. Choosing the former, he embarked in a ship and went through the Crimean campaign. Eventually arriving home, the ship lay off Cawsand for three months. No leave was given, owing to the certainty of desertion. The brandy smuggled into Cawsand went mainly to Plymouth, carried in slim bottles round women's waists, under their crinolines.

Senior officers had their horses and dogcarts,[34] and were allowed a groom in addition to their servant. Altogether it was a busy and happy time till I became available for sea service. Before I embarked, however, we had two more ceremonial parades: one in June 1903 for a visit by the Lord Commissioners of the Admiralty, and [the other] in July for our Colonel-in-Chief, the Prince of Wales. In the first, I had the honour of carrying the Regimental Colour, and in the second, the King's Colour.[35] Fortunately both days were fine and my full dress tunic remained intact; looked at financially, for however great the honour, carrying the Colours was not altogether a mixed blessing. At the best, I was lucky if I had a shilling or two a month to spend, and carrying the Colour entailed obligations as all honours of course do. The Regimental Colour cost you half a guinea to the Drum Major and a bottle of whiskey to each of the four colour sergeants of the escort. The King's Colour, a guinea and four bottles of whiskey. So I had little to spend that summer. A few years later, I carried the King's Colour in a Review of the whole garrison and Navy on the "Brickfields"[36] in a howling gale and pouring rain. The Colour once blew out of my hand as the corner I was holding gave way. A quick grab saved it, as I watched with horror the water pouring down my sleeve and out of the elbow of a brand new tunic that had just cost me 15 pounds!

On the whole, I was not sorry to get to sea,[37] where messing was only 2/- a day, subscriptions few, and you got 1/- a day ward room allowance. [On 10 December 1903,] I was appointed to HMS *Hogue*, one of a large class[38] of First Class Cruisers, carrying two 9.2" guns and twelve 6"s, of which the Marines manned three. The detachment consisted of a Captain,[39] one subaltern, me, and about 100 NCO's and men. I joined her lying in the Hamoaze [west of Devonport and south of Torpoint] where she was refitting after severe damage coming up across the Bay.

Most of the officers were on leave and there was time to look around before we were ready for sea. The Navy in general was a survivor of sail. Every officer and man was sail trained, and the life was far nearer akin to Nelson's time than to the present. No seaman ever wore boots summer or winter, and stokers when they came on deck had to leave their boots inside the casing doors. That was another grievance against Marines, who of course had to wear boots to keep their feet fit. Smart drill on a beautifully white deck simply didn't fit. The Marine officer naturally couldn't allow slovenly drill and the Commander [Edward Lowther-Crofton][40] couldn't allow slovenly decks if he was to stand any chance of promotion. A compromise of sorts was created by an issue of sea service boots with no nails in the soles. When you paraded to go ashore in nailed boots, you refrained from turning smartly about!

Yards were still carried on both masts, partly for signalling, but mainly because they looked right; and the yards were still fitted with jackstays and foot ropes. There was no electric light in the harbour when fires were drawn, and on going to sea you went onto salt grub and biscuit. An A.B. [Able Seaman] was still an A.B. in the true sense of the word and looked like it. Sail or pulling boat was the only way of going ashore, and in the Channel Fleet under "Tug" Wilson,[41] only one steam picket boat was allowed and that solely for strictly service use.

I was unlucky in my Captain of Marines. I saw him only once when I reported aboard and never saw him again. A week or so later, the Commander asked me where he was, and I had to say I didn't know. A Sergeant's guard was sent ashore to round him up; but what subsequently became of him I don't know. I think he was allowed to retire.[42]

There had recently been a conference as to the use to be made of Marine officers afloat, and an order [was] issued that subalterns were to keep watch in the harbour. I received this with open arms, not yet appreciating the snags. It never seemed to occur to anyone that they might usefully be employed with their men. It was many years later [after the First World War on HMS *Raleigh*] that I was able to put into effect an organization whereby the officers, NCO's, and men worked together in everything they did, and [it] wasn't very popular even then. However, it paid as will be seen. With no senior Marine officers to teach me my job, I naturally fell into the hands of three most gifted people who taught me everything they knew. The senior watch keeper was a very fine officer with a hatred of slipshod expressions, as applied to seafaring. I once referred to the "wave" which broke over the ship, and he sarcastically asked if I used curling tongs for it! I then learned that the mass of water which came aboard, and washed one into the lee scuppers, is a "sea." "Tieups" for "belay" and such unseamanlike expressions still make my back hair rise.

Watches were very strictly kept, night and day, and after a week I was allowed to keep watch by myself. There was far more to do than there can be in these days. Boats to lower and come alongside under sail. No centre boards in those days of lug rigged cutters and huge sloop rigged launch[es] and pinnace[s]. With the eye of everyone in the Fleet on you and your boats [and] ready to criticize, everything aboard the ship had to be perfect all the time; a lower boom or a gun out of true would result in a signal from the Flag if with the fleet, or a ticking off from the Captain or Commander if they saw anything wrong when going ashore. When hammocks or clothes were washed, they all had to be got up on the lines rigged on the fo'c's'l at the same time, and no one was allowed to touch them till they were piped down. Then all had to come down together. This led to one of my few downfalls. A stoker going on watch took down his washing and thereby left a gap. I couldn't possibly know it or see it from the quarterdeck, but it wasn't much use my saying so when sent for by the Captain.[43] He had just received a signal, "Report your reasons for having holidays in washing lines and name of officer of the watch."

Apart from sailorizing, the senior Colour Sergeant, always known as the "Sergeant-Major," was my best instructor. Marines being neither fish, flesh, nor fowl or good red herring, are always very military when afloat and the men, anyway, very nautical when ashore. Even when in barracks, my servant always asked if he could "go ashore," whilst the part of the ship where they live is always "The Barracks!" So even if he is only a Corporal, the senior NCO is always the "Sergeant-Major" and the Marine officer, "Soldier." In my dealings with the Sergeant Major, no-one could possibly have imagined that I was anything but an experienced officer. He never instructed me. His general method

2. Joining the Royal Marines, 1901–04

was to ask me when it would be convenient to do so and so. He knew his work from "A to Z," and in his most capable hands I learned far more than I should have from my Captain.

And lastly, my servant.[44] The worst thing a recent Labour government did was to abolish the officer's servant. He was one's greatest friend and helper. The chief duty of an officer is to look after the welfare of his men and to put them before himself. How in the world he can do that if he has not someone to look after him I cannot imagine. Take the simplest case. You've been for a long route march and get back about supper time. Before he can begin to think about himself, the officer must see [that] all his men's equipment [is] off and stowed, see that they wash their feet and inspect them for blisters, and see that they get their tea. In the meantime, his servant should be getting his officer's bath, change of clothes, and meal. If he doesn't, the officer must in time break down. On active service, it's impossible of course and we cheat, but it's not the same. A man detailed off as an officer's orderly can never be the same as the volunteer servant who looked after you as one of his own children. Years later [in 1912], when I married, old Wright,[45] my servant, adopted my wife as well.

We left Plymouth for Portland in February 1904, and then went south to Gibraltar, calling at Vigo, Spain, and Lisbon, Portugal. Off the Portuguese coast, we ran into an electric storm and saw something that can never be seen again. That was Corposants or St. Elmo's Fire: bluish lights at every yard arm and mast head, which ran along the lifts and triatic-stay. When wireless came in all stays and shrouds were insulated above the tops, so that could never happen again.

We fitted our first wireless during this cruise, and sent aloft a long gaff to the main top mast head. A single wire came down to a spare cabin on the upper deck, and the Torpedo Lieutenant [E.O. Ballantyne],[46] I, a signal yeoman, and [a] boy were appointed as the staff. None of us knew the first thing about wireless, and I nothing of signals. The wireless, when it came in at all, came in by dots and dashes on a long tape wound on a drum. But most of it was only electrical disturbance of the air. We did once receive a message from a ship 20 miles away, but as our mast head semaphore could do that a lot better, we were not much used.

Our chief trouble was constant breaking of the wire as it caught up on the main gaff and ensign, and the main job of the boy and myself was to keep it clear. There were ratlines to the top, and then a Jacob's ladder up the after side of the topmast. The main truck some 150 feet or more up made a wonderful seat. With one's back to the masthead semaphore, it was almost like an armchair, and I spent many hours there pretending to be doing something useful. The boy was a fine seaman and one day the wire caught at the very end of our immensely long gaff. We looked at it doubtfully from the top, and then he said "I can get it, Sir." This was a long climb up hill on a bare pole, but he made it all right.

Captain Marx[47] was one of the kindest of men, but a bit of a character. He must have been magnificent in sail, but he never really got used to engines. He nearly drove his Chief Engineer [Fred Worth][48] mad by going from full ahead to full astern. He was always putting officers under arrest and then forgetting all about them. One day it was the Commander. Evolution "Outsheet anchor and send to flagship." We Marines had done our job, getting the 6½ inch wire into the pinnace but on the fo'c's'l they were all at sixes and sevens. Captain, from the Bridge: "Commander, what are those men doing?"

Commander: "I don't know Sir, they are all a lot of bloody fools."

Captain: "Don't answer me like that Sir, go to your cabin."

At evening quarters the First Lieutenant reported, and the Captain asked where the Commander was.

"He's under arrest in his cabin, Sir," said No. 1.

"Oh, tell him not to be a damn fool and come and report," said the Captain.

One Sunday afternoon he sent for me on the Quarterdeck. Wondering what I had done wrong, I went up and saluted. Then he said, "My boy, never marry for money." "Aye, aye, Sir." said I.

Then he continued, "But make sure you go where money is. That will do." I've often wondered what sort of problem he had been thinking over. Captains led a lonely life. They never came into the ward room, and when he came on deck, the starboard side of the Quarterdeck was sacred to him, as everyone else had to move over to port.

We returned to Plymouth on May 15th [1904], and turned over to a brand new cruiser, HMS *Suffolk*,[49] and picked up a new Captain of Marines [John Dunstan].[50] As in the *Hogue*, we belonged to Home Fleet and painted in their colours, a rather dark gray with black funnel top and black gunwales round our boats. The *Suffolk* was one of the first of a large class, all with county names. Armed only with [fourteen] 6-inch guns and with a presumed speed of 21 knots, they were an answer to the new German cruisers with their 5.9-inch guns. As first turned out they were not beautiful with their three rather overgrown funnels and short topmasts. They were also the first ships with stockless anchors, which saved a lot of trouble but looked awkward at first.

Our shaking down and steam trials took us to Portland and then to Harwich, where the people of "Suffolk" presented us with a magnificent silk Ensign and Jack. When there was a breeze, one must have been able to hear the crack of those flags for miles. They also presented us with a fine piece of plate which was kept in a glass case on the Quarterdeck. Being a dockyard built ship, she was very badly finished and we much envied the *Lancaster* when we met her, for she was contract built and the contractors had done her well.[51]

Chapter 3

The Mediterranean Fleet, 1904–06

In July 1904, we left Portland to join the Mediterranean [and Red Sea] Fleet,[1] still the crack fleet of the Navy, so far as smartness went anyway. This was early in the Russo-Japanese War, and we had orders to keep a lookout for the British Steamer *Malacca*, which had been captured by the Russians. Looking in at Gibraltar, we learned that another ship had picked her up and proceeded on to Malta, where the fleet was lying. A new ship joining the Mediterranean Fleet had to be on her toes. Not only the Admiral from his mansion above the harbour, but every eye of every ship would be on you. There was nothing the matter with our seamanship, and all well reckoned we deserved a pat on the back for the way we picked up our berth, no easy job in a crowded harbour and in a ship, at the best, difficult to turn. She had in-turning propellers, the first in the Navy.

Sure enough, up went our number from the HQ Flagstaff. But it wasn't a pat on the back, but "Paint out the black on funnels and boats forthwith," and we just about to pipe down! Well, that was done and next day we repainted the ship in the light Mediterranean grey. The Chief Engineer[2] had had much criticism for allowing the funnels to blister whenever we steamed at any speed, [so] he invented a grey wash which looked very well indeed. Our stump topmasts also went, and the dockyard made us much larger ones. Getting the old masts down and the new ones up was a fine test of seamanship on the part of the First Lieutenant and the men who did the job, but I suppose more or less all in the day's work for men trained in sail. All this made a remarkable improvement to our looks, and from being a rather ugly duckling we became one of the finest looking cruisers I've seen.

Not long after this [in October 1904], our old Captain [Marx] left us and was superseded by David Beatty,[3] later to command the battle cruisers at the Battle of Jutland. The Commander,[4] always known as "Lousy," suddenly became an entirely different character. No one ever knew how he became a Commander; his nickname summed him up pretty well and he was generally unpopular, especially with the watch keeping Lieutenants, with whom he was always interfering. He stopped interfering with me in this way. When boom boats had to be hoisted in, that is the team picquet boat and pinnace and the sailing launch and pinnace, the job was carried out by the Commanding Officer and not by the officer of the watch. I was on watch one day when the picquet boat had

HMS *Suffolk*, the second ship on which the then-lieutenant Jerram, RMLI, served, 21 May 1904. Note the flags, funnels, and armament, including secondary guns on her port side. Although a new ship, within several years she would be obsolete for service with the main fleet when HMS *Dreadnought* and succeeding classes of capital ships appeared [© Trustees RMM].

to come in, and I duly reported to the Commander that she was ready for hoisting. He told me to carry on. It needed a bit of handling and I was surprised, as no watch officer had ever been allowed the job. The boat, 75 feet long and weighing several tons, was hoisted by a steam winch on the main boom rigged as a derrick. I had got the boat hoisted and topped up the boom and was giving orders for swinging her in, when the Commander came up and started giving orders. I returned to the Quarterdeck and the next thing I heard was a crash, and a shout from the Commander to ask what the hell I was doing. I told him, "You took over, Sir, so I went on with other duties." He hadn't anything to say, but he never interfered again with me.

I asked the others why they didn't do the same, but they said, "It's all very well for you, your promotion doesn't depend on how you keep in with the Commander." Promotion by selection [based on merit] is obviously the proper method, but it led to many abuses. A naval officer was entirely in the hands of his Commanding Officer, and it was pitiful to see how some of them made up to him. The wardroom a week before the half-yearly promotions came out was a place of gloom; and the arrival of the paper led to a rush to see whether you had been passed over or not.

David Beatty was a martinet.[5] Absolutely strict service all the time except when you were asked to dinner. Then he became the perfect host. But the instant you were outside the door you were on strict service terms at once. It suited me, as one knew

The cabin of Lieutenant Jerram on HMS *Suffolk*, circa 1904. Note the pictures, hats, spiked helmet, and other items in a very confined space. As he wrote, "Quilt made by my servant" [© Trustees RMM].

exactly where you were, and that was the more necessary as once more I was on my own, my captain [Dustan] having been sent home.[6] Captain Beatty was very good to me and to my men. And when I got a new Captain of Marines [John Deed],[7] we all backed him up in his aim to be the smartest ship on the station. Years later, when he became an Earl, he took a Marine for one of the supporters for his arms. It was a very high honour and one likes to think that the Marines of his first Captain's command[8] played some part in it.

The commander got hold of a Maltese carpenter who made beautiful white wood gratings to cover every coaming and bollard, after capstan, etc., on the Quarterdeck. The upper deck hammock nettings and engine room casings were white enamel, with all guns burnished [polished] inboard and the muzzles of the light guns browned. We were very beautiful indeed. Captain Beatty gave two cups, one for tug of war which the Marines won, and one to be competed for monthly for the cleanest 6-inch gun casemate, which we also won with our Y2 and second with Y1 every month.[9] My [gun] Captain put up enamel, burnishers, etc., and the inside was given six coats of white enamel and everything burnished that could be burnished, including the breach, pedestal, and platforms of the guns; whilst our working party sergeant got so high a polish on the corticene of the half deck, the First Lieutenant said it was positively dangerous and got strips of coconut matting for the principal "pathways."

August and September were spent cruising with the Fleet and visiting out of the way ports in Palestine, Cyprus, and Turkey. Whilst at Smyrna we received orders to proceed at full speed to Gibraltar to watch the activities of the Russian Baltic Fleet on their way out to Japan. They had panicked one night in the North Sea and fired on our fishing fleet.[10] They were not to be allowed to enter the Mediterranean.

We arrived at Gibraltar without a shovel full of coal left, and proceeded to coal [the] ship at once. Normally I rather liked coaling. It was a dirty job but exciting, with every part of the ship trying to be top each hour. We Marines worked[11] the second hold in the collier from aft. I supervised the hold and my Captain the inboard end. One worked four gangs, one in each corner, keeping the centre clear. Each gang filled twelve bags and strapped them together, whilst the centre party hurled them empty bags thrown down from the deck and brought the hook of the hoist down and hooked on. The moment that was done the shout "hoist away" was given and away she swung out of the corner with a crash and then aloft. There was no waiting till it was clear; if a bag or lump of coal fell on you, it was just too bad. But I never heard of an accident, you just kept nippy, and anyway you were out to beat the other holds. Inboard the hoist descended with a crash, unhooked, off strap, and away she went for another load. Hand trucks dashed in and bags wheeled at the rush to the bunker openings in the deck, and all had to be cleared in seconds before the next hoist came crashing down. How the stokers survived in the bunkers, I've never understood. They frequently got buried in and had to dig their way out, for every bag full had to be trimmed into the corners and bag fulls were hurtling down without ceasing.

But this coaling was a brute. It was very hot and we had 2,000 tons to get in. They were awkward ships to coal and we never succeeded in doing more than 200 tons an hour at best. With an occasional half hour for meals, we went right on through the night and, as the last bag came in, we weighed anchor and went to sea. The stokers, who had already kept her at full speed for 1770 miles and with this coaling on top of it, were now to keep us at full speed for another 600 miles.

Under the circumstances, the Captain sent for my C.O., Captain Dustan, and told him he would have to send the Marines to help. We told them off in three watches and at the end of it all, Captain Beatty paraded the whole ship's company and congratulated the Marines on their effort. The Chief Engineer was quite enthusiastic, [and] Captain Dustan had set the pace by going down with the first watch.

Off Arosa Bay in Spain, we picked up two small cruisers from the Channel Fleet and the Russians. At noon the Russians stopped and sent boats to the Flagship, and we wondered if they were conferring as to whether to attack or not. Captain Beatty had all [the] officers on the Quarterdeck and told us what he meant to do if they did. He said we had orders to stop them from entering the Mediterranean, so we couldn't run away. [However], our 6-inch guns were as useful as peashooters against their armour and 12-inch guns. So there was only one thing to do: Full speed and ram the biggest we could find! It meant suicide, of course, but with any luck we'd get in before being blown out of the water. However, they thought better of it, as their historian has said in his

Top: Lieutenant Jerram commanding the Guard of Honour during the visit of Kaiser Wilhelm II to Gibraltar Dockyard, 1904 [© Trustees RMM]. *Bottom:* The officers of HMS *Suffolk*, July 1904. Lieutenant Jerram, RMLI, is third row, third from left. The senior Royal Marine aboard was Captain John W. Dustan, RMLI, third row, fifth from right. The commanding officer, Captain John L. Marx, RN, is center, second row (with beard). Note the chaplain, seated, second row, far left [© Trustees RMM].

The Royal Marine Detachment, 55 strong, HMS *Suffolk*. Lieutenant Jerram is in the second row, seated, fifth from the right [© Trustees RMM].

book *From Libau to Tsushima*.[12] Having seen them clear of the Straits, we returned to Malta and, after another cruise with the fleet, we and the *Lancaster* were ordered to Marseilles in April 1905 to escort the King and Queen in the Royal Yacht for their holiday in the Western Mediterranean.

This was an interesting cruise. The King and Queen being on a holiday, there were few guards and we were able to get ashore at all the places visited. As those were mainly small ports not normally seen by the Fleet, it was more like a holiday for us too. Port Mahon in Minorca; Barcelona [in Spain]; Palma Bay in Majorca; Algiers, Bougie, and Philipville in Algeria; and Ajaccio in Corsica, were all delightful places where you could get out into the country.

In this commission we were always dashing off somewhere, and no sooner had we got back to Malta than we and the *Lancaster* were hurried off to Port Said to watch the activities of two Russian volunteer cruisers or armed merchantmen. The Russians duly arrived, but I fancy their one object in life was to keep as far away from the war as possible. But on leaving Port Said to return to Malta, we had a strange experience in the shape of a sandstorm. When about 200 miles out, on a fine sunny day, we ran into a circular storm of real sand. It was so thick that you could not see the length of the ship. Then we came out into the middle: A huge funnel with brilliant sunshine overhead and crammed with shore birds which could find no way out. Then we ran into the other side with the wind in the opposite direction and eventually left it behind. A few birds, including three hoopoes[13] stuck to us, and one hoopoe found its way home the next day.

Officers' mess tent ashore, Malta, spring 1905. Lieutenant Jerram is seated, far left. The other three officers are unidentified [© Trustees RMM].

The next day we started a full speed trial in a long beam swell, and during the night one of our privates was killed by a steel hatch cover falling on him. This led to my first experience of the amazing generosity of our men to a comrade. His kit was sold next day for the benefit of his mother. Every article went for about ten times its value, and was often put back to be auctioned again. His 18-penny cane, for instance, was sold five times for sums up to 10 shillings, and this by men whose pay was one shilling a day with few extras. In the last dog watch the next day we stopped to bury him, and when the funeral was over it was found that the engines were seized up and we couldn't move. [Neither] the Captain, Chief Engineer, nor Senior Engineer[14] ever got "hauled over the coals" [and], as they all went on to highest ranks, I suppose it was put down to the sand.

We had only just got back from this trip when we went off to Sfax in Tunisia with the Astronomer Royal for the total eclipse of the sun. It was very overcast and I don't think they did much of any use. I got two photographs, but the chief interest was watching all the birds go to sleep and seeing their astonishment at the shortness of the "night."

After another cruise with the fleet in the Eastern Mediterranean, we were sent off to Genoa to meet HMS *Renown*,[15] with the Prince and Princess of Wales aboard for their visit to India[16] and escorted them to Port Said where they were met by a ship from the East Indies squadron. The *Renown*, a small battleship, had been painted the old white colour with buff funnels and masts, and looked very well indeed. She was similar

HMS *Lancaster* and HMS *Suffolk*, Port Said, Egypt, 1905, assigned the task of guarding against possible Russian cruisers interfering with British shipping during the Russo-Japanese war. The pre–*Dreadnought* features of these two cruisers indicate their soon-to-be obsolescence [© Trustees RMM].

to the Majestic class [battleship], with two funnels athwartships and fighting tops on each mast. I think this was her last trip, as she was much too small to be [of] any use. Most of her guns had been taken out and she had become more or less a yacht. I suppose the Prince, as a sailor himself, preferred to go out in a naval ship rather than the Royal Yacht.

In February 1906, the whole fleet left Malta for the Atlantic for combined maneuvers with the Channel and Home [sic, presumably meaning the Atlantic] Fleets.[17] We left Malta in a gregale,[18] the local winter gale that wrecked St. Paul. Outside there was a very heavy sea and it was a fine sight seeing the ships taking up their positions, with seas breaking right over them. But it gave one [time] furiously to think. Up till now guns had remained very much in the same sort of way they had in sail. The only upper deck turrets which could be used in any weather were the ones on the fo'c's'le and quarterdeck, whether in a battleship or cruiser. The rest of the armament was in casemates, [running along the port and starboard sides] most of [them] on the main deck, a few feet above the water. With us, for instance, out of our broadside of six guns, four couldn't be used at all in any sea. And these were the ships with which we were to start a war in the stormy North Sea and still more stormy Atlantic; [however] most of these cruisers did in fact last right through the war.

My job in these maneuvers was up aloft, and able to report at once who any particular ship was and whether friend or enemy. With the Channel and Home [Atlantic] Fleets this was fairly easy, as [each vessel] of them purposely had something different, either bands on her funnels or different arrangement of yards on her masts. For instance,

Funeral of Rear Admiral James L. Hammet, CVO (1849–1905), Superintendent of the Malta Dockyard, in Malta, February 1905. Note the Royal Marines in column, in blue uniforms and white helmets with spikes. Another glimpse of a world now long gone [© Trustees RMM].

one ship would carry both lower and tops'l yards on each mast. The next, no tops'l yard on the main, etc., and I made a chart of all of them. When we finally anchored in Lagos Bay, Portugal, it was the biggest collection of ships since Trafalgar. The King of Portugal [Carlos I] was there in his yacht, and would often sail round us in his small sailing boat with one man.

We had a combined fleet regatta before we dispersed and I managed to win our class with our sailing pinnace, a rig similar to the Polperro fishing boat which I knew so well. But most of the kudos should go to the coxswain, who was an expert. In April 1906, [the *Suffolk*] went home to pay off and thus ended a rather unique first commission both for the ship and myself. A few weeks ago, in 1962, I had a letter from an old Marine who joined her for the second commission. His comment was, "Smartest ship I was ever in," so she kept up her reputation.

Amongst many other incidents which alone could fill a book, two might be worth recording. First, the honours paid by the Navy to an Admiral[19] who died on duty. Admiral Hammet's funeral must have been the biggest since that of Nelson. The whole fleet was in Malta, and everyone who could be landed was landed and took part in the procession.

It was a fine piece of staff work, whoever did it. I've no idea of the length of the procession; but, as a funeral, one marches in the reverse order of seniority, we Marines were well up, but the whole funeral service was over before we got there. By the time the high ranking officers arrived, the daisies must have been well up on the grave.

The other recollection is of the extraordinary behavior of a flash of lightning, when we were in camp one summer at Ghain Tuffieha, the Marines' musketry and field training camp [on the northwestern part of the island]. Across the valley was the camp of the mounted infantry, still in being after the South African war, and between us a small Maltese farm. Just before breakfast one morning, there was a terrific crash of thunder and a galloper from the M.I. Camp came over to get our doctor to the farm which had been struck, [for] a woman required attention. Later we learned the details and were able to see most of the [damage] to the house. Like all Maltese country houses, this one was of square cut stone with a flat roof and four rooms, [with the] downstairs being occupied by animals and upstairs by the family. The lightning had struck a top corner, knocked out a stone, passed over the woman lying in bed expecting a child, made a pencil sized hole in the stone floor and killed five out of about 20 hens in the lower floor. It had then knocked out a stone in the dividing wall, killed the middle animal of three, made another pencil sized hole in the stone floor above, and departed by knocking out another stone in the opposite corner. It all sounds quite impossible. Our doctor was required to [assist in the birth of] the baby, which seemed to have suffered no ill-effects.

Chapter 4

China Station, 1907–10[1]

To China, 1907

After a short spell of leave at home, I returned to the Barracks going through various courses, and met the other fort ghost. This was at Fort Stamford just across from the Barbican at Plymouth. Colonel Drury[2] brings it into one of his books, which I had not read at the time, so it's obviously an old story. Our experience was exactly the same as Drury's, only he had a dog which saw it. One Sunday sitting in the officers' mess and just before retreat which synchronized with 4 o'clock tea, someone came tramping down the passage and stopped outside the door. Anticipating tea, my C.O. called, "Come in," but nothing happened. So, thinking [the messman] couldn't open the door with a tray in his hands, I went across and opened it, to find no one there. I walked out to the gate where the bugler was getting ready for retreat, and asked him who had come out or in [but] no one had. It puzzled us until later I read Drury's account, which was exactly the same.[3]

On 10 January 1907, I embarked in HMS *Spartiate*[4] for passage to China. On that station[5] there was a squadron of [five] cruisers of the King Alfred and County classes, and also a whole crowd of small craft ranging from Second Class cruisers with 25 Marines, [to] sail and steam sloops and fore and aft rigged gunboats with about 10, down to river gunboats on the Yangtse and West Rivers which might contain six or none. Those on West River could be looked after adequately by the Major [William Dixon] at Hong Kong, but there had never been anyone to look after the Yangtse end. I was being sent out for the dual purpose of looking after these Marines and assisting, as to the northern post, the intelligence work carried out by the Major in Hong Kong.

The *Spartiate* was an even older ship than the *Hogue*; similar in appearance, but with only 6-inch guns, she was cram full of drafts. The only cabin available for me was a horrible stinking dog hole on the water line. I shouldn't think the scuttle had ever been open, as even a boat coming alongside would cause enough sea to flood it. The Commander [Ernest Loring][6] was a very nice chap and told me that a lot of people were only going as far as Malta, and then he'd give me something better. The first day I went down to dress for dinner and plunged my face into the basin and was nearly sick. Better not inquire what it had been used for! But I did get a new wash stand.

We had a fine passage across the Bay [of Biscay] with a long swell and, [later] calling at Gibraltar, duly arrived at Malta where the Commander did me proud. I got what used to be the Admiral's Secretary's cabin, right aft, and with two scuttles and any amount of [fresh] air. There was a northerly gale as we came to Port Said, and the passage through the Canal and Red Sea, of all places, was bitterly cold. We had fires in the wardroom until we were half way down the Red Sea. The day before we made Perim, [an island at the entrance to the Red Sea] I dined with the Captain, who still had a fire going; but that was rather too much. Captain [Cresswell] Eyres[7] was a friend of the May's; there were two captains of the same name, known as "Good Eyres" and "Foul Eyeres." This was the good one. Perim Island [off the southern coast of Yemen] is just a sand heap in the hottest part of the hottest sea in the world, and at that time only inhabited by a few Eastern Telegraph people. One of these I found was an old school fellow of my Bath days, one "Molly" Foster. We stayed two days and [our visit] must have been a Godsend in their monotonous existence, [for] one could hardly call it a life.

Then [on] to Bombay where the Amir of Afghanistan was making an official visit.[8] He was, we gathered, a holy terror; bought up all the musical boxes he could find and was very indignant when told he couldn't buy up the wives of the officials who were looking after him! A shoot from the forts was got up to impress him, and this resulted in my first and only naval command, for I was given the picquet boat to keep all comers off the firing area. Why, I cannot imagine, as there were plenty of naval officers available. These boats had a speed of 17 knots and could carry a 12 pounder, a maxim [machine gun], and two torpedoes.

[Then] I had an even better command that night: A whole squadron, no less, consisting of two picquet boats and two pinnaces, with which I was to make an attack on our ship. The chief trouble about any torpedo attack, as was later discovered, consisted of flaming funnels and shining bow wave. The part of the ship most vulnerable to attack was from dead ahead or dead astern, as the guns couldn't be depressed enough if you could get close. So I divided my squadron into two: The slower pinnaces to attack from ahead, whilst I with the picquet boats went right around the bay to attack from astern. Watches were synchronized and a time given for a start. All boats were to steam in dead slow until spotted and then go full speed, as close as possible to the ship before firing torpedoes, one group down the starboard side and one down the port. Torpedoes were to be represented by firing a red Very Light.[9] We were perfectly successful and the ship presumed sunk. But she wouldn't have been. If only we had had torpedoes, we might have saved our destroyers in the coming war from much mystified disappointment. In 1914, they carried out precisely the same procedure, and missed every time. It was then found that torpedoes with warheads [when launched] from upper decks sank under the target before attaining their right depth, and if you were too close you were bound to miss.

Our next port of call was Colombo where I, of course, walked out to Mount Lavinia for the famous fish lunch. The monsoon was blowing hard and it was strange to come straight in from rolling our guts out to the serene calm of the break water, over which huge seas were breaking. Calling at Singapore, we then headed north to Hong Kong, when three days out we ran into the tail of the typhoon which caused [such] enormous damage. There was a long following swell as I turned in for the night, but I had carried my scuttles all the way and it seemed safe to leave them open [for] it was very hot. Soon after midnight, I was washed out of bed, out of my cabin, and onto the Captain's flat, together with all my belongings! With the aid of the sentry, I screwed up the scuttles and then began to rescue my gear. Fortunately, the cabin coamings were very high and no one else was flooded out by my stupidity. What had happened was that we were pooped[10] and the whole quarterdeck was completely submerged. An officer sleeping on the quarterdeck awoke just in time to see a wall of water coming at him and jumped for the after bridge ladder. On arrival in Hong Kong, we saw some of the damage. The thing that impressed me most was the sight of a steamer high and dry in the middle of Kowloon Village. The force of the wind had piled the water against an 18 foot quay and forced her right into the middle and jammed her between two houses.

An idea of the size of China may be seen in the fact that we left Hong Kong in sweltering heat and arrived off Woosung[11] in a snowstorm. At Woosung, another officer and I were transferred to the *Clio* and taken up to Shanghai. *Clio* was one of three sloops[12] on the station, the others being *Cadmus* of the same class and *Algerine*. They were all barquentine rigged and in their white paint were pretty little ships. They carried little coal and therefore had to do a good deal of sailing. They were the last square rigged ships in the Navy, the training squadron of full rigged ships having been laid up about the time I joined, [with] the brigs and a barque rigged corvette in Malta soon to follow them.

Shanghai, a snow covered city as I first saw it, was in the height of its prosperity. During the Boxer War the foreign concessions, with the exception of the French, had amalgamated for better defence and organization, but still remained very much as they had been as regards inhabitants other than Chinese, who of course formed the bulk of the population. Down river on the west side was the Japanese quarter, then came the American; the Soochow Creek divided them from the British, much the best part. Then came the German and finally the French, abutting the walled Chinese city. The British senior naval officers' buoy was opposite the Bund, and the British Consulate in its gardens at the north end. North of Soochow Creek was looked upon "as beyond the pale," and as all the ladies of easy virtue or love were Americans, the inhabitants of that part were not known by the rest. The Chinese looked upon the Americans as an inferior race and it is not astonishing that in 1962 they can see no reason for loving them. On the other hand, the British were in high favour and probably still could be, without the Americans. British and Chinese commercial instincts were identical. Both would try and get a bargain, but once it was accepted it was final. An Englishman's word was always trusted, and so was that of a Chinaman.

These were the last years of the old Empress [Tzu Hsi, reigned 1898–1908], who may have ruled with a heavy hand but she did rule, and since she died there has never been peace. The Concession was ruled by a town council on which the British had the majority of seats and the Japanese the fewest. [It] ran a volunteer fire brigade and defence force, the British providing two companies and the other nations' one each. The fire brigade had the busiest time, especially at Chinese New Year. By that date all debts had to be paid or the Chinaman would "lose face." So they not infrequently burnt their houses for the insurance money. As these were crammed together and made of wood and paper, the firemen were frequently out all night. They were wonderful people; a gallop round the race course would put them right and they would be at their places of business by 9 a.m.

We did not of course learn all this on arrival; but as the *Clio* could not put us up, we were sent to the Astor House Hotel [the first western hotel in China and modernized in 1907] to await the arrival of HMS *Astraea*.[13] The British inhabitants consisted of the consular officials, businessmen, and the clergy of the cathedral, with a few retired people living in the country. A few merchant service officers, especially those of the China Merchant Company, kept houses for their wives. Other than these heads of departments, everyone was Chinese. There were no lower class or lower middle British, and that again tended to make us more respected, especially as the Chinese clerks, compradors [native house steward], etc., were implicitly trusted. At the Astor House, therefore, we found ourselves in a good English hotel where only the guests were English or American, and a better-run hotel it would be hard to find. At breakfast next morning I got a surprise, for sitting at a table across the room was a girl about 11 or 12 who was a strange mixture of my two youngest sisters [Winnie and Muriel] and dressed exactly as I had last seen them in sailor blue jumper and skirt. It was my first sight of Darcie Graham [who], later with her mother, [were] to become great friends and [she] eventually Godmother to one of my children. But at the moment I could only stare.

We had two or three days to explore Shanghai before the *Astraea* came in. The main shopping centre, club, offices, and cathedral were all centered near the Bund [the central waterfront area on the Huanpu River] in the British sector [of the former International Settlement]. The main street ran west from the riverside, the shops gradually becoming more Chinese till it became a purely Chinese street and then became the Bubbling Well Road. Here began the Europeans' country houses; and on the left a huge recreation ground, with golf course, race course, and every kind of sport available. Then came the Jessafield Road with the houses of the really rich Europeans, with their horses and carriages and mafoos (a general name for coachmen and grooms) dressed in picturesque Chinese long coats and fur capes. Beyond this, dirt roads, tracks, and footpaths went off in all directions and afforded some of the best riding country one could wish, as I discovered later.

Beyond the French concession, we entered into the Walled City through a gate and bridge over the most powerful-smelling creek in the world. At the gates stood, permanently, the most repulsive beggars in the world, the worst being advanced lepers with no faces. [Then,] ranged in a row, were usually men and women under punishment in the "cangue." This was a board with a hole in it which fitted over the head and rested on the shoulders. It was very heavy and of sufficient size so that you could not reach your face with your hands. As the flies were there in billions, it couldn't have been pleasant. However, it was not as bad as the English pillory, not so long given up, [and] neither were they pelted with rotten eggs as they had been in England.

In the centre of the city stood the original of the Willow Pattern: A tea house in the middle of a zig-zag wooden bridge just as you see it on a blue dinner plate. It must have been lovely at one time, when the latter was new. But alas, the lake, like every

4. China Station, 1907–10

Willow Pattern Tea House (or Huxinting Chashi), Shanghai, 1907. A former private turned public tea house on a lake in the Old City in Shanghai, it was approached by a zig-zag bridge over the water and was popular with Europeans and Chinese of Jerram's era and into the 21st century [© Trustees RMM].

other piece of water in a Chinese city, was now an open sewer. Still, it was a picturesque old town. It's all gone now in a disastrous fire which destroyed the whole city soon after I left the station. Up river above the city was the Chinese Arsenal and naval headquarters, and beyond that again the famous Loving Wa Pagoda. Only a few years back, China must have been a glorious country. But now most of its treasures were at least partly ruined, and nobody seemed to have the energy or money to keep them up.

The *Astraea* duly arrived and I commenced the best four years I've ever had. As there was no ship in which I could be accommodated on the Yangtse during the summer months, it meant in effect that I was to live in either *Astraea* or *Flora* (whichever was on the river all the winter, and cruise in the summer in the ship I happened to be in). So I remained at Shanghai till April when we started off on our summer cruise. We saw much of the East during this and subsequent cruises [as the following illustrates]:

HMS Astraea's Summer Cruise 1907

1–11 May—Yokohama, Japan
13–20 May—Kobe, Japan
21 May—Ibuki, Japan
21–23 May—Kitatsi, Japan,
23–24 May—Tsushima, Japan

1–5 Aug—Hakodate, Japan
6 Aug—Rikuoku Bay, Japan
7–8 Aug—Aomozi, Japan
8–12 Aug—Hakodate, Japan
13–17 Aug—Otaru, Japan

HMS *Astraea*, 1908, one of the cruisers on the China Station, 1908. By the time this photograph was taken, she was obsolete for service with the main battle fleet. Ships on the China Station moved along the coast and visited other countries of the Far East. The then-lieutenant Jerram served on her as well as smaller ships on the station for more than four years [© Trustees RMM].

24–26 May—Mesampo, Korea
27–31 May—Chemulpo [Inchon], Korea
1–5 June—Wei-hai-Wei, China
6–7 June—Wu Sung, China
9 June–22 July—Wei-hai-Wei, China
24–25 July—Aburatani, Japan
26–28 July—Miadzu, Japan
29–30 July—Niigata, Japan
30–31 July—Funakawa

18–19 Aug—Vladimir B., Manchuria
20–25 Aug—Vladivostock, Manchuria
25–26 Aug—Kopniloff, Korea
27–28 Aug—Gensam, Korea
8–30 Aug—Lazaroff, Korea
2–3 Sept—Imari, Japan
3–10 Sept—Nagasaki, Japan
12–16 Sept—San Tu, China
17 Sept—Hong Kong, China

From our point of view, the Chinese do everything backwards. The men wore skirts and the women trousers. They write from right to left. They shake hands with themselves and not with you, and if they want you to come they wave you away. They are always laughing, at you if you trip over a pig or at themselves if one of them falls off a ladder. In an accident they roar with laughter, always seeing the funny side first, but they would come and help you up. And they were absolutely honest; even the Japanese employed them as head clerks, cashiers, etc.

Officers on HMS *Astraea*, China Station, circa 1908. Lieutenant Jerram is in the fourth row, far left, in blue blouse and white cover. Note the chaplain and naval instructor, third row, third from right [© Trustees RMM].

The Japanese were none of these things. Japan was a complete contrast to China in every way. It was very clean and artistic in a rather "pretty-pretty" sort of way, and gave one the impression of being totally insincere. And this was borne out by its people. Before I went there, I was warned to see packed and taken away anything I bought, otherwise you'd find on opening it that it had been changed for something cheaper. And I found they always tried to take a purchase away to be packed. Superficially they were polite, but it was all bogus. On one occasion I was taking a photograph when I stepped backward, down a step. As I picked myself up, all the Japanese were looking very solemn and pretending they hadn't seen, but looking back as I went off they were all grinning. [The] Chinese would have roared with laughter, and come and helped me up. But the scenery [in Japan] certainly is beautiful.

Wei-hai-Wei[14] was leased to the British government and was the summer station for the Fleet. Also, in a hotel on the mainland, one of the summer places for the Europeans from Hong Kong and Shanghai. It consists of a large bay with the island across it. The island was purely naval and there were no civilians except the Chinese ships and farmers. It had been the headquarters of the Chinese Regiment[15] of the British Army, but this had been disbanded after the recent Boxer War, when the men were immediately snapped up by the Germans for their fortified base at Kiaochow, a port in Shantung province.

We were not to see much of Wei-hai-Wei then, for on arrival we were sent back to Woosung to tow up a huge lighter. But when we got back, we were there for nearly a fortnight before leaving for the rest of our cruise. The sea side of the island I found very much like the north coast of Cornwall, and the climate is also very much the same; hence, you might easily imagine you were there. As we arrived at Tsushima through the straits of that name, I couldn't help thinking of the Russian Fleet lying at the bottom of it after their defeat by the Japanese.[16] I had last seen them on their way out when we shadowed them in the *Suffolk*.

Korea was quite different again, a clean but rather more desolate country. The Koreans are probably the laziest people in the world, but at that time they hadn't much incentive to be otherwise. There was no army or navy, and their wants were few. I went up to the capital, Seoul. Wide earth streets, wooden houses, and picturesque wooden palaces. Most of them were empty, for when an Emperor died his palace was abandoned and became a sort of public garden, and a new one was built. But the loveliest thing to see was a group of children. After the drab blue of the Chinese and the variegated kimonos of the Japanese, these formed a complete contrast of the brightest primary colours. There was no pattern: bright red tops with bright yellow legs, bright green and red, the brightest of blue, and all mixed up together. Individually it was nothing striking,

Royal Marines training on Wei-hai-Wei, 1908. The white uniforms, with helmets and Corps badges, stand out against the ground. A standing officer or non-commissioned officer at the distant left is supervising what is occurring [© Trustees RMM].

4. China Station, 1907–10

Hong Kong Harbor, 1908. Royal Navy ships on the China Station often visited this crown colony. Another view of a vanished era [© Trustees RMM].

but in a group it was a charming sight. Men wore white exclusively with a black narrow top hat and chinstay, unless they were in mourning when they wore an enormous bowl shaped straw [hat]. It was a quiet, peaceful, and happy land, soon to be taken over by the Japanese, and years later to become a cockpit of war. To anyone who knew it then, it seems quite incredible.

The other place of great interest was Port Arthur. The Russo-Japanese War had only recently ended in the complete defeat of the Russian Navy and Army, and Port Arthur and its neighbourhood still showed the signs of the desperate fighting. The port was surrounded by a string of forts similar to those at Plymouth, and these had been stormed one by one. The Russians, abandoned by their field army, fought stubbornly for every foot. The Japanese approached in the recognized form of siege warfare by parallel trenches and drove the gaps forward. Eventually effecting a breach, the fight was by no means over: They had to fight their way step by step through every casemate and underground passage, and the Russians never surrendered; they were just wiped out.

Vladivostock was still Russian and I had a ride in one of their three-horse carriages, which worry about safety about as much as the Romans did. The streets were mostly

Residue of the Russo-Japanese War. The remains of the Russian defenses of the Eagle's Nest at Tung Chi-Kuan-Shan, China, include damaged naval guns. Note especially the barrel, rear gun. Visiting such sites of a recent war would have been of interest to individuals such as Jerram who studied and reflected on the profession of arms [© Trustees RMM].

dirt, but where they were paved you took them at full gallop. Going from a paved bit you dropped with a crash, and vice versa. It was like hitting a step!

On arrival at Hong Kong, I turned over to the *Flora* and we went back to the Yangtse River, and up to Hankow and Wu Chang.[17] It was now October and November, and the shooting was wonderful. For the first two days we were out of sight of land, which gives some idea of the size of the river, and at this time of year it was low. Further up you could not see over the banks. But in a month or two it would cause miles of floods. The river gunboats were flat bottomed and used to take shortcuts, but one [the following] spring nearly got left some miles inland! She came on a bank she couldn't cross and had to follow it all the way back to the river, just in time, for the next day the water fell several feet and there was dry land again where she had been.

Before leaving England I had been advised to take out as many cartridges as I could afford, eights, fives and fours,[18] and I had also brought out several hundred for the *Astraea* wardroom. But I had never imagined shooting where you never took less than 200 cartridges ashore. True, you might need none, but far more often you used the lot.

We left Shanghai on October 23 and arrived at Hankow on the 28th, after having only anchored one night at Chingkiang. Hankow was a treaty port and miniature Shanghai, with its European settlement and walled city. It is also the headquarters of the

Royal Marine detachment, totaling 30, HMS *Astraea*, circa 1908–12, all in white uniforms and cloth cover. Lieutenant Jerram is seated in the middle row, sixth from right. Marine Wright, his servant, is seated in the front row, far left. A close bond existed between Jerram and Wright, as he revealed in his memoir [© Trustees RMM].

lovely blue china. We went into a shop entirely filled with it, mostly modern but some old pieces if one was wise enough and rich enough to buy them. But my 5/3 a day wouldn't go far, and one longed in vain to fill the ship with Chinese crockery and lovely Hong Kong black wood furniture.

We crossed the river to Wuchang for an official call on the Chinese Naval Headquarters. Above this came the first rapids and then the upper river, which runs away nearly to Russia. We maintained four gunboats on the upper river and I begged to be allowed to go up. The Captain said that I could go if I could find one Marine to go and inspect. The hard line was that there had been one taken up as an unauthorized servant, and he had only just been sent back.

Leaving on the 31st of October, we spent a day at Kui Kiang, a hill station for Europeans at Shanghai. It is lovely, hilly country and the way to the hill residences is up a step road. Thousands upon thousands of steps about 2 or 3 yards apart, which can be used by pack mules. At Tung-lu Reach,[19] where we spent three days, the shooting really began. The chief difficulty was always the variety of game. If you were loaded for pheasant you would put up snipe and vice versa. But anyway the game was so mixed up that you were bound to be wrong, whatever you did. Further, you would just get your eye in on the rapid flying snipe then you'd get on to quail, and miss every shot as they flew too slow.

In general, the land was wet paddy-fields holding snipe. And these were divided by low grassy banks, out of which you could always kick a pheasant. On the dry bean fields you would get quail and red leg partridge, whilst any patch of water would be full of duck. At Wu-Hu we had another two days equally good. And a further two days at Nanking.

Nanking[20] is an old Chinese capital, and at one time must have been an immense city. But now it had entirely disappeared, except for the great wall, a mile each side, with a small village in one corner. Beyond the walls, across a flat plain, was the tomb of the last of the Ming Emperors. It was approached, a mile or more, by a double row of colossal stone figures. These were all different; two by two soldiers, camels, elephants, horses, and lions, some standing and some kneeling. The elephants' backs were covered with small stones, as it is apparently lucky if you throw one up and make it stay there. Each figure was carved out of one huge stone. It could be, if better known, one of the wonders of the world. But even then, no one ever went there except an occasional naval officer, and one wonders what had happened to it now that Emperors are in little favour.[21] We got back to Shanghai on November 10th and there I remained, alternating between the *Astraea* and *Flora* till the end of April 1908.

Shanghai, 1907–10

Now for the first time I was able to get down to the job for which I had been sent out, and at the same time get to know some of the people ashore. Indeed, my introduction to those who became my friends arose directly out of my job. As has been related, I had two main duties. One was to organize the Marines on the river for duties ashore; these duties were obviously the protection of consulates and British subjects in general, in addition to direct command of the Marines of [my] ship. Second, to supplement the work of the intelligence officer at Hong Kong, a Major of Marines.

During those four years I was to serve in two different ships, each a part of three different commissions. That is, I served under six different Captains and [ship's] First Lieutenants! Without exception they all did everything they could to help, and every suggestion I made was treated with sympathy and understanding. We were, I suppose, lucky in that we had no gunnery lieutenant as a possible "military" rival, though I must say in all fairness that I never, throughout my service, came across one of the bad type. But it stands to reason that it is possible to get friction, if on the one hand you have a trained soldier who has passed stiff exams in his trade and ought to know it backwards even if he doesn't; on the other hand, a naval officer senior to him who is responsible for the infantry training of the sailors in addition to his gunnery duties, and who has never had any training at all or even had to pass an exam. Further, the naval officer

4. China Station, 1907–10

Chinese Bridge, Soochow Creek, Shanghai, 1907. In planning to protect European nationals in Shanghai, consideration for moving over, around, or through such obstacles had to be considered—and reaction time accordingly considered. Jerram served on the China Station only several years after the 1905 anti-western Boxer Rebellion in China [© Trustees RMM].

knows that if he is landed on active service he is bound to be promoted. As I say, it stands to reason that he will want to take charge, and must, of course, if he is senior. In my case I ranked only with a Sub-Lieutenant and yet was older than most of the Lieutenants. Indeed, the "sub" of the *Astraea* was promoted whilst I was in the ship and at once jumped from being five years junior to me to a whole rank senior! This was all to be changed a few years hence, but that is how it stood at this time. So I was not sorry that there was no rival "expert" in the ship.

But I had no difficulties at all. Once I had explained what I was there for, [important since] nobody seems to have been told, the Captain laid it down that I was the military expert and it was up to me to make necessary plans and submit them directly to him. Moreover, he made it quite clear who would be in charge with a mixed landing by detailing the First Lieutenant who was senior to everyone. As I was unlikely to have an officer's command of Marines anyway, once the initial stages of a landing were over I should become the Commander's staff officer. From a Marine's point of view, nothing could be fairer or more satisfactory, and on that basis I got to work.

Our obvious first commitment in Shanghai, or any other treaty port for that matter, was the defence of the Consulate. In Shanghai, speed was the obvious necessity in order to give time for the volunteers and police to mobilize. The latter were all Sikhs under an English Lieutenant Colonel. So the three people to see were the British Consul General and the two Lieutenant Colonels of volunteers and police; [thus], a meeting was arranged at the consulate. As a result, naval commitments, in the first instance anyway, were confined to consulate protection and getting there, whilst the military and police took care of other strategic points, such as the station, bank, etc.

This meeting led to my first meeting with the Davidson family. He [John Davidson[22]] was the member of the Consulate delegated to put me in the picture, and after going round and fixing machine gun sites, guards, billets, and general defence, he took me home to tea. There I met Mrs. Davidson, a most charming lady, and their three year old son, a delightful child, and we became fine friends.

To return to the defence scheme: In general the naval companies would man the defence posts, whilst the Marines would form a mobile reserve, ready to either counter-attack or patrol. But the main difficulty was likely to be getting to the consulate. The ship or ships lay off the Centre of Bund, a wide promenade, garden, and road. Behind this were the main buildings, and right opposite [to] our usual landing [place] the main street ran straight ahead. Landing there one had to turn right, cross a bridge over the Soochow Creek [also known as the Woosung River] and, leaving the public gardens on our right, move to the consulate gate on our left. Altogether, only about half a mile, but a flank march across the Chinese quarter.

Not to go into too much detail, the Marines were to land first, pulling themselves "in" in one 32 foot cutter, and [then] hold a bridgehead, watching both ways and the main street; [this] left one section in reserve. The seamen would then land and pass through the Marines, who would then form a rear guard. It says something perhaps for our early training that I don't think I could improve on it now. And looking up the orders I wrote, signed by my first Captain, they don't look too bad either.

To carry out this duty the Marines obviously must be on their toes all the time. The shore, about one cable's distance, was separated from the ship by a tide which is notorious. That meant strenuous boat pulling exercise. Then again, the fighting equipment of those days consisted of pipeclayed belt and shoulder braces. These held up a folded coat and cape on the back, whilst water bottle and haversack were slung cross ways over the shoulders. It took about an hour to put it together, even in a hurry, and the men were given a whole day off if they had to parade for inspection. Obviously this wouldn't do, and I worked out something that could be all put on together after the fashion of the later web equipment. Somehow I scrounged from the base at Hong Kong extra belts, so that the men could keep theirs clean for walking out and parades, did away with coat and cape, put the water bottle and haversack on the belt and kept the whole thing in one, hung the rifles on the half deck, with a blanket rolled bandolier-fashion over all.

On the alert being sounded, the men assembled in any clothes they happened to be in, put on their gear, and went to the shore side gangway. In the meantime the boat keepers had brought the boat alongside, and the gunner and paymaster, one on each side, handed out 100 rounds of ammunition and three days' bully beef and biscuit to each man as he went over the side. The Captain gave us a surprise landing one day and timed it: 11½ minutes from the alert to taking up our positions ashore, which still sounds quite incredible to me; I don't think the modern commando could have done any better.

The intelligence duty was rather more complicated. It resolved itself mainly into

4. China Station, 1907–10

Officers, HMS *Astraea*, circa 1910. Lieutenant Jerram is in the middle, second row, wearing helmet with Royal Marine Light Infantry Emblem; his 1st Lieutenant's rank insignia of two pips can be seen on both epaulettes. The black mourning arm bands worn by the officers on their left arms pertain to the death of King Edward VII [© Trustees RMM].

movements of foreign men o'war, and shore batteries and forts, of which the German forts at Kiaochow seemed likely to be the most important nationally. But Chinese forts [were] more my business. There had been for some years a scheme by which merchant ships were requested to report to the nearest intelligence officer any man o'war they had seen, but it was very loosely carried out.

In this great port, which several lines visited frequently, there was a chance of getting something useful. Of the big [shipping] lines, there were the P and O [Peninsular and Oriental Steam Navigation Company], Blue Funnel, and Clan liners; of the coasters, Butterfield and Swire, Jardine Matheson, and the China Merchant. These were the most important, and I visited each agency and [received] official permission to visit their ships and [give] a directive to the captains to help all they could. The exception was the China Merchant.[23] As the Chinese owned it, I could not ask for official help. But they were all officered by British seamen, and were likely to be the most useful of the lot. So I visited each of them and summed the captains up before asking their assistance. This led to another friendship, as one of them introduced me to his wife, [who] lived in Shanghai; I frequently went there to tea when his ship was in, and was able to return this hospitality when we had parties on board.

It was interesting and amusing to note the different attitudes of the various companies' officers: The P and O very haughty and standoffish as successor to the old John

The China Fleet at Wei-hai-Wei on King's Ascension Day, 1909. Under British administration during Lieutenant Jerram's service on the China Station, the site and off shore island are on the northeastern shore of the Shantung peninsula. At this base Royal Marine detachments aboard ship conducted training ashore. From left to right: HMS *Astraea*, HMS *Kent*, HMS *Clio*, HMS *King Alfred*, HMS *Bedford*, and HMS *Monmouth*—all suitable for service on the China Station, but obsolete for service with the main battle fleet in the post–*Dreadnought* era [© Trustees RMM].

Company [East India Company], and Butterfields aped them as a sort of local P and O. Much the most helpful were Jardines and the Blue Funnel lines. I was generally turned over to the mate, and one of Jardines' mates entered into the spirit of the scheme wholeheartedly. Some time later I was able to make a personal reconnaissance of the Kiaochow forts, then in course of construction.[24] After I left I got on to this mate as his ship was a constant visitor to the port, and [after] every voyage he sent me a report of [the] progress and the movement of guns up the hills and into [their] positions. Between us we brought the intelligence report up to date, which must have been of great use in the capture of Kiaochow, or Tsingtao to give it its other name by the Japanese and British in the 1914–18 War.[25]

Through the Davidsons I got to know Mrs. Graham and her daughter, Darcie, the little girl I had seen on my first day in Shanghai, and we became great friends. On Saturdays, they used to go out to Jessafeld to the house of a rich widow, Mrs. Snethlager; she was English, though I fancy her husband must have been a German. She kept several hunters, and whilst the grown ups played bridge, Darcie was taken out for a ride by the head mafoo. One day I went with them, as Mrs. Snethlager asked me if I could ride as the mafoo wasn't available and she wouldn't trust the others. I admitted I could, after a fashion, and was given a grand steady hunter called "Portland" and went off with Darcie on a leading rein. After that the Saturday ride became a fixture when I could get away. [This] led to other horses, as few people could give their horses enough exercise and had to leave it to their mafoos.

One day three men were calling on the ship when one of them said to me, "I hear you ride. Would you like to exercise a pony for me?" Before thinking, I said I'd like to very much and then saw the faces of the other two! It looked as if there was some snag. These Chinese ponies of about 14 hands were notoriously hard mouthed and were not improved by the way they were ridden in the weekly paper hunts.[26] I should think the average owner of a pony in Shanghai must have been the worst horse master in the world. The Chinese, by the way, got a lot of amusement out of these paper hunts. They would watch the trail being laid and then get shovels and widen out the biggest ditch and collect there to see the fun!

One day I duly arrived at the stables at the end of Bubbling Well Road[27] and

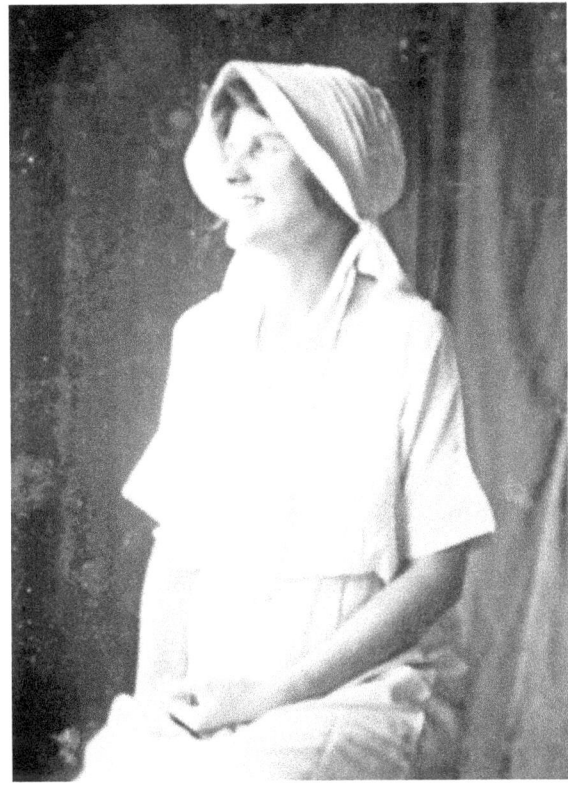

Darcie Graham, a young lady whom the then-lieutenant Jerram met in Shanghai and who later visited him in England after the First World War. Both shared an interest in horses and riding. She died just before the outbreak of the Second World War [© Trustees RMM].

said I'd come for the pony. I had my heart in my mouth as I had now learned that the pony was so hot that neither the owner nor anyone else would ride him, and he probably had not been out of the stable for some time. Sure enough, five mafoos brought out a kicking, rearing brute with a blanket over his eyes and head. I couldn't very well clear out as I should have liked to do so. He had the usual very short neck with nothing to hold on to, and it looked as if I was likely to go straight over his head, if I could even get up.

However, with the aid of the five grooms holding on to every bit of him they could reach, I did get into the saddle and they whipped off the blanket. In front was the compound gateway and beyond that all China, luckily straight ahead on a dirt road! After sticking out a lively circus performance, I got him headed for the gate and we were off. I let him go for half a mile and then gradually steadied him. His mouth had not been completely spoiled, and we had a very good 10 mile ride. It remained so until [he] saw [we] were going back to stables; [then] it started fighting again, and I last saw it kicking and squealing, being led off with the usual blanket over its eyes. I never saw [him] again, as we left soon after. But I strongly advised the owner merely to change his stables, and that the only thing the matter with the pony was that he was simply terrified of the people who were supposed to be looking after him.

During this long stay I made a survey of the Chinese forts at Woosung,[28] having found that the [current] intelligence report [was] very vague on the subject. This report, with accurate scale sketches, I sent in to the Major at Hong Kong. They were returned to me, together with an indignant letter from a Foreign Office intelligence official who said that my report was all wrong. My Major ordered me to check up again. However, I said it wasn't necessary; the F.O. report, made by a Chinese, was inaccurate in scale, the wrong shape, and left out several guns and the rest were inaccurate, and that if DX[29] would come up to Shanghai I would convince him by sight. This brought him along and I took him over the same ground I had previously travelled. It was difficult going and necessitated [moving] along the beach at low water, guarded by stakes, [but] saw for himself that I was right.

The result of this was that his source of information was obviously unreliable and involved me in an interesting trip to check-up on the forts around Ning-po.[30] I embarked in the river steamer *Pekin* for Ning-po, where I stayed with the consular agent. He was very inquisitive, so much so that I saw no reason to satisfy his curiosity as to what I was there for. A further trip up to Chinhai[31] in a Chinese launch satisfied me that the intelligence report was substantially correct, and I returned to Shanghai by the river steamer *Kiangtun*.

The stern, or aft, 6-inch gun, HMS *Flora*, manned by the Royal Marine detachment, one of the many roles of Royal Marines aboard ship. *Astraea* class ships had a primary armament of two 6-inch guns, one forward and one aft, with the crews protected by metal splinter screens [© Trustees RMM].

4. China Station, 1907–10

"Royal Marine Battalion" on parade in white uniforms, helmets, and with rifles, composed of detachments from ships on the China Station at Wei-hai-Wei, 1909. Note officers with swords and Sam Browne belts. Parade adjutant Lieutenant Jerram is in the background, far right [© Trustees RMM].

Not long after I left her, the *Pekin* was burnt out alongside the wharf at Shanghai. There were hundreds of Chinese passengers aboard and they panicked, jumping overboard with their possessions. A crowd of sampans collected, we thought to rescue them. But not they: It's bad joss [luck] to save anyone from drowning, [as] you offend the river god [of that name]. As a punishment you have to keep the person rescued all his life. So the sampan men just poked them in the eye with a boat hook and seized their belongings. Those that were rescued were by our boats, but in that tide there, not many.

[On] 4 February 1909, I found myself back in the *Astraea* at Shanghai; and we had another grand shooting trip round Nimrod Sound and the Chusan Lo.[32] And then up to Wei-hai-Wei for May to July. Here, after a fortnight in camp with my men, we returned to the ship in time for the annual gunnery, sports, and regatta. The *Astraea* had always, since I had known her, been a beautifully clean ship and I don't think the rest of the squadron gave much thought to her as a rival. And this impression was confirmed by my brother Rowland, who had now joined the Navy and was in the Flagship, the *King Alfred*.[33] So, when we settled down to win everything, there must have been a good deal of surprise. We had had little opportunity to fire our guns, and practically none in boat pulling and sailing, but we were all very proud of the ship and everyone was out to do their best.

The men won the soccer league, and the officers the tennis and golf. We won the gunlayers' shield and the Battle Practice Trophy, and made the most hits in night firing. Then came the pulling regatta. We were well up on points, when the Bo's'n discovered that no one had thought of an entry for the "All Comers" race. He tore round the ship and filled the pinnace with a scratch crew with double banked oars. They were too late to get a tow to the starting point three miles away, so away they went under oars. They got there just in time to start, and came home an easy winner, having rowed at racing speed for six miles! We won the cup for most points by 24 against the Flagship's 21; as she was big enough to pretty well hoist us on board, it was good going. In the sailing regatta we entered every boat and again got the highest points. I again got a first in the class for pinnaces.

Then came the Commander-in-Chief's Cup for any rig. We had a private rig for every boat, and we were confident of winning. The race was to be sailed next morning, when we got orders to return to Shanghai. It was quite unnecessary, and it looked as if the Admiral [Lambton][34] had had enough of us! However, our chummy ship for some unknown reason was the *Kent*.[35] She was as lousy as we were smart, and also in the Flagship's black book. So we hurriedly turned all our private sails over to her and learned later that she had won the race with one of them.

In September 1909, a very strong typhoon hit the coast between Hong Kong and the Yangtse, before bouncing off to Japan. We only got the tail end of it, but that was bad enough. I was on watch and standing in the starboard entry port, which was on the main deck, [with] the wind blowing a full gale on the starboard side. In the time I took to cross over and up the ladder to the upper deck, the wind went round eight points and was now blowing equally hard in the other direction. The *Clio* had left a few days before for Hong Kong and hadn't arrived. She had no wireless, carried little coal, and had to make most of her passages under sail. So we were ordered out to look for her. We looked into various inlets and eventually found her in Haitan Strait,[36] sheltering under an island. She was ordered to get under way as soon as the weather permitted, but I don't imagine that it was for a day or two, for we ran into a terrific sea on the way back and had to anchor off the Gutzlaff Light[37] on account of blinding solid rain. For six hours it was impossible to open one's eyes to windward.

Then in October, we had another shooting trip up the river. For some reason, *Astraea* was always a better sporting ship than *Flora*. On this occasion we anchored off the following places: North Tree Beacon, Nanking, Nganking, Kinkiang, Little Orphan Rock (a most astonishing place, an absolutely sheer rock about 300 feet high rising straight out of the river with a large temple on top of it; how they built it or how the monks lived was a mystery I never discovered), Tung Lin, Tung Ling, Wuhu, Heashan Bluff, and Chinkiang. Heashan Bluff was a masterpiece. We only had a short forenoon, and four of us landed, bringing back two hundred head of game of twenty varieties. I got a hog deer. These are queer little animals with two tusks like a wild pig and no horns.

At Wuhu[38] we met a party of Chinese farmers out shooting. We must have completely spoiled their sport and we rather wondered how they would take it. However, they were all friendliness: [They] examined our guns and we examined theirs. How they ever got anything I can't imagine, as it took all three of them to fire it: one to hold

4. China Station, 1907–10

Royal Marine Light Infantry, HMS *Flora*, China Station, 1908. Note the white uniforms, helmets, and Lee-Enfield Mark 1 long rifles [© Trustees RMM].

the butt, one the muzzle, and the third [to] put a slow match to the vent. Then they took us to their farm and handed out what we hoped would be tea. However, it was hot samshu, a most potent rice spirit. The mere smell nearly made you drunk and even old Wright, my servant, said he'd drunk most things but unless we were prepared to carry him home he couldn't tackle that. So the old lady by the fire, with a chuckle, drank the lot. We gave them a few cartridges and parted, wondering what would happen if an English squire out on his land after snipe came across a party of Chinese shooting them all!

My final cruise in the *Flora* in April-May 1910 took us to Chemulpo[39] in Korea, where we took part in the memorial service for King Edward VII. It was well on in May, very hot, and we had been in white clothing. However, this meant full dress, and for the Marines their scarlet tunics. My orders were to place guards on the Embassy compound to keep out unauthorized people and parade a guard for the catafalque on the same principle as that in Westminster Hall.[40] I found that an immense tent had been set up to accommodate about a thousand people for the service, with a draped catafalque before the altar. I had available two sergeants and two corporals, and placed them at each corner with myself in the centre facing the congregation. We had to be in position an hour before the service and remain till everyone had dispersed. Standing for some three hours without any relief, in tunic and helmet with arms reversed, in that climate

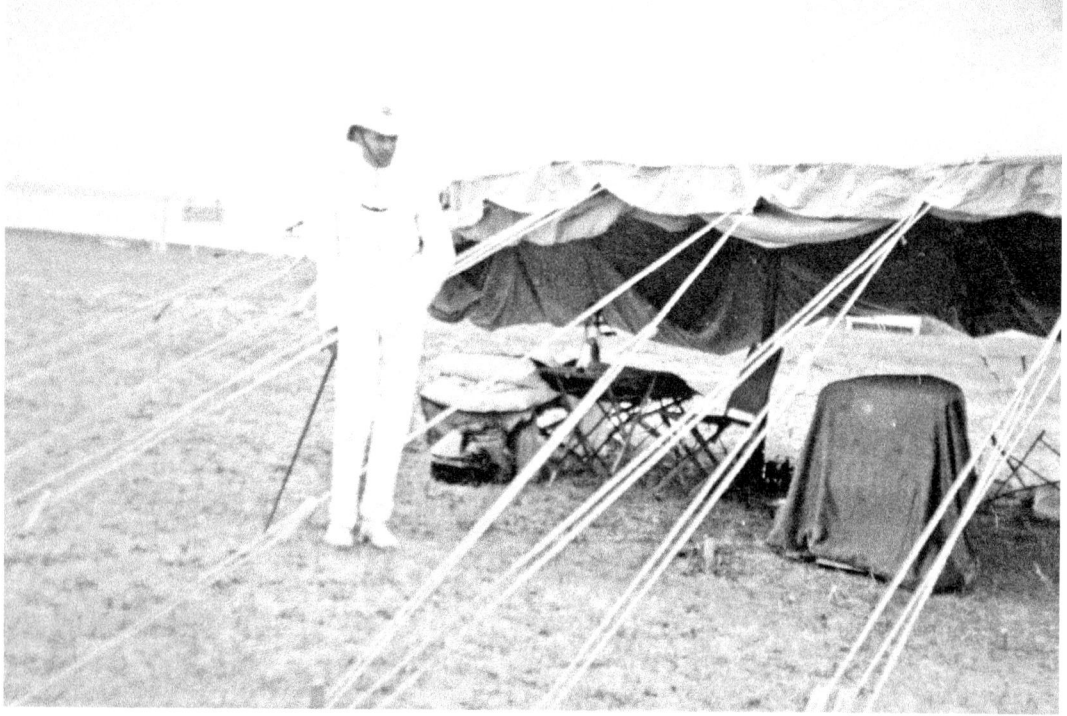

Top: Tent interior, Seoul, Korea, May 1910, at which a memorial service was held for Edward VII. Jerram recounts this ceremony in his memoir [© Trustees RMM]. *Bottom:* "My tent." The tent accommodation, with sleeping arrangements, of Lieutenant Jerram at the rifle range on Wei-hai-Wei, circa 1908. Jerram had the Royal Marine detachment of HMS *Astraea* ashore for training [© Trustees RMM].

was going to be tough. The guards' officers in London were relieved every half hour and found it enough.

So although we had to remain motionless with heads bowed, I ordered that during the singing of hymns heads were to be raised. But it wasn't much of a relief. One of my sergeants was very fat and I could only hope he wouldn't faint. I needn't have worried; out of the corner of my eye I could just see him. The sweat was pouring off the end of his nose, but he might have been carved out of a block of wood. The Captain[41] told me afterwards that there wasn't the slightest sign of a movement from the time he came in till he left. Next day we received a very nice compliment from the Ambassador, but I think we were the only five people [present] who didn't get any refreshment!

On our return to Wei-hai-Wei, we had a good example of the cheek of the Chinese pirates. Across the bay on the mainland side was a fleet of trading junks. In broad daylight and in full sight of [our] fleet, two pirate junks sailed in and looted them. No ship had steam up; and, as being the quickest, the dockyard tug was ordered to raise steam and we sent over 20 Marines to go in her. They never found the pirates and it remained a mystery where they had got to.

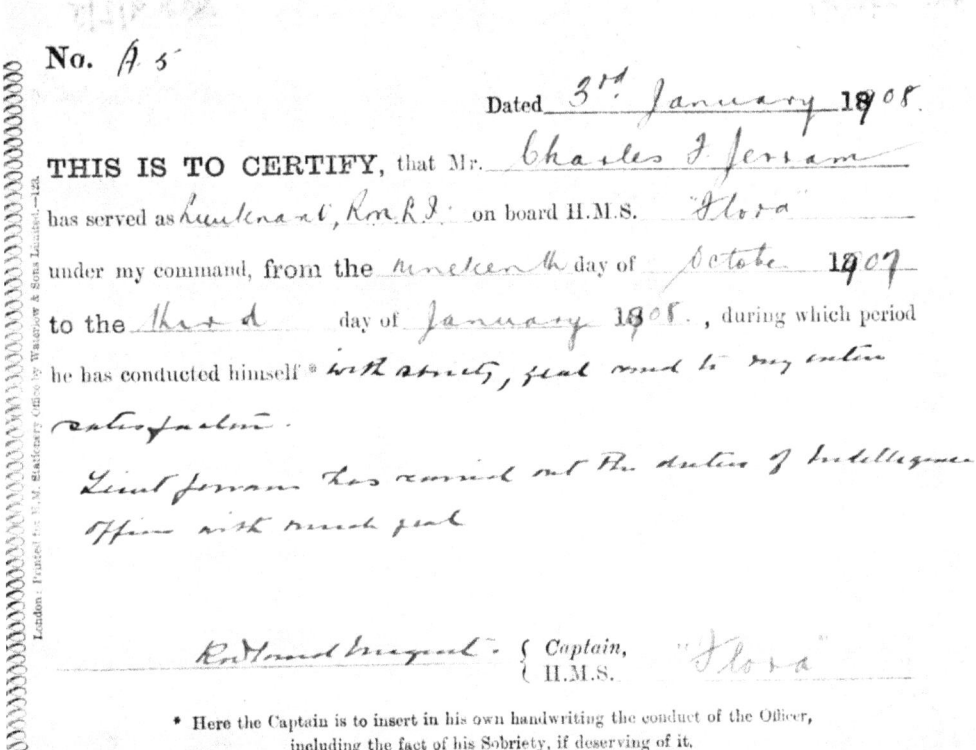

Flimsy given to Lieutenant Jerram by the Commanding Officer, HMS *Flora*, for the period of October 1907 to January 1908. Confidential reports on officers were literally confidential and submitted to the headquarters of the Royal Marines. Officers did not see them but were given a summary, called a "flimsy," on their performance of duty [© Trustees RMM].

In August 1910, the *Astraea* was due to pay off.[42] Thinking that it was about time, I went home [by way of] remaining in her. It is an astonishing fact that I never received any orders either to stay there all those four years or to come home! We went down through the fleet with our paying-off pendant flying and with manned yards. Calling in at Shanghai, Admiral Sah, Commander-in-Chief of the Chinese Navy, called and asked us all to a farewell dinner. Admiral Sah had been a midshipman in the British Navy and spoke perfect English. Under the regime of the Old Empress, he was a most picturesque and distinguished figure. His long black silk coat with its great golden dragon sleeves, his pigtail, and button cap all emphasized the fact that he was a great Chinese gentleman. [He had also] reminded us that his ancestors were civilized when ours were still living in trees! But now all this glory had gone, and we saw him for the first time in a bad copy of our uniform. To us who had known him before, he seemed to have shrunk.

However, he put up a wonderful dinner. As he said, a copy of an English dinner would be nothing to us; so we were invited to a Chinese restaurant, where we had all Chinese dishes and a Chinese play going on all the time. Captain Chang, our other host and the Admiral's Flag Captain, was a typical jolly, fat man who couldn't speak a word of English. He watched faces and when he saw by their expressions that a joke had been made, he roared with laughter.

Menu

1. Tea
2. Bamboo Shoots—Black Eggs (100 years old)—prawns—raw green crab—chicken—ham
3. Bird's nest soup
4. Pigeon's eggs in pigeon egg soup
5. Bamboo shoot soup
6. Shark's fin soup
7. Preserved oysters
8. Bean curd soup
9. Toadstool [mushroom] soup
10. Yangtse fish and cabbage
11. Varnished duck
12. Cabbage soup
13. Sweet ham
14. Sponge cake and orange syrup
15. Mincemeat pie and soup
16. Liver soup
17. Chinese unleavened bread
18. Stuffed cucumber
19. Ducks' brains
20. Shellfish stew
21. Six dishes set together from which you selected tid bits of fish, cabbage, sugar, ham, and cheese with rice

Drink

Hot Samshu

[Utensils]

Taken with chopsticks and china spoons.

    Before leaving Shanghai, I paid a last visit to the native city and saw in a shop a brass carved gong. I bought it after a bit of haggling, but the shop man said he'd like to polish it up before I had it. With complete faith in Chinese honesty, I paid for it and told him we were sailing at 2 p.m. and it must be on board by then. It turned up half an hour before we sailed and is the best witness to Chinese integrity one could want.

    We duly arrived at Colombo on August 30th, and turned over to the *Charybdis*, a sister ship, who had brought out the new crew. The *Charybdis* was a horror. One cannot expect a ship dragged out of the reserve for a trooping trip to be smart; but one does expect that dust from coal taken [aboard] at Aden would have disappeared before she arrived in Colombo! She was filthy and her crew apparently had been allowed to slack. I don't imagine that her First Lieutenant lasted long with our old Captain [Edward Kiddle],[43] who was staying in the *Astraea*. We duly paid off at Sheerness on October 17, 1910.

Chapter 5

Marking Time, 1910–14

On rejoining the Barracks at Stonehouse [Plymouth], I found that I was entitled to three months' leave and went home to Talland. But before doing so I ordered a boat to be built for me at the Cremyll Yard. They made a wonderful job of her and she was the best dinghy I've ever sailed. In the nearly four years I'd been away, I found many changes. The first aeroplane had recently flown the Channel. There were occasional motor cars. The Barracks had a Ford. It had only one gear and reverse, and when the hill was too steep for it, you turned it round and went up backwards. Gone was the Blue helmet, and [now] we had a better shaped wide one with the badge in front; not the flat monstrosity now worn, but something between that and the old one. Gone too was the men's red kersey, as blue became our normal dress. Scarlet was retained for full dress, with a slash cuff instead of the old pointed one. Also gone was the last of the civilian bandmasters, the new ones coming from the Military School of Music. And gone forever was the sense of security one had on joining [a] barracks [division] at the end of a commission afloat.

All officers came on the Sea Service Roster of their rank. When you disembarked you went to the bottom of the roster with a tour for every year over one; that is, when you got to the top, if you had two years to count, you went down to the bottom again. My three tours should have easily lasted me till I was promoted. But the Fleet was growing[1] daily with the menace from Germany, and our establishment was standing still.[2] I found only one other subaltern on the roster, B[ernard] Weller,[3] who had also two tours to count. Instead of a steady year or two in barracks, we turned round each other three times, and before long he was off to sea again. I was luckier, and as will be seen I got various short trips to sea which kept me from being appointed to one of the new *Dreadnoughts* now building, a job I would have hated after being so long on my own.

But at present I had my boat and my leave. I can only remember one incident of note which occurred during this time, and that was my first county ball. The Lygon-Cots of Traverbyn Vears asked me to a house party, and I found myself the only person at the ball with a black waistcoat with my tails! The white waistcoat came in that year and, being abroad, I didn't know it!

The social event of Barracks life, other than the Winter Ball, was the Monthly Matinee Musicale by the band. For this the mess room was always crowded, and it was an

5. Marking Time, 1910–14

excellent way of returning hospitality and getting to know people. The social aspect was very strictly observed, and one senior and two junior officers were on duty to make and return calls each month. There were still then county families living on their estates, and they were not averse to having their daughters invited to our "At Homes" and "Balls." So there was a lot of calling to be done. We bumped up against one snag I remember. It was the custom for a new regiment to call first; after a certain regiment had been in the garrison some time, it was gently hinted to them that we could not call on their mess until they had called on ours. The diplomat to whom we delegated this duty was informed that "The ____th do not call." Having met one of them later in the war, I don't think we missed much!

A fire in barracks, a fire on the docks, and a fire in the victualling yard all took place in this period. I do not know anything that gets you out of bed so quickly as the "fire call" as we used to sound it. The three groups of three notes long drawn out, with its "hurry, hurry, hurry come on" at the end made you jump. Nowadays they have ruined it by playing the notes short, and I don't think it would wake me up. Fires always seemed to come when my Company was on fire duty. In the one in barracks, I found myself sitting on a roof beam in the 1st Quartermaster's store, hauling up a hose to get at a place they couldn't reach from the floor. Next day I went to have a look at it and found that I had been sitting on a beam nearly burnt through at both ends and that a stream of molten lead had just missed me! "What the eye doesn't see, the mind needn't trouble about." The fire on the docks was a real blaze amongst huge piles of timber. On the dock were several small coasters, ketches mainly, with no one on board. As they were obviously in danger with the wind blowing straight towards them, I collected a few Marines, hoisted a stays'l, [and] sailed them over to the other side.

The [fire] in the Victualling Yard was a five story building [with the blaze] on the second floor. They were having a job with it and I went up to the next floor where I discovered that the floor was smouldering and the room full of clothing. Getting together a few men we started heaving bales out of the windows, many of them already smouldering, into the sea below. From nowhere dozens of boats gathered, picked them up, and took them home until the police arrived. At the subsequent Court of Inquiry, I was asked if I knew who was responsible for chucking them out. I said, "I was." "And who gave you an order to destroy government property?" I said, "I didn't need an order, I acted on common sense. The floor was already burning under our feet and if it collapsed with all those bales all the fire hoses in the town wouldn't put it out." After some argument the Court accepted my view, and the Marines were thanked for what they had done. On marching back to Barracks, we were all stopped and searched at the gate, and the men relieved of several extra shirts they had somehow acquired!

I was a good deal luckier than Weller as regards to being pushed off to sea again. Before I reached the top of the roster, I attended [in 1912] a Small Arms course at the Army School [of Musketry] at Hythe [Kent]. Unless you wanted to be at sea all your life, you had to qualify for a shore staff appointment. There was the Naval Gunnery course, which I didn't want as it meant big ships, and Army courses in small arms, signalling, etc. And I plumped for small arms as being most likely to keep me on the infantry side. It was an interesting course in two ways: One, it was a test out for the new rifle[4] to be used in the coming war; and two, because we were being treated as experimental experts, they qualified us as "instructor" without the usual exams! The other thing I managed to get through were my practical examinations for promotion, which was looming in the distance.

When I joined we were getting our companies in six years. But for a saving clause, things had got so sedentary now that I might still be a subaltern at 80.[5] The clause gave us our company after twelve years' service, IF you had passed for promotion. But you were on a supernumerary list and had to do subaltern's work. As a matter of fact, I have never been a substantive [permanent] Captain, for before I reached the bottom of the list the war came and I shortly became an acting Major. However, that was in the future and at present it was obviously wise to get qualified. This was the more necessary because I met my "fate" which was to change my whole life.

My brothers Rowland and Bertrand had been at King's School, Canterbury, and here they met the O'Neills, two boys and two girls. We looked on them as cousins but there was really no connection. Their mother was the sister of the wife of Charles Knight, my mother's cousin. I had met Leo, one of the boys, on several occasions when he had been staying with us; and in September 1911, he and his sister, Sibyl, had just completed a bicycle tour round England and he had left her in a farm at Talland. This coincided with my annual leave and the Talland Harvest Festival. I was decorating the [baptismal] font opposite the door [of the church] when Sibyl O'Neill walked in. Three days later we were engaged! I don't know how, it just happened and not until then did I even think what we were going to live on. My pay, by then 5/9, would go up to 12/1 a day on [my] promotion in a year's time. But that sort of thing happened in those days. If you couldn't afford to marry, you waited until you could. My Uncle Martyn was engaged for five years before his promotion to Commander. Nowadays every junior subaltern thinks he's ENTITLED to marry and that it's up to the government to give him the means to do so. But in those days, the government paid us for commanding our men, and not a whole family. Our private lives were our own concern.

However, I got a slight extension of leave on the strength of it and spent a fortnight at Canterbury. My greatest friends in the Regiment at this time were the Arbuthnots.[6] He was a senior Captain[7] with two charming children, Joan and Pat. Sailing my boat behind theirs out of Cawsand one day, I had noted how supremely happy they appeared to be; yet as far as I knew, they had little more than his pay to live on. So I wired to him, "Can you marry on a Captain's pay plus about 100 pounds a year?" The reply came back, "Yes at a push." So I didn't have to say I didn't mean it after all. But a staff appointment was even more necessary, and I was glad I had the prospects of being a small arms instructor some day. Little did I imagine how far off that was!

The year was filled in with the usual garrison life, but I was lucky in getting command of Renway Camp beyond Staddon Heights at Plymouth, where we did our small arms and field training. One evening it was blowing a full gale from the Southwest and I had a job to get across from the mess hall to my sleeping hut, and in the night I had a most vivid dream. A ship had gone ashore under the camp and I had done all the correct things: Told off rescue parties, gathered ropes and lanterns, and detailed a party to get fires going and hot drinks. At dawn I got up and looked out; it was still blowing

5. Marking Time, 1910–14

great guns, and there, sure enough on our end of the breakwater, was a big wooden sailing ship piled right up high and dry! We heard later that the King's Harbour Master in his picquet boat had rescued all the crew except the cook, who was drowned.

We arranged to be married at Talland on 15 August 1912, and spend our leave at Mylor[8] on the Carrick Road, Falmouth. I was, I believe, the first subaltern ever to be married. The O'Neills had no real home and old Uncle Charles Knight was an invalid. So they went to stay with Farmer Higman at Hendersick, which made it better for all of us, as they as well as we knew all the neighbourhood. Ralph was home on leave from India and [served as] best man. [He] did it so well that he had to buy my railway ticket, so as to leave me with enough for a cab at the other end! We hoped my next month's pay, plus a few wedding presents, would pay for the honeymoon!

August 15 was, I think, the only fine day in the month. I was to appear in Full Dress and old

Lieutenant Colonel Jerram (far right) on the date of his wedding, 15 August 1912, with three officers: two Royal Marines and one Royal Navy. The Royal Marine officers are wearing undress blue with frock coat. Note: All have swords [© Trustees RMM].

Wright, my servant, was staying in the house. The Service guests were to be in uniform frock coats, so I engaged a room in a Looe Hotel where they could change. Going up to change in good time, my father, who always expected everyone to miss trains, came up to give me a shake up. Finding me still in underclothes and playing on the mandolin "A Che la Morte" ("Why is death so long in coming"), he expected the whole show to be off. However, we got through [it] and Wright made a great hit in his livery, urging people to more champagne: "The best mess No. 1 Sir, it's good!"

Old Robert, the late Menheniot coach driver, now retired, brought over a pair of horse wagonettes for us. I got out at the first gate and removed all the old shoes tied on behind, and hoped that was the end of it. But at Liskeard the train taking my brother officers back to Plymouth left after ours, so they all came to see us off. Just as our train started they showered us and the whole train with rice! And when we went into the dining car for dinner, we were met by grins all round. Our landlady had never had

Mrs. Sibyl Jerram (1882–1952), wife of Lieutenant Colonel Jerram, at Trelew, near Falmouth, Cornwall, August 1912. They married when he was a First Lieutenant, unusual then because most officers did not marry until they were a Captain due to the need for adequate funds to support a family. Jerram did not have "independent means," i.e., an independent income [© Trustees RMM].

guests before, the house was quite new, and we were being furnished all the time. As we spent all our time out of doors, we usually came back to a new table or chair or something. [We] spent our leave between boat and bicycle, exploring miles of country. In the old *Queen of the Fal* under Captain Barney, you could go to the Lizard or Helford, and by taking your bicycle could explore all that country too. But it rained and it blew all the time. My wife was a philosophical person, and when commiserated later by other Barracks wives on being married to a lunatic boat sailor, said, "Oh, I don't think he wants to drown me." [Amidst much sailing and time ashore,] we eventually got up to Ruan[9] and in the church met a lady practicing the most dismal psalm tunes on a still more dismal harmonium. She was the vicar's wife and kindly asked us in to tea. There we met the Vicar, a charming old gentleman, and his curate son, who appeared to be only about half baked. But he was a great musician and had at least a dozen organs, harmoniums, and pianos scattered about the house, including a piano with stops. But how it worked, I don't know. We thought it a pity one of them wasn't put in the church.

We had taken very nice rooms at 51 Durnford Street with a Mrs. Davidson, a widow of one of our Warrant Officers. A delightful naval couple were in the rooms below.

5. Marking Time, 1910–14

After we had been there a few weeks, Mrs. Davidson took the lease of No. 76 and gave up 51. There was a good deal of amusement in Barracks circles upon reading the notice she stuck up: "Mrs. Davidson and Captain Jerram have moved to No. 76." My wife received much sympathy on the shortness of her married life!

On promotion to Captain (supernumerary),[10] I remained on the subaltern's Sea Roster, but the Royal Marine Office[11] was very kind in not sending me on a regular commission under a senior Captain, but kept me on a series of short trips on my own. Thus in March 1913 I had a week of manoeuvres, starting in the oldest battleship in the Navy, the *Nile*,[12] and ending in my old ship, [the] *Suffolk*.

Then it was decided to send the battleship *Swiftsure*[13] to the East Indies station and, as the Major [Hugh O'Sullivan][14] was staying out there, I took command of the detachment for the trip. It consisted of a RMA subaltern[15] and about 200 RMA and RMLI. This was my first and only dealing with the RMA. *Swiftsure* was built for the Brazilian [sic] government, [but] we took her over owning to the attitude of Germany [sic]. She was entirely different to any British ship, and had 11 inch [sic] and 7.5 inch guns. Her sister ship, *Triumph*, was sent out to China. They were no use as ships of the line, but could be quite valuable as a deterrent to raiding enemy cruisers.[16]

[But problems existed.] The[ir] 7.5-inch shell[s] weighed 200 pounds [each], and there was no means of getting [them] into the gun[s]. Hence, the Gunnery Lieutenant[17] asked all officers of quarters for suggestions, which he would come and see later. [With] no ideas of my own [but having] a very good artillery Sergeant, I left it to him. At that time the common practice of loading a 6-inch gun was to balance the 100 pounds on your left arm and throw it into the gun. It required a certain amount of strength, but more knack.

When the Gunnery Lieutenant came to our gun he asked me what we'd got and I referred him to my "gun captain." He closed up his gun crew of five strapping RMA and gave the order, "load." The two projectile members picked up their shells as if they were 6-inch and the first threw his into the breech, where it fetched up so hard that we had a job to get it out with the unloading rammer. "There you are, Sir," said the Sergeant, "That's the way to load her." Guns shook his head and said. "Yes, it's magnificent, but come and look at some of my seamen's gun crews!" They eventually invented some kind of platform to hold the shell whilst it was rammed home, but I always admired that bit of swank [of my gun crew]. At Bombay I turned over the *Swiftsure* and came home in the cruiser *Highflyer*.[18]

After that I had six months in the battleship *Exmouth*,[19] tender for gunnery trials at Devonport, which suited me perfectly. With our sea time limited to occasional days of gunnery, my C.O. more or less confined on board, and a sympathetically married commander,[20] things were made easy for me as to spending lunch time in our lodgings. All we married ones got to know each other and we formed friendships which [endured].

There were two of us there, and my C.O. was a senior Captain, one Strugnell,[21] or "Tubby Struggles," to give him his nickname. I'd heard of him as a very fat chap, and it was said that when he and "Skin Tight" White[22] were sent to the same ship, they had to keep them on opposite sides to prevent the ship from capsizing! But I never imagined anything approaching my first sight of my new C.O. I arrived at lunch and went in to the wardroom to see my new Captain at the head of the table. He couldn't sit anywhere else, and I nearly committed the indiscretion of collapsing with laughter. I've never imagined anything so enormous. It is quite impossible to describe; suffice it to say that if he landed in the Dockyard all the Dockyard mateys downed tools to collect round, and he seldom went ashore before dark. But he had plenty of guts, as I soon found out.

One day I suggested a long route march and said, "I suppose you won't come, Sir?" "Of course I'll come," said he. So I wickedly worked up a stinker: Landing at Saltash and coming off from Torpoint, which meant marching right round the head of the River Lynher and some pretty stiff hills.[23] I thought that by the time we got to South Germans, Tubby would drop out and come back by train. Not a bit of it, there he was all the way striding along at the head, and if anyone looked as if he'd had enough it was me, not him.

For our annual camp we had the Trevol Rifle range and I suggested a march to my home with a fight at the end. Tubby jumped at it and we went off on our 30 mile march, fought a night action up Hendersick Hill, and then arranged for a hay barn at the Barton for the men. My mother had arranged beds for Tubby and me, but he would have none of it. "You've got a loft over the stables, haven't you?," he said. "Well, we'll sleep there." And we did, rolled up in a blanket on the floor, whilst the men had hay! Next day we marched back. There was no softness about our Tubby. Nor was there for Skin Tight, for he later served with gallantry [at] Gallipoli. You could always be certain of a whiskey in his dugout. Where he got it nobody knew, but it was always said that if you hid a bottle of whiskey inside a 6" steel stanchion, Skin Tight would find it.

At Christmas we had a fortnight's leave, and my wife and I went off on a walking tour, mainly to take her mind off the death of our first child. It was gloriously fine, sunny, [and] crisp weather as we took it quietly along the North Cornish coast from Morwenstow to Boscastle, and thence across Brown Willy [to] Dozmary Pool and to Talland.[24]

Years before I had started ringing on the old decrepit ring of four bells at Talland, and had taken it up at Plymouth at St. George's Stonehouse, a ring of eight, and also joined Charles Church 10 under a grand old captain, Walter Mansh, where I had taken up change ringing.[25] Unfortunately, I never could progress very far as I was constantly being moved away. But I got our old Talland ringers under Tom Stephens interested in getting our bells increased to six with a new frame. We started a fund and put the job in the hands of Mears and Stainbank of Whitechapel.[26] They did a wonderful job, and we got it through just before the war. The new Tenor "Glory to God in the Highest" was bought from parish subscriptions, and we gave the Treble "Sanctus, Sanctus, Sanctus" in memory of our daughter. And we managed to be there for the opening.

The *Exmouth* paid off at the end of 1913. As I had not got a whole tour in, the Marine Office asked me if I'd like to go on a short trip in the cruiser *Eclipse*,[27] which it was hoped would make up my time. It was very good of them, and I accordingly joined *Eclipse* at the end of February and found that we were to escort the first two Australian submarines, *AE1* and *AE2*. I learned later that our RNR Sub-Lieutenant left the ship in Australia and joined their Navy. He commanded *AE2* and was lost in the coming war.[28]

After turning over to another ship at Colombo, we returned in the latter part of May 1914. We went to Talland for the dedication of the bells, and I got through my first peal at St. George's, 5040 changes Grandsire Triples, on the table. But the best part of this short period before the war was a field training company I was given at Fort Scrassdon. I had as my subalterns two newly joined officers, Morford[29] and Bath.[30] War by now seemed to be almost inevitable, and the thing that struck me most was the menace of the machine gun combined with the extreme difficulty of preventing men from bunching into the easiest places in which to advance or take cover. [Hence] I concentrated on this aspect [of tactics]. On the training mile square at Scrassdon there were good thick Cornish ledges, crowned with the usual thorn and bramble. [Consequently] I used to line up the men about two yards apart and make them [advance] straight ahead.

Undated photo of the then-major Jerram with one of his newborn daughters [© Trustees RMM].

Those that went through gaps had to go back again. Invariably through the very thickest part would come Morford, a magnificent example which quickly showed others both the possibility and probable advantages.

These early days formed a pattern for Morford's life, some of which I saw at first hand and some of which was told [to] me by General Blumberg[31] years later when he was commanding the Corps. Morford went out to Gallipoli with the Plymouth Battalion [of the Royal Naval Division] and was badly wounded. [Later in France he was] wounded in the foot, invalided home, and was told he could not be again employed on active service, even in a ship. He turned up at the Marine Office and asked to see General Blumberg, whom he asked if there was any objection to him joining the Royal Flying Corps. The General told him he hadn't any hope of passing the medical but, after renewed appeal, said he could try if he liked.

He eventually got an interview whilst still on crutches. Leaving these in the cab he went in to [face] the medical board. One look at his leg was enough for them but not for Morford, who assured them he could do anything with it. So they gave him another chance: "Jump on that foot" [and] "Climb that rope and drop on that foot." This was accomplished without a quiver, and they said, "Well, if you can do that you ought to be all right," and they passed him! Arriving in the dressing room the orderly found that he had fainted, but never told the doctors.

So Morford went out to France again, [this time] as an airman. Shot down eventually and badly wounded in the other leg, he made a perfect landing, saving his observer and his plane. He ended as he began. In World War II, he wished to demonstrate to his men that you could travel safely in a "Carrier," a small motor car with bullet proof sides and no top. So, getting his staff officer to drive him as a passenger, he drove across the front of his men [with them] firing at it! Now a carrier is safe if the top is not exposed to the fire, but unfortunately the driver let her go over the side of a hill and Morford was hit in the head and killed. Thus died a very brave man. No one ever saw him with the slightest limp or would imagine that one of his feet was more like a lump of pulp and the other leg not much better. But this was all to come, and at present he was the best subaltern I've ever had.

It was a grand company and I would have given almost anything to take it, as it stood, on active service. It had a sequel many years later in World War II. When riding into our new camp near Exmouth one day in 1944, a linesman of the G.P.O. [General

Undated family photograph of Lieutenant Colonel Jerram, Mrs. Jerram, two daughters, and one son (a second son was born later) [© Trustees RMM].

Post Office] shimmied down a telephone pole and came running up to me, saying, "You are Mr. Jerram, Sir! You remember me! I was in your Field Training Company at Scrassdon in 1914. Gawd it makes me feel hot all over to think of it!"

In July 1914 came the greatest review of the Navy at Spithead there has ever been. No need then, as in subsequent ones, to introduce merchant ships and fishing boats to make up something big enough to look at. It was a review of Britain's might upon the waters, commanded by a Sailor King [George V]. I was sent to the *Caesar*,[32] an ancient battleship of the same vintage as the cruiser in which I had first embarked. Many of the class did good work as bombarding ships at Gallipoli and elsewhere. It was a wonderful experience, that review: Miles and miles of ships from the great new *Dreadnoughts* down; all ships dressed overall and sides manned and with all the Marines as guards in their Blue and Scarlet; each ship in turn giving three cheers as the King came abreast of them.

And then, instead of dispersing, the whole Fleet was sent to its war stations. That was the first day of August 1914. It was said that it was Winston Churchill's own idea. It may have been; if so it was the only wise thing he was to do as First Lord of the Admiralty. He was hated in the Navy for his superior condescensions. My own experience of him, which was typical, was at Plymouth when he came to inspect us. I was carrying the Regimental Colour in the Guard of Honour. All the Civil Lords meticulously removed their hats as they passed, except Churchill; [he] took no notice whatever, but stopped a few files further along and lifted a private's trouser leg, presumably to see if he had on regulation socks. It says much for our discipline that he didn't get a kick in the eye! I do not suppose any greater insult could be committed at a Guard of Honour.

When my Uncle Martyn returned from his command of the China Station, Winston sent for him, kept him standing in front of him for fully five minutes, and then said, "Ah yes, Admiral Jerram, I think you are the only one of 'my' Admirals I've not met," and that was all. If it had not been war time I think my uncle would have told him very clearly that he was King George's Admiral and that Churchill wasn't a King yet! But anyway he was so taken aback that he just walked out and boiled over elsewhere.[33]

My war station was [on] the *Euryalus*, a sister of my first ship, and I went to Chatham Barracks to pick up my detachment. But first I had a couple of days at home. On the evening before I left we walked down to Devil's Point, and just at sunset we saw a flotilla of destroyers steaming out to sea, "Guardians of the Western Port." I turned to my wife and said, "That means war," and we turned home in silence.[34]

Chapter 6

War at Sea, 1914

I arrived at Chatham Barracks[1] next evening, the only time I've been there, by the way. The mess and [the entire] barracks were [organized] on a similar system to Plymouth, but in old red brick instead of our limestone. The mess room [was] smaller and [had] a band gallery. Here I found great activity: Officers were rejoining hourly, and the first person I met was my old Adjutant, Morres. On giving up his Adjutancy he had retired to British Columbia, [but] had dashed back to rejoin at the first threat of war. He had managed to find a uniform patrol jacket, but so far only plain clothes trousers. Many others hadn't even that and were taking up men's clothing and adding the necessary badges to the shoulder straps. I've never felt so sorry for anyone as I did for Morres. He was a grand officer and would have been a tremendous asset later. But in the scramble of the coming Antwerp expedition, he stepped unknowingly with most of his men into Holland, where he was interned for the rest of the war.[2]

We commissioned the *Euryalus*[3] on August 1. Practically all my men, and most of the seamen and stokers, were pensioner reservists with 21 years previous service. Most of mine had beards, the Marines being the only regiment to be allowed them. Normally they were not encouraged, but these men habitually [had] worn beards and I was very proud of my old timers. We coaled, ammunitioned, and stored in record time and put to sea the day war was declared. At noon the Captain [Leatham][4] had everyone aft and gave us the news, "We are now at war with Germany," and called for three cheers for the King! Just then there was a bang and the long drone of a big shell. It was only the artillery testing range at Shoeburymess [Essex] but it put an apt period to our cheers.

We went straight out into the North Sea, putting final touches to our preparation for battle. All rigging was snaked down with rope harness and rope mantlets rigged along the upper deck between the light guns to stop splinters, and a stack of filled coal sacks piled round the engine room casings. We were in three watches: Watch-on, stand-by, and watch-below. The first closed up round the guns, the stand-by slept where they could on deck, and the last turned in [below]. The Marines had the after 9.2-inch gun, but my daytime battle station was as spotting officer on the Fore Top, or, more generally, the Fore Tops'l yard as giving better view. From there I could give range corrections to the voice pipe number [sailor] to pass to the guns. There was, of course, at that time no system of control other than visual spotting and voice pipe.

For my stand-by I found a little cubby hole containing spare canvas under the conning tower. My first visit below showed me some of the "horrors of war." The North Sea as usual was revelling in a gale, and upper deck companion[way]s had to be kept open for getting about. Very cold and wet, I went down to my cabin to turn in, only to find it a foot deep in cold black sea water washing from side to side as we pitched and rolled. Indeed, one's watch below generally meant taking off one's oilskins, emptying the water out of one's boots, and turning-in "all standing," i.e., in your clothes.

We belonged to a cruiser squadron always at sea. There were four of us, all [of] the same class: *Euryalus* (the flag[ship]), *Aboukir*, *Hogue*, and *Cressy*. It was rather amusing [that] the Admiral [Arthur Christian],[5] [in] choosing our ship, [benefitted me]: [although] I was the Junior Marine officer in the Squadron, [I received] 5/- a day extra pay as Flag allowance. The senior Marine officer put in an application to [transfer] to the Flagship, but the Admiral said that he was quite satisfied with the officer he had and wouldn't grant it. So three senior [Marine] Captains[6] had to grin and bear seeing a newly promoted fledgling drawing the much coveted Flag allowance.

It was a tough time as we had to return to coal at least every week, and [then] went straight off to sea again before it was even swept down. This meant in effect that seldom more than three ships were on the patrol ground and one of these went in as the other came out. One day in the usual Northeast gale we met a submarine on the surface and went to quarters. She proved to be a damaged one of ours; but having run our [6-inch] maindeck guns out, we had a tremendous job getting them run in. The men were simply washed away from them and the ship [was] rapidly filling up. We did eventually get the ports closed, but in the meantime had lost our fore topgallant mast, with the wireless and Admiral's Flag, so we went in to coal and refit.

We were under the direct control of the Admiralty, which meant in effect Winston [Churchill], and were sent out to "trail our coats," [sailing] up and down the German coast from Heligoland to the Bovard 14 Shoal.[7] We couldn't fire our guns [nor] keep to sea for more than a week, even at 10 knots, and [we] were a sitting target for anything that came along. I think we were all quite philosophical on the matter. We knew we were bound to be sunk some day [and], if we thought of it at all, it was with a sense of derision of the vaunted German Navy being so dilatory about it. The Admiral told us once that he had been to the Admiralty and begged to be allowed to vary the patrol, but was told that it was Winston's orders. Looking back, it still seems to me to be pure murder. It is true that sometimes we had destroyers or submarines behind us, and there was sense in that even if we were "the live bait." We were of no value, and if we could lure a few German ships on to our destroyers it was worth while. But when we were alone, it was utterly senseless. We did occasionally get a reprieve, joining the Harwich forces[8] in a sweep round the Heligoland Bight. Not a solitary German did we ever see poke his nose out of harbour. It was the French wars of Napoleon all over again, with the [blockade in the] North Sea instead of off Brest.

We were, however, at the Battle of Heligoland [on 28 August 1914], though we never fired a shot. We were in support of the "L" class destroyers. They had been in action all night and fell back on us. Our first glimpse of real war! The *Laurel*, *Lurcher* and *Liberty*[9] had got it pretty badly going in at the shortest range and missing with their torpedoes. *Laurel* had lost all her guns and torpedo tubes. Her Commander, Rose, was wounded early on, but had [had] a chair [placed] on the bridge for him. Again wounded, he had remained in command till they came out of action. We made them a signal, "Do you require assistance?" In reply the Engineer Lieutenant [sic], the only officer left, replied, "We are still good for 10 knots if there is anything more we can do. But if we are to return to base, submit we may be towed, as our boilers are likely to blow up any minute!"[10] So we took them in tow. *Liberty* had lost her mast and all her funnels, and the crew was busy trying to get something round the stumps. *Lurcher*'s scuppers were literally "running with blood," having not only her own wounded but [also] the survivors of the German cruiser, [SMS] *Bismarck* [sic].[11] We took over the prisoners and returned to Sheerness after dropping them at Harwich.

On arrival at Sheerness, generally known as "Sheernasty" or "Sheernecessity," I heard of the birth of my son. As we should be in [port for] two days instead of the normal one or a bit, the Admiral very kindly allowed me to run home. My wife had taken a house in Yelverton, near Plymouth, and I could just get there and back at a push. Catching the midnight train from Paddington, I got to Plymouth in time to catch the 7 a.m. to Yelverton, where I found all well, and returned by the midnight, getting to Sheerness just in time to go to sea.

Steaming out to rejoin our squadron, we took in a wireless signal from the *Cressy*: "*Aboukir* and *Hogue* are sinking," and then silence. Working up to full speed, we were, however, recalled by the Admiralty, who informed us that destroyers had been sent. So it had happened at last.[12] A submarine had got the lot. *Aboukir* was the first, and the *Hogue* gallantly went in to help as did the *Cressy*. There were no [British] destroyers out and no submarines, [so] my old ship [*Hogue*] went down without hope of being able to retaliate. Such as were saved were rescued by Dutch fishing boats.[13] Ozanne, Captain of Marines of *Aboukir*, had a wonderful escape. Picked up by the *Hogue*, he was torpedoed again and was again picked up by the *Cressy*, and finally by a Dutch fishing boat.[14] As a result of this incident, an order was made forbidding ships to go to the rescue of others. It was a hard order, but obviously wise.

So we returned again to Sheerness, and were then ordered down to the Western Patrol.[15] Based at Plymouth, our beat was normally from the Start to the Scillies. My Midshipman assistant was a Williams, and from our perch in the fore top I would discourse on the beauty of Talland; whilst after rounding the "Deadman," he would proclaim the greater beauties of Caerhays, his ancestral castle.[16] We were, I suppose, the only two in the ship to call it the "Deadman," for we had a Chatham crew and all charts and maps mark[ed] it the "Dodman." But no local between Rame and Lizard ever called it anything but the "Deadman."

Before leaving Sheernasty we had a bit of a celebration, with which oysters were a feature. We had not been long on patrol when one of our midshipmen, son of the Commander-in-Chief, Plymouth,[17] was landed with enteric [i.e., typhoid] fever. Three more cases and then I succumbed. Carried out of my cabin on a stretcher, I begged them to carry me head first. But they couldn't, so out I went feet first, a sure sign that you are going to die! Lowered over the side into the hospital launch at Plymouth, I hoped I'd soon be in bed. Not a bit of it; I should think we must have visited every ship in the

Navy. However, we did eventually arrive at the Royal Naval Hospital pier—the creek is now filled in—and I was taken up under the arch. After a long time someone came along and asked me my religion. That certainly must mean an immediate funeral! On the way to the ward I was twice asked the same question; after being deposited, there was a sudden panic and I was whisked off again, it having been discovered that I was an enteric [case].

By the time I got to the zymotic ward [i.e., a ward for those with infectious diseases], I must have been half delirious. I remember an angelic vision of a girl in that most beautiful of all hospital uniforms to whom I begged not to be asked my religion, and [received] a soothing answer. [I also made] one last remark as I was put into lovely clean sheets: "I'm too dirty." [With] coal, sea water, and living in one's clothes, one doesn't notice much until you come up against something spotlessly clean. Then I suppose they must have given me something to ease my appalling head. And that's about all I remember until I was getting better. Eventually my wife was allowed to see me, and we got a good deal of amusement out of a violent flirtation between my charming sister [Posy] and a very redheaded and very Irish doctor.

I left the hospital, having seen all the others on the road to recovery, in late December. One of them was one of my Marines, a wardroom servant. When he mournfully [said], "I know I shouldn't have eaten the Officers' oysters!," I [replied] to him, "Oh you rascal, I've no sympathy for you." I went straight to Talland, where the family was staying, on six weeks leave, [after] being told that I must not come up for survey, [a medical evaluation to ascertain physical fitness for duty] before that. However, the very next day I [received] a telegram from the Marine Office: "You are appointed Staff Captain of the R[oyal] Marines Brigade [of the Royal Naval Division[18]] with temporary rank of Major. State when you can join." It was no use arguing with the hospital by letter, so I packed my bag and drove down to Looe.

In the train I handed two telegrams to a porter: One to the Marine Office to say I was joining at once, and one to the hospital to say I was coming up for survey. As luck would have it, the head[19] of the hospital was a great friend of my Uncle Martyn and also of ours. He greeted me with, "What the hell are you doing here, get out," but condescended to listen to my plea that this was my one chance that everyone was aching for; [so] he got hold of a surgeon to give me [the] necessary tests. Then I saw their faces fall, and had just given up hope when the surgeon said he'd made a mistake. "It might have been very serious," said his boss. Then I started in again, and pointed out that there could be no prospect of going overseas for some weeks, and eventually he said, "Well, all right we'll pass you, but God help you if you come back."

I duly arrived at Deal where we were assembling, and reported to Brigadier General Trotman,[20] an old friend, who promptly sent me home again on Christmas leave! During my time in the *Euryalus*, we had taken the [Royal] Marine Brigade, then under General Aston[21] to Ostende, on the first of its expeditions. General Aston had no staff and begged the Admiral to let him take me. Rightly, the Admiral would not let me go. I was his only Marine officer and had an important battle post. It was a great disappointment, but I spent the whole night making maps for [them] from the chart, so [I] was of some use. And now here I was in that very job. General Trotman had asked for either Weller or me. Now Weller was in a ship [HMS *Eclipse*] and I was in the hospital; therefore, in the typically muddled mind of the Royal Marine Office, I was available!

My old servant, Wright, was a problem and it was he who solved it. He knew and I knew the state of his feet; and he said that if he went before a Board they would invalid[22] him. That was the last thing he wanted and he could serve at sea quite well. I got him a job with my late subaltern, Bath, and he served in the Grand Fleet [throughout] the war. On his short leaves he always turned up at our house and went through all the clothes I left behind. He was a fine old man and a great friend of my wife and myself. "Don't you worry mum, the Captain will come back all right," [he always told her].

I rejoined the Brigade in Dorset where they were assembling for training and re[forming] after the disastrous Antwerp landing. [The Royal Naval] Division[23] was another of Winston's creations: A good idea in itself if it had been carried to a logical conclusion. The Division was made up of two so-called naval brigades and one of Marines. The naval brigades had originally been made up of stokers, unwanted on account of the new ships being oil fired. These had largely been interned in Holland during the retreat from Antwerp, [including] practically the whole of the First Brigade and the majority of the Portsmouth Battalion of the Marines. In fact, only one company, or a part of it, was saved when a young subaltern refused to cross the border and fought his way back.

In the [subsequent] reorganization, Brigadier General [Archibald] Paris[24] took command, and the [naval] Brigades were commanded by Commodore Backhouse, RN,[25] and General Mercer, Royal Marines[26]; the battalions by all sorts of people: Some of them by Marine officers, and some by officers of the Indian Army on leave, who found it the only way to get into the war. The remaining officers were largely Royal Naval Volunteer Reserve, who hated it and wanted

General Sir Charles Trotman, KCB. In 1915, he was Commanding Officer of the Royal Marine Brigade and, when its General Officer Commanding was on leave, Commanding General of the Royal Naval Division. He appointed Jerram as Brigade Major of the Royal Marine Brigade of the Royal Naval Division, serving in the grade of Temporary Major. His substantive promotion to Major occurred on 1 September 1917 [© Trustees RMM].

to serve at sea, [temporary Royal Marine officers commissioned for service in the division], and soldiers of fortune.

Such sailors as there had been had largely disappeared and had been replaced by Army recruits from the north [who were] surplus to their own regimental requirements. The Marines Brigade, now commanded by General Trotman, was better off though not [by] much. At least its officers were Marine officers, but most of the subalterns were completely untrained and, therefore, not available for sea [service]![27] [Also], about half of them were temporary officers straight from school.[28]

The Marine Artillery Battalion was disbanded and a fourth [one of infantry], Deal Battalion, formed. It was a pretty poor show. In effect, it was officered by all the left overs, and the men were raw recruits with one notable exception in its second in command [Major John Tupman].[29] This officer had retired to take on the job of paymaster, but at once gave up his cushy job and volunteered for active service, an example which might well have been followed by some much more junior officers at the Depot, two of whom sat there [throughout] the whole war. Of the other battalions, Colonel Parsons commanded the Chatham Battalion and Colonel Matthews, who had just returned from the Egyptian Army, the Plymouth Battalion, and Colonel Luard, the Portsmouth Battalion.[30] There was no question at all in anybody's mind that the whole force needed a great deal of training, even the Marines, 90% of whom had never even seen a battalion mobilized for war.

Still we were used to sudden calls; in every emergency there was always a call for a battalion, usually made up of a company from each division. So we were not unduly surprised, when we'd hardly settled down to train, to [receive] orders to embark forthwith for the Mediterranean. However, Portsmouth Battalion had hardly reformed and Deal was worse, so we were limited to Brigade Headquarters and Chatham and Plymouth Battalions. We embarked at Plymouth in the *Braemar Castle* and *Cawdor Castle*, arriving at Malta on the 14 February. There I experienced the uncanny memory of the Maltese dghaise man [,an operator of small boats in the harbour]. Last time I'd been in Malta was in 1906, a young subaltern in blue. [I] now [returned as] a Major in khaki looking over the side, [and] I was greeted by, "I know you, sah, you Marine officer in the *Suffolk*!"

We landed all the horses for exercise. My pony, "Bobby," had had a tough time cooped-up in a small box during a very rough trip. When it was time to re-embark, "Bobby" took one look at the ship, dived over board, and swam the whole of the Grand Harbour before he could land.

It was only now that we discovered what we had been sent out for. The Fleet had been bombarding the forts at the entrance to the Dardanelles and had landed some of its own Marines to complete their destruction. But they were not sufficient in number to undertake any operation further inland. We were, therefore, sent out to land and blow up forts and batteries, as required. [But] we were not really equipped, having no battalion stores and little ammunition.

We managed to get a few necessities at Malta and then proceed[ed] to join the Fleet off Imbros. Here General Trotman [received] his orders to land and destroy certain forts. Naturally his first request was, "What transport could he have?," pointing out that he must have sufficient boats to land his whole force AND to re-embark them if seriously opposed. Alternatively, he could only land sufficient numbers to ensure they could all land and come off together. So it transpired that as we could only use limited naval boats, the fleet was no better off than with its own Marines. For some reason, transport boats were not allowed to be used. It was therefore decided to use only two companies of Plymouth Battalion, one each side [of the entrance to the straits]—and they duly landed on March 4th, [1915], covering a naval demolition party. The party on the west side [i.e., the European] found no opposition and the Sedd el Bahr fort pretty well smashed up already, [hence] were withdrawn.

The force landing at Kum Kaleh on the Asiatic side had a tougher time and [in their experience] can be read in the history of the Campaign.[31] I am concerned here only with my own history.

LtColonel Matthews commanded the force which consisted of one company of Royal Marines, two machine guns, a doctor's party, and the naval demolition party [of] about 50 under a Lieutenant, R.N. From our destroyer we watched the leading platoon occupy the fort under a fairly heavy rifle and field gunfire, and then the remainder go off in the direction of the windmills. [This left] the demolition party about the spit, covered by one platoon; the rest of the company disappeared into the nullah [a dry river gully or ravine]. There was obviously a good deal of opposition and we could see a few casualties. About 2 p.m. the Brigadier decided to join the Admiral in the Flagship, and from the bridge I saw at least a battalion of the enemy emerge from trenches below the windmill and move off to the east. It looked as if they would work round out of sight and cut off our advanced units, and I reported [this] to the Brigadier.

After consultation with the Admiral, it was decided to re-embark. I was [then] sent in in a whaler, a small five oared boat, to inform Colonel Matthews and to remain to give any assistance. On the way in we came under shrapnel fire, and it was then that I remembered my old fights with Ralph and my need for "Dutch Courage." I found myself quite automatically tightening up the laces of my boots. I found a queer situation. Having once cleared the fort and houses, [while Lieutenant] May's[32] platoon had cleared up toward the north, these bits and pieces seemed to have collected round the landing under cover of the western wall of the fort. Apparently no one was watching the land side except to the south. However, the adjutant [Captain Reginald Lough[33]] was there somewhere and it [was] not my business.

I was told that Colonel Matthews was somewhere out to the south, but that there were snipers in the houses and I was sure to be hit if I went out. I hadn't time to ask what they were doing about it, and the only officer I saw was the doctor. Anyway the snipers were poor shots at less than 100 yards and I eventually found the Colonel, all alone, and gave him the message. He told me to do three things. One, send the naval party back to the landing place. Two, get a platoon, lying down in the sand, up on to the slight ridge to watch the east flank. And, [three], then go on to the nullah and tell [Major] Bewes[34] to withdraw through them. Sounds simple enough.

I [reached] the naval party without being hit and lay down alongside a sailor. Suddenly discovering that his idea of cover was a box of detonators, I hurriedly moved on! Passing the word for their withdrawal led to a "sauve qui peut" [everyman for himself], with the officer leading. I yelled to him to keep behind his men, without result. I only mention the incident as an example of a fish out of water, for the same officer [received] a Victoria Cross shortly after in a submarine!

To shift the platoon was another matter. The officer, a temporary Lieutenant, was completely paralyzed with fear and took no notice even when I kicked him. The platoon sergeant, a fine old soldier, had been hit in the head and was obviously not capable of taking charge. So there I stood, pretty helpless, asking if they were waiting for me to be shot. Eventually, a young soldier got up and said, "I'll go with you, Sir." I took him forward and told the rest to line up on him when we got there. That moved them. And then, as luck would have it, my volunteer was shot smack through the chest. I couldn't leave him, and had just finished patching him up when Colonel Matthews came up and asked me why I hadn't gone forward. I had neither time nor inclination to tell him and I don't know what happened to the subaltern, but he left the battalion and got a base job somehow.

Colonel Matthews and I went forward to the last bit of cover, if it could be called so. And he came to the conclusion that even if I got to the nullah, Bewes couldn't get his men out without adequate covering fire. So he sent me back with a message to the Flagship to bring fire down on the trenches beyond the nullah. I've never liked turning my back to fire. I don't know why, but one's back always feels more vulnerable than one's front. Anyway, being pretty blown [winded], I chucked myself down for a rest in what I fondly imagined was cover. A spurt of sand in my eyes disillusioned me, and two more shots on either side made me feel more kindly towards the platoon I'd been cursing. That was my first experience, and it taught me a lesson I've always passed on: NEVER lie down under fire if it is possible to avoid doing so. If you have to, it's the devil to get moving again. The subsequent landings of the 29th Division[35] more than proved it: On the centre and left of their attack nearly all their casualties were when lying down and they never did advance.

On getting back to the houses I met [Captain] Lough, the Adjutant, who asked if he could be [of] any use forward. I said I thought he would be [of] more use organizing the cover for the withdrawing troops. We decided not to cross the houses together. And, having given him the message in case, I went on. They were shouting to me from the fort to either run or crawl. But I couldn't have done either then to save the whole British Army. Wading up to my waist, [I] gave the blighters only my head and shoulders to aim at. And having missed me six or seven times, I got so angry that I stopped and gave each of six windows a shot from my revolver! Whether I got any one I don't know, but not another shot ever came from there.

Having got off the message, I found the two machine guns and got them up on the parapet. [I] told them to strafe the windows of the houses and then, at extreme range, [to] plaster the enemy trenches whilst Bewes was retiring. Conybeare[36] and Law,[37] the two machine gun officers, wanted to argue that it was not sound MG tactics. I said I didn't care a damn about that, and it was, I suppose, the first of the MG barrages with unobserved fire, which were to become common two years later. Anyway, Bewes said it was fine. When they heard those bullets going over, they realized that someone was at last trying to get them out of a hole.

We were all just reembarking when two "dead" sailors, left behind by the naval party, got up and started staggering home. Conybeare and Law immediately picked up stretchers and went out after them. A midshipman volunteered to come with me, but the Colonel recalled us and told us to embark and said he'd send a boat in for them. A destroyer sent in a whaler after dark and picked them up. The whole whaler's crew got a DCM,[38] [while] Conybeare and Law got nothing!

So ended our first scrap. Lots of guts—some funk and precious little result. But we had been shot over and, therefore, should be one up for any future occasion. When I met Lough again he said, "Hell of a lot of you thought about me, didn't you." It's true, I hadn't given him another thought. After I left him he was hit in the back by an expended shot and pitched into the sea, with nothing worse than a bruise. I enquired after my volunteer and heard that the bullet had not gone through, but only passed round his ribs.

Chapter 7

Gallipoli, 1915[1]

This was the end of our period of usefulness with the Fleet. The Plymouth Company had had 50 casualties, more than a quarter of its strength, and [was of] no real use. It is easy to be wise after the event, but even then it seemed as if someone ought to have been wise enough, in view of coming events, to keep us with the Fleet for hit-and-run tactics on the long exposed Turkish flanks, after the manner in which Commandos were used in [World] War II. But the whole Gallipoli Campaign was a muddle from start to finish[2]: Constant wrangling at home and diversities of opinions on the spot, a weak G.O.C. [General Officer Commanding] influenced by the last comer, a jealous shore commander, and troops almost without exception with no training at all. Even the 29th Division was made up of [six] individual battalions from India [and three from Burma, one each from China, Mauritius, and Scotland] and had no brigade or divisional training. However, this narrative is concerned not with the high command,[3] but how it affected us in general and me in particular. And the searcher for truth had better read Alan Moorehead's *Gallipoli*, [and Robert Rhodes] James' book [*Gallipoli*][4]—better still and very fair to Marines.

We returned to Mudros where we picked up the Portsmouth Battalion, and by 12 March [1915] the whole [Royal Naval] Division had collected [i.e. assembled]. It had neither artillery nor transport, and the idea still seemed to be to use it for naval purposes. We did practically everything we shouldn't have done in the way of keeping the Turk awake. [We also] made two demonstrations with the Fleet and transports, seemingly to ensure the enemy would be thoroughly prepared for any landing.

In the meantime, things were "going-on" in higher circles. The decision to land had been made and the troops allotted, and [only when the] force was assembled that it was discovered that all the transports had been loaded upside down and that everything we wanted first was at the bottom [i.e., not combat loaded]. So off we all went to Egypt to unload and reload. [While there] we had a camp in the desert and [endured] a sand storm and a locust plague.

The plan for landing [at Cape Helles] has to be touched upon because, owing to the jealousy of [A. C.] Hunter-Weston, the 29th Division Commander, it was so hopelessly mismanaged. He had no use for anyone except the 29th, and therefore used [it] in exactly the wrong way by giving them the initial landing and getting the [Division] almost completely destroyed. Had he had any forethought, he would have used the [Royal] Naval Division for this purpose, a Division quite useless if any great advance was made, and kept the 29th to exploit success.

So it happened that only the Plymouth Battalion was in the first landings [at Cape Helles], where they were delegated to a flank assault at "Y" Beach with the King's Own Scottish Borderers, Colonel Cole [sic, actually Koe, Commanding].[5] When Hunter-Weston was giving his orders to Cole, it was pointed out to him that Matthews was the senior. After that he took no further interest and, as is known, lost the whole advantage of this flank attack by ignoring their appeals for ammunition and stores. With all their officers' casualties the KOSB walked off and reembarked, and Matthews, finding [that] they had gone, sent one last message for help, [was] again ignored, and was forced to withdraw also, having no ammunition and no food.[6]

For the great day, Plymouth Battalion being detached, Brigade Headquarters transferred to the *Gloucester Castle* with Portsmouth Battalion, and the whole Division steamed north to make a demonstration of strength behind the Turkish lines [at Bulair]. [The] next day we were ordered to reinforce the Australian and New Zealand Corps (ANZAC) which had landed at Gaba Tepe and given it their name of Anzac. Although infantry brigades still consisted of four battalions, we [i.e., the Royal Marine Brigade] were reduced to three, for it had been found impossible to complete the First Naval Brigade and Deal Battalion had been sent to it. So at the moment we had only two Battalions, Chatham and Portsmouth.

We landed in a small cove and found complete chaos. The Australians and New Zealanders had made a most successful landing, and I don't believe any other men in the world could have done what they did. But they were individualists, especially the Australians. The New Zealanders were far better disciplined, but the Australians, up to the last day of the war, were always magnificent in attack but quite hopeless after it; they were as likely as not to walk away and hope some other mate would hold the line. So it was here, [where we] met them wandering around everywhere. Somewhere there was a line of sorts, and the first [task] was to find it, [and] then send the Australians back to reorganize. So we took over the centre of the position, at the head of a long deep valley. There wasn't even a goat track, and the only practical path was in the stream. With Chatham Battalion on the right and Portsmouth on the left, we consolidated a line that night [just] in time to repulse an attack [the] next day.

Two days later the 1st Brigade landed and took over to our right, and we had Deal Battalion next door. Everywhere hidden in the steep moorland country were enemy snipers and wandering Australians. I met one of the latter one day when very tired, on my way back from taking a message. He was quite unworried, cooking a billy[7] of tea and said, "Boy you look tired. Set down and have a mug of tea." It was hot, black, sweet, and a life saver; as was also the big pipe he gave me, which he had collected off a dead German officer. I had lost my own when landing.

After a few days the Australians sorted themselves out and relieved us. We [then] bivouacked that night down the valley. There had been some pretty stiff fighting as subsequent awards showed, including a Victoria Cross to Lance Corporal Parker.[8] Hatton[9] was the first of my batch to be killed, very gallantly leading a counterattack. The

Australian [official] history says, "The Marines bore the brunt of Mustafa Kemal's [i.e., Ataturk] third attack; though better timed and delivered than the last, it completely failed." But during this short period the two battalions had lost 10 officers and 337 men.

On 2 May the troops on the left flank had carried out an attack with little success, and in the middle of the night we had been relieved. We were [then] ordered up to dig in behind them. If the country where we were was difficult, what we now were coming [in]to was a nightmare, as we saw it in the first light of dawn. We were in a deep, winding valley. To our left, a very steep slope, and to our right and ahead, towering cliffs. As we got up to the head of it each man picked up a pick or shovel, with a view to digging in behind the line somewhere up the hill. Just then the Turks attacked and our front line came tumbling back, and orders were given to counterattack instead.

The two battalions were in single file for the best part of a mile. On their right was the cliff face, held by the New Zealanders. In front a steep-sided spur and beyond that an unclimbable cliff held by the enemy. As I watched, the last post along that cliff held by us was blown out by our own shells from the ships! The only thing to do was done by the two battalion commanders [LtColonels Parsons and Luard, respectively]. They led a charge with any men available, Chatham on our right and Portsmouth [on the] left, up the spur. Fired at from three directions, they lost heavily and, but for Lathbury[10] who got two machine guns up somehow, I don't know if we could have held.

The Brigadier [Trotman] sent me to help and let them know that it was urgent to get on. But I found that they were getting on as fast as anyone could. They stopped the gap in time, but poor Portsmouth Battalion was pretty nearly wiped out for the third time,[11] their strength being reduced to seven officers and about 300 men. Harold Armstrong[12] was among the killed, and I took over the remains of his company. The battalion [was] now reduced to two companies, and my company held Quinn's post, though Quinn was there and reorganizing it.

It was an amazing position. Between Quinn's and Courtenay's [post], to our left, the head of the nullah [ravine] was held by the enemy. Quinn's and all the ridge to our right was held along the extreme edge of the cliff, and the only way into the trenches was up ropes. The only bombs we had were those the enemy threw at us, caught, and thrown back before they exploded. Just below Quinn's was a tiny patch of level [ground] about the size of our dining room. On this the [troops] and I lived, when not in the actual line; and on it we cooked our food and buried our dead. Below us again was the only well, surrounded by [the] dead bodies of those who had been sent to draw water, under direct rifle fire at about 300 yards. My new servant was killed, shot through the head whilst putting on the kettle for breakfast!

Things became so impossible in the valley that I was sent away back to the other end of the position to get a battery to bring fire on the head of our valley. Getting there was some problem. Those who had to go down collected in groups behind a bit of cover, then one would volunteer to dash to the next and draw fire. A burst of rifle fire from the enemy, and the rest would [then] dash across. One was not encouraged much by the sight of those at every corner who had run too slow. Further down I met the Corps Commander[13] and two staff officers bound up. I told them that going up in daylight was plain suicide. However, they wanted to see [Brigadier] Trotman, and I advised keeping to the slope of the hill on their left where they would not easily be seen. I found the battery and it quieted things down for a bit. But the end of this nullah was to be a thorn in the side of the Anzacs for long after we left.

In conversation with Quinn, I said what a marvellous show they had put up in getting into these positions. He admitted that physically he didn't think any other troops could have done it, but said, "The bravest thing I've seen so far was the charge of your two battalions up that hill on Bloody Sunday," which was nice of him and in contrast to other remarks I also heard. But Quinn was a [good] man and got a very well earned V.C. [sic],[14] and I have always valued his remark.

On 12 May we reembarked and went down to [Cape] Helles. The casualties of Brigade Headquarters and the two battalions amounted to 33 officers and 510 men. Before the landing the Chief Officer of our transport had run us in for having a rugger match in the saloon with a waste paper basket. I met him as we reembarked, when he said how sorry he was when he saw most of those youngsters come back a few days later shot to bits. "I wouldn't have said anything if I'd known what it was going to be like," he said. I don't suppose there has ever been a campaign quite like Gallipoli, nor have any troops held a position quite like that of the Naval Division.

In general the ground rose gently at first; and then, after reaching the Turkish positions, more steeply to Achi Baba Hill.[15] On our right, held by the French, the ground was cut up into wadis, terminating in the Ravine des Morts, beyond which they never [advanced]. It got its name in an early attack I witnessed. The French, red trousered and blue coated, attacked and disappeared into the Ravine, whence they came pouring back a moment later, followed by the Turks. It was a regular stampede, when the French 75mm guns opened on the gap. At once the officers turned, flourished their swords, and the whole line turned about and captured the position. It was a most astonishing sight, and can only be explained by the fact that French infantry have unbounded confidence in their guns combined with some sort of second sight [called "coup d'oeil"]. I don't know how it works, and it's very confusing if you are working with them as to how they call off a battle. If we arrange one, it's got to go on—but not they. Somewhere miles back a General looks out of his Headquarters, doesn't like the look of the weather, and just cancels it at the last moment. But how they let everyone know is a mystery; certainly they never let us know!

Then in the centre of the line came the [Royal] Naval Division. And on our left eventually came the 42nd Division.[16] Our area was entirely open right back to the sea, with one shallow dry water course up the middle of it. The 42nd's area was much more broken. And beyond them to the sea came the 29th Division, with a superb nullah completely sheltered.

We were in fact much safer in the trenches than out. In our so called "rest area" we were under long-range rifle fire and easy shrapnel fire. It is necessary in these days to explain shrapnel. People talk glibly of being wounded by shrapnel, but there hasn't been any about since 1917![17] It was the invention [in 1784] of [British] Colonel [Henry] Shrapnel and consisted of a hollow shell with a small bursting charge in the base and fill[ed] with lead bullets. It was timed to go off when about 30 to 40 feet above ground, when it spat out its bullets in a cone roughly 150 feet long by 30 wide. It was an admirable shell against men attacking, [but] quite useless against trenches.

To return to our rest area: We could not dig more than two feet deep at most, as you came to water. So we had no protection. My sleeping place was a hole 6 feet by 2 by 2, over which I had pulled a blanket I had picked up riddled with holes. My groom was killed here whilst grooming my pony, Bobby, who also got two holes in him. And my late Company Sergeant Major Milne was wounded. Milne was a grand chap, he was one of five in three generations serving in the war. His father was my senior sergeant in the *Euryalus*, and his son a bugler in the Grand Fleet. Milne had been wounded three times, but flatly refused to go sick. One day in the rest camp he had his right arm blown off by a shell.

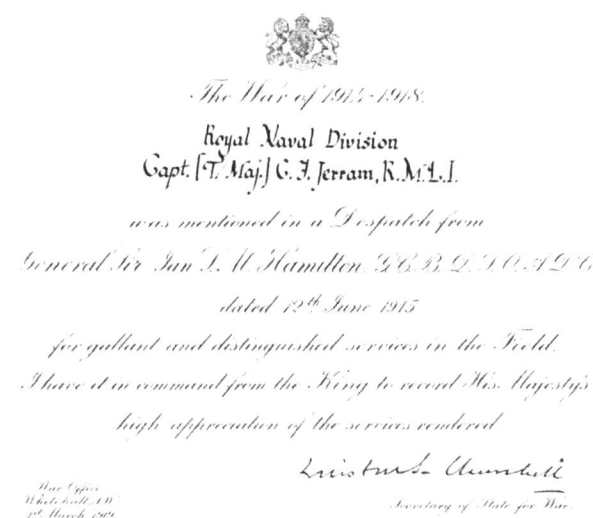

One of five Mentioned in Despatches certificates awarded to Lieutenant Colonel Jerram. This initial one pertains to his service at Gallipoli in which he was mentioned by name by the General Officer Commanding, Mediterranean Expeditionary Force General Sir Ian Hamilton, dispatch, i.e., report, of 16 June 1915. Note it was signed by Winston Churchill, Secretary of State for War, on 12 March 1919, who had returned to office in 1917 initially as Minister for Munitions in the David Lloyd George government [© Trustees RMM].

He picked himself up, saluted with his left hand, and said, "I'm afraid I'll have to go this time, Sir." Shortly after we got to Helles, the Brigade Major [Major Maurice C. Festing][18] went sick and I was appointed in his place.[19]

Normally we did a week in the line and a week out. But, unless there was an attack, our week out was far the most strenuous, owing to the enormous working parties we had to find. Food was bully beef and biscuit, with occasional bacon and a sort of tinned stew; jam occasionally and always the same, plum and apple.

The normal routine of the high command was to accumulate all the ammunition and men they could—ordinarily our guns were only allowed two rounds a day—then they staged an attack. The guns fired for about an hour, the [artillery] stopped and you went over the top, struggled with masses of barbed wire, and advanced anything from nothing to 50 yards before being wiped out by the machine guns which popped up as soon as our fire stopped. Then we'd wait another fortnight and do the same. If only there had been enough men and ammunition to attack two or three days together, we could have got through, but there never was. True, the Turk had just the same difficulty. But he, in the meantime, was putting up miles and miles of wire, till there was a blue mass all the way to Achi Baba.

As the summer got hotter, dysentery became a real problem. Practically every one had it. I put down my escape to the fact that I had just had enteric [fever]. The trenches had to be kept manned and everyone capable of staying had to stay, and the flies swarmed in billions on dead and rotting bodies, and then transferred themselves onto your food. Yet truth to tell, the men didn't want to go sick. I've seen men crawling back to the line, after this so called week of rest, rather than go sick.

All this sounds very horrible, but it isn't what you thought at the time, nor is it what you normally remember. It is said that the old Cape Horn seamen never remembered the bleak months off the Horn, but the fine weather of the Trades [trade winds]. So it is with us. With an effort, one remembers the day when crawling out on a reconnaissance one buried one's arm in a long defunct Turk. But when one doesn't think, it's the smell of a wood fire that brings back the memory of early dawn and the camp fires lighting up; or the early mass on a Sunday with the smell of the thyme on which you were kneeling. It does in fact take a very short time for one's life to adapt itself to almost any circumstances and become one's normal life. Even when we eventually left, we didn't want to go. I suppose if we'd been asked, "Do you want to go or stay," we should have said, "Go." But it wouldn't occur to anyone to ask to go.

By [July] we had received a new division,[The 52nd (Lowland) Division].[20] They were indeed very new and quite inexperienced, and they were put into an attack on [July] 12th, with us behind them in reserve.[21] They made a fine attack, but most of them disappeared into the blue and the remainder only stuck to the first Turkish trench. As Brigade Major[22] of the reserve, I went up to have a look. As I passed their Headquarters I met scores of men coming back, and went in and told their Commander, who sent his Brigade Major out to round them up. But there was no doubt that discipline had completely broken down and that they could not be relied upon.

Going on, I found a place whence I could view the ground, and I became certain of what I had been pretty sure of before: That the trench they were supposed to take wasn't a trench at all. It was merely a low bank, and that is why they had disappeared. Expecting to find a trench, they went on too far and were all wiped out.[23] I reported this to General Trotman, [now] temporarily commanding the [Royal Naval] Division [with] General Paris being on leave, and he to the Corps Commander.[24] [The latter] sent for me and "pooh poo[hed]" it, [saying] the aeroplane photos showed it as a trench. I insisted that it wasn't and offered to show him, but this was refused. It was the ONLY time I saw the Corps Commander. Whether he ever visited any part of the line, I don't know, but it's quite certain he never visited ours!

On the morning of 13 [July], the situation on our front was that the 52nd Division held what had been the first Turkish trench, with Plymouth Battalion, RMLI, on their left, and Chatham, Portsmouth, and Nelson Naval Battalions close up behind them. Sketchley,[25] our GSO-2, was going round, when the whole 52nd poured back, followed by a Turkish attack. They were stopped by our battalions and Sketchley [received] a DSO[26] for rallying them, whilst Plymouth Battalion from the flank repelled the Turks.

As a result, we were told in the afternoon to retake the trench AND their original objective, the "dummy." In our front line, I wrote the orders for Chatham and Portsmouth Battalions, RMLI, and Nelson Naval Battalion in the presence of their Commanding

Officers from General Trotman's dictation. General Paris being on leave, General Trotman was still in command. The CO's left at 4 p.m. to attack at 4:30. This time, quite inadequate, was forced on us by the Corps Commander as the French on our right were to attack at that time. General Trotman left me, with his ADC,[27] on the forward end of a telephone in the front line at the junction of Chatham and Portsmouth Battalions.

We had very poor artillery preparation, which as usual ceased as the troops assaulted at zero hour. Immediately the Turks opened a terrific artillery and machine gun fire, and our whole front line was plastered. The ADC and I were comparatively safe under a sheltering bank, but the advancing troops got it full in the face.

Nelson and Portsmouth Battalions, both commanded by Marines, Col[onels] Evelegh[28] and Luard respectively, went off led by their Colonels, as being the only practical way to lead at no notice. Chatham's Commanding Officer [Parsons] tried to give orders in the more normal way, with unfortunate results. The French made no effort to advance, which affected this wing. I went out to see what was happening and found the [Chatham] Battalion still struggling up the communication trenches, instead of going straight overland as the others had done. There were many killed and wounded, and a disabled Colour Sergeant was encouraging them to get on, but it was too late to do anything. I, therefore, rang up General Trotman and told him that as far as I could see there had been no advance on our right, and that Portsmouth and Nelson Battalions had disappeared into the blue, precisely as had the 52nd Division before them, and that I was going forward to find out the position.

Miraculously, I got across "No-man's Land" to the Turkish trench and at first could find no one at all, except dead and wounded. At last I found Captain Gowney[29] and six men, with the dead body of young Dougherty,[30] the last of my old subalterns. Gowney said so far as he knew he was the only officer left, which proved to be true, and he was wounded [the] next day.

Collecting what men we could in groups, I left Gowney to organise the defence and passed on to the Nelson Battalion area. Here things were slightly, but not much, better. There were few [troops] in the front line, but going back I found several more in our old front line and one or two officers. Meeting my old friend Weller, temporarily in command of Plymouth Battalion, I gave him the situation and left him to give what help he could. It was now dark and, returning to my telephone, I reported that (a) Portsmouth and Nelson had retaken the Turkish front line and, as anticipated, gone on to try and find the nonexistent trench; (b) Portsmouth had ceased to exist and were quite incapable of holding the line or getting a communication trench through; (c) Nelson Battalion could be organized if someone was put in command; (d) Portsmouth had one officer left and Nelson probably four, all junior [in rank]; (e) our right flank was intact in its old positions and there were remnants of the 52nd Division, quite unorganized, in [the] rear, mainly of Nelson; [and (f)] a new battalion to take over from Portsmouth was essential.

On this, the Drake Naval Battalion under Commander King[31] was sent up and reported to me at 2 a.m. on the 14th. King did a marvellous job. No regular soldier anywhere could have done more. By daylight he had sent back the remnants of Portsmouth Battalion, established his own, relieved Nelson Battalion, and dug two communication trenches back. It was a wonderful achievement in the dark and strange surroundings. He got a very well merited DSO.

That was the end of the [Royal] Marines Brigade. Portsmouth had gone into action with 27 officers and 720 men, and came out with none and 125. Nelson Battalion had five officers and about 240 men left. So the Division was reduced to two brigades, [with] the Marines organized in[to] two battalions, [and the] two naval battalions formed the second brigade, but with the same frontage to hold! Indeed more, because when the Suvla landings [of 6–8 August 1915] came off and disastrously failed, the 29th Division was sent up there and we, with only two brigades, took over their front and most of [that of] the 42nd Division front as well.

Although we had some nasty [and] sticky battles, it was heaven compared with our old area. Lovely deep ravines with a mule track right up to the front and no casualties behind the lines. When the 29th returned and we had to go back, we were not pleased, especially as now the broiling sun had given place to winter. A blizzard from the north flooded our trenches and then froze. The Turks on the uphill side had the best of it, but for us it was a nightmare. Then Anzac was evacuated and the Turks moved all their heavy guns down against us.

Finally, it was time for us to go. The French couldn't be trusted and we took over their front, leaving the 42nd Division to hold the centre and the 29th the left. I had a "nice" job organizing the destruction of the stores, animals, etc. I found huge dumps of food which had never reached the forward troops. Lovely tinned foods and strawberry jam, all kept back for the beachcombers.

Riding back from the old French positions one day, the Turks started shelling with 21-inch guns and one [round] landed on a low bank right alongside us. Being alongside the stalk of the umbrella, "Bobby" and I waited whilst all the world crashed round us. Just beyond was a RASC[32] officer with the unenviable job of shooting 200 mules, but the Turks were making a pretty good job of it already. As I rode down the track to our Headquarters, a shell burst right under "Bobby's" nose, and I turned him over to my groom with a remark that if he could find a handful of oats poor old "Bobby" deserved them, for he hadn't turned a hair.

One more adventure I had. That was a toothache, for which I visited a dentist's tent above "W" Beach.[33] Just as he got the thing opened up, "Asiatic Annie," a big gun across the Dardanelles, opened up. After one or two near misses the dentist asked me what about it. "Well," I said, "I can stick it out if you can, and anything's better than an exposed nerve." So we carried on and a jolly good job he made of it. When it was done, he said, "I'm clearing out," and sent the rest of his patients away. We had gone about 100 yards when the whole tent was blown sky high!

With a new Commander-in-Chief and a new Corps Commander,[34] everything went much more smoothly. There were no more battles just for the sake of giving us something to do. And everyone had more confidence. If we were to go now, we knew that everything possible would be done to ensure success. Of all things in those last days, we missed most the support of the French guns. They had all gone, and most of ours [as well], when the Turks made a final effort to throw us out. I stood by the one remaining 18-pounder out of a battery, and watched with admiration the gunners' efforts to make it appear that all six guns were there! [The attack] was repulsed and we [evacuated Gallipoli on 8–9 January 1916] without a single casualty. The 2/RMLI (Old Portsmouth and Plymouth Battalions) form[ed] the final rear guard, so the two battalions which had been the first ashore, were the last to leave!

I had been ashore from first to last, without having my foot off it, and must have been the only person who did! Every headquarters and every battalion had been away on a fortnight's rest in Mudros (Lemnos Island), [but] when our turn came I had to stay because General Trotman had gone sick. But I was not the last to leave, as practically everyone else says he was. I reached the final rendezvous at midnight and then formed one of a solid block, eight deep, down to the beach and along the shore to the old *River Clyde*,[35] now a pier. We were the last of the main body.

It had been blowing hard and only at the last moment had it been decided to take us off. The only sound one heard was the crack of our dummy rifles going off up in the trenches. These were rather ingenious. Old rifles were loaded and a string tied to the trigger with an empty can tied to it. Above this was a big can of water with a small hole; when the trigger can filled, it fired the rifle! It completely deceived the Turks as to the "manning" of the now empty trenches. "Asiatic Annie" gave us a farewell, firing every minute, [with] the shells all falling in the water. A correction of 10 yards right would have ploughed them right into us!

We embarked in the HMS *Prince George*,[36] an ancient battleship of the Caesar [*sic*] class. They gave us a wonderful supper, [with] tablecloths, knives, and forks, things we'd forgotten existed. Then I rolled up in my great coat on the half deck by the "C" door [which led] to the Marines' flat or Barracks. We left the shore at 2 a.m., and at 3 a.m. a torpedo hit us [but] didn't go off. But the bump swung the armoured door on to my head, [giving me] the first of the headaches I've had ever since. We landed at Mudros and went into camp and the whole divisional staff went home to feather their own nests, leaving me the sole staff officer to deal with getting us together, getting us relieved by new troops, and [moving] the Naval Division to France. I don't think anyone ever appreciated what all that entailed.

Here [were] some of the problems. A ship is due to arrive and must not be detained. The battalion to embark on her cannot be relieved until another battalion in another ship [has] arrived. The ship can take 500 men, but there are only 475 in the unit [and taking] 25 more will mean splitting units. She can't take any horses, [but the] next ship which can take them hasn't yet left England. Who is to look after the horses and wagons? One ship can take a crowd of officers [but] few men, and that's one hell of a useful ship! So it's not surprising that one day, after a bellyful of all this, I turned over the day's sailing's message to the Admiralty to the Signals Officer with orders to put [it] in cypher and get [it] off, and [then] went down to see how the embarkation was going.

Getting back a couple of hours later, I sent for the cypher to check it up, to be told that the Signals Officer had forgotten to cypher it! Here was a pretty mess. The largest ship in the world[37] was going off with everyone in Greece, Italy, and France knowing when and where and what she was carrying. My Commanding Officer, Colonel Stroud,[38] after checking that the wire had already reached Greece, wisely took no action to stop it and therefore draw attention to it, and sent me off to the Flagship to explain. I have never in my life admired anyone so much as I do that Admiral [John de Robeck].[39] Not one word of criticism. I think he realized, even better than I did, what an impossible job I had been given. He concentrated on doing what he could to ensure the safety of the ship, and that consisted mainly of altering her route. But I didn't get much sleep for some days until I heard she had arrived safely.

The last of us got away eventually, and I [finally] had no one to worry about. I was, for the first time for many years, merely a passenger. On arrival at Genoa some of us were given leave to go home overland. As this would give us three extra days, I took advantage of it. Our train did not leave till midnight, so I with three others went out in the town. Passing a group of Italian officers, one [of them] came over and spoke to us. His Colonel, he said, spoke little English but would like to entertain us in his box that night at the opera. Naturally we accepted. The play was "Il Trovatore," and the tenor had been released from active service on the Northern Front to sing in it. We were most hospitably entertained, with refreshments in the interval; I certainly thoroughly enjoyed seeing an Italian opera in its own country. The audience showed their appreciation in cries of "Bravissima." I got a fortnight's leave, and then left for France: The Division was assembling near Amiens.

Chapter 8

The Western Front, I—1915–18[1]

With the Marines in France, 1915–16

Our casualties in Gallipoli had been very high. In officers alone we had lost 53 [*sic*] killed and 66 wounded, mostly regulars[2]; and there were few indeed of the old Gallipoli veterans left. Indeed of the original [Marine] Brigade of Chatham, Portsmouth and Plymouth Battalions, out of 147 officers who landed, only 20 took part in the evacuation. Those not killed or wounded had been invalided [i.e., medically evacuated], mainly with dysentery or frostbite. My sister, "Posy," then at Rockhampton Hospital, told me that nearly all their leg cases at this time were amputations due to frozen legs after the blizzard.[3]

The [Royal Naval] Division [now] was reconstituted on Army lines, and [had] artillery attached to it. The two Marine battalions [and the] two naval ones became the 188th Brigade. The 189th [Brigade] was purely naval, [but] all naval battalions were commanded by Marine officers. Not long after, General Trotman, myself as Brigade Major, and Tagg,[4] Staff Captain, were taken from our command and sent to England to organize and bring over four new army Battalions, [these] to become the 190th Brigade.[5]

They were the queerest lot I've ever come across, and were scattered over the whole of Britain, from Falmouth to the east and north to Ireland. The 7th Battalion of the 7th Royal Fusiliers and the 4th Bedfords were both militia battalions and had [had] some training. But the 10th Royal Dublin Fusiliers were perfectly hopeless from their Commanding Officer down. However, we got them to France somehow in July 1916 and there picked up the infantry battalion of the Honourable Artillery Company. This battalion had volunteered for active service and had seen some fighting; but being considered too valuable, [it] had been turned into an officers' training corps. Now they were to go into the line again.

But prior to this, whilst still with our old brigade, we had our first taste of trench warfare as conducted in France, in the Angres sector [northwest of Arras] amongst the coal fields. My first reaction was one of surprise at the complete silence and difficulty of discovering any defenders! No one looked for possible targets for one's rifle, [while] the trenches were held in small posts, as few as possible in the front line.

There was one stretch of trench through a coal dump which was smouldering, known as the "Burning Bin," in which you never needed a fire to cook by. All you had to do was to scoop out the back of the trench and put your Billy on. But men couldn't live in it for long and no one could suggest anything till I got a brain wave. This was to import clay and fill sandbags with it and pack them in. The bags would burn out and the clay set like bricks, and this was eventually done. Other than that, it wasn't a very exciting time. We got our new brigade into the line in August, and it was probably fortunate that we had little to do, whilst at the same time getting enough shelling to get our new troops used to it. It was in this sector that Morford, my old subaltern, got his ankle mashed during a reconnaissance between the lines and received a Military Cross.[6]

In September we marched away to the Monchy Breton training area, already beginning to feel like units of some sort—but our Dublin Fusiliers especially were very raw still. And in October we moved down to the Somme, in the Mailly Maillet–Engelbelmer area north of the River Ancre. Here we were to take part in the next great Somme battle against the German positions round Serre–Beaumont Hamel–Beaucourt–St. Pierre Divion, [and hence] took over the sector from the R[iver] Ancre to opposite Beaumont Hamel.[7] We were already half buried in mud, and it rained steadily and remorselessly. To witness an attack by troops on our right [on 12 October 1916], Tagg and I went up to a point I knew, and on the way met General Paris and Sketchley, the GSO[2] bound the same way. On the principle of not having too many people together, we went off further to our right, and just after we left heard a 5.9" shell. There were plenty about and we didn't think anything of it. But [we] heard later that it had got them both. General Paris[8] lost a leg and Sketchley was killed. He was a great loss, a fine and fearless staff officer.

The new Commander of the Division was General Shute,[9] the most hated man in his regiment, and known as the "Barnshute," which I believe in India means something pretty horrible.[10] He came to us with the avowed intention of creating something out of an unruly mob, which was by no means the case. The one bright spot was that [LtColonel] Aspinall[11] was still our GSO [chief of staff]. He came to us after Gallipoli from Corps Headquarters, and very soon came to know our increasingly good qualities.

Then, after getting out the Brigade orders for the coming battle, my Brigadier, Trotman, had to go sick. Sometime before this his horse, "Surefoot," had thrown him and injured his leg. He wasn't a good horseman, and I took over "Surefoot" as my second horse. But [his] leg got worse until he couldn't walk, and he was relieved temporarily by Colonel Hutchinson[12] from the 2/RMLI and he in turn by General Sackville West[13] from the Army, who had different ideas as to our orders, and wanted to get a view of the ground over which we were to attack.

On our right was the muddy, boggy river with small bits of firm ground, occupied by the enemy in strong posts. The remains of a road and railway ran up the valley to the village of Beaucourt, our objective. To the north the ground rose fairly steeply to Beaumont-Hamel and beyond. Our bit of the attack lay between the river, entailing some sticky mopping up, and to about half way up the hill. An awkward place at best, as the sort of attack needed for the river was totally different to that of the hill. Our brigade was to be in reserve, and push through after the first objectives had been captured, with the H[onourable] A[rtillery] C[ompany battalion] on our right to mop up the river and then leapfrog through to Beaucourt. But there is a good account of the battle [in] the History of the Royal Marines.[14]

In the meantime General Sackville-West wanted to see, and I took him up to a place I had previously had a good look from. On the way we met another Brigadier and his machine gun officer, and they decided to come too. I was afraid it was rather a crowd and said so, but they didn't seem to worry. However, a 5.9 [inch] howitzer opened up and dropped a shell about 200 yards to our left [and then one within] 100 yards. I was just saying that they were ranging on us and we'd better split up, when the next landed right on top of the bank we were looking over. We all got partly buried, and the Machine Gun officer and I [received] a knock on the head; but my Brigadier got a piece right through his face. Then we got Heneker,[15] another Army chap, who again of course had ideas of his own. But he was a grand chap and it was well he came, for he feared no one, let alone a divisional commander. [For example], when General Shute wanted to chuck out various battalion commanders, Heneker stood up for them and insisted on their rights. But that came later.

In the meantime we were in and out of the line. Fighting, when in, for the strong points of the river which had to be cleared before the attack, and wallowing in [the] mud in ruins of villages when out. The HAC put in some good work capturing one important post and even the Dublin Fusiliers were improving. But it still rained more and more, and the ground was getting worse and worse. Four times did we get into position, only to be told the battle was postponed. It eventually took place on my [34th] birthday, November 13, [1916]. It was a pretty sticky show. On our right, things had gone well and the HAC did good work in their follow-up and were in a position to leapfrog forward when ordered. But the centre had encountered a "brute" of a strong point. The Marines lost heavily here but pushed on round it.

The rest of our Brigade, thinking it was all clear, followed up and bumped right into it. By dark, our Brigade was, I'm afraid, in a hell of a mess, and we had a job to extricate them. There was a mass of untended wounded round our Headquarters close to where the advanced field dressing station was. But all the doctors had been killed and many of the horsed ambulances put out of action. So we telephoned to Division to send more doctors and suggested moving the station further back.

By dawn we had got under control the HAC, about a quarter of the Fusiliers, 40 Bedfords and a few Dubliners. After another artillery [preparation, we] pushed forward through Freyberg's Battalion and took Beaucourt. Freyberg had orders to let us through, but went forward with us and some of his battalion. He got wounded and went into divisional Headquarters on his way back and gave the impression that he alone had taken the village, for which he got a Victoria Cross! No one minded that, Freyberg earned a VC pretty well every time he went into action. But it was grossly unfair on the HAC, who were the only battalion in the whole outfit to do exactly what they had been told to.[16] Shute wanted to sack their Commanding Officer, [but] it was here that Heneker put his foot down and incidentally got me a quite undeserved DSO.

The Marines had lost heavily, having 37 officers killed and wounded. Colonel Hutchinson had only one officer left. We were pulled out the next day, being relieved by the 37th Division.[17] Our brigade camped in tents near our old line, and I won undying fame next morning by having a bath in a snowstorm, as I discovered years later when at the Staff College[18] I was asked if I was that lunatic! If [the questioner] had seen me before I had the bath, he wouldn't have been so surprised.

But the two Marine battalions, or what was left of them, earned real fame. Their quartermasters had brought up a complete set of clean clothes. They spent most of the night cleaning their equipment, polishing brass and boots, and [then] marched back past the Divisional Commander next morning as if on a full dress parade. The biggest compliment they got was being booed by the French villagers, who thought they were going back without fighting!

Shute left at the end of the month, being relieved by General Lawrie,[19] a very different sort [of officer]. The cold now set in properly. Up to February [1917] we were in and out of the line, fighting forward and digging in. The ground was so hard that the steel heads of [our] picks broke. It was a snorter of a winter. [Then] on 13 February,[20] I left to join the 31st Division as GSO-2.

With the Army: The 31st Division, 1917

The 31st was a Midland Division[21] commanded by General [R.] Wanless-O'Gowan.[22] It had never done much and I don't think O'Gowan was ever likely to "set the Thames on fire," [but] he had been blessed by a good staff.[23] For Spender,[24] the GSO [or chief of staff], was outstanding and the most energetic man I ever knew. The GSO-2, whom I only saw one day, had been promoted to XVIII Corps, and young Stafford,[25] the GSO-3, was an obvious candidate for a rise. We were in the same area on the Ancre, and the fighting was still going on on both sides of the river, but it was slow work and abnormally cold. One day the temperature was down to zero, 32 degrees of frost, and Spender dragged me out for a walk up to and all round our lines. I doubt if we ever touched less than five miles an hour where walking was possible. But I'd had enough of the Ancre and I wasn't sorry when we had orders to move, which we received on Feb[ruary] 12th, [1917].[26]

Thinking it a good time to get his leave in, Spender went home leaving me to get on with the move. As we were moving into the Hebuterne area [north of Albert and southwest of Arras and near Gommecourt], which had been held by the 31st Division before, they knew all about it. [Hence], we had the defence scheme, [but] little did Spender know that we weren't going to want it, [for] it was going to be a question of attacking [because] our constant pressure was about to [force a] German withdrawal. On 13 February, therefore, I wrote my first divisional order, and now looking at it again, it seems quite creditable. Over a three day march, divisional headquarters arrived at Authie, which was to be our headquarters, in an abandoned chateau. For the final move the roads were so bad that our baggage got stuck about a mile away and was transferred to G.S. wagons drawn by four horses. But the village street was too much for them and it was transferred again to half limbers [i.e., horse drawn vehicles for carrying artillery ammunition], and for the last half mile had to be manhandled.

We took over command of the sector on 22 February, coming under V Corps of the 5th Army.²⁷ There was a good deal of artillery shelling of our lines and back areas. But the high ups were pretty sure that the enemy were giving, and on the 24th all divisions in the line were ordered to push out strong patrols to test the enemy strength and take advantage of any withdrawal. It was during this period that the 31st Division really found itself, getting great fighting encouragement from the result of these patrols. On the first night, although all patrols came up against strong resistance, the 92nd Brigade sent in a machine gun and two prisoners, and each night we had successful raids.

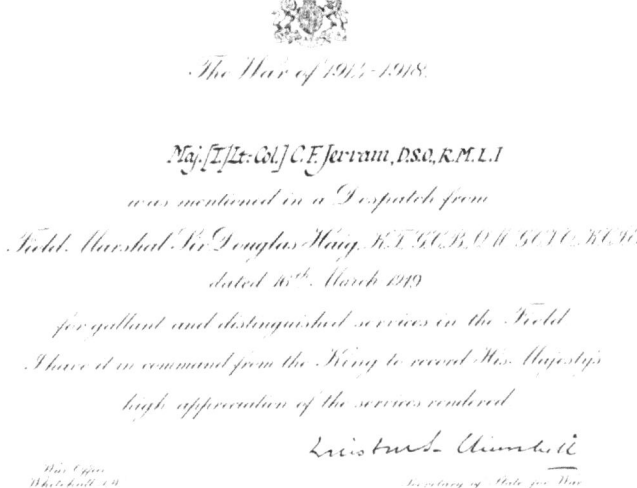

Another Mention in Despatch certificate for Lieutenant Colonel Jerram for his services on the Western Front. Here he was mentioned by name by the Commanding General of British forces on the Western Front, Field Marshal Sir Douglas Haig, in his despatch dated 16 March 1919. Certificate also signed by Churchill on 1 July 1919. Personnel "Mentioned in Despatches" (abbreviated MiD) wear a bronze oak leaf on the appropriate campaign medal ribbon [© Trustees RMM].

News from the south was also good, and we learned from prisoners that the enemy was withdrawing to the Hindenburg Line,²⁸ assumed at that time by both sides to be almost impregnable. On the 26th, I attended a conference at [V] Corps Headquarters at which we received instructions to push boldly on, but when we came up against severe opposition to do nothing without artillery cover. The 92nd and 93rd Brigades were in the line, with [the] 94th in reserve. And on this day most of the enemy front lines were occupied by us. But we were now left at the bottom of a shallow valley, which had been churned into a complete bog. It was dominated by the Germans around a large copse, Rossignol Wood, and our junction [tie-up] with the [19th] Division²⁹ on our right was always in doubt. They were constantly telling us that they had advanced much further than they really had, and I do not think their staff made any personal reconnaissance[s] at all.

We attacked the Wood but didn't get very far. And our right junction with the 19th Division was so obscure that I decided to go and have a look myself. We had strict orders from [5th] Army that staff officers were always to be accompanied by an orderly. I'm afraid I ignored this entirely. I found quite enough to do looking after myself and, like the American cowboy, I didn't want any band playing me into action. There were two trenches on our right, "Dugout" near the bottom of the valley and "Slug" half way up. It was constantly reported that we held "Slug," and yet neither Division could get in touch with the other.

I found the going very heavy. It often took me half an hour to get 50 yards, sinking up to [my] thighs in ghuey mud at every step. I found our position was in "Dugout," not "Slug," and it lay at the foot of a steep slope on top of which was "Slug," protected by very heavy wire entanglements. It was strongly held and the intervening ground enfiladed by machine gun fire from the Wood. The garrison of "Dugout" was literally up to their waists in mud, and the position was an impossible one to attack from and not really even tenable. To our right again was La Louviere Farm, at present an impassable bog.

I reported that the proper way to get "Slug," as a prelude to the Wood, was to take it from the rear. But to enable us to do this, the 19th Division must push on so as to allow us to get round by Star Wood in this sector. This they were reluctant to do. The difficulty of ascertaining the exact position of this Division's left is shown in the fact that had they held the position they said they did, it would have materially helped our attack on Rossignol Wood. During the night two of our scouts [penetrated] into Gommecourt on our left during a heavy shelling of it by the 58th Division[30] and reported it evacuated. Both men were promoted to Corporal and given the DCM. We asked the 58th to stop shelling, and sent in two platoons to occupy it.

On the 28th our line was shortened by the 46th Division[31] taking over Gommecourt, and I issued orders for a determined attack on Rossignol Wood to take place on March 3rd. That night Spender returned from leave, very annoyed that the war had been going on without him. But not nearly so annoyed as I was in having to take a back seat again. But we were the best of friends, and I don't think I'd done anything very reprehensible, and these few days certainly gave me a confidence I'd never had before.

On March 2, we had orders to relieve the 19th Division. This, whilst materially extending our frontage, at least allowed us to know where [our] flank was. In the meantime, another abortive effort was made against "Slug Street," and little sense could be got out of the 19th Division. During a reconnaissance to find out where we really were, I [became] completely bogged down. I found that I was in front of our positions, and every time I tried to get a leg free, I was fired at by a sniper at about 50 yards range. At length I got hold of an old trench boot and forced it down under my foot and got it out. Working back to get in touch, I found a wounded Sergeant who had been there three days. I could do nothing for him, and [I didn't] even [have] a water bottle. However, I found our advanced post with an officer and he sent men off to bring him in, after I'd warned them about my friend the sniper.

Our attack on Rossignol Wood was completely successful and we got about 30 prisoners, and the tails of the Division were right up in consequence. The next day we had a message from General Gough,[32] the 5th Army Commander, congratulating the [31st] Division on its work. We again extended our front to our right but continued to fight forward, usually by strong fighting patrols. On 12 March, we were relieved in the line, and reports from the whole front south of Arras showed that the enemy [was] retiring. We being on the fringe of the withdrawal, it [was] naturally a good deal slower here. By 21 March, we had moved back to the Pernes Area and were in General Headquarters reserve [on] 24 hours notice. And on the 28th, we were ordered to reconnoitre the country round the Vimy Ridge against which the Canadian Corps were to attack in a few days. The Canadians' attack, as is known, was almost completely successful, with 11,000 prisoners and 169 guns.[33]

On 23 April, we heard that the [63rd Royal] Naval Division had followed through and that the Marines had taken Gavrelle.[34] We were now up in support of this sector, and some of our battalions [were] under the orders of the 63rd (Royal Naval Division). It is odd that both [divisions] should have come up here. The Naval Division really found itself in the Vimy Ridge battles; and at Gavrelle the 2nd Royal Marines had withstood ten major counterattacks. Just north of the village was a small knoll and the remains of a windmill. Every German attack swept over and around it. But at night the remains of one platoon which had held it all day were relieved: One officer and ten men. North of this again were a series of trenches, and then came Oppy Wood with the village behind it. Against this position the Naval Division launched an attack on the 28th, but ended up where they started.[35] Whatever the Germans might be doing on the Somme, they were certainly holding on to every inch of ground here.

We relieved the Naval Division after this attack, and of course had a snowstorm. In the morning report to Corps, I called it a blizzard and was later rung up by the Brigadier General, General Staff, and told not to exaggerate. So I altered it to snow flurry but, as I said it to him, it might be a snow shower in the Corps Headquarters Chateau! It was a pretty hard snowstorm on top of our hill, and I'd bet it felt like a blizzard to the poor devils in the line! Anyway, there were drifts seven feet deep.

This was a more or less standstill month for us, yet our casualties had been 11 officers and 163 men. [This] gives some idea of normal "wastage" [i.e., casualties] in trench warfare, with nothing going on. We relieved the Naval Division and in our turn staged an attack on Oppy Wood area.[36] Our right brigade got on well from Gavrelle, but Oppy was a death trap. All night long we had been heavily shelled, and the packed troops waiting for zero [hour] lost heavily. Oppy Wood, when reached, was a nightmare. Conceive a wood of high pines, wasted and lying over each other on the ground; the ground, continuous shell holes filled with mud. Add to that a tangle of wire, and even then one cannot visualize it. What we should have done was to ignore it and go round, but at that time we had been so badly bitten by strong points left behind that it was considered essential to mop up as you [advanced]. It has to be remembered that at that time no German troops ever gave in, and you simply didn't dare leave any behind you.

Anyway, the holdup here left the right brigade open and the Germans counterattacked and rolled them up. Gavrelle was fiercely contested and the windmill changed hands eight times, finally remaining in our[s]. The final result was "as you were." Attack and counterattack continued [until] 20 May, when the Naval Division relieved us again. Our casualties for the month, or 20 days of it, had been 146 officers and 3,107 men, about a third of our strength! On June 10, we went back to relieve the Naval Division and found a great change. Enemy shelling was almost nil and we had a fairly easy time devoted to patrols and raids. [An example]: One by 200 men in which we captured several prisoners and wiped out the garrison of a second line trench.

One snag we had was a German link trench between Gavrelle and Oppy, known to us as "Cadorna." We badly wanted it, to give access to Oppy Wood, but the troops in the line said they couldn't make any daylight reconnaissance owing to the standing barley. So I was sent up to see what I could do. I was rather pressed for time, as we were due to shell the position at 10 a.m. The distance between our front line and "Cadorna" was about 100 yards. Getting out through our wire was a bit of a job, but the barley was more simple. The standing corn could be avoided and I got right up inside the enemy wire, where I could see the whole length of trench. Here I found a sniper's post. He had obviously recently been killed and I grabbed his broken rifle and helmet for a souvenir and started back. I have said before that I hate turning my back on an enemy. One has not been given eyes in one's backside, and it was 9:45 a.m. and I was in a hurry. Anyway I missed my point of exit and had to come in at a place [where] I was not known to be out. My last ten yards was a rush over the top of the parapet, and there were four men with their bayonets stuck up to catch me, whilst a German machine gun started to shoot me up the tail! However, all was well and I [submitted] my report and we took "Cadorna" in a very successful attack on 28 June.

That was my last effort in the 31st Division, [for] on 1 July I was appointed GSO-2 (Training) of the XIII Corps. I protested, but one had to go where one was sent. To cut a long story short, that infernal Oppy Wood never was taken until a year or more later [when] the Germans began their final retreat. The broken rifle and helmet [from the sniper's nest] are in the Regimental Museum at Eastney Barracks.[37]

With the Army: XIII Corps, 1917–18

I joined the XIII Corps Headquarters[38] at Ecoivres, near Arras, on July 3, 1917, and entered into an entirely new life which I didn't know existed. As GSO-2 Training, I had apparently no part in the war at all. But as no one gave me any information as to what I was supposed to do, I am equally ignorant to this day. There was, of course, the Corps School[39] for which I was responsible, and to which junior officers had to be drafted from the various divisions. But I had little to say as to who went there or what instructors were employed. Naturally there was a good deal of difference of opinion. I wanted the best of their officers as instructors, preferably those with a DSO or MC.[40] And for pupils, those who really needed a rest. Equally obvious, these were just the officers the battalions wanted to keep. But I did eventually ou[s]t the school Commandant, who had been there long enough. [I also wanted] to gradually get rid of those [instructors and staff] who only wanted a cushy job.

My other job obviously would seem to be providing training grounds and facilities, and allotting them to units. So one of my first jobs was to try and work up something there. To [achieve] some sort of connection, I set out to visit each division and each brigade, at least. Of these I knew two, the 31st and 63rd (Naval); the other, the 5th [Division],[41] I didn't know at all. I could always get a car, so visits were fairly easy, but any sort of [ensuing] result very difficult indeed, for hard-worked divisional and brigade staffs could see as little use for a Staff Officer for Training as I could myself![42] It [also] occurred to me that all the time I had been a Brigade Major and GSO-2 of a division, I had never seen a corps staff officer. This held good to the end when I was a GSO-1 [Chief of Staff] of a division, so I must have caused some surprise, I suppose. As it was obvious that if the war went on long enough I should eventually return to the front, and equally obvious that that was about the last thing many staff officers desired, I kept my "hand in" by allotting Sunday to a visit to some part of the front line.

This led to an amusing incident. Over the Vimy Ridge ran a straight road past the Point de Jour and down the hill to Gavrelle. To the north of it was a communication trench. To walk down the road was plain suicide as you were in full view, [but] the communication trench meant a much longer time than I could afford; so I used to go down over the open [ground]. We had recently invented the instantaneous fuse [i.e., point detonating] for shells, which replaced the shrapnel shell. The new shell exploded on the slightest contact and made no crater, and was [thus] quite devastating to anyone within 50 yards of it. So far the Germans had nothing like it, and when they did invent one it was not as good as ours.

Well, this time I was about halfway down the hill, the enemy was shelling the road as usual, and I wasn't worrying much. Suddenly the ground was cut up all round me by a shell which had exploded a good 50 yards away. "Hulloh," I said to myself, "the Boche has discovered the 106 fuse; you'd better hop it," and I made a dive for the trench. Just before I reached it another [shell] burst just behind me [and] lifted me up and dumped me in headfirst. A Sergeant came running up and asked me if I was hurt. "Like hell I am," I said. "What the blazes did I hit with my shoulder?" "That was my barrel," he said. I then learned that the Territorial Battalion in the line took its canteen up with it on which companies could draw: This was the beer barrel, so I hastily ordered a pint of Shandy [i.e., beer and lemonade].

One day the BGGS (Chief of Staff)[43] sent for me and asked me what I was doing with my time. This was pretty good, considering he had never told me to do anything at all! So I said I would give him a weekly return, which seemed reasonable. On the following Monday, therefore, I had ready a report showing everything I had done. He was rather taken aback, starting with my Sunday adventures, and hastened to tell me that he had not meant to imply that I hadn't done anything, which of course *is* what he meant. However, he had asked for a report and I insisted on reciting the whole of it.

In the line this was a time of continuous fighting, mainly by raids on our part. The Germans had retreated to the south right back to their main Hindenburg line; but there was the hinge of the retreat and it was obvious that they were not going back on our front. Mines and gas shelling added to the "general amusements," and everyone was becoming convinced that we were getting the upper hand. This confidence in our superior fighting ability was probably the reason why the line held when the enemy did deliver their great assault later in the year [1918].[44]

In the meantime, the Corps Commander conceived the idea of mixing his staff up more. I'm sure he was right, but the result was merely to move me from "A" to "B" Mess. I protested that as all the fighting part of the war was carried on from "A" Mess, I couldn't possibly keep in touch with it. However, I retained my office but had to go to "B" Mess. Here was something still more strange, and [it] showed the Corps Commander's wisdom, for I for one had never met the strange people I did now. The French word "embusque"[45] adequately describes them. Even now I have no notion whatsoever as to what they did, if anything. At meals they spent all their time running down the "G" staff and calling them "embusque." [Then] one day I went off the deep end and said, "If we are cowards what the hell are you?," and gave [them] a general invitation to accompany me on my next Sunday walk! Only one offered to come. It was next day as it happened, and I took him down to Gavrelle.

It was now March [1918] and the German counter-offensive was in full swing to the south of us. So far it had only meant additional shelling on our front. I don't think my companion had ever seen a front line. I told him not to bother about shells unless he saw me dive for cover, and then dive as fast as he could for the nearest shell hole. Soon one came that was obviously going to be a near thing and I went to ground with a dive. On to my back came my companion [who] nearly drowned me in the mud. "Well, you told me to get down quick," he said, "and I thought you'd pick the best hole!" He was a good chap and we became great friends, and [this] ended "G" staff baiting. I didn't realize it, but this was to be my last visit to Gavrelle. My regiment [the Marines] had captured it, my old 31st Division had held it, and now I was in the Corps which lost it: For the next day was 28 March [1918] when the German offensive spread to our front, and they made a great final effort to retake the Ridge.

We were in our advanced Headquarters in the Chateau Ecoivres at the foot of the west side of the Ridge, and I had a wooden hut in the garden. All night there had been terrific crashings, which I put down to two 6-inch guns in [the] rear of us. However, as I came out of my hut, something enormous crashed out of the sky about five yards in front of me. It was a 15-inch shell! They made a terrific noise and completely flattened out anything they hit, but in comparison with their size killed very few people. One hit our signal billets and laid the house out flat, and another hit a house in which four officers were sleeping upstairs, without causing a single casualty! The enemy opened a terrific fire on our front, all headquarters and batteries from 3 a.m. to 7 a.m. when they advanced under a creeping barrage, but gained very little. The 56th (London) Division,[46] holding the Gavrelle Sector, and the 3rd Canadian Division north of them held out well. And although we lost Gavrelle, Oppy Wood, and Arlewt, we held on to the main battle position; and the result, as far as the Germans were concerned, amounted to the fact that they had put themselves into a worse position than before.[47]

I was sent as Liaison Officer to the XVIIth Corps[48] on our right, and had some job getting there. A 15-inch shell burst in the road just ahead of the car, so I had to get out and walk. Then another blew up the road behind it. How the driver extricated the car I never found out. [Meanwhile], our own headquarters staff moved to Acq as the 15-inch crumps were rapidly reducing the place to dust; and on March 30, we moved back to Tincques and came into Army Reserve.

During this period out of the line I got two jobs, both interesting. A course on open fighting was started for battalion commanders under a most charming Brigadier and I was lent as his staff officer. It was a good course, [designed] to take us away from

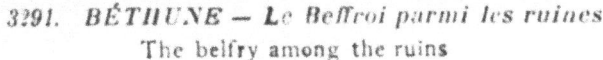

"BETHUNE—Le Beffroi parmi les ruines. The Belfry among the Ruins," Bethune, France. This undated postcard is from the Jerram personal papers and photo albums collection. Jerram's papers had no photographs from the war; instead, he retained a few postcards and many newspaper accounts. This card reflects the severe damage to cities, villages, towns, and the landscape on, near, and behind the lines of the Western Front [© Trustees RMM].

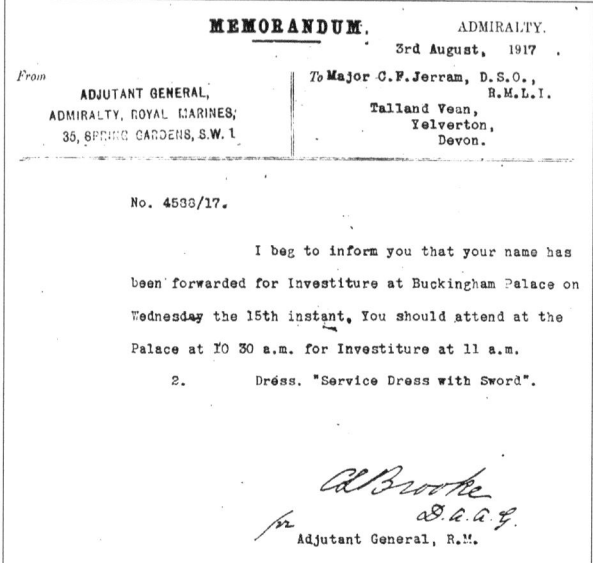

Cable to Lieutenant Colonel Jerram references his official investiture of the Distinguished Service Order (DSO) at Buckingham Palace, 15 August 1917. Note the signature of the sender, an officer whom Jerram commented upon in his memoir, and the dress requirements, to include sword [© Trustees RMM].

siege warfare. One day the Corps Commander came to have a look at us. What he thought we were I don't know, but the class contained, amongst others, three Lieutenant Colonels of Marines including Hutchinson, later to become a General [and Adjutant General, Royal Marines]. The Corps Commander gathered us round and started to preach map reading. That was all right until he started to specialize. Quite rightly he emphasized the reading of ground rather than objects, and to emphasize his point said, "Of course we can all recognize that copse over there," and gave a map reference. I looked at my map and then at Colonel Hutchinson and said nothing. However, he sensed our doubt and said, "Well it is, isn't it?," to me. "Well, no sir," I said; "Actually that copse is hidden by a rise in the ground at so and so," [to which he replied,] "Oh well, you see what I mean."

But he gave up teaching us map reading, which we had learned as Second Lieutenants! The next day I got a test. I had to accompany him on a visit to a brigade exercise [at] a distance of about 40 miles, with only a quarter inch map and most of the road unrecognizable. I'm glad to say we got there without having to stop.

The other job I had was quite a good one. I was ordered to prepare a full scale exercise for the brigade in reserve to counterattack and retake Vimy Ridge, supposing it to have been taken by the enemy. For this I had the collaboration of a grand Sapper [Royal Engineer] officer. The normal way of showing an artillery moving barrage was by flags waved by lines of men, and I always thought it looked silly. The obvious remedy was some sort of "puff" bomb, and here my sapper friend came in with 1,000 or more Bickford's safety fuse[s, i.e., a slow burning fuse], which had a self-lighting gadget. The whole affair went off very well, and the Artillery General said the whole barrage was the most life-like thing he'd ever seen.

On April 24 [1918], we took over the line in the Bethune area with the 3rd, 4th, and 15th Divisions,[49] later joined by the 46th. [Then] in July I went on a fortnight's leave to England. But I think it was my peace time battle and the report I got from my Commanding Officer of the [Corps] Senior Officers' Course that decided the "high ups" to promote me. For I returned from leave to a chorus of congratulations and was told that I had been appointed GSO [i.e., Chief of Staff] of the 46th Division.

Chapter 9

The Western Front, II—1918

With the 46th (North Midland) Division

I do not think anyone could have been more fortunate than I was in joining this Division at this particular time. The 46th (North Midland) Division was proud of the fact that it had been the first complete Territorial Division to go on active service.[1] But it had never had a chance. Every battle it had been in had been a bloody failure. In spite of this, it was in good shape and had lately come into the limelight in two different ways, both showing a pride by the men in themselves. We had recently had the Corps Horse Show, and a battery of the 46th Division had walked off with the best turnout for a complete battery. This battery had been relieved in the line at 2 a.m.; marched back to its reserve area; cleaned men, horses, [and] wagons; burnish[ed] the guns, axles, chains, etc.; and arrived on the show ground in spotless condition at 2 p.m.! So much for the gunners. The infantry had made a name for themselves in numerous raids, and whilst recording their exploits I had often thought I'd like to be with them. But I never even dreamed of having the honour to be their GSO^1 [i.e., Chief of Staff].[2]

The GOC was Major General W. Thwaites, CB,[3] and the Brigades were commanded [as follows]: the 137th, Brigadier General J. V. Campbell, VC, CMG, DSO[4]; the 138th, Brigadier General F. G. M. Rowley, CMG, DSO[5]; the 139th, Brigadier General J. Harington, DSO[6]; and the Artillery by Brigadier General Sir Hill Child, Bt, CMG, MVO, DSO.[7] We were holding the right sector (Gorre-Essaro) of XIII Corps Section, [with] divisional headquarters in a small chateau of Les Charmeux in Gosnay near Bruay.[8]

Feeling rather lost, I came down to dinner and was stared at by my new General with an eyeglass, who looked as if he was wondering what the hell he had been sent. However, things cheered up a bit when a shell burst just outside the window and blew the General into his soup! Hearing a good deal of commotion, I went out to assess the damage. There wasn't much, but the power lines were cut and live wires snaking round, so I got hold of the interpreter to get on to the civil authorities. This interpreter, a French Officer,[9] was a first class chap and we became great friends. He was a good rider and no "embusque," for he was always ready for a visit to front line troops. Later, when we got into open warfare alongside the French, he proved invaluable.

I had kept my groom, servant, and "Surefoot," but poor old "Bobby," my Gallipoli pony, had to leave when I was at Corps Headquarters as they cut us down to one horse. The "Q" staff [i.e., logistics] were very sympathetic and got him a job with a Padre [i.e., chaplain]. I've always hoped he didn't survive the war, for the horses left behind came in for a rough deal. Now I had a new horse and named him "Joe the Marine," [or] "Joe" for short.

I spent the night reading the defence scheme, which seemed to me a pretty poor effort. I don't think attack or fighting patrols [were] once mentioned in it, and [I immediately] looked up the brigade staffs. 137 Brigade had, as its Brigadier, J. V. Campbell, a Coldstream Guardsman who had won his Victoria Cross in the early days of the war rallying his men with a hunting horn. He had the horn still, and, as I learned later, when you dined with him it had a cork put in the mouthpiece. It was then filled up with Brandy and passed round. His Brigade Major was also a VC and MC [with] Bar, and the Staff Captain a MC and Bar.[10] A pretty hot lot, so I thought I'd start with them. Ringing up the Brigade Major, I asked him what time the Brigadier went round his lines in the morning and asked if I could come with him. He seemed very astonished and asked again who I was. So I said, "Sorry, I've only just joined as GSO." Anyway, he said I should be at their Headquarters at 6 a.m.

Just then the GOC looked in and asked why I hadn't gone to bed. So I said it was hardly worth while as by the time I'd got the defence scheme into my head and a general idea of the defences, it would be time to go round part of the line. He also seemed astonished! Something was up, [but] I couldn't think why. It seemed and still seems the obvious thing for a new Chief of Staff to do. Anyway I set off and met the fiercest looking General I'd ever seen in Campbell, who also looked at me as if I was something that had crawled out of a cabbage. However, he was quite pleasant and when we'd been the rounds he gave me breakfast.

The next evening the mystery was solved. I was busy rewriting the defence scheme, more on the lines Colonel Spender had put into the 31st Division Scheme, when in walked a very angry officer[11] demanding to know who the hell I was and what was I doing in his room! I said, "I'm very sorry, I don't know in the least who you are, but I was given this room and I am the GSO of this Division." "No you aren't," he said, "I am." Just then General Thwaites came in and took him off. Next morning I heard that he had been given the sack whilst on leave and the news hadn't reached him. I was sorry for the General, who [thus] had to explain to him. I never saw him again or asked about him, but I learned that he had never been nearer the front than Divisional Headquarters. No wonder there was a certain stir when I said I was going round the line. I seemed to have started on the right foot, anyway.

The line we were holding was that from which the Portuguese had bolted when attacked.[12] [It then] had been held by the Corps cavalry dashing to stop the gap and then the 46th had taken over. The enemy had got themselves into a mess, on flat ground, very swampy, and almost surrounded by low hills which we held. But for prestige, I expect they would have been glad to get out of it. It proved magnificent training ground for us, and every night our patrols were out: Fighting and driving the enemy out of trenches, and bringing in prisoners and occasional machine guns. Occasionally we would put up a bigger raid and on August 20, we staged a divisional advance. General

St. Quentin Canal, showing the brick facing and its steep banks. In the distance are the remains of a German footbridge [*History of the 46th Division*, 1919, p. 34].

fighting took place every day with considerable advances and little loss to us till September 6. It was splendid training for what was to follow.

In all this, I had the help of the best staff anyone could have. Neilson,[13] the GSO-2, was outstanding and had been, I imagine, the mainstay of the staff under an incompetent GSO. Burns-Lindow,[14] [the GSO-3 and] brother of an Irish Master of the Foxhounds and with only one eye, had guts enough in him to make up for all of us, whilst Freestun,[15] the AA&QMG [i.e., Assistant Adjutant General and Quartermaster General] and his assistant, were grand chaps to work with. On September 7, we [were] pulled out of the line and entrained for the Corbie area,[16] ideal for training in open warfare: [A] lovely rolling down [open pasture] intersected by copses, where we remained till the 18th.

I took advantage of this period to see all the troops, other than [the] infantry, and impressed on the Royal Engineers that they must be prepared for much bridging and river crossings. One young Sapper officer said, "We've been hearing that for three years and have never used even our pontoons once." So I said, "Well, you'll use them soon; anyway practice and practice and practice." About a month later I was to meet the same officer and asked him what about it now? They had used not only our own pontoons, but those of four other divisions as well! But that was to come. In the meantime we

St. Quentin Canal with Requeval Bridge [*History of the 46th Division*, 1919, p. 58].

moved into the line with Headquarters at Vraignes and relieved the right of the Australian Corps opposite the St. Quentin Canal with our right on the Village of Pontruet.[17] The Germans had shot their bolt. [French Marshal Ferdinand] Foch's great counter-attack had taken place. On this front, the Australians had fought their way to their present position, opposed by the strongest defen[sive] area ever known, the Hindenburg Line.

Just before we went back into the line, I had examples of good and bad staff work. It is the sort of things that follow that caused the natural hatred of "Brass Hats" amongst so many fighting soldiers, and the further one got from the fighting area, the worse it got. I had gone on a short leave, and on the way back through London thought it polite to call in at the Royal Marines' office [then located at 35 Spring Gardens Road] where General Blumberg, an old friend, was in charge [at this time, a Colonel serving as Assistant Adjutant General, Royal Marines]. Unfortunately, he was away sick and I saw his deputy.[18] Here is the conversation that took place: "Well, what do you want?" "I don't want anything, I really called in to see the General, thought I ought to as I was passing through." "Well, if you haven't anything to do, I have. I suppose you know there's a war on!"

[Then, when] reaching France I passed by the headquarters of a division in the line and went in to get the latest news, only to find they were in the middle of a big battle. I was just saying I wouldn't stop as they were so busy when the GSO-1, a perfect stranger, saw me and insisted on my going in and [he] went over the whole battle for my benefit. Here there was certainly a war on, but it didn't prevent a busy staff officer from being polite.

Further on at the outskirts of St. Pol[19] my car lost a wheel and crashed. Walking on, I found the town mayor's office and asked if I might use his telephone. "Where do you come from?," [this British officer] barked at me. I said I didn't see what that had to do with what I had asked. "Did you get here by rail or road?" "By road," I said, "but I still can't see that it matters." "You may use the phone. If you'd come by rail you could have gone to the Rail Transport Officer." So I told him exactly what he could do with his phone and walked out. If he treated a Lieutenant Colonel in that way, how would he treat an unfortunate Second Lieutenant, one wondered? No wonder dugout Colonels of the "Blimp" type were hated. Just beyond I found the Cavalry Corps Headquarters where I was given tea, a lorry [was] despatched to rescue my car, and I was given a car to complete my journey.

I think it is worthwhile recording these incidents to show that it was not the staff of the fighting units which made the name of "Brass Hat" stink like mud. But a change was coming in my own unit. On September 5, General Thwaites had left on appointment to the War Office, and General G. F. Boyd, CMG, DSO, DCM,[20] had joined. I was very sorry to see General Thwaites leave. He had been very good indeed to me. But I never imagined he thought much of me until he said goodbye, and then he was kind enough to say how much he appreciated what I had done. He had brought the [46th] Division into a high state of efficiency and now was not to reap the benefit.

However, in General Boyd we got the very best General I've ever met. And I learnt more [about] real soldiering and staff work in the last few weeks of the war than in all the rest put together. The staff is there to help the regimental officer and soldier. That was the basis of everything. Even when living in a trench, the divisional staff lived in luxury compared with brigades, battalions, and companies. It had more people and more facilities. It is so easy to send an order to brigades to be handed on to battalions. That wouldn't do for Boyd. If any information had to be passed down even to platoons, we, the divisional staff, had to send out sufficient copies so that every platoon would get one.[21]

It entailed a good deal of work for our clerks, but the results were almost immediate. Here was a General Officer taking a personal interest in every unit, down to the smallest. And I'm certain that this and other similar action[s] were largely responsible for our future successes. Every man recognized that in our GOC we had a leader, not a pusher. Indeed, he was so often in the forefront of the battle that I had to complain that I couldn't adequately keep in touch with things if I was confined to the office; we then arranged to take alternate days, when possible. But our other changes were not nearly so happy. My splendid GSO-2 [Major J. W. Nielson] left on well deserved promotion,[22] and we got a misfit of the kind I most detested.

Immaculate pomposity best describes Major Hay.[23] Where he came from I don't know, but he soon made it clear that he was the person who ought to be in my place. His job, amongst others, was the Divisional School, and I soon found that he had no intention of getting nearer to the front than that if he could help it. The consequence was that I was often driven to send him out on jobs I should have preferred to do myself, and the General never, I think, understood my reasons. General Boyd's method was to give an order, and he trusted his staff too well to know that that order was not necessarily carried out by the person to whom it was directed.

The other change was the AA&QMG. Freestun went and we got a complete dud, who was not only an "embusque" but lazy.[24] So here was I on the eve of what was to be the biggest battle in history and the final defeat of the Boche with a GSO-2 whom I couldn't trust and the head of the "Q" side of the staff who would never attempt anything more than routine work. Eventually I ignored him and dealt with his admirable assistant.[25] But I couldn't say anything. It was the General's business to sum up his staff, not mine, and he never knew that the DAA&QMG did all the "Q" work, or of my difficulties with Master Hay, of which more later. Fortunately, we still had Burns-Lindow who made up in guts what was lacking elsewhere!

On September 11, I issued, as a result of a conference with General Boyd, the first indication of mobile war, under the heading "Notes from Recent Operations, Applying to a War of Movement."[26] The Australian and New Zealand Corps had, in a series of battles, advanced to within striking distance of the main Hindenburg Line northwest of St. Quentin. On September 21 we took over from them from opposite the village of Pontruet[27] to a point opposite the south end of the Bellicourt (Canal) Tunnel. On our right was the 1st Division[28] and on our left an American Corps[29] had replaced the 4th Australian Division, which was in close support of them. Behind us was the 32nd Division.[30]

In general, on this front, the German line ran from north to south, across the area of the Riqueval Tunnel and behind the St. Quentin Canal to the village of Bellenglise, and thence south across open country opposite the 1st Division. At Bellenglise the canal turned abruptly southeast and then round through the city of St. Quentin. This was the [Germans'] last and [most] "impregnable" position, but for some further lines of trenches still being dug in rear. In front of this was a formidable outpost area of many trenches and thick wire, which would have been a notable feat to capture without anything else. Our part of the battle was from Bellenglise, inclusive on the south, to the south entrance of the Bellicourt Tunnel.[31]

The general outlook was as follows:

[1] In the enemy outpost line was the very strongly fortified village of Pontruet, with two other major strong points to the north. An advance of one mile brought you to the canal, guarded at its southern and by the village of Bellenglise, in which there was known to be a tunnel with its other entrance a mile back, and underground accommodation for a garrison of 3,000 men. The road bridge across the canal was destroyed, but there was little or no water for the next 1,000 yards.

[2] Here also the banks were low. But north of this for another 2,000 yards the ground rose rapidly to a narrow road viaduct near Riqueval Farm, 1,000 yards beyond which it ran into the tunnel. This part of the canal had from 6 to 12 feet of water. There

9. The Western Front, II—1918

Aerial photograph of Bellenglise and the St. Quentin Canal from above the Hindenburg defenses west of the canal [*History of the 46th Division*, 1919, p. 56].

were solid brick sides 10 to 15 feet high, above which, on both sides, the cutting rose some 50 feet smothered in wire. Behind this ran the three parallel trenches of the main line, with deep concrete dugouts and a mass of concrete machine gun posts.

[3] This was the position we were to take, and [then] advance another 7,000 yards, including two entrenched villages, Lehancourt on the south and Sequehart to the north. On reaching our objectives, the 32nd Division was to pass through.

[4] On our right the 1st Division was not to advance until our objectives were reached, when it would move up its left flank to join up.

[5] On our left there was to be no attack between the road bridge and the tunnel. Beyond this the Americans had a straightforward attack over the tunnel and would then link up with our left.

It seemed to me then, and still does, that this was to be a set piece for the Americans and that it was not really expected that we should get across. However, one couldn't work on that basis, and my first worry was the 1,000 yards on our left flank, which was not only not going to be attacked but which was not even going to be shot over. At the General's suggestion, I therefore rode over to their Headquarters and pointed out that it was in their area, and if it was not shot up we would be badly enfiladed. They were

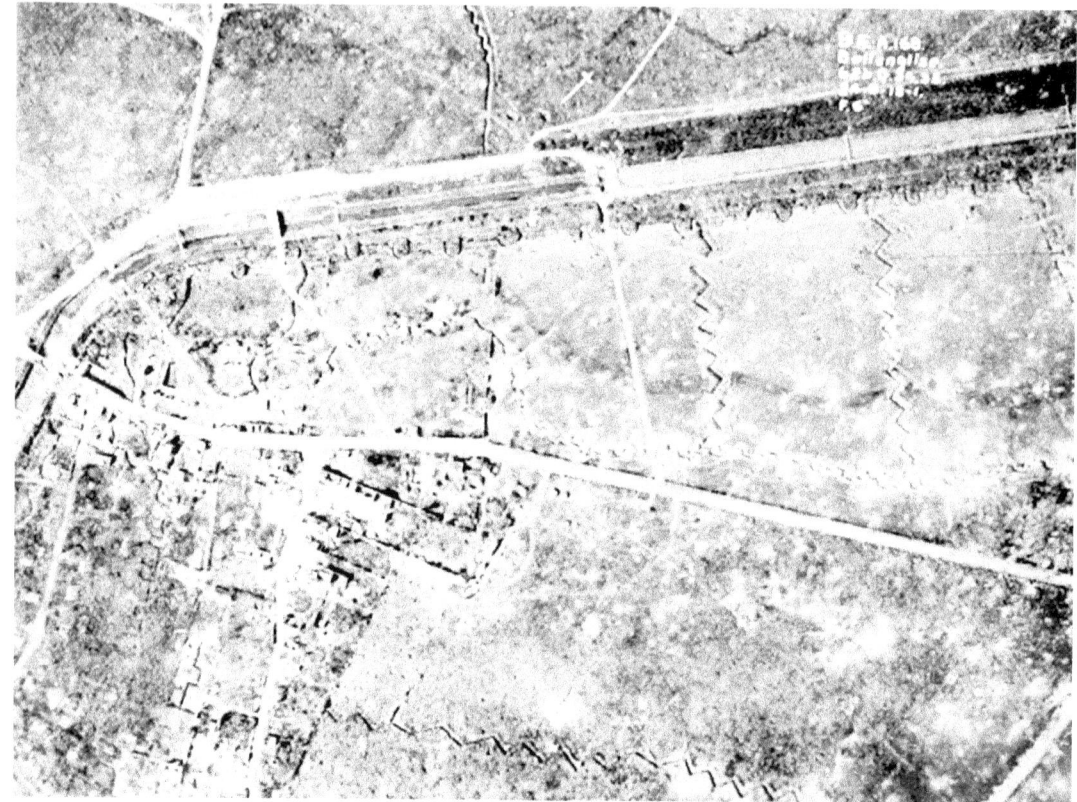

Aerial photograph of St. Quentin Canal at Bellenglise showing the defense system east of the canal and the German bridges [*History of the 46th Division*, 1919, p. 32].

not co-operative, so we got "direct-on" to the Army and eventually they were ordered to include it in their barrage.

The next headache was how to get a straight jumping off place. General Boyd, in all his battles, was adamant on the subject of getting the men started off in the right direction, and would abandon many yards of trench to get a straight line for the start of the barrage. All one had to do then was to line up in a straight line as the barrage opened and follow it when it advanced. This might be in front of our trenches or even well behind. And it thus had another advantage in that the enemy barrage directed on our front lines would miss most of our men. This straightening up entailed three attacks on Pontruet, which was eventually taken after heavy casualties, and attacks on other strong points.

Eventually, we got things straightened up as well as we could. In the meantime, of course, [we] had been considering the major problem of the canal and orders were going out to the brigades. We had been given, in addition to our own, three artillery brigades, an additional machine gun battalion, and an Army Field Company, Royal Engineers.[32] I'm still rather proud of the opening paragraph of the orders I wrote on notes taken at a conference: "At a time and date to be specified later the 46th Div, as part of a major operation, will cross the St. Quentin Canal between ... and ..., capture the Hindenburg Line and advance to a position shown on the map." There was at any rate no "if possible" so common [at] Gallipoli![33]

There is in my copy of the Official War Diary a full account of the battle,[34] with orders and maps, so there is no need to go into detail here.[35] But in general the plan was to attack with the 137th Brigade, assisted by every gun. They, covering the whole frontage, were to overrun the outpost position, cross the canal, and occupy the main Hindenburg Line. The other two brigades would then follow through to the final objective. The two machine gun battalions, after firing an intense barrage on probable approach roads for reinforcements, were to form a protective right flank in echelon. The Royal Engineers of the Army field companies were to build a bridge at Bellenglise, whilst our own were to go with the leading infantry to seize the Riqueval Bridge, carry rafts, ladders, etc., and repair a few dams in the canal to be used as crossings. The long advance would entail a good deal of movement forward of artillery, and I subsequently saw a sight, never to be seen again, of a [horse drawn] battery galloping into action. It was the most thrilling sight one could ever see.

Of the immense amount of preparations required, I will only mention one item. I was busy jotting down a list of things to be provided for crossing the canal. Burns-Lindow and Hay were present, and I was naturally consulting them as to details. There were rafts to be made, scaling ladders, hook ropes [to be obtained], etc., and I was turning over [in my mind] the kit for the individual soldier. As a Marine, the naval Gieve waistcoat[36] which you blew up to form a lifebelt, occurred to me, only to be abandoned owing to the impossibility of getting enough. Then I said "leave boats," [and] that was it. They all had at least 1,000 kapok [flotation] life belts on board. Just then I noticed that Hay had picked up some papers and taken them in to the General, which incidentally he had no business to do. To anticipate, when the General was later making out the list of rewards and consulting me, he said, "One thing, Hay must have a DSO. That idea of his as to the life belts was a life saver!!!" It was one of three occasions where I was completely at a loss. I could say nothing without appearing to blow my own horn![37]

[An]other occasion was on the same subject. It was "Q's" job to get the life belts, and next day I found he had done nothing except indent [requisition] for them. Even if that had ever got through, we couldn't possibly have [obtained] them in time and we only had a few days. So I rang up Corps "G" myself and told them that it was vital that we should have 2,000 in two days, explaining why and where to get them. They arrived and the AA&QMG got a decoration! As I shall be dead years before this is read by anyone, I can't be accused of blowing my own horn now. But I have always wished that those two honours could have gone to the DAA&QMG and to Burns-Lindow, who had earned them.[38]

The attack started at 5:50 a.m. on September 29, 1918, in a thick mist which rapidly turned to fog as it was thickened by [the] many smoke shells in our barrage. For us it was a time of waiting. We had two additional means of information direct to us. One, under Burns-Lindow, consisted of all the grooms mounted, and the other, under the Intelligence Officer, [who had] one of the first portable wireless [radio] sets. At last Burns-Lindow sent in a report that he had met a Sergeant who had been wounded in a village. That could only be Bellenglise. And on that information the 138th and 139th Brigades were let loose. At 1 a.m. General Boyd, attended by his groom with a lance carrying the Green and Red of the Division, rode forward and, as the fog lifted, saw the entire world moving forward. For the [46th] Division had achieved the impossible,[39] and when the aeroplanes were able to go up they reported that we were on our final objectives "as if the line had been chalked out on the ground."

[However,] the Americans on our left had achieved nothing at all and were back in their original positions.[40] So both our flanks were in the air and we had to make provision for the left flank in a hurry. This was made easier as the 32nd Division moved forward and relieved us, but they were too late to exploit success. The 1st Division rapidly closed the gap on our right, and by dark we were well established. We had taken between 4,000 and 5,000 prisoners and 70 guns![41] I don't think the machine guns were ever counted! And we had earned five VCs. One cannot detail every gallant action but [several] are worth recording.

[1] First and best, I think, was the leadership of the company commanders of the 138th and 139th Brigades. When one realizes that their job was to lead their companies in thick fog across a mile of unknown country, heavily wired, crisscrossed by trenches, sodden with shell holes, and under artillery fire, to crossing points over a deep canal, and deploy them ready to carry on the attack on the other side, it is a miracle that they ever got there. It [was] the finest exhibition of regimental leadership I have ever experienced.

[2] [And to] another bit of leadership: our right flank battalion was commanded by LtColonel Vann, MC.[42] In private life he was a priest of the Church of England and the tone of his unit was a fine advertisement to the Church. At the final objective he found himself faced by a German battery just beyond our protective barrage. It was firing at point blank range and the situation was critical. Vann gathered a dozen men together and charged through our own barrage, killed the gunners, and removed the breech blocks of the guns. He was one of the VCs, but never knew it as he was killed in the next battle saving the situation again.

[3] The last is that of a subaltern. It will be remembered that our right flank was open and that the canal, dry here, was its only protection. A German battery about 200 yards away was slewed [i.e., swung] round and was enfilading our flank. This young officer took his platoon across the canal and captured the battery.

For the first time in the war the name of the Division was published, and a steady stream of congratulations poured in from the Army commanders down or up to local schools in the Midlands.[43] One of the happiest was from the 1st Division, the premier division of the Army, as General Boyd called them in his reply. They had fought hard to help us, especially in our troubles round Pontruet, and they had to watch us take the plums.

They were pinched out by our joining up with the French after they entered St. Quentin. The GOC of the 126th French Division, General Mathieu, sent us a message: "We entered St. Quentin today, but it was your 46th Division which enabled us to do so when they stormed the Hindenburg Line at Bellenglise." We paraded for him a few days later when he presented ten Croix de Guerre[44] [to us], of which I was one of the recipients. It cannot be often in these days that one receives a decoration on the field of battle for which it was granted! To end up this battle, the Australian 4th Division attacked through the Americans [the] next day and linked up. They said the Americans were starving and couldn't even feed themselves. So much for their boast that they won the war![45]

Open Warfare, 1918

On October 1, the 32nd Division made an attack to gain the high ground they were meant to take on September 29. They failed to advance a yard and [IX] Corps[46] immediately ordered us to take it on the 3 October. This was far from being a straight forward affair, but I do not think that anyone of us imagined that we should not succeed. We had just won the greatest battle of the war with absurdly few casualties, and our tails were right up.

It is surprising therefore that the High Command,[47] who had been drumming into us that we must become open war minded, entirely failed to become so themselves.[48] In front of us, save for defended villages, there was lovely open rolling country, without hedges or obstacles, and ideally suited to cavalry. If we got through, there was no defensive position left; and if we didn't get through, no one would be any worse off. Yet, as we learned later, the cavalry, far from sitting on our tails, had been told that they need not consider our front at all.

The situation as we saw it was as follows: To our immediate right front was the defensive village of Sequehart, whence a ridge ran diagonally across our front. This ridge fell away to the extensive village of Montbrehain, a distance of 5,000 yards, and this formed our left objective. Nearer to our left flank was the village of Ramicourt, after which the battle was named.[49] On our right, in more or less doubtful positions, were the French. And on our left the Australian 4th Division, which was not to attack but to link up with our left flank later.

As can be imagined, it was an awkward attack both for the infantry and guns. The latter had to come into position in unknown territory and had no opportunity of registering. Indeed, some of them were only in position just in time to open fire at zero hour. The advance entailed a swing to the right, pivoting on Sequehart, to seize the high ground; a steady advance up the centre of some 5,000 yards to capture Montbrehain; and a defensive flank to be formed on our left as we advanced. In spite of this, the whole thing was completely successful. From the high ground our troops saw the whole German force pouring to the rear and guns galloping away; we shrieked for cavalry to come up and end the war, [but] in vain.

The 5th Cavalry Brigade GOC, Neill Haig,[50] and his Brigade Major arrived at our Headquarters at 3 p.m. on completely exhausted horses. [They] said that their Brigade could not possibly arrive for at least three hours and then would be in no position to charge. Poor Neill Haig. Here, as he admitted, was the one opportunity in the whole war, and owing to the orders he had received he had arrived too late, for by that time the Germans had brought up a new division and were heavily counterattacking. The brunt of this attack fell on Colonel Vann's battalion in Montbrehain, and [the Germans] drove them back to Ramicourt. But here they stuck, though Vann was killed in the fighting. Everywhere else we held. But again we were strung out with both flanks open. The Cavalry [thus] had to be used, dismounted, [i.e., fought as dragoons] to help hold our left. As the Australians fought their way up on our left flank, we continued to hold out over the next two days and then turned over to the 6th Division,[51] [after] having captured another 2,000 prisoners. I [also] had an interesting encounter. Riding over the battlefield, I met a Royal Marine Artillery Sergeant. I asked him what on earth he was doing. It appear[ed] that their 15-inch howitzers, being now of no more value, the crews were being sent forward to bring into action any German guns!

On the 6th [of October], the Australians re-occupied Montbrehain, and our centre of advance was switched slightly south with the 6th Division advancing on our left and the French on our right. One brigade was detailed as advanced guard and we were given two squadrons of cavalry; one of the Greys and one of the Lancers. Advanced guard fighting brought us into the village of Fresnoy [northeast of St. Quentin], where we found our first few civilians on 8 October, and were then held up for some hours along a railway embankment. I sent Burns-Lindow with a squadron of the Greys to find out if the bridge carrying the railway over the road was intact, and to report on how the embankment was held. They made a very good reconnaissance, galloping across the front at 300 yards range when about 30 machine guns opened on them, with only one horse slightly wounded.

The next day, [October] 9th, we overcame this obstacle and entered the town of Bohain [approximately 15 and a half miles or 25 kilometers from Cambrai], where some 5,000 civilians were still living. They had not been badly treated themselves, but all testified to the brutal treatment of prisoners. Our next obstacle was the Bois de Requeval right across our front, where the Germans, French, and ourselves played hide and seek for two days, [before] we bumped into a very strong rear guard position round the village of Regnicourt [located between St. Quentin and Le Cateau]. Our first attempt to take it failed, mainly owing to intense machine gun fire against the French. [Then,] at a Corps conference, it was decided to attack it from our left flank without involving the French. The position was a long spur running directly towards us from the village of Andigny-les-Fermes to Regnicourt [south of Le Cateau]. With the 6th Division on our left, we were to disengage, move off to our left, and attack from the North. To deceive the enemy, we arranged a dummy attack from our present positions; the Royal Engineers made dummy men on sleighs, which could be pulled forward from blocks and ropes previously laid out.

The flank march led to a jumping off line taped on the ground during the night. The GSO-2, Hay, hadn't done anything whatever during the advance, and, now that he had come up to Advanced Headquarters, I was determined that he should at least smell powder. So I sent him with the sappers who were marking the line. As a matter of fact all was peace, but he had a night out. It was quite wrong. I should have gone myself, but I had a tremendous amount to do [and] I think General Boyd didn't like it. He never realized the complete uselessness of this most useless officer, or the great work of the

9. The Western Front, II—1918

number two of the "Q" Staff. It was [Boyd's] one failing: He simply could not appreciate the fact that an officer could exist who was not out to do his best.

During the preparations for this battle, I pointed out to General Boyd that one of the 6th Division tanks was due to come very near our flank where there was a rather sticky fortified farm. [I] said I'd ride over to Tank Corps camp and see if he could help us, as we had no tanks. On arrival, I asked for the officer of this tank and was told, "Oh, I think Jerram is doing that." Wondering who this "Jerram" was, I was directed to his tank and found my cousin, Roy,[52] son of the Admiral! I had no idea he was even in the Tank Corps, and I hadn't met him since he was about five. In the subsequent battle, his tank was knocked out but he got his crew out and took our Farm, for which he got a very well earned Military Cross.

This attack was entirely successful. [Then with] the French having captured Mennevret [east of Bohain], we had a day or two [of] forest fighting with them through the large forest of Andigny, [finally] ending up on its eastern ridge. Here the 1st Division, having passed through the 6th Division, came up on our left flank and squeezed us out. We [then] withdrew into a well merited rest and clean up [until] 31 October, when we received the Corps' orders for the attack of the Sambre-Oise Canal, for which we were in reserve to exploit success. This attack was successful and we passed through the 1st Division on November 4th.

With a Squadron of the 20th Hussars and another of the Greys, we followed up the enemy as fast as we could advance, much hampered by the fact that every bridge, culvert, and crossroad was blown up. We were now in a country of orchards, and our cavalry had more difficulty. The German rear guard worked well. In general every crossroad and farm was held by machine gunners, whilst the main body of the rear guard was establishing itself on river obstacles. To deal with these machine guns, we had a field battery with [our] vanguard, with one section as close up to the leading infantry as they could get. And in this country that was very close.

Burns-Lindow and I had a close call one day and I mention it because of the very fine effort of my groom, in private life a young farm labourer. We had ridden up as far as we could, on a look round our advanced posts, and left our horses with my groom in a long depression whilst we walked through a small copse to the front. As we were coming back, the enemy put down a fairly heavy barrage across the valley where our horses were. For a bit we couldn't find them and thought they had stampeded, but eventually found them in a small quarry. How my groom had controlled three horses and got them there, I don't know. It was a pretty good effort.

We decided to gallop on and risk the shells. It was close country with good stiff quickset hedges. Just as we came up to one, my groom on "Surefoot" cleared it and then I saw that it was just the sort of fence "Joe" wouldn't bother about. A thin hedge he could see through. But I could see a solid stake in the hedge and gave him a shake up. At the last moment he decided to jump and at the same time a shell landed just behind him and we came a complete [word illegible] over the stake. Burns-Lindow fared no better: He made for a gap, and just as he reached it, a shell fell right under his nose. Luckily both shells were ground burst shrapnel and we all escaped without a scratch, [while] my groom gave a good exhibition by catching both horses under considerable fire. "Joe" never got over his laziness, and during the Armistice when we had a paper hunt he let me down in exactly the same way.

On November 6, I had an interesting day. Having sent out orders to push on towards the town of Avesnes [about 11 miles or 19 kilometers northeast of Montreuil-sur-Mer], I rode up to the advanced guard. On reaching [the] vanguard headquarters, the battalion commander told me that he was hung up at a crossroad 200 yards ahead. So I stupidly left my horse whilst I went up to see. Just as I got there we began to move and I went on with the leading platoon. But our guns were still shelling behind us, and I was rather torn between going on and going back to tell them. However, thinking they must soon find out, I went on as it was important to know if the bridge over the river at Cartignies (due east of Le Cateau] was blown.

Arriving at the town, we drove the Germans out of the houses, [but] were much delayed by the inhabitants. [They] came out and passed apples and coffee on our men till I thought of telling them that the French Army was only two kilometers away on our right. Then they all streaked off to meet them. In the meantime the squadron of the Greys rode on to the bridge, but it was blown up just as they [arrived] there. So I hurried back to report, cursing the fact that I had left my horse. During the night we got pontoons across below the town, and at dawn attacked across the river and that night, the 9th [two days before the Armistice], we established an outpost line with Cavalry Vedettes [i.e., guarded posts leading into a military area] pushed well forward.

On November 10, our cavalry and cyclists were transferred to Bethell's Force,[53] [which] consist[ed] of a brigade each of artillery, cavalry and infantry. This force pushed through us to keep touch with the enemy. Indeed,

Jerram's diary, November 1918. He penned no entry for 11 November 1918, the day of the Armistice. However, his entry for the following day addresses when the fighting ceased: "12 Nov. So here's the end of it after four years. At 11. A.M. yesterday we were ordered to cease fire & at that time had the honour of being the most easterly troops in the British Army." At the time, Jerram was Chief of Staff of the 46th North Midland Division, with the rank of Temporary Lieutenant Colonel [© Trustees RMM].

9. The Western Front, II—1918

it had become difficult to keep us fed. We were 87 miles from our railhead,[54] and although troops were working like mad to clear the roads behind us, only light limbers could get within an appreciable distance. And the last few miles meant pack horses. [For the status of divisions on the Western Front on Armistice Day, see Appendix VIII.]

The Armistice of November 11th found us occupying an outpost position east of the little town of Sains du Nord [15 and a half miles or 25 kilometers south of Maubeuge, or just over 68 miles or 110 from Brusells or Reims], and not far from Mons where it all began in 1914! The next day the General and I rode into Mons where I bought a length of Valenciennes lace for my wife. We went over the old battlefield where General Boyd had fought as a company commander. He showed me how they withdrew up the hill in full view of the enemy, who had [had] such a hammering from our rifle fire that they would not come on. The old regular Army marksmanship was the fastest and most accurate ever known and compares well with the English Archery at Crecy [in 1341]. Curiously enough, the two battlefields are very similar. Getting your musketry penny and your marksman's three-pence depended almost entirely on the 300 yards rapid. Fifteen rounds in 40 seconds, and unless they were all bullseyes you hadn't a hope.[55]

Official warrant of the Distinguished Service Order (DSO) awarded to Captain (Temporary Major) Jerram, dated 1 January 1917 [© Trustees RMM].

The [46th North Midland] Division deserved to march into Germany. Since the end of September we had fought several major battles without a single setback and advanced 50 miles.[56] It was a wonderful achievement. We had a very nice message from the 4th Army Commander, General Rawlinson,[57] in which he expressed his deep regret that it had not been his good fortune to take us. One paragraph read: "The forcing of the main Hindenburg Line on the Canal ranks as one of the finest and most dashing exploits in the war. The attacks of Oct. 3 and the subsequent operations round Bohain together with the advance beyond the Sambre Canal constitute a record of which all ranks of the Division may feel justly proud. I offer to all ranks my warmest thanks for their great gallantry and to the leaders and staffs my admiration of their skillful direction and staff work throughout these battles."

To the historian it is interesting to compare the battles and advances [of the First World War] with those of World War II as described by General [Brian] Horrocks[58] in his book *A Full Life*. The advance from Caen to the final defeat of the Germans by his Corps in 1945 is almost exactly similar, allowing of course for difference of weapons, armoured cars for horses, and self propelled guns for horse drawn. For every mile we advanced, they made 20, but in essentials the two campaigns [*sic*, actually operations] are the exactly the same.

On November 22, I was sent home to attend the first post war course at the Staff College, [Camberley]. I [received] a very charming letter of farewell from General Boyd, whom I look upon as one of the finest divisional commanders of all time. [But I] thereby miss[ed] the visit of His Majesty the King to the Division.[59] Later I attended a levee at Buckingham Palace, where the King decorated me with the insignia of the Order of Saint Michael and Saint George[60] and the Distinguished Service Order [DSO].

In the meantime the rest of my family had not been idle. My father was lecturing on current events. My sister "Posy" was a VAD [Volunteer Ambulance Driver] at Rockhampton Hospital. Ralph had joined a Gurkha Regiment and served in France and Mesopotamia, where he was wounded and earned a Military Cross. Winnie was still in India; Muriel a VAD in Egypt and in the Hospital at Bologne; Rowland on Admiral Beatty's staff in HMS *Lion* [and had] gained a DSO; and Bertrand was busy getting people away from the Bolsheviks at Odessa, got imprisoned, and somehow managed to get away. Surprisingly, we all came back, having accumulated five decorations between us! [See Appendices IV and V for the war services of the families of Lieutenant Colonel Jerram and his wife].

Chapter 10

Between the Wars, 1919–40

Staff College, Camberley

I didn't really want to go to the Staff College. I knew that it would do me no good to have "psc"[1] after my name, but General Boyd had been so good in recommending me that it would have been churlish to refuse. To an Army officer it was essential for a command, but to us [Royal Marines] it meant nothing at all[2] and was a hindrance, if anything, owing to the stupid jealousies in the Corps. As I [discovered] later, the Royal Marine Office resented my being sent there by the Army and refused to pay me [until] forced to do so by the War Office. My pay as a Major of Marines was much more than an Army Major's and obviously I could not afford to be paid by the Army.

Immediately I knew of my appointment, I wrote to my wife telling her to go to Camberley and take a house for a year before they were all snapped up. She wisely went at once and got a nice little house very cheaply and got the lease signed at once. Just as well, as about a fortnight later I had a letter from the owner saying she had just heard that the Staff College was reopening and could not possibly let us have the house on those terms and asked for three times the amount. Needless to say, I ignored the letter completely. This avarice amongst house holders led to their undoing, for the War Office started building bungalows of their own for married officers. We brought the family, nurse, and a maid up from Devon, but were not allowed to bring our soldier servant. Anyway, he had been demobilized. But we were given a servant, groom, and a horse. Mine was a "Hairy," out of a gun team I should think, and we had to learn how to jump the Berkshire fences together.

There were 200 students,[3] all of whom had been in high positions either in command or on the staff but had not got the coveted "psc." [Thus] the course was shortened from two years to one to suit us. We had, of course, to revert to our substantive [permanent] rank, and there were Captains who had been Brigadier Generals! A good many of us were consequently thinking in terms of retirement until [Major] General Anderson[4] gave us his opening talk. He pointed out that we pre-war officers were essential to bring up the new entry, and I decided that I would at least stay on as long as I was wanted. Lord Gort[5] told me that he was in the same position and had likewise decided to stay, and he eventually commanded our Army in France in the early days of [World]

War II. They were a distinguished company and included such people later to become famous as Dill[6] and Alexander.[7]

But I for one learned absolutely nothing at all. There was literally nothing that I had not learned as a Second Lieutenant at Greenwich, and I was appalled at the complete ignorance of many of the students who had held staff appointments in the war. To mention but one or two things, we were instructed as to the value of "graphs" and given a simple exercise. [However], whilst a GSO-2 in XIII Corps I had the job of working out the March Tables of a division coming out of the line being relieved by one marching up, whilst the whole Canadian Corps was moving across our area between them! I defy anyone to work that out without a "graph," which I had of course learned to do when a Second Lieutenant.

On another occasion we were given an advanced guard exercise with cavalry. This was right up my street, [as] I had just been doing it for weeks, but I was not head of my syndicate [seminar group] of six. Naturally, as I had learned at Greenwich and practiced in the war, I worked out the bounds for the cavalry with their report centre and follow up headquarters lines, etc. But I was completely overruled by the other five, who insisted on sending the cavalry off into the blue. When the directing staff came out with the only possible solution, the leader did have the grace to say, "Sorry, Jerram." But what amazed me was what they could possibly have learned at Sandhurst or Woolwich!

[Then] we had to write a paper on "Artillery in Support of an Advanced Guard." Here again was something right up my street, and I pointed out the absolute necessity of having [the] guns right forward to blast machine guns at point blank range. My essay was taken by a gunner [artilleryman] instructor who could never have been in any war of movement, for he plastered it with jeers such as, "What do you think the machine guns would be doing in the meantime?" And my paper was sent to the Commandant, who interviewed me. I pointed out that in his opening lecture he had said that we were preparing for a war in 10 years, that I had seen guns used in this way with horsed artillery, [and] that if in 10 years they still had horsed artillery, then heaven help the Army. I visualized something on the lines of the Whippet Tank.[8] But it wasn't any use. We were purely 1914, and I cannot remember tanks being brought into any exercise. As everyone knows, we *did* have horses in the next war, not 10 but 20 years later, and had to learn from the Germans that guns must be in the front line. So much for our instruction, but it was a very pleasant year and we made many friends.

Much the most dangerous part of the whole [year] was the Paper Hunt. Owing to foot and mouth disease, the College drag hunt[9] couldn't be revived, so we had the paper hunt in which everyone had to ride whether he could or not. Many, of course, had their own horses, but most of us merely had what we had been issued with. Imagine, therefore, 200 of us lined up 50 yards from the first jump waiting an order [to] "Go." I found that the safest plan was to let well mounted experts get away and keep close on their heels before the ugly rush of the remainder crashed into you from behind and ground you into the mud!

The "Berkshire Double" defeated my horse and myself. We never did learn to negotiate it without a fall. It consists of a ditch, a bank with a hedge on it, and another ditch. A small grass ride about the width of a horse's length and then a repetition of ditch,

Warrant for Lieutenant Colonel Jerram's Award of the Order of St. Michael and St. George, 11 June 1919 [© Trustees RMM].

hedge, ditch. If you took it slowly, as one would a double, you fell into ditch two. So next time you took it a bit faster and fell into ditch three. Whatever we did we always came a cropper [i.e., to fall from a horse.] One day riding out I asked Gort if he knew what the course was like. "Oh, it's all right," he said. "One fence and ditch you've got to go at." I looked envyingly at his hunter and said, "Your horse or mine?" Then he laughed and said, "Yes, it does make a difference."

Anyway, into the middle of the jump he mentioned, fell my pet aversion of instructors. He lay cursing at the bottom of the ditch whilst about 50 horses jumped over him. I jumped quite nicely over a gap where someone else had crashed and made a nice hole in the hedge. But I got a stinker later on. We came to a bank under an oak tree with a low branch. Whether my old "Hairy" jumped too high or I got up from my crouch too soon, I don't know. But I came to myself three fields further on having taken two jumps I hadn't even seen, with a cut in the top of my head and blood pouring down my face. Carinna, my wife's sister and a doctor, plastered me up when I got home.

Outside Staff College work, I joined the local church bell ringers under a most delightful leader who was struggling to reorganize his tower. With him I visited many towers for ringing, including Winchester Cathedral. He [also] got up a peal of 5040 Grandsire Triples at my father's old house at Chobham, which we brought round in three hours and five minutes. Altogether it was a very pleasant year indeed and I enjoyed every minute of it.

Then came the aftermath. I was offered in turn four Army staff appointments. One of them [was] as Brigade Major to my old divisional commander, Boyd, who had a Brigade in Ireland; I should have loved to have gone back to him, but [financially] I simply could not afford it.[10] After all, I was a Marine and it didn't matter what the Army gave me, at the end of it I should have to come back and command 50 to 100 men at sea. The only thing to do would be to transfer to the Army and join a line regiment. Then, with my "psc" and war record, I could accept a junior staff job with the certainty of a future command. But this I was very loath to do. I loved my own Regiment [the Royal Marines], and in addition what was I going to live on until I did get a command, for my pay as a Marine was nearly as much again as I should get in the Army. I tried to explain all this to General Thwaites, my old commander, when I met him in London. "What's the matter with you," he said, "that you turn down all the jobs we offer you; aren't they good enough?" But I don't think he understood. It is difficult for them to see any reason for turning down a job that every Army officer was trying to get without success.[11]

Eventually I was appointed to a brand new Cruiser, HMS *Raleigh*.[12] Almost immediately afterwards the Marine Office asked me to go to Deal as Assistant Military Instructor under Major [Maurice C.] Festing, my first Brigade Major in Gallipoli [and a fellow student at Camberley]. He had very kindly asked for me, but I didn't like him and I'm sure we should not have got on, so I made excuses.[13] Then I was offered GSO-2, Hong Kong, as the War Office wanted a Marine for the job. But the situation remained the same. Either I had to take my family out there or keep up two establishments, all on less pay. By that time everyone was no doubt pretty well fed up with me. But the proof of the pudding is in the eating. The only "psc" officers [of the Royal Marines] of those two post war [staff college] courses who rose above Lieutenant Colonel were those who left the Corps and joined the Army.[14]

Towards the end of our time at Camberley, some of us were sent by the War Office to advise County Lieutenants on the formation of Citizen Guards, and Lieutenant Colonel G. C. Williams, CMG, DSO,[15] and myself were sent to Dorset. It was an interesting experience and we received a very flattering report from Admiral Parry, the Lord Lieutenant, in which he reported the "high opinion that I formed of the abilities and qualifications of both the staff officers with whom I had the good fortune to be associated."[16] As the *Raleigh* was not commissioning till July 1921, I returned to Plymouth and soon found myself let in for the great railway strike.[17]

Reserves were being called up, and it was generally assumed that the strike would become general. Two battalions were forming at Plymouth, one of regulars and the other of reservists, and I was appointed adjutant of the latter [the 13th Battalion].[18] It was interesting and rather frightening, as every single man was either on strike or was a potential striker. As a supposed Staff College expert, I was told to lecture to the battalion on "military aid to [the] civil power." At the end I said that I was prepared to answer any questions on law, but not on any controversial question. At the back of the theatre a man got up and started on a stump "Hyde Park" speech. So I told him to sit down. He didn't do so [until] his comrades pulled him down. Pointing out that I had made it plain that I was not there to alter the law but to explain it, [this] brought to my surprise a cheer from the whole house. And I again asked if there were any questions. One man got up and said that he was a transport driver, [and] what would happen if they struck and he was ordered to drive transport? That was a good question and easily answered. Military transport was a military commitment. If we wanted drivers for civil purposes, we'd call for volunteers. I saved the life of my "bolshie" [Bolshevik] by transferring him to another unit. I found out that they were all waiting for him in the canteen!

A few days after my lecture I was sent to give it to the Naval Barracks. The one question I was asked there was "Should Lewis guns[19] be loaded!!!" My reply to that was, "If you are let loose on strike duty, for heavens sake leave the damn things behind; and preferably all ammunition." I think he must have gone to sleep during the entire lecture!

The [troops] were a wonderful crowd. Every single man had joined, but there were some very hard cases of men with sick wives, etc., and we

Except for one tour at the Royal Marine Division, i.e., barracks, Chatham, Jerram's home division remained Plymouth, Stonehouse Barracks. Mrs. Sibyl Jerram actively supported her husband in his career. A talented artist, she produced a book of sketches of the barracks. The badge in the center was and is that of Britain's Corps of Royal Marines [© Trustees RMM].

were forbidden to give leave. Finally my Commanding Officer took matters into his own hands and sent really hard liner cases off. To keep the men amused, I took a line out of the policy of the Brigade Major[20] of the 138th Brigade during the Armistice when "he started" Brigade Dis-Orders. I started "Battalion Dis-Orders," in which we cracked jokes on the other battalion; divisional [barracks] orders, etc. One day outside the orderly room I was very busy when I heard, "What are you waiting for, chum?" "I'm waiting for orders to be posted up." "Why, there's orders there." "Oh not them. Its the dis-orders I'm waiting for." So I shouted out, "Sorry, too busy." We lasted about three weeks till the strike ended, and every single railway and transport man volunteered for service. I doubt if any reserve battalion could show the same record, and the high state of morale was due first to my Commanding Officer and to the very fine company commanders from the reserve, of whom my old friend Nutt was the best.[21]

Barracks life as I had known it had gone. I arrived on a guest night and, having a Mess bedroom and nowhere to go, I sent a message to the President asking permission to go to the smoking room. To my horror and surprise, immediately after [the toast to]

"The King" all the officers left the Mess except the President! Later he told me how glad he was to [have] another pre war officer to back him up. He had tried in vain to get some sort of Mess discipline going and had lost heart. Between us, we did get things gradually improved.

Back to the Sea

We had bought a house in Falmouth next to Penwerris Church, and here I left my family, Jon, Morwenna, and Jennifer. Anthony was born soon after I sailed. The *Raleigh*, Flagship of the North America and West Indies Station,[22] was a fine looking cruiser carrying 7.5-inch guns. She was brand new and had been long building, [but] was a beast to keep clean. Indeed, no one except the Commander[23] and myself tried very hard. All the lieutenants had been brought up in war conditions, and only we two knew anything of a peacetime Navy. All the old traditions seemed to have gone, and there was little resemblance to anything I had known before. I was almost wishing that I hadn't stayed on till I remembered General Anderson's talk at the Staff College: That we must bring up the new Army [or], in this case, the Navy, and remembered my introduction to the post war mess at Plymouth.

There were four ships on the station. We had about 50 Marines and the others about 30. My second in command was Captain [sic] Spraggett, MC,[24] who had been adjutant of our battalion in France but who had never been to sea. I had to start teaching him from scratch. But he was a very able officer and, having no preconceived ideas of his own, was able to give me a good backing in my revolutionary ideas, which were quite in keeping with his military ones. In Ronald Fraser, the Commander, I found a fellow spirit. He didn't care what I did, only [that] it had to be efficient or he would have to go back to old and tried customs. That was fair enough.

For what I wanted was an organization in which units worked under their own Noncommissioned Officers in whatever they did on board or ashore, ate together, and slept together. And the first thing to do was to get away from the two chief obstructions: One, that every Warrant Officer had always had a Marine storeman, and two, that in telling off the hands for work it had been the custom to detail one or two from each part of the ship. Thus the Marines' working party would be split up all over the ship, working with different petty officers. The first was the hardest to crack, but we did it. The other was easy, once I had convinced Fraser. What I asked him was, if a number of men were wanted for a particular job, don't bring [some] Marines in but give them the whole job. Then I could detail a section under their own NCO.

Working out the Watch and Station Bill with Spraggett before commissioning was a nightmare. What I had arranged in my mind was that we would form a [squadron] company. One platoon in each ship, [with] the Flagship to [also have] company Headquarters. For naval commitments, we were given one 7.5-inch gun, two antiaircraft [guns], and a shell room and magazine. For cleaning we had the aft deck.[25] Perfectly simple in theory: The company headquarters takes the 7.5-inch gun, [and] the sections the anti-aircraft guns, shell room, and magazine, until you found that your best gun

10. Between the Wars, 1919–40

While on the west coast of the United States in 1922, the officers of HMS *Raleigh* visited the Paramount Mack Sennett comedy studio in Hollywood, California—and posed for a group photograph. Then-major Jerram is in the bottom (front) row, third from the right. Note the Sam Browne belt he is wearing [© Trustees RMM].

layer was an infantry Lewis gun expert, [plus] a dozen similar headaches. However, we got it taped at last, and then had to deal with the NCOs.

In my Sergeant Major I had a first class man.[26] Naturally he raised all sorts of objections [and] that was his business, but he loyally backed me up. The Second Sergeant was a big, blustering, beer-swilling chap. A grand chap in a scrap, but quite untrustworthy as a peacetime NCO, and openly hostile. Number three, a Lance Sergeant, was inclined to follow him, till I had him in my cabin and told him he was backing the wrong horse, [after which] he became one of the best of NCOs. Of the eight corporals, I soon found that four were useless—and they were reduced and better men promoted in their place. Being half a world from Headquarters had its advantages!

Our first call was at Bermuda, and here we were able to go into camp at Warwick[27] and get a good shakedown whilst the ship was in dry dock. Here my number two Sergeant was run in for drinking in the Canteen after lights out, and the Captain [Arthur Bromley][28] reduced him to Corporal. He was allowed to join the police at their request, and I was not asked to give him a character [reference], thank goodness.

After that we settled down very happily. With one exception, the lieutenants were a very nice crowd; [this] was fortunate because the Commander constantly held up the Marines as being the only people in the ship who were trying to get her smart, which was quite true but perhaps not very tactful. But the thing I couldn't understand was that they didn't seem to care. Thus, when we had an evolution "away all boats and pull round the fleet," the Commander gave us the second cutter.[29] I had my crew told off

HMS *Raleigh* berthed alongside a pier at the U.S. Marine Corps Marine Barracks, Quantico, Virginia. Note the U.S. Navy destroyer in the boat basin. In 2016, both the pier and boat basin remain, the latter now a marina [© Trustees RMM].

[i.e., called] and led them along the lower boom, and we were first away and got back half a mile ahead of anyone else. No other officer went with his boat, [and] there were many other similar incidents.[30]

After Bermuda we went through the Panama Canal and up the West Coast [of North America]. San Diego at that time was quite a small place and only just beginning to be the Headquarters of the Pacific Base [of the] U.S. Marine Corps.[31] America was still "dry,"[32] and the First Lieutenant and I had a sample of it when asked to dine by a U.S. Navy Captain. On our way he stopped at a Chemist's shop and came out with a bottle of sherry. On arrival at his house, his small son came to meet us and said, "Oh, I know what that is. Daddy calls it his medicine." "That's what we have to put up [with]," said his father, "One's children's' first lesson is how to break the law!" We spent Christmas at Esquimalt,[33] where there was a lovely little barquentine with a skysail yard. I didn't know there was one left, but I've heard since that there were three similar ships. But the change in the Navy from that which I had known was shown in the fact that no one in the ship could even name the sails, except I suppose the Admiral [William Pakenham]³⁴ and Captain.

Crossing over to Vancouver, we arrived in time for New Year's Day. The Warrant Officer, Carpenter, was a fellow ringer and we helped the local band to ring in the year with a touch of Grandsire Triples at the Roman Catholic Cathedral. At midnight the priests brought in whiskey and cigars, which seemed strange to us, until they told us that in R.C. churches the tower was not part of the consecrated building. We [also] had some good duck shooting, both here and on the island, and everyone was very good to us. Plenty of parties for those who liked them. I met a very nice family going round the ship and took them in tow, and had a very pleasant day with them in return.

On our way [back] south, amongst other places, we stopped at Monterey, [California], [the post of the 11th] U.S. Cavalry Regiment. They got up a game of polo for us and, whilst watching it, a cowpuncher [cowboy] came galloping up on a lovely black horse, which he pulled up in a sliding halt. I got talking to him and he said, "That was just swank to impress your boys. It's not the way I generally pull up." He was a nice chap and we asked him off to lunch, to the amusement of the cutter's crew at seeing a cowpuncher in full regalia in a boat. In return, he took two of us for a ride [the] next day.

While at Quantico, the officers of HMS *Raleigh* on 6 June 1922 attended a parade and review of the U.S. Marine Corps East Coast Expeditionary Force, a precursor of what would be the American Corps' amphibious assault force in World War II. Although neither Corps had "horse Marines," officers could and were expected to ride—including on parade and, if necessary, in the field. Note the Royal Navy's White Ensign flying from the reviewing stand [© Trustees RMM].

He was a most interesting chap and the exact spit[ting image] of Johnny Nelson, black horse and all, in the Hopalong Cassidy novels.[35]

[Then to] Santa Monica, Santa Barbara, and a trip to movie town [Hollywood], and back to [the east coast] and Quantico[36] and Washington, [D.C.]. There were, of course, numerous guards and an official dinner at the Embassy [and] as one of the Admiral's staff, I was included ... the major of U.S. Marines in charge of their Depot asked me up there and introduced me to the G.O.C. [Major General Commandant John A. Lejeune] of the Marine Corps. And at Quantico they had a parade of the Marines Division and march past for the Admiral, who took me with him, which made me green with envy.[37]

[We passed] some lovely country harbours on the way north and then [went] up the river to Quebec and Montreal. Here I met Colonel Alexander of the Canadian Army, who had been at the Staff College with me. He not only arranged some good field days for us, in conjunction with the Army, but took me down to his father-in-law's house on the Saguenay River. Mrs. Alexander and her two children were charming and the father, a Bishop, a perfect host; I had a most delightful week, [and] rejoin[ed] the ship at Quebec by river steamer. At that time the country north of the river was quite wild, and there was nothing but virgin forest till you came to the snow, between us and the North Pole, but for a few Hudson Bay Company's settlements.

The Admiral left us to join [HMS] *Capetown* for a trip up north, and we, after wandering round the islands in the Gulf of St. Lawrence, headed north across to Forteau,[38] a small fishing village on the south coast of Labrador. It was very thick weather as we closed [on] the land in the afternoon watch and we passed several icebergs. At 7 bells, when I went down to tea, you couldn't see the length of the quarterdeck. I had hardly sat down when there was a terrific crash. Thinking we had hit an iceberg, after seeing the scuttles screwed up, I went on deck and collected the Marines for our collision station's job of getting the collision net out. We got it to the focs'l and there met the First Lieutenant who said, "It's no use soldier, look," and pointed over the side where you could just see the heads of rocks in the smother [a surging of foam and water].[39]

The sea, which seemed slight when we were afloat, now made itself felt. It seemed impossible that water could lift that huge ship and dump her again and again on the rocks. My men, who[m] I had sent aft to fall in on the quarterdeck, were hanging on to anything they could, and being shaken off like rats. In the meantime we were firing minute guns, but you couldn't see the shore or whether anyone was there or not. The Captain told me, but to keep it to myself, that we were held up by two rocks each side of the engine room and had 20 fathoms under our stern. If we slid off we should go to the bottom, so he wanted to get everyone ashore. The difficulty was to get a line over. And eventually he decided to send in the lee cutter, [for] all the weather side boats had gone.

The lieutenant who went in charge had never been in charge of a boat at any time in the commission [cruise] and would have done better to leave it to the Midshipman, Hutton,[40] who was my racing helmsman and a first class boat handler. No steering oar was shipped, and the boat went straight in. Needless to say, she broached to and was swamped. Four men were drowned [but] the rest got ashore. Hutton gallantly went back and grabbed a man just as he was being swept past our bows and hung on to a lower scuttle. They were pulled aboard nearly dead with fuel oil, and the doctors had a job with them. In the meantime we were not much better off, except that there was now someone to take a line. But no one seemed to know how to get it there till I got hold of the gunner and said, "We were practicing the other day with that line throwing gun, now seems to be the time it should be useful." So he got it and we got our first line ashore. After that, it was merely a question of ferrying by Carley rafts.[41]

Working to make sure that my Marines had done their job of shutting all cabin scuttles, I went below and crossed the Aft Deck. It was pitch dark and, as the ship lifted, I heard a tearing crash just behind me and realized that the four torpedoes had got adrift and were charging from side to side. The worst of it was that I had to come back the same way. Perhaps it was as well I couldn't see!

I spent the rest of the time tending the back ropes of the rafts. The bottoms of them had gone to bits with the first trip, but the rest was all right. As more got ashore, the job of hauling them became easier, but of course eventually more difficult for us. The Captain had sent Spraggett ashore early on to find out where we were and make his way to Forteau and see what facilities they had. And at 9:30 p.m. the only people left on board were the Captain, Navigator,[42] First Lieutenant, Chief Bo's'n mate, and myself. We had the devil of a job hauling the raft back, and there was of course no one to tend the back rope to steady it as we went on shore. I had thought it out as to how to coil it to give the most steadying power without catching up, and said I'd do it and then jump. But the Navigator said he'd put the ship ashore and should be last off, and took over. As we were pulled clear, a sea broke over us and we were of course like drowned rats.

On landing, my Sergeant Major came up and reported, "Marines present, Sir," and I reported to the Captain. "What do you mean," he said, "None of them drowned?" "No," I told him, "they are there all fallen in, you can just see them against the snow." "Well," he said, "no one else knows where any of their men are, let alone all of them; Spraggett has just reported that there is a barn full of hay at Forteau, you'd better go and occupy it." So my organisation and drill

R.M.L.I. Detachment H.M.S. "Raleigh."

In saying good-bye to the Detachment, I wish to congratulate them on the fine soldierly spirit, which they shewed during and after the wreck of our ship. At all times it was simplicity itself to detail a unit for any work; guards were well carried out, smartness was maintained and a very fine example was set which was noted in more than one quarter. To the N.C.O's I wish to point out that this would have been impossible without thorough organisation, and to thank them for the loyal way in which they assisted in making that organisation perfect against many odds. Organisation makes for discipline and comradeship, and the three together make it certain that a force will not become a rabble in an emergency. In wishing good-bye to those who are leaving the Corps I trust they will remember with pride our short commission in H.M.S. "Raleigh."

C. F. JERRAM,
Major.
1st September, 1922. R.M.L.I.

Major Jerram's final communication to his Royal Marine detachment on HMS *Raleigh* after her loss, 1 September 1922. Note his emphasis on organization, discipline, and comradeship—all necessary traits associated with the profession of arms [© Trustees RMM].

had borne fruit. The men naturally turned to their own NCOs, and every NCO knew every individual man. In consequence, the Marines slept in hay that night and had something to eat, whilst the sailors wandered round in the deep snow. But first we had to get there. The three miles cross country in deep snow was rather like the retreat from Moscow!

The fishermen at Forteau had just got their winter supplies from the Grenville mission and generously brought out food. I hope someone eventually got paid for it. Spraggett and I shared a bed with a red hot stove pipe within a foot of it! This being the 19th of August, it isn't a country I should choose to live in. [The] next day was spent salv[ag]ing food and clothing. And later the *Capetown* arrived. We found that we were within half a mile of Point Amour Lighthouse, [but] they heard nothing of our guns, nor did we hear their fog signals. So much for fog.

My cabin proved water tight and I saved all my gear, including a model brig[antine] I had been building. A few days later we embarked in a Canadian Pacific Railroad liner and returned to Liverpool. [There] I bade goodbye to Spraggett and the detachment and went to Plymouth, having been notified that I had been appointed Instructor of

No. 36

Dated 19 August 1922

THIS IS TO CERTIFY that Mr. Charles F. Jerram, CMG, DSO has served as Major R.M.L.I. on board H.M.S. "RALEIGH" under my command, from the 23rd day of July 1921 to the 19th day of August 1922, during which period he has conducted himself*

To my satisfaction.

A very capable and energetic officer.

A. Bromley { Captain
              { H.M.S. "RALEIGH"

*Here the Captain is to insert in his own handwriting the conduct of the Officer.

Another "flimsy" on Major Jerram's performance of duty, dated 19 August 1922, from his tour on HMS *Raleigh*. Commanding officers could be as specific or general as they deemed appropriate [© Trustees RMM].

Small Arms [i.e., official title "Instructor of Musketry, Plymouth Division" on 22 September 1922]....

Between the Wars, 1922–40

The Instructor of Small Arms job at one of our headquarters was an interesting one, and kept me in one place for two years. So far, I had been married for nearly ten years and the longest time my wife and I had ever spent together was about two months! We had a flat in Barracks, [and I had] a horse and groom. On settling down we bought a 20 foot half-decked boat in which we cruised round the coast. During this time the Grahams from Shanghai paid a visit to England, and we asked them to stay. I renewed my riding with Darcie, giving her my horse, "Kelfoie." On return[ing] to Shanghai she was married, and to my sorrow died shortly before [World] War II. It may of course have been a blessing, for I do not imagine that life in Shanghai under the Japanese was much joy....

In addition to my job, I was responsible for Scraesdon Fort in which our men lived, doing their firing on Tregantle Ranges.[43] But Plymouth was no longer the home of the 8th Infantry Brigade, so we had it pretty much to ourselves. My assistant was also the garrison officer responsible for the ranges. [Each one of] my assistants were to become famous. Archie Craig,[44] the first, who brought Plymouth Division back into the top of the prize list at Bisley, became a General. And "Jo" Hollis, who succeeded him, became Sir Leslie Hollis, Mr. Churchill's Military Secretary in World War II.[45]

At the end of my term as Instructor of Small Arms [in March 1926], I was appointed to the Staff of the Commander-in-Chief, Plymouth,[46] to look after the Marines in various harbour ships. Here I came up against something I've never understood in the way of beastliness from the Royal Marine Office, and from especially Royal Marine Artillery officers in particular. For the Corps had now been amalgamated.[47] I don't think that they ever forgave me for my report to the Admiralty in 1922 or thereabouts.[48] Certain officers, of which I was one, had been told to put forward their ideas as to the future of the Corps, and with special reference to the employment of senior officers. The Royal Marine Artillery had been pushing for all they were worth [for] the Mobile Naval Base [Defence] Organisation.[49] I could never see it being used, and, if it was, it gave the infantry a purely static job and practically turned us into a garrison regiment, the most despised thing in the Army.

My plan was, in a nutshell, exactly the same organisation that we have today, [in] 1962-3. First and foremost, that our Chief[50] should cease to be an Adjutant General and should COMMAND the Corps, whether ashore or afloat. [Next,] many of our establishments could be abolished, as they were invented in the days of marching when we had to be in or near the great ports. And a Light Brigade should be formed ready to go anywhere at a moment's notice. My old friend, General Blumberg, was our Chief [i.e., Adjutant General, Royal Marines, between 1920 and 1924] at this time and he had me up to read my report to the Board of Admiralty.

When I had finished, the First Sea Lord [Admiral of the Fleet Earl Beatty, my former

Captain on HMS *Suffolk*] asked me where I proposed to get the men for my Brigade. And I told him from the ships, [as] all ships were over manned and hundreds of small ships didn't need any Marines at all! Also, if we concentrated on two headquarters and a depot instead of five,[51] we could economize very greatly. "Oh," said he, "but if I say we don't want them for the ships, my friend here," pointing to the Treasury Official, "will take their pay." So I said, "Well, Sir, that is your fault." "What d'you mean, my fault?" "Well, not yours personally, Sir; but it's the fault of the system. You say I want so many Marines for HMS X and so many for Y. If you added, I want so many for HM Royal Marines, your Treasury friend wouldn't have a leg to stand on."

It took a long time to come, and because it didn't come in time the Army had to form Commandos,[52] essentially a job for us, and the one I had visualized in my Light Battalions. General Blumberg sent me the following letter, which in view of subsequent events, is worth quoting: "Dear Jerram, Ormsby[53] told me about your letter, but your last word was wrong, it ought to have been 'Vinci.' The Admiral[54] and Committee were very taken with your paper and it is going to be included in the Report as an Appendix. The Striking Force is the ideal to be worked to and would give an object to which all training could be directed." Then he [wrote] of the MNBDO, and continue[d], "Probably as the RM Artillery feeling dies away the Corps will realize that its real role is the Striking Force; and possibly it will come into Naval heads too." Then he talk[ed] of manning difficulties and [the] education of high[er] authorities, and end[ed] as follows: "However, the Report is gradually taking shape and it may do some good. You can congratulate yourself on having sent in the most valuable constructive proposal yet."

General Sir Herbert Blumberg, KCB, former Adjutant General, Royal Marines and historian of his Corps in the First World War. Blumberg was a supporter of Jerram and believed he might have been a future Commandant General of the Corps. Blumberg was on the Madden Committee in 1924 to which Jerram in 1923 submitted a controversial paper on the future role and organization of the Royal Marines.

And there you have all my future troubles in a nutshell. A senior ex–RM Artillery officer told me that I had ruined all the chances of the Corps! It was nice to know that I was considered to be of so much importance.

10. Between the Wars, 1919–40

Back to Barracks duty at Plymouth Division (Stonehouse Barracks), 1925, for these machine gun instructors. Major Jerram is seated in the center, second row [© Trustees RMM].

But the proof of the pudding is in the eating. Two Mobile Naval Base Defence Organisations were in existence during World War II. Neither was ever used and kept locked up [i.e., committed] several thousand officers and men. Some of the personnel were hastily thrown into Crete as infantry, for which they had never been trained. They behaved with great individual gallantry and formed the rear guard of the retreat. Most of them remained there, [captured by the Germans].[55]

But, as I have said, my proposed organisation is now that of the Corps from the Commandant General downwards! But here is what happened, after General Blumberg retired, to any suggestions I might make. It seemed ridiculous to me that the Chief of the Royal Marines, the Adjutant General, should come all the way down to Plymouth to inspect our barracks and completely ignore the Marines in the harbour. I knew that he could not inspect them as a right, for they came directly under the Admiral and were subject to the Naval Discipline Act, whereas in barracks [ashore] we came under the Army Act. So I tested the feelings of the Admiral, Commander-in-Chief. He, Admiral Phillimore, was extremely good to me and always welcomed any suggestions, as did his successor, Admiral Bentinck.[56] And I was quickly assured that if the Adjutant General [then Lieutenant General Alexander R. H. Hutchinson, CB, CMG, DSO, who succeeded General Blumberg.] did come, he would be made very welcome and receive every facility. So I put the suggestion up to the Royal Marines Office and had a very curt reply from the Chief of Staff[57] that when they wanted any suggestions from me they would ask me. In the meantime, would I confine myself to my job! That put the lid on any further suggestions, but again it is interesting to note that the Commandant General does now visit all Marines, ashore and afloat, as a matter of right.

But the thing that really did get my goat arose out of my first annual report. I made it a very full one on every aspect of training. [I] point[ed] out that for generations "up the harbour" [i.e., service in a detachment aboard a ship which spent most or all of its time in port] was looked upon as a sort of rest cure, with long weekend leave a necessity. [However,] it could be, and my Adjutant, Sergeant Major, and I were trying to make it [into], a useful training ground, in the doing of which I had the full support of the Admiral. My officers and NCOs were fully backing me up, [but] the chief trouble was in the men who were apt to resent too much drill. This was a confidential report, only seen by myself at my end.

I [received] a reply in an open letter read by my Adjutant and clerk, to the effect that my report was likely to have an adverse effect on the discipline of the Corps. One couldn't overlook that, and I at once sent a copy of my report and the reply to the Commander-in-Chief, together with a letter in which I asked him to forward my resignation of my commission in the Corps. Pointing out that if it was the considered opinion of my superiors that I was undermining the discipline of the Corps, the sooner I got out the better. [But I also] ask[ed] which letter was mo[re] subversive of discipline: mine, [a] confidential [one], or theirs, an open letter? A week later the Admiral sent for me and showed me a letter from the Admiralty, [which] he said was the nearest approach to an apology he had ever heard of from "My Lords," and he [asked] me to withdraw my resignation. I would far sooner have had some recognition from the Marine Office, as they were the people responsible, but I couldn't ignore the Admiral's advice. He, and every naval officer I had ever served under, had always given me such good reports and been so kind and understanding, that one had to take this advice.

Six months later when my admirable Port Adjutant[58] had really got going, I asked the Commander-in-Chief [Admiral Phillimore] if he would honour us by inspecting the detachments. His only possible day was a Monday. My only possible day for practice and rehearsal [was] the previous Friday. I had one rehearsal of what I wanted to do. An inspection, a march past by detachment, form up in line, and advance in review order, with one command only. This was an invention of mine and, if properly done, ought to be spectacular: Give the order, "Advance in Review, Order and Present Arms, by the Centre, Quick March." The band then plays the first few bars of the British Grenadiers and, when it stops, you take two more paces, halt, and present arms without any further command. We ran through it once and then I said, "Well, there you are, you know what to do, and if we practiced for a month you wouldn't know any more. I'm not stopping your weekend leave, and I trust you all to turn up properly on Monday afternoon."

Well, we had our parade. I could only say it sounded all right behind me, [but] it was not until I turned about after reporting to the Admiral that I was able to see an absolutely perfect line. Then the Admiral did us a great honour. He told us that he had made a rule all his life never to say anything to men on parade, good or bad; if he had anything to say, he would embody it in a report. He was now going to break his rule for the first time, and he [then] told them that he had just witnessed the smartest turnout and drill he had ever seen! It was a great feather in our caps. Incidentally, the smartest detachment of all was one of 12 men under a Corporal in HMS *Defiance*, an old wooden hulk and the Torpedo Training School. Her Captain and Commander were enthusiastic about their Marines, and it was always a joy to go and inspect them....⁵⁹

At the end of my two years "up the harbour," I returned to Barracks at the end of the period of command of the last of my old friends, General Mullins.⁶⁰ [He] gave me the best of [Confidential] Reports as, without boasting, I had [ever] received. Ever since my promotion to Major I had always been recommended for accelerated promotion, but again a change was coming and with it an Ex–RM Artillery Commandant.⁶¹ Having been given the job of Assistant to the Chief Instructor, I thought I was getting on pretty well and doing my job by helping officers readying for their promotion and Staff College entrance exams. So when I was shown, by an indignant Brigade Major, my annual report from my new Commanding Officer, I was somewhat more than surprised!

In it he stated that I was averse to taking the decisions of my superiors in tactical matters. This I still look upon as one of the best opinions I could receive as, in effect, it said I was not a "yes man." But that it was not meant as a compliment was shown by the paragraph, "whether recommended for promotion," which read "Yes, in due course."⁶² That ended for me any possibility of promotion to top rank; and it was and is the more puzzling because although I might easily differ on tactical matters from my superiors, I had actually never even had the opportunity to do so! I believe that the cause of this report was general dislike by my immediate superior, who had never been in action ashore or afloat, and the fact that young officers came to me for instruction. It seemed to me then, as it does now, that experience in war and at the Staff College was meant to be passed on. But there were at that time a few

General Sir Alexander R. H. Hutchinson, KCB, CMG, DSO, successor to General Blumberg as Adjutant General of the Corps. Jerram had extensive ground combat service with Hutchinson in Gallipoli and France during the First World War [© Trustees RMM].

officers who, from no fault of their own, had not had these advantages and were deeply jealous of those who had. And as bad luck befell [me], I bumped into two of them.

It was 1928 and I had reached the period for the maximum pension for a Major. I had decided in 1919 to stay as long as I was wanted, and it had now been made pretty clear that I was not. I didn't take the usual step of questioning my Commandant as to his report. I am quite incapable of ever trying to excuse myself, but I waited till they posted me to the Mediterranean as Second-in-Command of the Marines, and then sent in my [retirement] papers. To go away for another two years, with my children all going to schools without the smallest hope of any future, would not [have been] fair to my wife and family.

I received a letter from my old friend, General Blumberg, in which he deplored my decision and said that he had always looked upon me as a future head of the Corps! I didn't tell him my reasons or that any hopes of becoming a General [Officer] had gone. But I should have made a very bad Adjutant General, for I should never have [accepted] the absurdities of the appointment. Either "command the Corps or get out" had been my attitude to this anomaly since I had begun to think about it many years before. It's now come, owing to really strong men in the position after [World] War II. And they have done it by tact and a thorough knowledge of what was wanted. And I'm pretty sure that I could not have made the grade. Actually, command of small units has always been my strong point, and where I have had any success in higher jobs it has always been because I've had a first class staff. So we went off to live at Falmouth in our house next door to Penwarren Church, which we called "Talland Vean," or Little Talland, after my old home.

Pensioned Off

We went to live at Falmouth and found no difficulty in finding something to do. We had a big, old fashioned, terrace garden that had been very neglected, and I had my boat. Also we bought a bit of land near Helford[63] and built a cottage for the children's holidays. It wasn't long before the Falmouth Corporation built a huge and intensely ugly mass of workmen's houses round us, and imported all the hard cases from the Clyde [in Scotland], whom no one wanted up there. So we built on to our cottage and went to live there.

I soon found that day sailing and fishing suited me a lot more than cruising, and [I] bought one of the old Polperro boats, most of which were laid up. The war [had] killed all Cornish fishing by the fact that the government gave them engines on a sort of hire purchase. The men were never able to pay off the debt, and I believe the government eventually dropped the demand for it. But the motor killed the pilchard fishing, which had always been pretty precarious anyway. But in the sailing days, even if you came home empty handed, it hadn't cost you anything. But for the motor you had to pay for oil and petrol. Of the 50 odd boats at Polperro in 1914, by 1930 there were only five left and every Cornish port was in the same state. My boat cost me 80 pounds and I got Jack Bassett, an old Looe sailmaker who had made my sails for years, to make a complete suit of sails for her. Pat Phibbs,[64] a brother officer, also bought one, and we had an annual 18 mile race.

One rather amusing thing happened to my wife. She was travelling by bus from Falmouth to Truro when a ticket inspector stepped on. Hearing someone call her Mrs. Jerram, he asked if she was any relation to a Marine Officer of that name. [After] being told that I was her husband, [he] said that he had always wanted to meet me again for my kindness in pulling him up when he was a boy bugler in the *Astraea*. It cured him, and he had now retired and got a responsible job.

Here is the story. We were in camp at Wei-hai-Wei when he came in drunk. Being only 15, the legal method of dealing with him was to send him on board, when the Captain would have ordered him a dozen strokes and his conduct sheet would be smeared by a red "D" for drunk. I told him this, but I would give him the choice of [that or] taking a dozen from the Sergeant Major's cane and we would forget about the incident. He chose the latter, and there was no reporter from the "Daily Howl," nor did he write to his Member of Parliament. If he had, there would have been pages of "sadistic brutal assault on a poor little drummer boy." He would have become a "hero" and probably ended on the hangman's rope, and I should have lost my commission! As it was, a young rapscallion, perfectly sound at heart, became a decent, sober, and hard working citizen. But I do not recommend this life saving practice in these days!

Come to think of it, I did one thing [in 1936] during my retirement which nobody will ever be able to do again, that is going to sea in a sailing ship. I did two short trips in the Finnish mast barque *Pommern*: From Falmouth to London, and Falmouth to Ipswich, working with the crew, and [I] must be the only retired Lieutenant Colonel, I should think, to get an ordinary Seaman's Discharge from a sailing ship! The war [then] prevented a passage to Australia and back.

CHAPTER 11

Epilogue—World War II and Beyond, 1940–69

Back to the Regiment: World War II

So life went on in peace till 1939 when war broke out again. I had been promoted to Lieutenant Colonel on the retired list,[1] and sent my name in for a job. I realized of course that I was too old in that rank to get an active service [assignment]. I was a contemporary of Dill, Gort, and Neame[2] [and] they were Generals! And there were plenty more about, so there wasn't the smallest possible opportunity there. But the War Office might give me a staff or training job if the Marine Office didn't want me.

Curiously enough, on the day the Marine Office offered me the post of Military Instructor, the War Office also asked me if I was available. But I thought I could do the Marine's job, which meant bringing up all our regular Second Lieutenants, plus any other military course they gave me, in spite of my ten years retirement. So I joined at [the Depot,] Deal,[3] and there learned how I had got the job. My old Subaltern, Morford, was now a Brigadier and wanted the present Military Instructor to command a battalion. The Royal Marine Office said they had no one to replace him, and Morford said, "Why not call up Jerram?" So my old Subaltern had given me as good a report as I had given him many years before!

Whatever may have been the state of mind as regards myself in the "high[er] ups" in 1928, there was no doubt at all as to 1939. No one could possibly have been kinder. Right through the war with various Adjutants General, Commandants, and Commanding Officers, I only had one very slight difference of opinion. It could have been a difficult position for there was only one person, the then Adjutant General,[4] who was senior to me in service, and all my commanding officers were years junior. But the Adjutant General had been the Military Instructor himself, and had also been a victim of the absurd jealousies after [World] War I. However, he had stayed on, and was now at the top of the tree. Even my own staff, who could very well have resented an old "Dugout" put in over them, made me more than welcome. They consisted, at that time, of two Captains and a subaltern, instructors, who knew their job[s] from "A to Z"; three WRNS[5] clerks just relieving the last Sergeant clerk; and a Corporal storeman and general help.

I was told I could have three weeks with my predecessor, but I've never been able to take over someone else's ideas. [Hence], after a couple of days to find my feet, I said I was ready to take over. Naturally, I altered things gradually. I have always had a great respect for our training at [the Royal Naval College], Greenwich nearly 40 years before; and, from my own experience, I knew that after the Military Course very few of us were ever taught anything. So in the short time at our disposal, 15 weeks instead of 52, I set out to teach as much as possible of the theory and practice of war, and not merely turn out platoon commanders.[6] That is what they did in 1914–18, with disastrous results....

As soon as we got settled down I took a small house and sent for the family. At the moment they were disposed as follows: My wife and daughter, Morwenna, at Helford, my wife's health needing someone to help her[7]; Jennifer in the Land Army; Jon (John) had enlisted in the Gunners [Royal Artillery,] and was later given a commission and joined the Intelligence Corps; [and] Anthony at Blundell's

General Sir Alan George B. Bourne, KCB, DSO, MVO, Adjutant General, Royal Marines, during most of the Second World War. Bourne placed Jerram in charge of young officer instruction. Among officers on active service, only Bourne was senior to Jerram in date of commission in the Corps [© Trustees RMM].

[School, Tiverton, Devon]. There was nothing much to get excited about till the great German attack commenced.

Everyone seemed to think in terms of the Maginot Line, that great concrete breastwork across the borders of France. But I had been with the Division which broke through the Hindenburg Line, and made a point of pointing out that no line was impregnable, and further that the Maginot Line ended just where it was most badly needed.[8] But in our office, we had the establishment of the 10th Armoured Division.[9] If we had ten of these held in reserve, obviously we were in a pretty good position. [But] how were we to know that we had not even one armoured Regiment? But Gort knew, and how he could have accepted command of our Expeditionary Force knowing it, I cannot imagine.[10] But Gort I could never see as a great General.[11] He was cram full of courage, and in his later appointment as Governor of Malta[12] he found his proper sphere. As the Germans pushed their necks into the great bulge, just as they did in 1918, I preached, "let them come on, somewhere—we don't kn ow where, there is a great reserve waiting

Retired and recalled to active service in World War II, Major C. F. Jerram, CMG, DSO, instructs a class of young Royal Marine 2nd Lieutenants in the use of the prism compass, circa 1943. Note the maps in the hands of the young officers. Even in the 21st century, the Corps emphasizes map reading and terrain analysis for all Marines [© Trustees RMM].

to swoop on their flank and crush them." How should we know that there wasn't any reserve, and that one of the first principles of war had been forgotten or neglected? And of course there was no General Foch.[13] But the war staff and Gort must have known.[14]

So I had to preach the "principles of war"[15] to Second Lieutenants, who must have been fully aware that the high[er] ups had forgotten all about them! However, when my unfortunate students had to guard beaches all night and listen to five lectures in the day, I got in touch with the Royal Marine Office. [I then] told them that either my class must go out and fight, or else learn how to; but they couldn't combine the two.

Wisely they decided that they must be taught, and we moved to Lympstone,[16] near Exeter, where we had built a new training centre for war time recruits. I do not know anyone I admire so much as the various members of my staff, from top to bottom. Naturally they were constantly changing,[17] and so were the various organisations of the Army and Marines, [and] their equipment and tactics. My instructors not only had to be word perfect in everything they taught, but had to be constantly forgetting one thing

11. Epilogue—World War II and Beyond, 1940–69

Royal Marines Military School, Thurlstone, Devon, 2nd Military Class, 1942. Jerram is shown here with staff and students (young lieutenants). He is seated at center. His daughter, Rosemary Morwenna, seated in the first row, far left, is one of three WRENS [© Trustees RMM].

and being word perfect in something different. It meant hours of night work "sweating up" new books and pamphlets, and they never failed. One who came to us [was] "Woolly" Gardiner, the one survivor of his [gun] turret aboard ship, when blown up, only just out of the hospital. He always had dreadful headaches and had the worst of the lectures, the "Q" side, to keep going. He stuck it out and became an expert in organisation, etc. Later he got a decoration [an OBE] after leaving us, and is now a Church of England priest.[18]

When a new staff officer was needed, I made a point of insisting on one who had been in action [combat]. Obviously, to the Second Lieutenant, an instructor who had smelt powder was more to be respected than one who had sat in a soft job. I only had one failure, an officer who had been wished [forced] on me. He was exactly in looks and manner the dead spit of my GSO-2 in the 46th Division: A useless swank, who fortunately only stayed a month and then somehow wangled himself into a junior chair at the Royal Marine Office, where he sat for the rest of the war!

Another move to Thurlstone,[19] where the School for Temporary Officers had been established, gave us a few more headaches and trouble about the WRNS staff. Their Commanding Officers could never appreciate the fact that our clerks had to be something special. They had to be word and letter perfect in a language and abbreviations they had never heard of; and the best shorthand-typist in the world was perfectly useless until taught. So when they put in a Leading WREN over my two clerks, she had to be taught by her inferiors in rank. Eventually I managed to wangle my daughter, Morwenna, into the job, who, although she was not a typist, knew the work from "A to Z" by working it up as a junior. There was great uproar from the head of the WRNS [Mrs. Vera Mathews], who said that it was forbidden for a daughter to serve under her father. I said I had a war to get on with and couldn't be bound by any regulation that interfered with it, and incidentally pointed out that her own daughter had got a very cushy job as her staff officer, which put an end to the argument.[20]

Other than the job itself, I managed two things of lasting benefit to the Corps. At each of our Headquarters there was a military library, and for some years that at Deal had been in charge of the Military Instructor. It was in an awful mess and the [card] catalogue was hopeless. I roped in Morwenna to sort it out; she completely reorganized the whole library and kept it together with all the new books we amassed during the war. It is now the official Corps military library under the management of the Officer Commanding, The Officers School, as they call my job now,[21] and with a civilian trained librarian! If we had not taken charge of it, it would have been completely destroyed by a bomb which hit its old quarters.

The other thing was the horses. Robert Sturges[22] was the [Colonel] Second Commandant at Deal and had continued the riding courses for Second Lieutenants after the Royal Artillery gave up their horses. He had collected most of the regimental chargers. When he left to command the [Royal Marine] Division,[23] I took over the horses and riding lessons.[24] I looked upon such riding as we could manage as a useful guide to an officer's value. And of all soldiers, it is most useful for a Marine to be able to ride because he may be landed in all sorts of out of the way places where riding may be the only means of transport. If we could hold on to these or any animals through the war, there was a possibility that we might continue to keep them. But if they went, there was no possibility at all of reviving

Major General Sir Campbell Hardy, KCB, CBE, DSO, Commandant General, Royal Marines, 1955–59. At Normandy, he commanded 46 Commando, Royal Marines—the unit in which Jerram's son, Anthony, served and was killed in action. Hardy escorted Jerram over the ground near Caen where his son died [© Trustees RMM].

them. So each move we made, we took the horses and the library with us. It became increasingly difficult to obtain remounts, and we had to fall back on the larger pack animals. But as long as I could keep 12 animals of sorts with four legs, it didn't matter what they looked like.

The result is that the Corps still, in 1963, has twelve horses, and a Regimental Horse Master responsible for teaching young officers.[25] [We also] probably [have] the best military library in the country outside the Staff College, [Camberley].[26] [These] two items may perhaps make up for many sins of omission or commission during my service. As for the amazingly kind letters I received on my final retirement from the [Corps, those from the] [Commandant] General,[27] the Marine Office staff, and others, more than compensate for the rather nasty taste left by 1928.

The End

After the war we returned to live at Helford, and I became a farm labourer, tractor driver, and hedge builder on my daughter's little farm. Broken down turf hedges are now all stone faced, which also perhaps may be put on the credit side. On the amusement side, I had my boat with her old Polperro rig, sailing and fishing usually alone, as my wife, after several operations, became more of an invalid. [I also had] a truly wonderful horse. A grey I had wouldn't face stone faced hedges, and one day I saw a list of 10 horses being sold in Essex, of all places, one of which, three years old, sounded possible.

The people were very honest; [said s]he'd never seen a bank, but was the right shape and [lived] in western Ireland, so I said send her down. I met her at Helston station with a lorry. She hadn't turned a hair and walked straight off the train into the lorry. Next day I took her out. She'd never seen a hill, let alone a bank. But she had perfect manoeuver, a perfect mouth, and was obviously out to do her best. Joe Collins, a farmer about 10 miles away, [was] a great man with horses and I

Church War Memorial, Manaccan, Cornwall, to the dead of the First and Second World Wars. Included is the son of Lieutenant Colonel Jerram, Lieutenant Anthony Patrick Jerram, RM (seventh name from the top), killed in action at Normandy, 11 June 1944 [editor's collection].

took the mare over for a fortnight's training. A week later he rang and said he could teach her nothing more, she was a born banker and only wanted experience; and she was not yet three years old. So I gave her a very easy season with hounds, after which she gained the [reputation] of being the best horse in the Cury Hunt.[28] When in trouble with a new horse, the master would call, "Come on, Colonel, give us a lead." She never refused a thing, and my end to hunting was *not* her fault.

At the age of 75, Jennifer on her cob [a thickset horse with short legs] and I on "Foxtrot" went to the opening meet and, leading the way over a bank, failed to see a stout wire hidden in the brambles. I dislocated my neck, and "Foxtrot" and I had to part. She was bought by a member for a girl who had lost her nerve. "Foxtrot" recovered it for her and became famous with the Four Borrow [Hunt] as she had been with the Cury. She's still going in 1963 as a brood mare.

Helford, at the time we went there was completely unspoiled. With one exception, every cottage was occupied by village people, one of whom was an old schooner captain. There was only one modern house on the north bank and none on the south. The quay, originally a sail loft, was now a coal store, as was that at Porth Navas,[29] and schooners discharged coal at the latter and shipped granite. Timber ships discharged huge pit props for the mines in the river, and these were formed into rafts and towed to Gweek.[30] Sailing barges landed manure for the farms in Penarvon[31] and loaded wheat.

About the same time that we arrived, the last owner of the Manor House overlooking Porth Navas died and left the estate to the farmer. He quickly sold all the riverside to various people, who built on it, and then sold out the rest, including the house,

Modern view of the retirement area where Lieutenant Colonel Jerram lived, Helford, Cornwall. The water and boat reflect two of the area's attractions for him and his family [editor's collection].

to a syndicate. They split it up in small plots and the manor house became a hotel. An occasional yacht used to come in, and that was all.

Since the 1939–45 war the whole place has been "developed." There are now in 1963 only two cottages occupied by locals, and one of these has just died. Every inch available for building has been built on by people who have no interest whatever in the place or the people. They stay a year or two, and then sell to someone else. The winter is the best time, when all the houses and cottages are empty. As the old people die, their cottages are sold. Who can blame [the heirs], when they can get 5,000 pounds for a cottage, on which the summer visitor is prepared to spend a further 5,000 pounds on improvements! And the old owners can, for a few hundred [pounds], build and live in a wooden shack till they too become to[o] valuable to keep.[32]

My connection with the Regiment [Royal Marines] still continues. We formed a branch of the Royal Marines Association in Cornwall and I had the honour of being the first President, and also have the honour to be a life member of the Plymouth and Lympstone Officers' Messes. In 1964, at the age of 82, I was able to take a small part in the 300th Centenary Celebrations of the Regiment. A big parade was held at Buckingham Palace and Her Majesty honoured us by taking the salute. A small party from the Royal Marine Associations paraded on the flank, and as President I paraded with about half a dozen of my Cornish Marines. Her Majesty inspect[ed] us and talk[ed] to several of the men, including myself.[33] And if I was offered the chance of beginning my life again, I would not want it any different.

Appendix I

Lieutenant Colonel Jerram: An Historian's Assessment of an Officer and His Career[1]

Donald F. Bittner

During World War II, Lieutenant Colonel Charles Frederic Jerram, CMG, DSO, Royal Marines, was recalled to active service. Commissioned in 1901, the Corps used him in a most appropriate way: It placed him in charge of various aspects of young officer training. In 1991, members of a "batch" of officers who were commissioned on the same date in 1941 and trained together held a 50th reunion anniversary dinner at the Royal Marines Museum, formerly the officers' mess of the Royal Marine Barracks, Eastney. These officers had been trained by Jerram; five decades later and now in their 70's, they still spoke of him with awe and respect. This was very evident in the tone of their voices, with all references to him reduced to one word—"Jerram!"

Such responses provide a clue to both his personality and aurora as a career Marine. As a leader, Jerram stressed a sense of responsibility and professionalism in his subordinates. Young officers who initially served under him would not have looked upon such an initial relationship as an enjoyable one. In retrospect, however, they would comprehend that such a demanding commander with high standards made them better professionals and leaders. If these officers responded as he demanded, they acquired his respect and became colleagues in the "brotherhood of arms." Jerram then followed their subsequent careers with great pride and interest.

Jerram's high professional and ethical standards clearly conveyed that an officer had an intertwined primary duty: his men and profession, regardless of rank, posting, or social status. He believed that officers should be more than just courageous commanders leading from the front; they also had to *know their profession*. The lives of men in combat were not to be wasted through the incompetence, ignorance, or stupidity of their commanders or staff officers. Training and discipline were the key elements. Even in retirement this emphasis continued; three years before his death, in an article for the Corps' journal, *The Globe and Laurel*, he linked leadership, clarity of communication, and a commander's responsibility. Jerram did so by responding to a piece which had used the phrase "if possible" in orders. He wrote such verbiage had been the cause of "great disasters," including the operation at Suvla Bay at Gallipoli. Such words were "taboo," for "no-one can achieve the impossible." Conceding that the phrase in the subject article might have been the slip of the pen, Jerram nonetheless was unforgiving; he concluded, "if it had slipped in to a paper by a 1940–45 2/Lt he'd had a 0 for the whole show."[2]

As early as July 1917 while serving on the staff of XIII Corps in France, Jerram emphasized these key elements inherent in the profession of arms. In his "Notes on Musketry for Company and Platoon Commanders," he wrote: "ESSENTIALS—INTEREST—DISCIPLINE. The last two of course being essentials ... the beginning and end of everything is discipline.... Always remember a reason for everything, even discipline itself.... This is a matter of habit, and habit is instilled through discipline."[3]

In 1922 he returned to this theme after the loss of the cruiser HMS *Raleigh*. In a final communication to the Marine detachment which he commanded and had performed admirably in that crisis, Jerram wrote: "Organization makes for discipline and comradeship, and the three together make it certain that a force will not become a rabble in an emergency."[4] Of course, such self-discipline when expanded to unit cohesion had to be instilled by its leaders—professionals who knew what was needed, demanded it, and ensured such was achieved.

Jerram was truly a "Soldier Gone to Sea." He strongly believed in the linkage between his Corps and the Royal Navy. Although often committed ashore, the Royal Marines were still a maritime service. However, he also served in an outstanding manner when seconded to the Army during World War I and after it the War Office later offered him a staff position in Ireland following his graduation from the Army Staff College, Camberley. Yet Jerram refused the posting in Dublin and remained with his Corps, always loyal to his "sea" regiment.[5] During World War II, when he could have again served with the Army, he opted for his Corps. Ultimately, he had few difficulties either at sea with the Royal Navy or ashore with the Royal Marines or British Army for one basic reason: Jerram mastered the professional skills required of both services.

Jerram was also a staunch traditionalist, both within the messes of the Royal Marines and with regard to naval customs aboard ship. However, he did not believe in useless traditions, to include the outmoded traditional roles and functions of the Royal Marines in the 20th century. This surfaced in 1923, when the Admiralty formed the Madden Committee to study and ascertain the Corps role—and reaffirmed its traditional missions.[6] As part of its proceedings, Jerram both appeared before the committee and submitted a paper with his views on the Corps—and its poor state and role in Britain's defence establishment as of that year.

In Jerram's view, during the period between 1815 and 1939, the true nature of the Royal Marines, a force equally at home ashore and at sea operating skillfully in both environments, had become obscure. In reality, they had merged with sailors and became interchangeable with them; hence, when serving at sea Marines were members of gun crews, butchers, storekeepers, officers' servants, and wardroom attendants. Meanwhile, their military training and capabilities diminished. Thus, during the era of the *Pax Britannia*, Marines remained aboard ship but their distinct roles at sea and on land had become unclear. Simultaneously, naval officers and sailors in the 19th century formed major parts of landing parties ashore, further obfuscating the role of the Corps who also did this. In an unpublished essay, Jerram addressed the situation in the early 20th century by recounting an old adage reference who was the most useless officer aboard ship: the chaplain or the senior Marine? However, in answering this old query Jerram a more devastating: "The old story of two seamen arguing as to who had least to do had an element of truth in it. It went in favor of the Marine officer; for the Chaplain had nothing to do, whilst the Marine officer also had nothing to do and had a Subaltern to help him do it."[7]

Ultimately, why were Marines aboard ship? Jerram wrote that if only to maintain order and discipline, then they were really useless—and provided no capable force for needed ground operations. They did naval duties and thus their military skills eroded; even if training could be done, the Marines had no role or mission for which to train. The officers, moreover, did not really perform naval duties and had no command over their own detachments. Using intemperate language, he said the Royal Marine officer became an "idle figurehead and more often than not a drunkard and waster." Jerram's conclusion: "They have at present no official status; no end towards which they may train has ever been pointed out to them and it would appear that they [sic], for whom alone they exist, look upon them in the light of a cheap, well disciplined, and small force which helps them to keep up the Navy's prestige at small expense." Retaining the Corps in its current structure and role was a waste, uneconomical, and counter to training and ascertaining a proper role for it.

In his view, Britain was a maritime empire—and in this lay the Corps' real function. Jerram was clear he did not envision it as a branch of the Army; rather, its linkage with the Royal Navy was the key to its existence and value—but it was still a military organization with soldier skills. Hence, the Royal Marines should have a capability for operating in small wars from a naval base, operating against an enemy with no naval force, or conducting landing operations and seizing ports through which Army follow-on forces would move. As he wrote, "The landing must be a naval operation and it should have its own troops to do it with."

Avoiding a roles and mission fight with the Army, he continued, "It must be clearly understood that the Marine force would not be mobile on land and would not join the Army, but having done its work would be reorganized and probably be re-embarked to be used again when and where required." As he also penned, "For it must be kept in mind that the Marines are to be a naval force whose base is the sea and mobility dependent on the sea." This meant an ability to embark, move, land, threaten, and withdraw, with bases at home and abroad. The current problem existed because ships' detachments had onboard priorities and individual, let alone collective, efficiency, was nil; alas, no permanently organized ground force existed to embark and perform such needed duties as Britain would require in modern warfare.

Jerram, of course, had a solution: Reform via elimination of the current organizational structure, retained linkages with the Royal Navy, and the formation of a permanent ground force with a specific role and capability. As he stressed, "Except as a Naval Force the Royal Marines can have no justification for their continued existence." Thus,

Jerram advocated the creation of a permanently organized tactical ground force capable of immediate operations or, in case of major war, expandable. In this, he was influenced by some pre–World War I ideas and reflection on operations in that conflict (especially Gallipoli and Zeebrugge). Further inspiration came from a visit to Quantico, Virginia, the home of the United States Marine Corps' East Coast Expeditionary Force. As he wrote, "These are admittedly a magnificently organized and efficient body, and the sight of their Expeditionary Force on parade would make the average Royal Marine envious." Still, he acknowledged that the commitments of Britain's American cousins partly differed from those of Royal Marines, "but there seems no reason why we should be too proud to pick the best of their brains and leave what we do not want."[8]

Jerram was specific in his recommendations. Elimination of the three administrative barracks,[9] and forming one by the sea with an appropriate training area; creation of a permanent ground force of four infantry battalions, with artillery, signal, engineer, and pioneer units; in the Royal Marine office, operations and training sections in addition to personnel and logistics; the commander of the ground force to have a seat on the Admiralty board; Royal Marine officers at the staff colleges to study "Marine," i.e., amphibious, operations; senior officers to be employed within and outside the Corps; and retained linkages with the Royal Navy, as each officer would spend a tour in each rank at sea, as ships' detachments would remain. However, there would be a cost: Although his proposal would see two general officers serving, the number of colonels commandant would be reduced from five to two, colonel/lieutenant colonel positions reduced by one from 16 to 15, and a reduction in the number of majors. Still, those remaining would be fully employed in meaningful ways. As he concluded:

> It is the proud boast of England that her frontiers are the coasts of her enemies. It is our duty, the Royal Navy and Royal Marines, to carry the wars into and across those frontiers. Are we doing everything possible to this effect? So long as the Navy look upon their ships as their only assets it is obvious that we are not. It is the Navy's duty and proud privilege to be able to carry a threat against any part of a frontier. There is no threat in the presence of a few ships as was seen at Gallipoli; but when those ships carry a Striking Force the threat becomes a very real one and one which the enemy cannot ignore. The threat must be a combination of ships and Striking Force, [and] when the Navy and the country recognize this, the problem of the Royal Marines is solved.[10]

Jerram's proposal, conceptual or its details, was not accepted. The Madden Committee embraced the Corps' traditional functions; however, in the Interwar years one major change did occur. The Royal Marines moved to a base defense mission via development of the Mobile Naval Base Defence Organization—a completely different tasking and capability. However, the Second World War produced the force which Jerram advocated, the commandos—and it has been retained since then.[11]

Ultimately, Jerram believed this ruined his career because some senior Royal Marine officers disagreed with his views.[12] Actually, a combination of his proposals coupled with blunt language might have done this. Even when trying to make a positive point, Jerram used less than tactful verbiage. In stressing the overall abilities of senior Marine officers, their versatility could be most value "for more appointments and would be sought for as Military and Colonial Governors. Even present Senior Officers of the

Corps might be employed; they are not nearly as useless as seems to be generally supposed." He then continued, "The majority are men of wide experience are certainly capable of taking such appointments as Governor of smaller Colonies, etc., especially where the object is mainly naval. Sir M. Hankey and Sir. L. Wilson were very ordinary Marine officers, neither any better nor any worse than the hundreds of others." (NOTE: The references are to Colonel Maurice Hankey, RMA, 1877–1963, whose career was in government, especially as Cabinet Secretary; and to Colonel Leslie Orme Wilson, RMLI, 1876–1955, with civilian government service in Britain, India, and Australia.) Still, he had no regrets for candidness on the Corps' role and the resultant needed organization.

Jerram's Early Life

Charles Frederic Jerram was born into a middle-class family on 13 November 1882, at Godalming, Surrey. The Jerram extended family "served the crown" in both the armed forces and civil government. Only his entry into the Royal Marines could be considered unusual, as opposed to the Royal Navy, the Army, or a civil service career. The son of a schoolmaster, he spent most of his early years in Cornwall. Throughout his life, he considered the West Country home and lived in Cornwall or Devon. The family, although not wealthy, had close ties to the gentry. Jerram also associated with many famous personages of his time, met through either his family or career, e.g., Sir Winston Churchill, Admiral of the Fleet Earl Beatty, Field Marshal Viscount Gort, Field Marshal Sir John Dill, and General Baron Freyberg.

Still, money was not plentiful, and Jerram described his parents in the following manner: "Goodness knows mine were poor enough and Victorian enough." Despite this, the family provided him with a proper education which prepared Jerram for and enabled him to pass the examinations which led to his entry into and be commissioned as a Lieutenant of Royal Marines. Jerram preserved one example, with comments, from his early years in school. The master at Hillside in Godalming penned a report to Charles Frederic and Ralph Jerram's father dated 12 August 1895 on the academic progress of his two sons. As one of the Master's wrote, he was in a meeting of the master's as a "minority of one" in his belief that "Freddy was the ablest of your two boys." He indeed commented that Ralph "has worked very steadily & extra hours at Arithmetic have enabled him to forge ahead of his brother in that subject." However, there was more to their academic studies and implied sibling competition, for he continued, "But judged by Euclid & Latin Prose (the best prejudice of all tests) Freddy's superiority is unquestionable." As Lieutenant Colonel Jerram wrote on this letter in 1963, "It didn't prevent him from beating me every day! But I've always said that I worked hard and wasn't lazy, whereas they all said Ralph was clever but lazy. Anyway I got nearly full marks for Latin in my Entrance exam for the Army [i.e., the Marines]."[13]

Jerram's childhood experiences and holidays in France and Britain (aptly recounted in his memoir) were in stark contrast with parental and societal attitudes of today.[14] Ultimately, they provided the foundation of confidence, initiative, and resourcefulness so necessary in a career military officer. None-the-less, a shortage of funds was a continual problem in his adult life, and, in common with so many officers of the Royal Marines, Jerram lacked "independent means." As he later commented, "To the newly commissioned officer not the least of his embarrassements [sic] was one of finances."[15] Monetary concerns later had direct and indirect influences on his career decisions.

Royal Marines Career: Pre–World War I

After achieving appropriate marks on the Civil Service Examinations for the Royal Marines, the Royal Military Academy, Woolwich, and the Royal Military College, Sandhurst, Charles Frederic Jerram opted for the Royal Marines. He was commissioned in the Royal Marine Light Infantry on 1 September 1901, and studied at the Royal Naval College, Greenwich, from 30 September 1901 to 30 June 1902. Jerram considered this initial education and training to be the most significant of his military career:

> It will seem strange in these days that we were taught to be theoretical Napoleons before we had seen a single soldier. But I still think that it was a first class training for officers.... As to the results, I can only say that from the day I left Greenwich till today I have never received a single day's instruction in the theory of war, yet managed to get through the 1914–1918 War on what I learnt there, I hope without disgrace, and later to teach what I learnt during the 1940–1945 War, at any rate without being chucked out; and my thanks go out now to those admirable instructors.[16]

On 1 July 1902, he was promoted to Lieutenant and appointed to Plymouth Division[17] in Devon. He remained with this barracks throughout his Royal Marine career except for a brief period in 1914 when at Chatham Division, Kent. He remained at Plymouth until December 1903. His confidential report marks were brief for this essentially training period, with one reporting senior commenting, "A very good all round young officer of more than ordinary ability/zealous, capable and takes a keen interest in his work."[18]

In 1903 Jerram went to sea. However, the Royal Navy at the turn of the century was not that of 1914: "My introduction to the sea, although to a nearly new cruiser, was far more Nelsonian than modern. The Navy in general was a survivor of sail." He also described the service as "between the end of the mast and yard Ironclads and the 'Dreadnought' era of World War I," and then wrote of his first ship, HMS *Hogue* of the Channel Fleet: "Every officer and man was sail trained and the life was much nearer that of Nelson's time than the present."[19] After *Hogue* came HMS *Suffolk* in both the Channel and Mediterranean Fleets from December 1903 to April 1906. Jerram thought enough of his service in *Hogue* and *Suffolk* that in his final entry in *Who's Who* he cited these ships and continued, "...in Mediterranean under late Earl Beatty."[20] One reporting senior from the *Suffolk* presciently noted in his comments: "Has a good way with men." He also developed a special qualification: Wireless telegraphy. Jerram was candid as to why: Both he and the torpedo officer did so, for the former, "as the only person with any knowledge of electricity, [for] myself as being supposed to have nothing else to do."[21]

While with the *Suffolk*, in 1904 Jerram commanded a guard of honor when Kaiser Wilhelm II visited Gibraltar. About this event, he later wrote that the Emperor, "passed us looking very glum indeed at being shown round a few old railway sleepers and other junk, instead of what he wanted to see, the secret galleries in The Rock. He wasn't allowed to see them and was, I believe, very cross." His concluding comment about William II, Germany's naval ambitions, the British fleet, and the *Pax Britannia* was succinct: "Without the German Emperor's ambition to defeat that fleet, we should, I suppose, have continued to keep the peace."[22]

In January 1907 the China station beckoned, for he departed Britain for three years of duty in the "Senior Officer's Ship Yangtse River." His primary duty was overseeing the many Royal Marine detachments in the area, ranging in size from 10 to 25 men—none of which was commanded by an officer. He rotated among HMS *Astraea*, HMS *Flora*, and HMS *Tamar*. Based in Shanghai, he spent nine months cruising on the Yangtse River on a 2nd Class Cruiser and three months sailing in Far Eastern waters. During these years, Jerram traveled extensively in China, Korea, and Japan; he also performed intelligence work, submitting reports on German and Chinese military positions. The Admiralty duly acknowledged his endeavors, for on 19 May 1909 Jerram, "Received expression of their Lordship's appreciation of assistance rendered to Senior Naval Intell. Officer [Major H. C. Evans, RMLI] in preparing report on several Chinese forts."[23]

In September 1910 Jerram's China service ended when he boarded HMS *Charybdis* for passage home, arriving in Britain the following month. A senior's assessment of 1 August 1910 succinctly addressed the developing soldier of the sea: "An excellent officer full of zeal. Fond of exercise & out of door life afloat or on shore. V.G. at boat work and understands it." A notation also succinctly stated his intelligence duties on the Yangtse River.

In 1912, a significant event occurred in his life: On 15 August he married Sibyl Victoria Greys O'Neill, the daughter of Dr. J. H. O'Neill of Auckland, New Zealand. Eventually, the Jerrams had two sons (one of whom was killed in World War II), and two daughters. Before and after his marriage, between October 1910 and February 1913, Jerram served with Plymouth Division. He also passed his final examinations for promotion to Captain and was duly promoted on 1 September 1912. In February 1912, he also passed the Musketry Qualification Course at Hythe, and a report of that year stressed, "An excellent instructor." In the 18 months before the outbreak of World War I, Jerram rotated between division duty and short tours at sea in six ships, including a ten-week cruise in HMS *Swiftsure* in temporary command of the Marine detachment for the East Indies Station. Hence, as war neared in the summer of 1914, he was technically ashore.

The First World War: Service with the Fleet and the Royal Marines

Lieutenant Colonel Jerram served with the Royal Marines in World War I from August 1914 to January 1917. This "Corps" duty had three distinct phases: (1) at sea as senior Marine aboard HMS *Euryalus* from 1 August to 7 November 1914; (2) service with the Royal Marine Brigade and then on the staff of the Royal Naval Division (both later renumbered 190 Brigade of 63rd Royal Naval Division), at Gallipoli; and, (3) on the Western Front with it until when seconded to the British Army on 24 January 1917.

Jerram's war mobilization assignment was aboard HMS *Euryalus* and he reported aboard her on 1 August 1914. He served on this ship until 7 November 1914, primarily in North Sea operations close to the German coast. She was the fourth vessel of a squadron labeled the "live bait squadron" by the Royal Marine officers who served in it, for all were of the same obsolete class. The others were HMS *Aboukir*, HMS *Cressy*, and HMS *Hogue*—and the German submarine U-9 sunk the latter three on 22 September 1914. The *Euryalus* was not with them, but what occurred did not surprise Jerram, and why was reflected in a later description of *Euryalus* preparing for battle in the "old fashioned way": A detachment composed of retirees, the crew going to battle stations due to a false enemy sighting during a gale, running out the deck guns and then being unable to bring them in again, and the vessel nearly foundering with the loss of the fore t'gallant mast with her wireless aerial. She thus returned to port for coal and refit, and while preparing for return to station received the signal "*Cressy, Aboukir,* and *Hogue* are sinking."[24]

Then, in December 1914, a major change occurred: Jerram was promoted temporary Major and appointed Staff Captain of the Royal Marine Brigade of the Royal Naval Division. On 18 June 1915, he assumed the duties as its Brigade Major, and on 27 December of that year became the Deputy Assistant Adjutant and Quartermaster General (DAA&QMG) of the Royal Naval Division. As an overwhelmed staff officer, he later recalled his frustration about what happened after the withdrawal of the division from Gallipoli to the islands of Lemnos, Tenedos, and Imbros:

> Subsequently the two R. Marine Bns went to Salonika & took part in operations there—I was left at Lemnos. The whole Divl Staff left and Gen Trotman [the brigade commander] was recalled to take command, with me as his sole staff officer. I had, subsequently, the whole of the staff work for relieving the various island garrisons ... and embarking the Division for France.[25]

In these staff appointments, Jerram served at Gallipoli, going ashore with a naval and Marine force before and after the major amphibious landing, and then on the Western Front.[26] He observed, and later recorded, courage, sacrifice, and skill when he saw it. Accordingly, he wrote the following about troops at ANZAC Cove:

> June 1st, [1915]. I am glad to see that there are good accounts of the Australians and New Zealanders. They were simply *magnificent*, and I do not believe that any other troops in the world, even the very best, could have done what they did. Its bad enough *walking* up these hills, but to charge against an hell of fire and keep it up, as some of them had for 5 miles, is perfectly marvelous. I can tell you we are proud of having them over here.[27]

Although a staff officer, he saw extensive front line service and was under fire on many occasions. These included the landings at Kum Kale (4 March) and at Anzac Cove (3 May), and engagements at Cape Helles (4 June and 13 July), and, in France at Calonne, Redan, Hamel, and Ancre, all during the Somme offensive. For his services in these years, Jerram was twice Mentioned in Despatches, in 1915 by the General Commanding the Mediterranean Expeditionary Force (General Sir Ian Hamilton), and then in 1916 by the Commander of the British Expeditionary Force in France (General Sir Douglas Haig). On 1 January 1917, Jerram was awarded the Distinguished Service Order (DSO), "for meritorious service in the field."[28] On his service, Brigadier Trotman wrote Mrs. Jerram, "C.F.J. is getting o[n] splendidly, I think, he well deserves it. DSO and GSO2 are small rewards for what he has done continuously under the most difficult circumstances."[29]

During these years, Jerram received two confidential reports. Both were quite candid, thus providing a balanced view of him. Major General Sir Archibald Paris, the Royal Naval Division commander, on 6 April 1916 wrote: "His tact in dealing with officers leaves something to be desired. This will probably improve with increased experience. Very energetic, self-reliant, & reliable & is excellent leader of men. Recommended for employment on General Staff duties or as a Brigade Major. I recommend him for promotion."[30] On 23 March 1917, Brigadier C. N. Trotman, commander of 190 Infantry Brigade, evaluated his key staff officer with this honest assessment:

> Has been on the staff since the commencement of my command. As Staff Captain, RM Bde. He was energetic and successful as Brigade Major. He quickly grasped, though not accustomed to it, the "Office" portion of his duties, whilst in "operations" he was very good indeed. This officer is particularly good in handling men; as a staff officer, he can be recommended for G[eneral] S[taff] rather than administrative duties.[31]

For Jerram, Gallipoli remained a seminal event in his personal and professional life. In the 1960s, he and Major General James L. Moulton, CB, DSO, OBE, corresponded extensively about this campaign. In Jerram's view, Robert Rhodes James' *Gallipoli* (New York, 1965) was the best book on this subject. As he wrote,

> Yes, it is very good indeed. In a few chapters it manages to combine every aspect, from the high political and strategic, through the tactical to the efforts of the individual soldier. And this without missing anything or making it look like a précis although it is very readable.... I think his main object was to put in right proportion certain injustices & lack of justice, & gives a truer perspective of various commanders & troops as seen through the eyes of the fighting men.[32]

Then came a major change of duty with different responsibilities.

The Western Front: Seconded to the Army

The recommendations of Major General Paris and Brigadier Trotman were soon implemented: Jerram was "seconded" to the British Army from 21 January 1917 to 31 March 1919. He served in three diverse and increasingly responsible assignments at division, corps, and division levels, respectively. For these two years, only two excerpts from his confidential reports are extant. The first, dated 20 June 1920, simply noted, "A very good leader. Has sound common sense, good judgment, and self-reliant." The second, dated 31 December 1920 and written by Major General Sir Gerald Boyd, former General Officer Commanding, 46th Division, was more specific: "One of the best and most zealous officers I have ever come across. A good leader, can get the best out of those under his command. Has tact and is self-reliant. Has great experience in staff work."³³

Jerram had three assignments with the Army. On 24 January 1917, he joined the 31st Division as its GSO-2. Five months later, on 2 July, he was assigned to XIII Corps and on 2 August assumed duties as its GSO-2. He stayed with it until 23 July 1918. Jerram then became GSO-1, or Chief of Staff, of the 46th (North Midland) Division. He retained this post until after the November 1918 armistice, when he departed to attend the Army Staff College at Camberley.

During this period, Jerram continued to experience the effects of conventional symmetrical warfare in the industrial age. His professional assessments and personal efforts at coping with the Western Front are apparent. On 14 April 1918, during the German spring offensive, he noted the pleasure of the unfolding new season and then continued:

> We came up the road down which all the refugees were streaming from the battle. Old men and women, and little children and babies, with all they possessed in their hands. Home gone for good—some of them lucky enough to have saved a horse and wagon to carry their gear, some had perambulators, some bicycles, and most nothing at all. But they are brave; they are really the most wonderful people there are. They must have walked miles and miles babies and all—yet they were quite cheery, tired of course, but "c'est la Guerre," quite philosophical about it all.

On 8 October he then wrote about the inhabitants of villages near the Bois de Riqueval: "Many civilians were found in these villages, in BOMAIN over 3000. Their welcome to our troops was most enthusiastic. They do not appear to have been badly treated generally, but all testify to the generally brutal treatment of British prisoners." A month later, on 6 November, he recorded his thoughts as combat operations:

> We have now got into enclosed country with many farms, good villages, orchards and hedges. Enclosed grazing country. The land is untroubled by war except for the fact that the enemy has driven off all the cattle and horses & blown up all the bridge and cross roads. During the day we entered CARTIGNLES, having overcome considerable rear guard opposition. Our troops are proving themselves more than equal to the enemy in open warfare. The villages and farms are full of civilians, who enthusiastically cheered our men as they passed through, pressing on them coffee, apples, and cyder ... it was a wonderful sight.... On the way back I told the villagers that the French were on our right & they all streamed off across the fields to find them.

Jerram tried to cope with such conditions in various ways. For him, horses were both a working necessity (transportation), as well as a means of personal relaxation. Thus, on 30 May 1918 he reacted to having to lose of one of his beloved mounts:

> We are not in the latest push. The saddest thing that happened lately, as far as I am concerned, is that poor little Bobbie and I have had to part. All our horses have been cut down and we have little control over those that are left, and Bobbie was one of those which were packed off. The Corps Commander, a great lover of horses, was awfully good about it and has got him a good master behind somewhere. So I hope he will be all right. He told him that I had been with him since the beginning of the war, both here and in Gallipoli, and he assured me he would be well looked after. Rixon, my groom, is very sad and Sugarfoot neighs for him all day. It's a rotten war.³⁴

While with the Army, on 1 September 1917 Jerram was promoted to substantive Major. Then, when appointed as the GSO-1 of the 46th Division, he was advanced to Temporary Lieutenant Colonel, to hold this rank whilst so employed. He also saw considerable combat, with 12 actions listed in his Statement of War Services: 3 March 1917 (Ressignac Wood, Part of German Advance), 3 May 1917 (Oppy Wood), 28–29 March 1918 (Arras), 28 August 1918 (Rue de Bois-General Advance), 24 September 1918 (Pontruet), 29 September 1918 (Bellenglise), 3 October 1918 (Ramicourt), 8 October 1918 (Fresnoy), 12 October 1918 (Riqueval Wood), 17 October 1918 (Regnicourt), 20 October 1918 (Catillon), and "Advance in November [1918]." For this, Jerram was Mentioned in Despatches three times by The Field Marshal Commander-in-Chief, British Forces in France, "for gallant service and devotion to duty."[35]

Other awards were conferred on Jerram for his World War I service: In June 1919 he was appointed Companion of the Order of St. Michael and St. George, "for valuable services as General Staff Officer, 1st Grade, 46th Division," and in July France awarded him the Croix de Guerre.[36] In a 1968 letter, Jerram reflected on the latter award. He wrote that it was a Croix de Guerre with Silver Star, one of ten awarded for the crossing of the St. Quentin Canal, and received by him for his service as Chief of Staff of the 46th Division. He noted this was for service at a lower level of command than a General Headquarters (the latter the cross with "Palm Leaf"), but Jerram continued it was "…to me at least, of far greater value than the Palm Leaf out of the lucky bag." Presented to him by the French General Mathieu personally on the field of battle, this led to further meaningful comments: "I think that this must have been the first time for many generations that the recipients actually received their awards on the Field of Battle for which they were awarded."[37] In addition to these awards (and the previously DSO), Jerram also received three World War I medals: the 1914–15 Star, the British War Medal, and the Victory Medal.

The Corps' unofficial history of the war noted that Jerram had served as Chief of Staff of the 46th Division and that it had achieved one of the main operational victories of the war. As General Sir H. E. Blumberg succinctly wrote: "In the latter capacity made the arrangements for crossing the Canal de St. Quentin at Bellenglise, the men swimming across the Canal with the aid of the lifebelts of the Cross Channel Steamers."[38] Jerram recorded his assessment of this operation on 1 October 1918:

> We have just achieved the impossible, and without any doubt in anybodies [sic] mind have done the finest thing done in this war. Zeebrugge and the landings in Gallipoli, though more expensive in men, were nothing compared to the job we were given to do, and the storming of the S. Quentin Canal and Bellenglise will go down in history. If you can imagine to yourself a fairly strong line of trenches well wired; then a canal with 10 feet of water, a bank 15 to 20 feet high on each side and sheer down to the water inside, 30 to 40 feet in some places. The bank wired on both sides; on the far side the main Hindenburg line, the strongest line that has ever been built; Beleglise [sic], a wonderful work of tunnel and concrete—then over line upon line of the strongest trenches ever made, and through two more villages, if you can see this, you can imagine a part of what we were called upon to face, and our fellows never made the slightest hesitation, and at 2 p.m. when the aeroplanes went along over the line some five miles from the start, there they were in the final objective. In all the world as if they had found it chalked out for them…. By Jove they are perfectly magnificent fellows and all done in a fog in which you couldn't see your hand.[39]

In a communication published to the 46th Division, the commander of the 4th Army, Lord Rawlinson, said: "The forcing of the main Hindenburg line on the canal, and the capture of Bellenglise rank as one of the finest, and most dashing exploits of the war." General Headquarters Report of 1100, 29 September 1918, "STORMING THE CANAL***Troops with Lifebelts," reported the operation in the following manner:

> The 46th North Midland Division, provided with lifebelts, mats, portable bridging material and rafts, and under cover of concentrated artillery and machine gun fire, stormed the main HINDENBURG Defences, which here run along the Eastern bank of the Canal. Notwithstanding the depth of the water, the breadth of the CANAL and the strength of the enemy defences, which include the Village of BELLENGLISE and numerous tunnels and concrete works, the men of this division succeeded in capturing the whole of the German position opposed to them. They then pressed forward with great bravery and determination up the slope of the hills beyond the CANAL making many prisoners in the course of their advance. BELLENGLISE, LEHAUCOURT and MAGNY-LA-FOSSE are now in our possession.[40]

On Armistice Day, 11 November 1918, Jerram recorded no private thoughts in his personal diary although he bracketed that day with comments about the weather, terrain, accommodations, a parade, and riding on horseback through the 46th Division's operational area. His official war diary entry was brief: "Nov 11th at 11AM hostilities ceased along the whole front, the German delegates having agreed to the terms of an armistice." The previous day, however, he recorded his last comments on operations before the end of the fighting, noting a still dangerous foe:

> Owing to the constant destruction of railways in back areas by enemy delay[ing] actions and his thorough system of destroying all bridges & crossroads on his retreat, the feeding of advance troops is becoming more & more difficult. We are at present 87 miles from our own railhead with all roads destroyed in numerous places. In spite of this our rations & ammunition have come up daily. The enemy's defensive policy is of a nature which shews clearly that he has no intention of attempting an organised resistance—still he is attempting to hold us off by means of machine gun posts placed in carefully selected positions & fight sufficiently long to enable his main body to retire in order. He is carrying out a [???] & well ordered rear guard action; his artillery fire being negligible except for occasional bursts chiefly directed against main roads.[41]

Personal comments came after the armistice. On 12 November, he reflected upon the end of combat operations:

> So here's the end of it after 4 years. At 11:00 a.m. yesterday, we were ordered to cease fire, & at that time had the honour of being the most easterly troops in the British Army. It seems curious being, at any rate, temporarily at peace after 4 or more years of it. It's only an Armistice, of course, but with the break up in Germany it can hardly break out again. I expect some of us will have to go & keep order in Germany though. I don't think we are going, for which I'm sorry in many ways, still no doubt all is for the best.

Jerram was right: Neither he nor the 46th Division would go to Germany: "November 13, 1918. Sains-du-Nord. It has been a glorious day today, & I had a good ride this morning, & saw some of our people on the March. I've heard that we are not going into Germany, rather sad after 4 years of it—still it can't be helped, & we can't all go."[42] He also missed the visit of King George V to his division, for another change in his life occurred: Orders to the Army Staff College at Camberley.

Post Great War Years: Return to Traditional Duty

Jerram was a student in the first postwar Army Staff College class at Camberley. Major General Sir Gerald F. Boyd, the commander of the 46th Division, strongly supported his attending this course. Boyd's final Army evaluation of his Chief of Staff, in addition to the copy that went to the Royal Marine Office, reflected the high regard in which he held his Marine subordinate:

> Lieut-Col. Jerram is a very able Staff Officer and I have strongly recommended him for the Staff College. He has been highly tried as GSO (I) and has carried out his work entirely to my satisfaction. He is very quick, active and energetic: Thoroughly fit and possessed of considerable character, confidence and initiative. He should I consider make a name for himself either on the Staff or in command of troops.[43]

Thus, between 1 April and 22 December 1919, Jerram studied at Camberley. He was also awarded a King George V Scholarship Prize for the year (one of two), from a fund specially established after the George V's coronation, to help defray expenses of Royal Marine officers at staff college associated with one or two years of such higher education.[44] His class at the Army Staff College was composed of combat experienced and decorated officers, many of whom already had had extensive staff experience.[45] His experience there involved such diversions as fox hunting and riding, where his lack of an independent income, in contrast to many Army officers, manifested itself: he rode College horses while some of his fellow officers who had their own personal mounts. In the student publication for that year, the *Owl Pie*, Jerram was one of the few officers listed by name in a humorous "next assignment" section. His peers projected the following: "Major Jerram—To be Riding Master, R[oyal] M[ilitary] C[ollege], [Sandhurst]." Mrs. Jerram also was mentioned in a student publication produced by the wives, *An Owl's Wife*. The distaff publication's anonymous writer recorded: "Mrs. Jerram—A breath from the ocean. Keeps a perpetual smile on her face and talks like a Rolls Royce—never breaks down. Is the wife of The Mad Marine & is to be pitied therefore."[46]

More significant were the classroom conflicts between the combat experienced students and the staff college's theoretical school solutions, with the faculty demanding adherence to the latter. After graduation, Jerram confronted a difficult professional career choice. The War Office offered him the post of GSO-2 of an Irish command in Dublin. However, he refused this and the official reply of the Corps simply stated, "Regretted cannot be spared."

Rejecting a transfer to the Army, Jerram returned to Plymouth Division, serving there from January 1920 to 22 July 1921. A significant event occurred in April 1921: With the threat of a general strike looming, 13 Royal Marine Battalion was raised and Jerram was appointed its adjutant. Although the strike did not occur and the battalion was disbanded, he recorded his thoughts on this experience:

No uniforms, no stores, no accommodations, no messing arrangements.... Today we took them for a 6 mile route march. I had the adjutant's horse, which behaved pretty well on the whole. The men were splendid, and I'll bet no one would have guessed we were only a 1 day old battalion.... We have been for several route marches, and not a man has fallen out, and today we put up a show for Zeebrugge Day. We had the colours out and a march past. The men were splendid, played up like anything.[47]

On the battalion's dissolution, its commander [Lieutenant Colonel Percy Molloy] wrote a candid assessment of Jerram's accomplishments in a most laudatory personal letter to him:

Your wide experience made you infinitely better-fitted to command the battalion than I and on this account I'm afraid I put a great deal more work on your shoulders than I should have done.... Personally, I feel that I have learnt more in the last 2 months than I could have picked up in a year's study of handbooks, & I am safe in saying that Coy. & Platoon Commanders feel the same, so that your labours have been far from wasted.[48]

This was Jerram's second such venture into possible "aid to the civil power." In October 1919, he and Lieutenant Colonel G. C. Williams, CMG, DSO, RE, were sent to Dorset from the Staff College to prepare for potential unrest, and both received noteworthy comments from that county:

I specially desire to report the exceedingly high opinion that I formed of the abilities and qualifications of both staff officers with whom I had the good fortune to be associated. I venture to suggest that they should be called upon to make a formal report on the subject of the formation of a Citizen guard for the County of Dorset.[49]

Jerram's official evaluation for this period dated 22 July 1921 succinctly noted the traits previously recorded: "Good leader. Controls men well. Good instructor. Has had considerable experience on the Staff of the Army and has done well. Has plenty of self-reliance and common sense."

Next came a traditional posting: On 23 July 1921, Jerram assumed command of the Marine detachment on board the new cruiser HMS *Raleigh*, assigned to the North America and West Indies station. Although such an assignment did not have the challenge of his war postings or what the Irish Command would have had, Jerram performed in his usual efficient and demanding manner. Frustration arose, however, as he had to adjust to a post-war Royal Navy vastly different from that of his prewar experiences. He late reflected on this: "I didn't go to sea again till 1920 [sic], about which least said soonest mended. It was something absolutely and entirely different with apparently no connection whatever with anything that had preceeded [sic] it. I suppose the change was more noticable [sic] if you'd been away from it, as I had, for 6 years."[50]

Still, it had its positive aspects, for *Raleigh* made many port calls on the west and east coasts of the United States and Canada. However, his time on *Raleigh* ended abruptly on 8 August 1922 when the new cruiser went on the rocks in the St. Lawrence River near Labrador and was lost! Jerram ensured that none of his Marines died and helped in the abandon ship action for the crew. He described the cruise, with special attention to the loss of the ship, in written reports to journal of the Corps, *The Globe and Laurel*.[51]

Jerram then returned to Plymouth Division, serving there from 20 August 1922 to

28 February 1926. During most of this time, from 17 September 1922 to 16 September 1925, he functioned as Instructor of Musketry with primary responsibility for small arms training. For a short period in 1925 he was also the division paymaster.[52] Amongst the five confidential reports he received while at Plymouth, that of 31 December 1925, added the perspective of a strong personality to previously noted strengths: "An exceptionally good type of Officer. Takes the greatest interest in his men and is a very good Instructor. Is the greatest assistance in not hesitating to give an opinion on any service matter which may call for discussion."[53]

Jerram's career was now nearing its end, although he would not retire until 1929. From 1 March 1926 to 2 January 1928, he served as the Senior Officer, Royal Marines, in HMS *Impregnable*, a boys' training establishment of four ships at Devonport, and from 3 January to 23 April 1928, he was Senior [Marine] Officer on the Staff of the Commander-in-Chief, Plymouth. From these assignments came the last informal indication of his performance of duty. The Chief of Staff to the Commander-in-Chief, Plymouth, wrote on 25 April 1928 that from March 1926 to April 1928 Jerram had, "conducted himself entirely to my satisfaction. A most zealous & able staff officer who has done much to promote efficiency in the small & scattered Marine Detachments in the Plymouth Command." After this, he returned to Plymouth Division, serving there until 17 January 1929. Finally, his last day of active service arrived: On 18 January 1929, by his own request, Jerram retired from the Corps he so dearly loved.

Retirement and Return to Active Service: World War II

In retirement, Jerram and his family remained in the West Country. In the 1930s, he worked on his home, participated in change ringing, rode his horse, and indulged in his love of sailing. Meanwhile, links to the Corps continued. On 30 March 1931, Jerram was promoted to Lieutenant Colonel on the retired list, and in 1938 he returned to active duty from 28 September to 6 October in HMS *Drake*, a major training establishment in the Devonport area, as the Senior Royal Marine again on the staff of the Commander-in-Chief, Plymouth.

With the start of World War II, Jerram again had the option of serving with the Army but instead remained with his Corps. Initially serving in the grade of Major, he was promoted to Acting Lieutenant Colonel on 4 September 1944. His orders were issued on 1 January 1940, with the clear intention of utilizing his best skills: "You will be attached to the Military Instructor [initially at the Depot, Deal], with a view to eventually being employed as such."[54] He served there from 14 January to 3 June 1940, with an official staff appointment as Military Instructor at the Royal Marine Military School dating from 10 September 1940. In reality, he trained young officers.[55] But the war was costly for him in a personal way; his son, Patrick Anthony Jerram, had entered the Royal Marines and was killed in Normandy in June 1944.[56] Jerram remained on active service until after V-E Day, finally reverting to the retired list on 1 July 1945. For his service in World War II, he received the France and Germany Star, the War Medal, and the Defence Medal.

In March 1945, Jerram reverted to the retired after his service as "Military Instructor to Probationary 2nd Lieutenants."[57] Upon leaving active duty, the General Officer Commanding, Royal Marines, General Sir Thomas L. Hunton wrote to him. The head of his Corps expressed his appreciation for Jerram's support and work. Hunton stressed, "the great importance of the post, and the great responsibility carried by the officer holding it. In the Military Class one lays the foundation on which each individual can build ... officers carry with them into the service much of the system they serve under in the Military Class." Hunton's assistant and successor, Dallas Brooks, also wrote to him and likewise addressed the significance of his recent service:

> The value of your work in the last few years is impossible to assess. But, in my opinion, no-one could have brought along our probationary officers as efficiently, and firmly and objectively as you have done, and that in spite of the many difficulties of organization, of location, and of the material which you have had to handle.
>
> It was very interesting for me to see the highstandard on which you so rightly insist; and to know that "nothing but the best" is still the Military Instructor's slogan. We will do our best to keep it so.[58]

Jerram also received a letter from the "G" (Training) Branch of the Corps Headquarters as he left active service for the last time. From five officers junior to him in rank and grade but with responsibilities for training, their lead-in words conceptually addressed his role: "to thank you for the very valuable work you have carried out in the education [and training] of the young regular officers of the Corps." Then it transitioned into a theme of Jerram's life throughout his service, easily recognized by all who had served with or under him in any capacity: "We feel that it will be very difficult to find a successor for you, who will be able to maintain the same high standard as you did." The officers then extended their best wishes to him and his family—concluding that once retired they would have to come to see him across the River Tamar, "as we know that once you have returned to Cornwall you don't intend to come to 'foreign' again!"[59] Significantly, all were of a younger generation than Jerram and were serving in an acting rank one step higher than that of their permanent grade.

After the war, Jerram remained in the West Country. From then until his death, his Corps activities were with the Royal Marines Association[60]; he also wrote pieces about the Corps, some of which appeared in *The Globe and Laurel*. He continued to sail and ride until his age precluded such strenuous activities. His final home was at Pengwedhen, Helford, Helston, near the River Hal, in Cornwall. Lieutenant Colonel Jerram died on 12 January 1969.[61]

Upon Jerram's death, commentary in *The Globe and Laurel* addressed his last major contribution to his Corps:

> C. F. Jerram made a remarkable and important contribution to the Corps ... to take charge of the military instruction of young officers. This was the final course for subalterns before they went off to join their operational units. Jerram's impact was extraordinary.... He was in his every fibre a soldier and had the rare knack of being able to communicate the clear essence and reality of his art. This compassionate, shrewd, and highly intelligent man ... was not content to impart the mere mechanics of warfare. He explained the very nature of battle, its disparate spirit in attack and defence, its unpredictability and its heartbreak. The young men

who heeded his words and then went out to fight on land drew immeasurable strength from his wise counsel.[62]

Jerram himself would probably have been most proud of remarks made not by his fellow officers, but by one of his Marines a "Soldier of the Sea" from the ranks. As E. R. Roullier wrote:

> Major Jerram was looked up to and admired by every NCO and RM. He was, in that hackneyed phrase, an officer and a gentleman. He was as much at home giving lectures about the Dardanelles and actions in France as he was giving sailing instructions to matelots.... His 'next of kin' should be very proud of the fact that he was admired and respected by all who had the honour to serve with him, of the Lower Deck as well as the Wardroom.[63]

Appendix II

Career Chronology

Dates: From/To	Assignment	Comments
1 Sept–29 Sept 1901	On Leave	Commissioned 2nd Lieutenant, RMLI, 1 September 1901
30 Sept 1901–30 June 1902	Royal Naval College, Greenwich	Student—Initial training
1 July 1902–9 Dec 1903	Plymouth Division	Promoted Lieutenant, 1 July 1902; further training and initial duties
10 Dec 1903–20 May 1904	HMS *Hogue* (Channel Fleet)	Initial sea duty
21 May 1904–9 April 1906	HMS *Suffolk* (Channel and Mediterranean Fleets)	For part of this period, the future Earl Beatty commanded the *Suffolk*; qualified in wireless telegraphy
10 April–13 June 1906	Plymouth Division	
14 June–17 June 1906	HMS *Nile* (Channel Fleet)	For naval maneuvers
18 June 1906–9 Jan 1907	Plymouth Division	
10 Jan–16 March 1907	HMS *Spartiate*	Enroute for China Station, "For senior officer's ship, Yangtze River," HMS *Tamar*.
17 March–18 Oct 1907	HMS *Astraea* (China Station)	
19 Oct 1907–3 Jan 1908	HMS *Flora* (China Station)	
4 Jan–5 March 1908	HMS *Astraea* (China Station)	
6 March–5 June 1908	HMS *Flora* (China Station)	
6 June–19 July 1908	HMS *Astraea* (China Station)	
20 July–16 Nov 1908	HMS *Flora* (China Station)	
17 Nov–17 Dec 1908	HMS *Tamar* (China Station)	
18 Dec 1908–27 Jan 1910	HMS *Astraea* (China Station)	Received commendation from the Admiralty for intelligence work in the Far East, 19 May 1909

Appendix II: Career Chronology

Dates: From/To	Assignment	Comments
28 Jan–31 July 1910	HMS *Flora* (China Station)	
1 Aug–8 Sept 1910	HMS *Astraea* (China Station)	
9 Sept–18 Oct 1910	HMS *Charybdis*	Passage home from the China Station.
19 Oct 1910–28 Feb 1913	Plymouth Division	Promoted Captain, 1 September 1912; passed Musketry Qualification Course, Hythe, February 1912.
1 March–5 March 1913	HMS *Suffolk* (Home Fleet)	
6 March–25 March 1913	Plymouth Division	
26 March–24 April 1913	HMS *Swiftsure*	In charge of Royal Marine Detachment for the East Indies
25 April–30 May 1913	HMS *Highflyer*	
1 June–30 June 1913	Plymouth Division	
1 July–28 Dec 1913	HMS *Exmouth* (Devonport)	
29 Dec 1913–23 Feb 1914	Plymouth Division	
24 Feb–21 May 1914	HMS *Eclipse*	Conveying reliefs
22 May–12 July 1914	Plymouth Division	
13 July–31 July 1914	HMS *Caesar*	Naval Maneuvers
1 Aug–7 Nov 1914	HMS *Euryalus*	Flagship of squadron operating in the English Channel; sister ships (*Hogue, Cressy,* and *Aboukir*) in the squadron sunk by the German submarine U-9, 22 September 1922
8 Nov–15 Dec 1914	Plymouth Division	
16 Dec 1914–23 Jan 1917	Royal Marine Brigade	Served at Gallipoli and on the Western Front. Promoted Temporary Major, 16 December 1914; appointed DAA&QMG, Royal Naval Division, 27 December 1915; awarded DSO "for distinguished service in the field," 1 January 1917
24 Jan–1 July 1917	31st Division (Western Front)	Seconded to the Army; Staff appointment: GSO^2
2 July 1917–22 July 1918	XIII Corps (Western Front)	Seconded to the Army; Assumed staff appointment as GSO^2 (Training) on 2 August 1917; promoted substantive Major, 1 September 1917

Appendix II: Career Chronology

Dates: From/To	Assignment	Comments
23 July 1918–31 March 1919	46th (North Midland) Division (Western Front)	Seconded to the Army; Staff appointment: GSO^1 (Chief of Staff)
1 April–31 Dec 1919	Staff College, Camberley	Passed (Army) Staff College; Appointed Companion of St. Michael and St. George (CMG), 10 June 1919; awarded the Croix de Guerre, 18 July 1919; temporary duty in Dorset during period of potential unrest
1 Jan 1920–22 July 1921	Plymouth Division	Adjutant, 13 Royal Marine Battalion, April 1921, during threat of general strike
23 July 1921–19 Aug 1922	HMS *Raleigh* (North America and West Indies Station)	Vessel sunk in the St. Lawrence River, August 1922
20 Aug 1922–28 Feb 1926	Plymouth Division	Primary duty: Instructor of Musketry; attended Senior Officers' Course in Land Artillery
1 March 1926–23 Apr 1928	HMS *Impregnable* (Training Establishment, Plymouth)	Senior Officer, Royal Marines, Staff of the Commander-in-Chief, Plymouth
24 Apr 1928–17 Jan 1929	Plymouth Division	Attended Senior Officers' Course in Land Artillery
18 January 1929	Retired List	Retired at own request in the grade of Major.
30 November 1931	Retired List	Promoted Lieutenant Colonel, Retired List
28 Sept–29 Sept 1938	Plymouth Division	Recalled for service
30 Sept–5 Oct 1938	HMS *Drake* (Training Establishment, Plymouth)	Senior Officer, Royal Marines, Staff of the Commander-in-Chief, Plymouth
6 October 1938	Plymouth Division	Reverted to Retired List
19 Jan–3 June 1940	Royal Marines Depot, Deal	Recalled to active service in the grade of Major
4 June 1940–30 June 1945	Royal Marines Recruiting District, Exeter (Royal Marines Military School)	Military Instructor (for young officer training); promoted Acting Lieutenant Colonel, 10 June 1944
1 July 1945	Retired List	Reverted to Retired List

Born–Married–Died

Born	13 November 1882	Godalming, Surrey

Married	15 August 1912	To Sibyl Victoria O'Neill (died 1953)
Died	12 January 1969	Pengwedhen, Helford, Helston, Cornwall

Editor's Note: This career summary is based primarily on the official record of service of Lieutenant Colonel Charles Frederic Jerram, ADM 196/63, pp. 155 and 146. How Lieutenant Colonel summarized his "Service Career" in his memoir follows as Appendix III. Appendices IV and V are two other appendices relating to his family's war services and are as he essentially wrote them.—D.F.B.

Appendix III

Service Career of Lieutenant Colonel Charles Frederic Jerram, DSO, CMG, RM, as Drafted by Him

1901: Commissioned as 2nd Lieutenant, Royal Marines, Light Infantry

1902: Promoted to Lieutenant. Royal Marines Barracks, Plymouth.

1903: HMS *Hogue*.

1904: HMS *Suffolk*. Mediterranean.

1906: Royal Marines, Plymouth.

1907: HMS *Spartiate, Clio, Astraea, Flora, Charybdis*. China. Thanks of Admiralty for Reconnaissance work.

1911: Royal Marines, Plymouth. School of Musketry, Hythe.

1913: HMS *Suffolk, Swiftsure, Highflyer, Exmouth*. Promoted [to Captain].

1914: HMS *Eclipse, Caesar, Euryalus*. North Sea, Landing Royal Marines Brigade, Battle of Heligoland. Western Patrol.

1915: Staff Captain, Royal Marines Brigade. Brigade Major.
  Promoted Major. Actions: Kum Kaleh, Anzac, Helles during whole campaign. Mentioned in Despatches.

1915: France. Brigade Major, 190 Infantry Brigade. Battle of Ancre. Granted DSO. Mentioned in Despatches.
  GSO-2, 31st Division. Mentioned in Despatches.
  GSO-2, XIII Corps. Mentioned in Despatches.
  GSO-1, 46th Division. Battle of Bellenglise.

1918: Granted CMG. Mentioned in Despatches.

1919: Staff College, Camberley.

1920: Royal Marines, Plymouth.

1921: HMS *Raleigh*.

1922: Instructor of Small Arms, Plymouth.

1925: Senior Officer, Royal Marines. Staff of Commander-in-Chief, Plymouth
1928: Retired.
1939: Military Instructor, Royal Marines.
1945: Retired, Lieutenant Colonel.
Companion of the Order of Saints Michael and George. [CMG]
Distinguished Service Order [DSO]
Croix de Guerre, France
Mentioned in Despatches: Five (5) times.

Appendix IV

War and Other Services of My Family

Catherine Florence [also Posy and Kitty] Jerram (sister), VAD nurse in Egypt and at Rockhampton Hospital in [World] War I.

Agnes Winifred [also Winnie Jerram (sister)], married in India. Her son Dennis entered the Navy and was lost in a submarine in [World] War II after gaining the Distinguished Service Cross [DSC] and OBE.

Helen Muriel [Jerram] (sister), VAD nurse in Egypt and France in [World] War I. Ran an orphanage in Serbia between the wars. Serbian decorations.

Martin Ralph Knight Jerram (brother). Indian Forest Service. Joined a Gurkha Regiment in [World] War I and served in France and Mesopotamia. Appointed Adjutant. [Received the] Military Cross [MC] and wounded. In [World] War II he was told he was too old to rejoin, so he put his age back 10 years and enlisted. Subsequently given a commission. Seconded to the Navy for small boat work, landing and bringing off agents to and from France.

Rowland Christopher [Jerram] (brother). Served as a junior officer on Admiral Beatty's staff in the Battle Cruiser Squadron. Distinguished Service Order. [DSO] In [World] War II, Chief Operations Officer at the Admiralty and Chief of Staff Mediterranean. Knight of the British Empire. [KBE]

Cecil Bertrand [Jerram] (brother). In [World] War I was serving in Middle East in Levant Consular Service, saved and embarked many people from Odessa during early [part of the] Bolshevik Revolution. Imprisoned by Russians. Subsequently [held] several diplomatic appointments, ending as Ambassador in Chile. Knight of St. Michael and St. George. [KCMG]

Family Decorations. KCMG: one. KBE: one. CMG: two.

DSO: two. Military Cross: one. Foreign: Two, or more?

My Mother, in [World] War I ran a canteen for munitions workers. My father gave many lectures to schools and services.

Appendix V

[World] War [II] Services of My Wife's and My Own Family

Frederic O'Neill [Jon] Jerram (son). Was teaching in Austria when war broke out. Came home and enlisted in Royal Artillery. Commissioned and seconded to Intelligence Corps. Invasion of Normandy. Mentioned in Despatches. Promoted to Major.

Rosemary Morwenna [Jerram] (daughter). WRNS for duty with Royal Marines. Promoted to Leading Wren.

Lowena Jennifer [Jerram] (daughter). Joined Land Army and served all through the war.

Anthony Patrick Jerram (son). Joined Royal Marines as a Second Lieutenant. 46 Royal Marines Commando. Normandy assault. Killed in action leading his troop into the final objective at the flank guard action up the River Rue towards Caen.*

*—General [Robert] Sturges [Commander, Commando Group] got me a temporary job to carry despatches to France; and I went all over this action with the Commanding Officer, Colonel [Campbell] Hardy, and spent a few days in the line with them.

Editor's Note: Lieutenant Colonel Campbell R. Hardy (1906–1984), at the time the Commanding Officer, 46 Commando. Later General Sir Campbell R. Hardy, KCB, CBE, DSO, commissioned (RM) in 1924, Commandant General, Royal Marines, 1955 to 1959, retired 1959.—D.F.B.

Appendix VI

Abbreviations

ADC—Aid-de-camp
ADM—Admiralty
AEF—American Expeditionary Force
BEF—British Expeditionary Force
Bt—Baronet (Can also be abbreviated as Bart.)
CB—Companion of the Bath
CBE—Commander Order of the British Empire
CIE—Companion of the Order of the Indian Empire (???)
CMG—Companion of St. Michael and St. George
COMUKAMPHIBFOR—Commander United Kingdom Amphibious Force
CVO—Commander of the Royal Victorian Order
DBE—Dame Commander of the Order of the British Empire
DCM—Distinguished Conduct Medal
DL—Deputy Lieutenant
DSC—Distinguished Service Cross
DSM—Distinguished Service Medal
DSO—Distinguished Service Order
FRGS—Fellow of the Royal Geographical Society
GBE—Knight Grand Cross Order of the British Empire
GCB—Knight Grand Cross of the Bath
GCMG—Knight Grand Cross of St. Michael and St. George
GCSI—Knight Grand Commander of the Star of India
GCVO—Knight Grand Cross of Victorian Order
GOC—General Officer Commanding
JP—Justice of the Peace

Appendix VI: Abbreviations

KBE—Knight Commander Order of the British Empire
KCB—Knight Commander of the Bath
KCMG—Knight Commander of St. Michael and St. George
KCVO—Knight Commander of the Royal Victorian Order
KG—Knight of the Order of the Garter
LLD—Doctor of Laws
MBE—Member of the Order of the British Empire
MP—Member of Parliament
MVO—Member of the Royal Victorian Order
OBE—Officer Order of the British Empire
OM—Order of Merit
PC—Privy Councilor
psc—Passed Staff College
Ret'd—Retired
RM—Royal Marines
RMA—Royal Marine Artillery; also Royal Marines Association
RMLI—Royal Marine Light Infantry
RN—Royal Navy
RND—Royal Naval Division
RNR—Royal Naval Reserve
RNVR—Royal Naval Volunteer Reserve
VC—Victoria Cross
WO—War Office
WRNS—Women's Royal Naval Service

Appendix VII

Royal Marine Light Infantry Batch, 1 September 1901

Editor's Note: The information provided for the following officers is in their initial order of Civil Service exam standing (see Notes at end) • Initial and altered seniority, 2nd Lieutenant/Lieutenant • Highest Rank attained • Fate

Barker, Godfrey • 5th—6,159 Marks • 5th/7th • Captain, retired 1 September 1913 (temporary Major, 9 November 1914) • Retired, 13 January 1912. Reserve of officers and recalled, 31 March 1914. Killed, Gallipoli, 29 April 1915.

Brewer, Herbert Reginald • 13th—5,575 Marks • 13th/10th • Major, 1 September 1917 • Retired, 31 January 1932. Recalled, World War II, 1939–1945. Physical training specialist and intelligence trained.

Burton, Reginald Edward George • 12th—5,624 Marks • 12th/8th • Captain, 1 September 1912 • Died in Malta, 1 April 1915, of wounds received in the sinking of HMS *Irresistible*, 18 March 1915. Also served in China.

Cheesman, Ernest George • 2nd—6,437 Marks • 2nd/3rd • Major, 1 September 1917 (Lieutenant Colonel on retirement, 11 May 1933) • Retired, 11 May 1933. Wireless specialist—served in that specialty before, during and after World War I and, when recalled, in World War II, 1939–45. Died 15 August 1971.

Durst, Alan Lydiat • 9th—5,812 Marks • 9th/9th • Captain, 1 September 1912 (major, 1 April 1919) • Retired, 1 September 1913; Sculptor with a national reputation for working in stone, wood, and ivory; work in galleries (e.g., The Tate), and churches and cathedrals. Reserve of officers and recalled, World War I, July 1914–March 1919; coal strike, 1921; Munich crisis, and World War II, June 1940–January 1945. Died December 1970.

Eagles, Charles Edward Campbell • 3rd—6,313 Marks • 3rd/11th • Major, 1 September 1917 • Killed in action, Zeebrugge, 23 August 1918, serving as the second in command of 4 RM Battalion.

Evans, Arthur Kelly • 7th—6,116 Marks • 7th/2nd • Major, 1 September 1917 • Retired, 12 November 1922. Reserve of officers, 3 November 1927. Musketry specialist, served with Royal Naval Division at Gallipoli and in France. OBE, MC. Died in Birr, Ireland, 13 November 1947.

Hatton, Edward Allen Smeathman • 1st—6,874 Marks • 1st/12th • Captain, 1 September 1912 • Killed in action, Gallipoli, 29 April 1915.

Jerram, Charles Frederic • 6th—6,125 Marks • 6th/1st • Major, 1 September 1917 (Temporary Major, 16 December 1914; Temporary Lieutenant Colonel, 23 July 1918–31 March 1919; Lieutenant Colonel, 30 November 1931) • Retired, 18 January 1929; recalled as Major, World War II, 10 January 1940–30 June 1945. Acting Lieutenant Colonel, 4 September 1944. CMG, DSO.

Appendix VII: Royal Marine Light Infantry Batch

Rees, Harold Frank Pemberton • 4th—6,215 Marks • 4th/4th • Major, 1 September 1917 • Retired, 7 September 1921. Reserve of officers, 3 November 1927. Died 3 November 1944. Traditional career pattern of sea service before, during and after World War I.

Risk, Charles Erskine • 8th—5.977 Marks • 8th/6th • Major, RM, 1 September 1917. Wing commander, RAF • Transfer to Royal Air Force, 1 August 1919. Pilot, RM and RAF. Retired, Wing Commander, RAF. Served in France before and after Gallipoli; wounded at Gallipoli. Died 26 January 1926, in Paris, France. DSO.

Shewell, Arthur Meade Moore • 10th—5,637 Marks • 10th/14th • Major, 1 September 1917 • Retired, 5 August 1919. Reserve of officers, 3 November 1927. Traditional career pattern of sea service before, during and after World War I. Died 1928.

Sinclair, Robert • 14th—No score given • 14th/5th • Major, 1 September 1917 • Retired, 18 January 1932. Traditional career afloat, including World War I. Also intelligence duty. Drafting officer, Plymouth, four times. Recalled, World War II, 31 July 1939–1 July 1944. Died 25 December 1973.

Welch, Alfred Davis • 11th—5,635 Marks • 11th/13th • Lieutenant Colonel, 22 December 1931 • Traditional career at sea, although once served as superintendent of the Royal Naval School of Music, 1930–32. Retired, 1 October 1934. Died 21 May 1960.

Sources: *The Times*, 2 August and 7 September 1901; *The Navy List*, October 1901, July 1902, August 1902, October 1902, and January 1903; ARCHIVES 9/2/28, Vols. I and II; ADM 196/63, Official Records of Service; and *The Globe and Laurel*, the journal of the Royal Marines.

Notes: (1) The Civil Service Examination standings, with examination marks, as reported in *The Times*, 2 August 1901. The listing posted in *The Times* includes all who passed for the Army, i.e., Royal Military Academy Sandhurst (with the Royal Marines an option to select for those so inclined), i.e., infantry or cavalry listed in order of merit. Candidates for the Guards, infantry and cavalry, were listed separately with each candidate's marks. Scores were also listed separately for the West India Regiment. For those who did not qualify, private notice was sent to those individuals. (2) Initial seniority standing as 2nd Lieutenants in the official *Navy List* from October 1901 through October 1902, page 212, coincided with the list of commissions in *The Times*, 7 September 1901. (3) Official seniority ranking for Lieutenants, promoted after completion of one year of initial training and education at the Royal Naval College, Greenwich, in *The Navy List*, January 1903, page 212a, reflected the order of merit for the officers after the end of their studies there in June 1902. Note that Jerram had moved from 6th to 1st in seniority in his batch. (4) Royal Marine Artillery officers are not included as they were on a separate seniority list reflective of their branch within the Corps; RMA officers had their own division, i.e., barracks, at Eastney, Southsea, Portsmouth, Hampshire, and had separate dates of seniority, promotion timing, uniforms, pay, and initial training (two years as opposed to one for RMLI officers at the Royal Naval College, Greenwich). Three RMA officers had dates of rank of 1 September 1901, the same as Jerram's batch, but they are not included in this table.

Appendix VIII

Status of Divisions on the Western Front, 11 November 1918

	In Line			In Reserve			
	Fresh	Tired	Total	Fresh	Tired	Total	Total Available
United States	4	12	16	3	11	14	30
French	19	17	36	19	53	72	108
British	5	24	29	6	29	35	64
Belgian	3	1	4	2	1	3	7
Italian	1	0	1	0	1	1	2
Portuguese	0	0	0	2	0	2	2
TOTAL ALLIED	32	54	86	32	95	127	213
German	*47*	*97*	*144*	*8*	*35*	*41*	*185*

Source: "Secret War Room, G-3, General Headquarters. Order of Battle on Western Front, 11 A.M., Nov. 11, 1918"—Compiled from a map showing locations of the divisions, with the title table matrix on it. Original in the Soldiers Memorial Military Museum, St. Louis, Missouri.

Notes: (1) The scale of the forces committed and from which nations reveals the magnitude and scope of the Great War. (2) As Lieutenant Colonel Jerram noted in his diary of 1918 and later in his memoir, at the tactical level of war even in October and November of the last months of the conflict—the Germans remained, especially in the defense, a very dangerous and capable foe. (3) United States Army divisions were generally double the size of European Divisions, formed around an infantry organization of two brigades per Division with each brigade consisting of two infantry regiments and one machine gun battalion.

Appendix IX

King George V Prize Recipients, 1914 to 1923

Editor's Note: The information provided for the following men is in this order: Rank • Year • Fate • Comment

Aman, Dudley L. • Captain, RMA • 1914 • Retired Major, DSC, 1920 • Created Baron Marley of Marley, 1930 (Labour).

Bourne, Alan G. B. • Captain, MVO, RMA • 1914 & 1915 • General, KCB; retired, 1943 • Adjutant General, Royal Marines; also initial Director, Combined Operations. Both in World War II.

Festing, Maurice C. • Major, DSO, RMLI • 1919 • Transferred to Royal Tank Corps, 1923. Corps Rank: Brevet Lieutenant Colonel • Died in Burma while serving as Chief of Staff, 4th Indian Division, in the rank of Colonel, British Army.

Jerram, Charles F. • Major, CMG, DSO, RMLI • 1919 • Retired, Major, 1929; Lieutenant Colonel, 1931 • Recalled and served during World War II.

Harrison, Harold C. • Captain (Brevet Major), DSO, RMA • 1921 & 1922 • Appointed Major, East Yorkshire Regiment, 1924; died, Brigadier, 1940 • Noted for rugby, intellect, and professionalism. One Army officer said, "Either Gort of Harrison will one day be head of the Army." Awarded CB. "In Memoriam. Brigadier H. C. Harrison, CB, DSO," *Globe and Laurel*, Vol. XLVIII, No. 5, May 1940, 251.

Coode, Cuthbert H. • Captain, RMLI • 1921 • Retired, Lieutenant Colonel, 1936 • Received prize sword after completing training at the Royal Naval College, Greenwich. Attended Army Staff College, Camberley.

Bamford, Edward • Captain (Brevet Major), VC, RMLI • 1922 • Major, 1936; died, Hong Kong 1928 • Awarded Victoria Cross, Zeebrugge Raid, 23 April 1918.

Weston, Eric C. • Captain, RMA • 1922 • Retired, Lieutenant General, 1943 • Commandant, Deal, 1939–40; commanded II Mobile Naval Base Defence Organisation I, Crete, 1941.

Glunicke, Robert C.A. • Captain, RMLI • 1923 • Major General, Retired, 1940 • Colonel Commandant, Plymouth, 1939–1941.

Seath, Gordon H. • Captain, (Brevet Major), DSO, RMLI • 1923 • Major General, Retired, 1941 • Colonel Commandant, Chatham, 1939–1942; recalled, 1942–44.

Source: ARCHIVES 9/2/28, Vols. I and II, augmented by obituaries in the journal of the Corps, *The Globe and Laurel*.

Appendix X

British Army Armoured Divisions of World War II

Editor's Note: The information provided for the following divisions is in this order (and see Notes at end):
Division • *Active duty* • *Theatres* • *Comments*

Guards Armoured • 17 June 1941–12 June 1945 • UK and NW Europe • In existence through the end of the war; reorganized as an infantry division and redesignated the Guards Division, 12 June 1945.

1st Armoured • September 1939–29 October 1944 • UK, France, At Sea, Egypt, Libya, North Africa, Italy • Div HQ disbanded: 11 Jan 1945 (in Italy)

2nd Armoured • 15 December 1939–8 April 1941 • UK, At Sea, Egypt, Libya • Div HQ disbanded: 10 May 1941 (in Egypt)

6th Armoured • 12 September 1940 through V-E Day • UK, At Sea, North Africa, Italy, Austria • In existence through the end of the war and post-conflict months.

7th Armoured • September 1939 through V-E Day • Egypt, Libya, North Africa, At Sea, Italy, UK, Northwest Europe • Regular division in Egypt, as the Mobile Division, and on outbreak of war redesignated The Armoured Division (Egypt), and on 16 February 1940 redesignated 7th Armoured Division. In existence through the end of the war and post-conflict months.

8th Armoured • 4 November 1940–1 January 1943 • UK, At Sea, Egypt • Never operated in Egypt as a complete division.

9th Armoured • 1 December 1940–31 July 1941 • UK • Never left the UK

10th Armoured • 1 August 1941–15 June 1944 • Palestine, Egypt, Syria • Operated only in Middle East; redesignated and formed, with reorganization, from the 1st Cavalry Division (in Palestine)

11th Armoured • 9 March 1941 through V-E Day • UK, At Sea, Northwest Europe • In existence through the end of the war and post-conflict months.

42nd Armoured • 1 November 1941–17 October 1943 • UK • Never left the UK; formed from the 42nd Infantry Division

79th Armoured • 14 August 1942 through V-E Day • UK, Northwest Europe • In existence through the end of the war and post-conflict months. In April 1943 its composition and organization changed so as to include development of specialized equipment and ensuing techniques. It also fought in Northwest Europe until V-E Day.

Source: Table compiled from Lieut-Col H. J. Joslen, *Orders of Battle, Second World War, 1939–1945*, I (London, 1960), pp. 3–33.

Appendix X: British Armoured Divisions of World War II

Notes: (1) From May 1939 through May 1945, British Armoured divisions had nine changes in their basic organization. (2) Does not include the only Cavalry Division of the British Army, which had a separate organization, formed in Britain on 31 October 1939 until redesignated as an armoured division on 1 August 1941. As a cavalry division, it served in UK, At Sea, Palestine, Transjordan, Iraq, and Syria. See 10th Armoured Division above. (3) Theatres are as designated by official British designation. With respect to this, Northwest Europe (officially "NW Europe") meant France, Belgium, Holland, Denmark, and Germany from 6 June to the end of the war; "North Africa" meant Algeria and Tunisia; and "Libya" meant Cyrenaica and Tripolitania.

Notes

Preface

1. Such views of the Great War are, of course, hardly new. A recent comment reflecting this appeared in the welcoming comments to the Annual Congress of the International Commission of Military History held in Varna, Bulgaria, 1–5 September 2014: As Dobromir Totev, Permanent Undersecretary of Defense, Bulgarian Ministry of Defense, wrote: "That is why we highly appreciate the will of the international military history community to devote its XL Congress to the 100-anniversary from the outbreak of the First World War.... The First World War and its consequences reshaped radically the geopolitical map and went across the whole XX century. In fact, the 'Great War' changed the world forever, and its effects are all around us." Dobromir Totev, "Welcome," *Program of the 40th Congress of the ICMH: World War One, 1914–1918*, 7. The congress convened in August and September 2014 in Varna, Bulgaria.
2. Gordon Corrigon, *Mud, Blood and Poppycock: Britain and the First World War* (London, 2003), 11. Corrigan also stresses a basic Clausewitzian point: An Army may be used for many purposes, but ultimately it exists to win a war, a trial of strength between opposing forces via the use of force, i.e., violence.
3. "Editorial," *Napoleonic Society Bulletin*, No. 688, 1–7 November 2013.
4. David Lloyd George, *War Memoirs of David Lloyd George*, VI (London, 1936), vii–viii. The former Prime Minister's exact verbiage: "I was the only Minister in any country who had some share throughout the whole of the War in its direction.... No other minister in any of the belligerent countries held an official position from the 1st of August 1914, to the 11th of November 1918." George differentiates himself and other political ministers from four heads of state: King George V of Britain, King Albert of the Belgians, Kaiser Wilhelm II of Germany, and President Raymond Poincare of France.
5. Commander the Hon. R. Plunkett, RN, "The Staff College," *The Naval Review*, III, No. 1, Feb. 1915, 91–92. The author was eventually Admiral the Hon. Sir Reginald Aylmer Ranfurly Plunkett-Ernle-Erle-Drax, KCB, DSO, JP, DL (28 August 1880–16 October 1967).
6. Edmund Venables, rev. Timothy C.F. Stunt, "Jerram, Charles (1770–1853)"; Donald F. Bittner, "Jerram, Charles Frederic (1882–1969)"; and H.G. Thursfield, rev. Paul G. Halpern, "Jerram, Sir (Thomas Henry) Martyn (1858–1933)," H.C.G. Matthew and Brian Harrison, eds., *Oxford Dictionary of National Biography*, XXX (Oxford, 2004), 56–57, 57–58, and 58–59, respectively.
7. Bittner, "Jerram, Charles Frederic (1882–1969)," 58.

Chapter 1

1. Chobham, Surrey, is eight miles north and west of Guildford and two and a half miles northwest of Woking. *The Times Gazetteer of the World* (London, 1895). Subsequent identifications of locations are from this source published during Jerram's youth.
2. The lineage of the Knight family is in Sir Bernard Burke, CB, LLD, edited by his sons, *A Genealogical and Heraldic History of the Landed Gentry of Great Britain and Ireland.* Vol. I, 8th ed. (London, 1894), 1124.
3. For a brief overview of Charterhouse written during Jerram's lifetime, with insight into that public school, see F.A.M. Webster, *Our Great Public Schools: Their Traditions, Customs and Games* (London, 1937), 57–81. An interesting comparison and contrast exists considering Jerram's comments on his father's view of the public schools, Jerram's own comments on sport and his later career, and Webster's account of Charterhouse's 19th century move to Surrey, military training offered, and emphasis on sport.
4. Edward Frederick Knight (1852–1925), *Who Was Who, Vol. II, 1916 1928* (London, 1929), 592. Knight listed his professions as "Morning Post special war correspondent in S. Africa; barrister, journalist and author." He also covered wars in India and the Russo-Japanese War, as well as serving as a volunteer with the French during the Franco-Prussian War.
5. The church of Saints Peter and Paul, whose origins date back to the 9th century.
6. For a view of Cornwall and descriptions (with illustrations) of many of the localities and sites mentioned by Lieutenant Colonel Jerram in his memoir, see Arthur Mee, ed., *Cornwall: England's Farthest*

South (London, 1937). This is a volume in the Interwar series titled *The King's England.*

7. See footnote 22 and Appendices I through IV, plus appropriate entries in *Who's Who* or *Who Was Who* for three of the four Jerram brothers: Sir Cecil Bertrand Jerram, KCMG; Lieutenant Colonel Charles Frederic Jerram, CMG, DSO; and Rear Admiral Sir Rowland Christopher Jerram, KBE, DSO; although eligible for inclusion, Martin Ralph Knight Jerram has no an entry. Another branch of the family had a tradition of military service, and three generations were listed in these references: an uncle, Admiral Sir Martyn Jerram, GCMG, KCB; his son, Brigadier Roy Martyn Jerram, DSO, MC; and his son, Major General Richard Martyn Jerram, CB, MBE.

8. Wrecking: Finding, keeping, and/or using material worth saving from wrecks or other wreckage washed up along the beach.

9. Much of Jerram's original third chapter, "Description of Talland," contains details on local families, farming, roads, and fishing boats. These sections have been edited out, but are available for perusal in the original manuscript.

10. As in the previous section, the original chapter 4 contains much detail on life and personalities of interest to local historians; hence, most of this has been edited out. What has been retained gives an indication of childhood in the late 19th century and Jerram's early life experiences.

11. Hansom-Cab: A covered two-wheeled passenger vehicle, with the driver's seat elevated behind the passenger compartment, with the reins to the horse passing over the occupant's roof. A hansom-cab is part of a famous London scene in the Fred Astaire–Ginger Rogers film *Top Hat* (1935), or the lesser known David Niven–Olivia de Havilland film, *Raffles* (1939).

12. An Eton jacket had an open front, broad lapels, and was cut square at the hips; the collar was large, stiff, turned over, and worn with the jacket.

13. The East Surrey Regiment, formed the year prior to Jerram's birth by the linking of the 31st Huntingshire Regiment of Foot and the 20th (Surrey) Regiment of Foot.

14. This section is considerably reduced from Jerram's original chapter 6 of the same name. In the original, he wrote in detail about fishing, boats, ground transportation, personalities, and incidents. Of interest to specialists of the locality or period, this is available in the original manuscript.

15. Frank Lethbridge (??–1922), British Vice Consul at Caen, transferred there from Honfleur in February 1893. Ouistreham is a coastal town in Normandy, Northeast of Caen and West Southwest of Honfleur, population in the 1890s approximately 1200.

16. Rear Admiral James Tobin Bush, CBE (1874–1949).

17. Service examinations were administered by the Civil Service to candidates desiring appointments to the Royal Military Academy, Woolwich; the Royal Military College, Sandhurst; or probationary commissions in the Royal Marines. Candidates listed their choice(s) in order of precedence, and those who qualified were placed on an order of merit list.

18. For Sir Frederic Winn Knight, KCB, JP, DL (1812–1897), see *Who Was Who. Vol. I. 1897–1915* (London, 1920), 293.

19. Simon's Bath House, called Simonsbath Lodge, Exmoor, Southmelton.

20. Probably a local reference to Dodman Point, northeast of Falmouth; Polperro is due northeast.

21. Admiral Sir (Thomas Henry) Martyn Jerram, GCMG, KCB (1858–1933), had a diverse career, including many foreign postings, duty with colonial expeditions, and service at sea; the latter included command of the Second Battle Squadron at the Battle of Jutland. H.G. Thursfield, rev. Paul G. Halpern, "Jerram, Sir (Thomas Henry) Martyn (1858–1933)," *Oxford Dictionary of National Biography*, XXX (Oxford, 2004), 58–59.

22. The referenced brothers: Sir Cecil Bertrand Jerram, KCMG (1891–1971), a diplomat who had extensive service in Russia (including a brief imprisonment by the Bolsheviks), and later served in diplomatic posts in Europe and Latin America (*Who Was Who, Vol. VII, 1971–1980*, 413). Rear Admiral Sir Rowland Christopher Jerram, KBE, DSO, RN (1890–1981), commissioned in 1907 and served in World Wars I and II; secretary to Admiral Ernle Chatfield (later Lord Chatfield), 1919–40 (*Who Was Who, Vol. VIII, 1981–1990*, 395). Martyn Ralph Knight Jerram, MC, joined the India Forest Service in November 1907 and retired in March 1925, with military service between March 1915 to January 1919 (Reserve of Officers, India Army); he wrote three books on forestry: *A Textbook on Forest Management* (1935), *An Outline of Forestry*, with Thomas Thomson (1938), and *Elementary Forest Mensuration* (1939). See also Appendix IV.

23. Crammer: When a young man failed the Civil Service exams or needed extra schooling before taking them, he studied with a "Crammer," who prepared him for the tests for entry into the forces. Crammers are addressed in Winston Churchill, *My Early Life: A Roving Commission* (New York, 1958), chap. 3; for a Royal Marine view, see General Sir Leslie Hollis, KCB, KBE, *One Marine's Tale* (London, 1956), 17–18.

24. Hyderabad, a state in India of approximately 82,698 square miles, with a population in 1891 of 11,537,000.

25. The Royal Military Academy, Woolwich, trained young men destined for the Royal Artillery or the Royal Engineers, whereas the Royal Military College, Sandhurst, trained cadets for the infantry or cavalry. The appeal of the Royal Marines was financial: Men were commissioned immediately and drew the appropriate pay and allowances of a Second Lieutenant, whereas at Woolwich and Sandhurst families of cadets paid fees.

26. At this time the Royal Marines had two branches: Royal Marine Light Infantry (RMLI) and Royal Marine Artillery (RMA). Each had separate lists for ranks, seniority, and promotion. Uniforms, pay, and professional schooling were also different. Amalgamation occurred in 1923.

27. Batch is a Royal Marine term meaning a group of officers with whom one was commissioned, went through initial training, and maintained strong personal ties. There were 17 officers in Jerram's batch, i.e., those commissioned on 1 September 1901. Of these, 14 were RMLI and three RMA. Their highest substantive Corps ranks: Captain—5; Major—10; Lieutenant Colonel—1; and Colonel Second Commandant—1; and their fates: Retirement—11; Battle deaths—4; Non-Combat death—1; Transfer to the Royal Air Force—1.

28. Major Stephen C. Wace, CBE, RMA (1883–1920). Commissioned in September 1901, promoted Major in September 1917, and died of acute pneumonia on 21 May 1920. Head of the Admiralty W/T Board when he died.

Chapter 2

1. Royal Marine Second Lieutenants drew pay upon commissioning. The Admiralty's 19th century policy of requiring their parents or guardians to deposit 60 pounds to cover both initial expenses and as a financial reserve ended in 1901. RMA and RMLI officers were initially paid 5/3 per day; however, RMA officers remained at Greenwich for four terms and their RMLI peers for only two. Hence, at the end of the former's second term, they received an additional mess allowance of 1/6 per day. The two terms of the RMLI officers were the same as the last two of the RMA; the officers then proceeded to their divisional headquarters and to HMS *Excellent* for instruction in gunnery. The courses of study were: RMA First Year—Algebra; Trigonometry; Statics; Euclid IV; Mensurations, Dynamics, Hydrostatics; Physics I, II, and practicals; Chemistry I, II, and practicals; French or German; and Artillery. RMA, Second Year, and RMLI—Permanent Fortifications; Strategy and Military History; Theodolite Surveying; Field Fortifications; Military Law; Tactics; Topography; French or German; Freehand Drawing; and Riding and Gymnastics.

2. The Admiral President: Admiral Sir Robert Henry More-Molyneux, KCB (1838–1904), later GCB; the Captain of the College was Captain Henry John May, CB (1853–1904), later Rear Admiral. Jerram is only partly correct with respect to the Commander. In September 1901, the Commander was Commander Henry Pelly, MVO (1867–1942), later Admiral, KCVO, CB, MVO; Commander John Nicholas (1865–??), later Vice Admiral, had served as the Commander until joining the Naval War Course which convened that month. Jerram would later serve under Nicholas in HMS *Flora* on the China Station.

3. In December 1901, 12 captains and 11 commanders were studying at the College in the cited course, eventually titled the Senior Officers War Course. Officers on it were on full pay.

4. Jerram here is expressing a traditional view, now challenged by recent scholarship on aspects of training and professional military education in the Royal Navy; See Harry W. Dickinson, *Educating the Royal Navy: Eighteenth-and Nineteenth-Century Education for Officers* (London, 2007), and *Wisdom and War: The Royal Naval College, Greenwich, 1873–1998* (London, 2012). Jerram believed his own time at the College provided the foundation for his professional career of almost three decades.

5. In 1901, 34 Second Lieutenants had been commissioned in the Royal Marines: 1 January 1901: RMA—2, RMLI—15; 1 September 1901: RMA—3, RMLI—14. But numbers at the College varied, as officers commenced their studies in January and September, hence came and departed accordingly.

6. Royal Marine instructors were in the Department of Fortifications. However, there were four on the staff, one Major and three Captains: Major Henry D. Drake, RMA (1854–1931), commissioned in September 1877, promoted Lieutenant Colonel in December 1907 and Brevet Colonel in May 1908, and retired in 1911, with a CBE; Captain John Brough, RMA (1874–1917), commissioned in September 1891, promoted Lieutenant Colonel in June 1916 for distinguished service in the field and transferred to the Royal Artillery that month, and committed suicide on 20 July 1917; Captain Robert C. Colquhoun, RMLI (1873–1916), commissioned in September 1890, promoted Major in August 1909, and killed in action at Jutland on 31 May 1916; and Captain Percy W. Simmons (1875–19??), RMLI, commissioned in February 1894, promoted Captain in July 1900, and transferred to the Army Ordnance Department and promoted Major in February 1911.

7. Jerram is partly in error here, as Royal Marines from ships on the China station served ashore—with attendant casualties. The Boxer Rebellion was suppressed with the capture of Peking by an allied force on 14 August 1901. For one account, see Donald F. Bittner, "Bored in Bermuda, Died in China: The Military Career (1890–1900) of Captain H.T.R. Lloyd, Royal Marine Light Infantry," *The Mariner's Mirror*, Vol. 90, No. 4, November 2004, 410–426. A fictional account, in the second of a series of Royal Marine family novels, is set in China during this period: Douglas Reeman, *The First to Land* (London, 1984).

8. For a succinct analysis of these "colonial wars," see Hew Strachan, *European Armies and the Conduct of War* (London, 1983); and for the naval brigades in the 19th century, Richard Brooks, *The Long Arm of Empire: Naval Brigades from the Crimea to the Boxer Rebellion* (London, 1999).

9. For an historical comment on this, see Major General J.L. Moulton, CB, DSO, OBE, *The Royal Marines* (London, 1972), 43. For personal commentary on the same subject, see Colonel Sam Bassett, CBE, *Royal Marine: The Autobiography of Colonel Sam Bassett, CBE, RM* (New York, 1965), 42–54.

10. At this time, promotion in the Royal Marines to Major was by seniority and vacancy. Promotion was slow; the few deaths, resignations, service transfers, or early retirements had limited significant effect on advancement; also, retirement for age at specific ranks had been introduced in the late 19th century. This system remained in effect, with consequential problems, until after World War I.

11. A prize sword was awarded to the top RMA and RMLI student at the end of their batch's course of instruction, if they had marks of 60% or higher on tests and were favorably recommended by the Professor of Fortification, i.e., the senior Marine.

12. Second Lieutenant Alfred Denis Bertram Godfray, RMA (1882–1950), commissioned in September 1900, promoted Major in June 1917, and retired in September 1920.

13. Henry William Meads May, commissioned a 2nd Lieutenant in the Hampshire Regiment, 6 March 1915, and Captain retired, 4 June 1930; awarded the Military Cross with two bars for service with the 2nd Battalion in North Russia, 1919.

14. Major Henry Dowrish Drake, psc, RMA, Professor of Fortifications, Greenwich, October 1899 to September 1904. Specially promoted Lieutenant Colonel in December 1907 in recognition for service at the Indian Staff College, Deotaki; awarded Royal Humane Society Bronze Medal, 1892.

15. In his annual report to the Admiralty, the Admiral President, Royal Naval College, Greenwich, indirectly referred to what occurred: "The prize of a sword was by their Lordships' directions withheld, as the conduct of the Officer who would, under ordinary circumstances, have been entitled to it, could not be considered 'exemplary' as required by the Instructions." Admiral President, Royal Naval College, Greenwich, to the Admiralty, Twenty-Seventh Annual Report on Royal Naval College, Greenwich, November 1902. National Maritime Museum, Greenwich. Naish Papers—NAI/3/29. There are no negative comments with respect to Greenwich in Jerram's official record of service.

16. Major Robert Kevern Clarke Nutt, RMLI (1881–1962). Commissioned Second Lieutenant in January 1901, promoted Major June 1917, and retired August 1920.

17. The extensive regulations, requirements, and descriptions for 1902 can be found in *The Navy List, July 1902*, pp. 683–689. The rate of pay for a Lieutenant, RMLI: Under one year of service, 95 pounds, 16 shillings, and 3 pence per annum (or 5 shillings, 3 pence per day); for three to ten years of service, 118 pounds, 12 shillings, 6 pence per year (6 shillings, 6 pence per day); and over ten years of service, 136 pounds, 17 shillings, 6 pence annually (or 7 shillings, six pence per day). Second Lieutenants had the same rate of pay as Lieutenants under three years of service. *The Navy List, July 1902*, 641.

18. Even in a maritime "regiment," equestrian skills were important to an officer's career, especially for an adjutant on parade. Such was noted in reports and recorded in official records of service.

19. Honorary Lieutenant J. Learmont, RA, appointed Riding Master on 17 January 1894. Woolwich is east of Greenwich.

20. Major Charles Erskine Risk, DSO, RMLI (1882–1926), commissioned Second Lieutenant in September 1901, promoted temporary Lieutenant Colonel in December 1916, and substantive Major in September 1917. One of the first Royal Marine flying officers, Risk transferred to the Royal Air Force in August 1919, retired on 7 December 1922 as a Wing Commander, and died in Paris in January 1926. "Obituary, Lt-Col. Charles E. Risk, DSO, RAF (Retd.)," *The Globe and Laurel*, Vol. XXXIV, March 1926, No. 3, 53; and *The Times*, 10 January 1923.

21. Lieutenant Colonel Jerram when in Britain spent almost his entire career ashore at Plymouth Division, located at Plymouth, Devon. A reference with many photographs to the many locations and sites about which he writes, written during his life, is: Arthur Mee, ed., *Devon: Cradle of Our Seamen* (London, 1938). This is a volume in a series titled *The King's England*.

22. Captain Eric Hody Morres (1870–1920), commissioned Second Lieutenant, RMLI, in September 1889, promoted Captain in March 1898, and retired in September 1904. Adjutant, Plymouth Division, from 30 March 1901 into 1904. Recalled for World War I, promoted Temporary Major in November 1916, and placed on the Major's Retired List, in July 1919.

23. The Venezuela Campaign was a five-ship blockade from 20 December 1902 to 14 February 1903. Colonel Cyril Field, RMLI, *Britain's Sea Soldiers, A History of the Royal Marines, Vol. II* (Liverpool, 1924), 340.

24. A fifth Royal Marine division existed at Woolwich from 1805 to 1869.

25. Colonel Commandant Frederick Baldwin (1845–1925), RMLI, Plymouth Division, commissioned in December 1864, promoted Colonel Commandant in November 1898 and General on 19 May 1910, and retired that November.

26. The Battle of Bunker Hill, actually fought on Breed's Hill, occurred on 19 June 1775. The hills overlooked the port of Boston and controlled the harbor. A tactical victory for the British, the attacking force of 2,200 men suffered almost 50% casualties due to frontal assaults on the entrenched Americans.

27. Major John Pitcairn (1713?–1775), commissioned Second Lieutenant in November 1755, promoted Major in April 1771, died of wounds received at Bunker Hill, and buried in Old North Church, Boston, Massachusetts. He also commanded the troops tasked to seize militia weapons and stores which resulted in the battles of Lexington and Concord on 19 April 1775.

28. For another officer's recounting of his initial view of his division's mess, see Lieutenant Colonel W.P. Drury, CBE, RM, *In Many Parts: Memoir of a Marine* (London, 1926), 32–33. Although Drury described the Chatham Division officers' mess of 1881, little had changed between both officers early garrison life, to include initial division training and financial issues.

29. An unsigned commentary by a "Major who as a recruit officer first made the acquaintance of the late Major Morres" after his obituary in the Corps' journal was probably written by Jerram for its comments and assessment reads very similar to the above. See "Biographical Notes. [Major Eric Hody Morres, RMLI]," *The Globe and Laurel*, October 1920, Vol. XXVII, No. 10, 153.

30. The 8th Brigade reference for 1902–03 is erroneous. According to *The Army List, January 1903*, Plymouth was home to the 6th Division and the 12th Brigade, with appropriate headquarters, plus combat and supporting units. However, *The Army List, January 1914*, reflects a reorganization referenced by Jerram: The Southern Command with the 2nd Cavalry Brigade and the 3rd Division, the latter consisting of the 7th, 8th, and 9th Infantry Brigades, plus supporting troops. In his recollection, Jerram has described the Plymouth garrison of 1914 as opposed to the specifics of 1902–03; but in concept, his point is valid. See also note 36.

31. Drake Island: An island, with extensive seaward defenses by the early 20th century, in the middle of the channel approaches to the Plymouth/Devonport harbor area.

32. HMS *Impregnable*, formerly HMS *Howe/Bulwark*, built in 1860, a training ship for boys with no armament.

33. Lieutenant Francis Wyville Home, RMLI (1882–1943), commissioned in January 1901 and retired as a Lieutenant Colonel in October 1934. A wireless specialist, he spent most of his career in communications while serving at sea and ashore, including the Wireless Board of the Admiralty between 1923–37. Recalled for

World War II, Home was head of the Admiralty Wireless Board, promoted Acting Colonel Commandant and Temporary Brigadier, and served with the British Admiralty Delegation, Washington, till his death there in March 1943.

34. Despite its name, the dogcart was a two-wheeled horse-drawn vehicle. It had a seat for the driver and an accompanying dog, or for two people.

35. The colours of a unit were carried by a subaltern. The King's (or Queen's) Colour is paraded alone for a member of the royal family or a visiting head of state, the regimental colour for other distinguished persons; in the Corps, each division had its own "regimental" colours. When an entire unit is on parade, both are carried. For a history of the Corps' colours, see Major Alistair Donald, RM, *The Story of Colours in the Royal Marines. Royal Marines Historical Society Special Publication No. 23* (Portsmouth, Hampshire, 2001).

36. Brickfields was an open field area outside the old walls of Plymouth, near the Devonport area. As a garrison town, major military reviews were held there—and well attended by the public. For a discussion, with photos to include one from a 1912 garrison review when Lieutenant Jerram was in barracks, see "Plymouth Dock—A Garrison Town," http://www.devonportonline.co.uk/historic_devonport/military/garrison_town.aspx, accessed 20 September 2014. The site is now the grounds of the Devonport Albion Rugby Football Club.

37. "Going to sea": Each division maintained a sea register and officers, i.e., Majors, Captains, and Lieutenants, moved from the bottom to the top. When at the head of the register for his rank, when a ship was being commissioned he went to it and assigned to duty appropriate to his rank. Troops and non-commissioned officers likewise rotated between ships and barracks.

38. HMS *Hogue*, one of a class of six armoured cruisers constructed between 1898 and 1904, was laid down in July 1898 and completed in 1902. Jerram inadvertently conveys the impression she was old and obsolete. When he joined her, she was new but rendered obsolete by HMS *Dreadnought* (1906). For a description of *Hogue* and her class, see Fred T. Jane, ed., *Jane's Fighting Ships, 1906–07* (London, 1907), 62. A picture of any ship of the class reveals their transitional nature in an era of rapid technological and design change. See also note 3, chapter 6.

39. Captain Moore H. Marshman, RMLI (1877–1929), commissioned in September 1895, promoted Captain in July 1901, retired in June 1911, recalled during World War I, promoted Temporary Major in February 1916, and retired as a Major in June 1917.

40. Commander Edward G. Lowther-Crofton, DSO, RN (1873–1942), later Vice Admiral.

41. Vice Admiral Sir Arthur K. Wilson, VC, KCB, KCVO, Bt. (1842–1921), Commander Channel Squadron, 1901–03; later First Sea Lord (1909–1912), and Admiral of the Fleet, VC, GCB, OM, GCVO.

42. This passage is unclear or the time sequence is misleading. Captain Marshman remained in HMS *Hogue* until transferred, with most of the crew, to HMS *Suffolk* in May 1904.

43. Aboard Royal Navy vessels, by tradition the senior Royal Marine officer was always called "The Major," even if his rank was "Captain." This avoided confusion as there was only one "Captain" aboard ship—he of the Royal Navy who commanded it.

44. Jerram has made and would continue to make frequent references to his "servant"—and he explains this relationship throughout his memoir. For a fictional portrayal mirroring his real life, see the many references to an officer's "Marine Officer's Attendant" in the fourth volume of Douglas Reeman's Blackwood Royal Marine family saga: Douglas Reeman, *Dust on the Sea* (New York, 2002), especially page 169. Two generations of the close association of two officers, two servants, and their families are portrayed in this book which covers the years 1940 to 1943, with references to the previous generation.

45. Jerram later wrote of Wright, "My soldier servant, old 'Shiner' Wright, the grandest and loyalist of all men I had to honour to meet...," Referenced in "Our Forebears," *The Globe and Laurel*, Vol. LXXVI, No. 4. August 1968, 222.

46. Lieutenant Ernest O. Ballantyne, RN.

47. Captain John L. Marx, MVO, RN (1852–1939), naval cadet in December 1865, promoted to Captain in June 1895, and retired as Admiral in September 1913. Later, CB, DSO, MVO.

48. Engineer Commander Frederick Worth, RN.

49. HMS *Suffolk*: Twin screw, First Class Armoured Cruiser, the last of 10 Monmouth class vessels built between 1899 and 1904—soon to be obsolete with the launching of HMS *Dreadnought*. 9,800 tons with 14 six-inch guns, two forward, two aft, and five each port and starboard. For a description of the class and photograph, see *Jane's Fighting Ships, 1906–07*, 6.

50. Captain John W. Dustan, RMLI (1873–1917), commissioned in September 1892, promoted Captain in March 1900 and Major in May 1911, retired due to ill health in January 1917, and died of Tuberculosis on 2 July 1917. Served in the Boxer Rebellion in China while serving on board HMS *Centurion*, and from 1908 to 1910 as Commandant, Ascension Island.

51. HMS *Suffolk* was built at Portsmouth Dockyard. Her sister ship, HMS *Lancaster*, was constructed by Armstrong-Whitworth (Elswick & Walker), Newcastle-Upon-Tyne and commissioned in 1904 at Chatham.

Chapter 3

1. In 1904 when *Suffolk* first appears in the list of ships of that fleet, 53 ships were in the Mediterranean and Red Sea. *The Navy List*, October 1904, p. 269.

2. The Royal Navy then had a professional (and social) split between two branches: The executive (those who commanded a vessel and fought her) and the engineer (those who operated the engines which propelled the ship). For a pertinent discussion, including failed efforts to remedy the situation, see Vice Admiral Sir Louis de Bailly, KBE, CB, *From Fisher to the Falklands* (London, 1991), chaps. 1 to 5.

3. Captain David Beatty, MVO, DSO, RN (1871–1956). He commanded HMS *Suffolk* from 25 October 1904 to 19 September 1905. An appraisal of his tour is in Stephen Roskill, *Admiral of the Fleet Earl Beatty: The Last Naval Hero* (London, 1980), 40–41. Later First Sea Lord, Admiral of the Fleet, and Earl of the

North Sea and Brooksby, OM, PC, GCB, GCVO, KCVO, DSO, MVO.

4. Since the officers and crew of HMS *Suffolk* were transferred from HMS *Hogue*, the reference is to Commander Lowther-Crofton.

5. Beatty was rotating in command of three ships on the Mediterranean station: HMS *Juno* June-December 1902; HMS *Arrogant*, November 1903-September 1904; and thence to HMS *Suffolk*, with brief periods in HMS *Diana* and HMS *Mars* (September-October 1904); see Bryan Ranft, ed., *The Beatty Papers, Vol. I, 1902–1918* (Aldershot, Hants, 1989), xvi; *Suffolk* is mentioned very briefly in two of the published papers and twice in Ranft's assessment of the future Earl's career. In this period, he also addresses in his introduction (pages 3 and 4), like Roskill, Beatty's approach to training, assessments, and hospitality—all seen in Jerram's recollections. See also Rear Admiral William Scott Chalmers, CBE, DSC, RN, *The life and letters of David, Earl Beatty, Admiral of the Fleet, Viscount Borodale of Wexford, Baron Beatty of the North Sea and of Brooksby* (London, 1951), 88–89. Chalmers includes a succinct discussion of changes in naval warfare due to technology, including wireless telegraphy (p. 89), also addressed by Jerram in his memoir. HMS *Suffolk* is not mentioned in the short biography of Beatty written by his nephew: Charles Beatty, *Our Admiral: A Biography of Admiral of the Fleet Earl Beatty* (London, 1980). Beatty made more of an impression on Jerram than *Suffolk* and her crew, including the commander of the Royal Marine detachment, did on the future Admiral and earl.

6. The rapid sequence of Jerram's Royal Marine senior officers is unclear as to why. He implies some problems, but this is not really clear from the named officers' records of service.

7. Captain John C. Deed, RMLI (1876–1915), joined HMS *Suffolk* in February 1905. Commissioned in February 1894, promoted Captain in October 1900, and retired in August 1906; recalled for World War I, he drowned in the loss of HMS *Formidable*, 1 January 1915.

8. Jerram is claiming too much for his detachment during Beatty's short command tour in *Suffolk*. Beatty had served with Marines in combat ashore in and around Tientsin in the summer of 1899 during the Boxer rebellion, and in his service afloat in many ships—many of which he commanded. Still, his point is made—as a Marine is one of the supporters of his arms: The right supporter is a Royal Marine, enlisted, standing at attention with rifle and ammunition belt; the left supporter is a sailor. For a good picture, see Sir Bernard Burke, CB, LL.D, and Ashworth Burke, and E.M. Swinhoe, ed., *A Genealogical and Heraldic History of the Peerage and Baronetage, The Privy Council, and Knightage* (London, 1937), 240. See also Charles Kidd and David Williamson, eds., *Debrett's Peerage and Barontage* (London, 1995), 100.

9. In addition to other duties when afloat, Royal Marines manned guns, which could include one of the main batteries. "Y" turret would be the last one closest to the stern of the ship.

10. The reference is to the Dogger Bank Incident of 21 October 1904.

11. Jerram here addresses a central issue affecting the Corps: What were the roles and missions of Marines in the post age of sail era? Generally, Marines disliked, if not despised, coaling. The shift to oil fueled major combatants eliminated this issue.

12. Eugene S. Politovsky, *From Libau to Tsushima: A Narrative of the Voyage of Admiral Rojdestvensky's Fleet to Eastern Seas, Including a Detailed Account of the Dogger Bank Incident*, Trans. Major F.R. Godfrey (London, 1907).

13. Hoopoe: A crested bird related to the hornbills.

14. Engineer Commander William W. Lawrance and Engineer Lieutenant Henry W. Grant. Both retired as Engineer Captains. Beatty was still in command.

15. HMS *Renown*: Twin screw battleship, 1st class, armoured, 12,350 tons, 14 guns. Commissioned in 1895, sold in 1913.

16. For a brief description of this Royal Tour, see John Fabb, *Royal Tours of the British Empire, 1860–1927* (London, 1989).

17. Presumably, Jerram is referring to the three major fleets of 1906: The Channel, Atlantic, and Mediterranean Fleets. In that year, the Channel Fleet had 51 vessels (16 battleships, nine cruisers, 24 destroyers, and two attached ships); the Atlantic Fleet, 26 ships (eight battleships, eight cruisers, six destroyers, two special service vessels, and two attached ships); and the Mediterranean Fleet, 42 vessels (eight battleships, seven cruisers, 22 destroyers, two attached ships, and three special service ships). A major reorganization occurred in 1912 with the formation of the Home Fleet. *The Navy List*, March 1906, 269. *Suffolk* and *Lancaster* were in the four ship 3rd Cruise Squadron.

18. Gregagle: A strong and cold northeastern wind of the Central Mediterranean Sea, somewhat resembling the foehn (Fohn) of Switzerland and the Santa Ana of Southern California.

19. Rear Admiral James L. Hammet, CVO (1849–1905), Superintendent of the Malta Dockyard from 1902, who died on 15 February 1905.

Chapter 4

1. Jerram wrote these sections in 1962, and some of his comments on Chinese–United States relations are reflective of that era. Some of these have been retained, as they represent both his views and the context of the decade in which they were written.

2. Lieutenant Colonel William Price Drury, CBE, RMLI (1861–1949). Son of Royal Navy and grandson of Royal Marine officers, Drury was commissioned in September 1880, promoted Major in December 1898, retired in July 1903, recalled to active service during World War I, promoted Lieutenant Colonel in May 1919, and died in January 1949. He wrote 18 books between 1899 and 1939, plus his memoir, *In Many Parts: The Memoirs of a Marine* (London, 1926), three plays, and one screen play. He also wrote poetry and historical essays, directed theatrical productions, and served as editor of the Corps journal, *The Globe and Laurel*.

3. Major W.P. Drury, Royal Marine Light Infantry (Retired), "Greyfellow," *The Tadpole of an Archangel, The Petrified Eye, and other Naval Stories* (London, 1904), 207–218. Editor's Note: The volume of Drury's writings in the library of the Royal Marines Museum in which this story was verified has enscribed in it "C.

F. Jerram, H.M.S. 'Astraea,' -/10." The library had five books with Lieutenant Colonel Jerram's signature, assigned postings, and dates.

4. HMS *Spartiate:* Twin screw protected cruiser, 1st Class (of 1898), 11,000 tons, 16 guns of 6-inch caliber.

5. In 1907, the Eastern Fleet consisted of 28 vessels on the China Station (five cruisers, six attached ships, 10 river gunboats, and seven destroyers), plus seven in the East Indies, and nine in Australia. By April 1907, Jerram was carried on the roll of HMS *Tamar*, a receiving ship of 4,650 tons, based in Hong Kong, but was assigned for service in the senior officer's vessel, Yangtze River. (*The Navy List, April 1907*, 382.).

6. Commander Ernest K. Loring, RN (1869–1945); eventually, Vice Admiral, CB.

7. Captain Cresswell J. Eyres, RN (1862–1949); eventually Admiral, DSO, OBE.

8. "News of the Week. The Visit of the Amir to the Viceroy," *The Spectator*, 12 January 1907.

9. Very Light: Colored pyrotechnic lights or flares, fired from a pistol.

10. Pooped: A wall of water coming over the rear or front of a ship.

11. Also Wusung: A river in Southern Kiangsu, flowing north of Shanghai. It enters the Yangtze River just below the town of Woosung (Wusung).

12. HMS *Clio:* Screw sloop (1903), of 1,070 tons, with six guns of 4-inch caliber or larger. HMS *Algerine* and HMS *Cadmus* had similar armament and tonnage.

13. HMS *Astraea*, HMS *Flora*, and later HMS *Charybdis:* Twin screw Protected Cruisers, Second Class (1893), 4,360 tons, 10 guns of 4-inch caliber or larger.

14. Wei-hai-Wei: A British naval station, north central Shantung Province, southwest (by land) from Port Arthur with southern Korea due east.

15. The Chinese Regiment had British officers but was composed of Chinese troops and noncommissioned officers, except for four British NCOs: one Sergeant Major, one Colour Sergeant, one orderly room clerk, and one armorer. It was raised in 1899 but disbanded after the Boxer Rebellion. Anthony Gero, "1219. 1st Battalion, Chinese Regiment," *Journal of the Society for Army Historical Research*, Vo. LXV, No. 262, Autumn 1987, 184; and William Y. Carman, "The Wei-Hai-Wei Regiment of the 1st Chinese Regiment," *Journal of the Military Historical Society*, Bulletin Issue 137, Vol. XXXV, August 1984, 7–11.

16. The reference is to the battle of Tsushima Strait of 27–28 May 1905 in which Admiral Togo's Japanese fleet destroyed the Russian Baltic Fleet which had sailed from Northern Europe.

17. Hankow, on the left bank of the Yangtze 700 miles from its mouth, became a treaty port in 1861 and was the focus of trade with the central and western provinces of China. Wu Chang is across the Yangtze, on the right bank of the river.

18. Eights, fives and fours: Shotgun cartridge loads related to shooting. Eights were the smallest and considered ideal for snipe and sand grouse (abundant in China), while shot fives were used for rabbits, pheasants, and duck. Fours would be too heavy for fowl and smaller game.

19. Tung-lu Reach: Gazetteers of the period do not list this.

20. Nanking: In Kiangsu province, on the right bank of the Yangtze River, 130 miles from its mouth and 194 miles west of Shanghai. A description of this city in the 1890s is in *The Times Gazetteer of the World* (London, 1895), 1065.

21. Nanking: In the 21st century, now a developing and thriving major city, whilst also a major historical and cultural tourist site in China. See, for example, http://www.travelchinaguide.com/cityguides/nanjing.htm.

22. John Wallace Ord Davidson (1888–1973), in 1909 a student interpreter in China. Eventually, CMG, OBE.

23. China Merchant: The official name listed in *Lloyd's Register of Shipping*, was the China Merchants' Navigation Company, based in Shanghai.

24. Kiaochow Forts: For a succinct background, see Bascom Barry Hayes, "Kiaochow," *Historical Dictionary of European Imperialism*, James Olsen, ed.(Greenwood, Ct: 1991), 342–345.

25. Kiaochow, now called Qingdao, besieged by Japanese and British forces on 2 September and capitulated on 7 November 1914.

26. Paper Hunt: Or "Paper Chase" evolved from the "Hare and Hound" paper chase from boys' schools of the mid–19th century. Usually two horsemen (the hares) set a trail of cut-up paper, the hounds (horsemen) then gave chase, and the hunt terminated at a clubhouse.

27. Bubbling Well Road: Extension of the Nanking Road to the Jing'An Temple, by the time Jerram was in China it had been incorporated into the International Settlement. Prominent thoroughfare on which the International Settlement police station was located.

28. For a contemporary view, see "The Woosung Forts," *The Otago Witness*, 28 June 1900, available via "Papers Past" from the National Library of New Zealand: http://paperspast.natlib.govt.nz/cgi-bin/paperspast?a=d&d=OW19000628.2.291.

29. Major William Dixon, RMA (1868–1958). Commissioned in September 1886, promoted brevet Major in September 1907 and substantive Major in August 1910, and retired in April 1920. Between August 1901 and March 1907, on temporary service with the Naval Intelligence Department as a specialist in foreign ordnance and explosives. On 30 May 1919 he received the CMG for service as Governor of St. Helena, 1917 to 1919.

30. Ning-Po: Another treaty port in Chekiang Province, on the Ning-po (Takin) River, approximately 100 miles south of Shanghai.

31. Chinhai: A town on Hangchow Bay, at the mouth of the Yung-Kiang River, 18 miles northeast of Ning-po.

32. Nimrod Bay is south of Hangchow, in Chekiang Province. Chusan Lo is a group of islands off the coast of China, east-northeast of Ning-po.

33. HMS *King Alfred:* Twin screw armored cruiser (1902), 14,000 tons and 18 guns of 4-inch caliber or higher. At this time, Rowland Jerram was listed as "clerk" in *King Alfred*, having joined her on 16 January 1908.

34. Vice Admiral the Honourable Sir Hedworth

Lambton, KCB, CVO (1856–1929), Commander-in-Chief, Eastern Fleet. Later, Admiral of the Fleet Sir Hedworth Meux, GCB, KCVO, assuming the name Meux in 1911.

35. HMS *Kent:* Twin screw armored cruiser (1901), 9,800 tons, 14 guns of 4-inch caliber or higher.

36. Haitan Strait: Probable reference is to Haitan Island, in the Formosa Straits.

37. Gutzlaff Light on the island of the same name, in Hangchow Bay.

38. WuHu: Another treaty port in Anhwei Province, approximately 55 miles south-south east of Nanking, on a tributary of the Yangtse.

39. Chemulpo: Meaning "muddy harbor," a seaport in Korea, southwest of Seoul, on a sheltered bay to the south of the Han River, 55 miles by water from Mapu, the port of Seoul. 20th century name: Inchon.

40. Adjoining Parliament, now the vestibule to the House of Commons. Built in 1097 as an extension to Edward the Confessor's Palace, it was restored during the reign of Richard II, to include an extensive oak hammer-beam roof.

41. Captain John Nicholas, RN, in command of HMS *Flora* since 7 September 1909.

42. Pay off (or paid off) was the end of a ship's commission, prior to the vessel's refit, recommission, sale, or other disposal.

43. Captain Edward B. Kiddle, RN (1866–1933), was the last commanding officer of HMS *Astraea* under whom Jerram served. Later Admiral, KBE, CB.

Chapter 5

1. From 1880 to 1905, Britain built 63 pre–*Dreadnought* "battleships," while from 1905 to 1914, 45 post–*Dreadnought* battleships and battle cruisers joined the fleet. All of these vessels had Marine detachments. A.J. Marder, *The Anatomy of British Sea Power: A History of British Naval Policy in the Pre-Dreadnought Era, 1880–1905* (New York, 1940), Appendix I, and *From the Dreadnought to Scapa Flow. The Royal Navy in the Fisher Era. Vol. I. The Road to War, 1904–1914* (London, 1961), Appendix.

2. In 1906, the Admiralty implemented a new officer accession program called "The Selborne Scheme." All "naval" officers would enter the service via a common training program, then serve with the fleet as a "naval officer." After several years of duty, each would then select a specialty, i.e., executive, engineer, or Marine. For details, see "Naval Training. New Admiralty Scheme. Memorandum by the First Lord," *The Times*, 25 December 1902. For the Corps, it was a disaster: From 1906 to 1911, only 15 officers joined: 1906—6; 190—6; 1908 and 1909—0; 1910—2; and 1911—1. Direct entry based upon competitive examination returned in 1912, with 23 joining that year and 24 in 1913. For the public announcement, see "Naval and Military Intelligence. First Appointments in the Royal Marines," *The Times*, 7 November 1911.

3. Lieutenant Bernard Weller, RMLI (1881–1941), commissioned in September 1900, promoted brevet Lieutenant Colonel in 1918, and retired in August 1922. Most of his career was spent at sea, although in World War I he served with the Royal Marine Brigade at Gallipoli in 1915 and 4 Royal Marine Battalion on the Zeebrugge Raid in April 1918. Awarded the DSC (1916) and CB (1918), and the Croix de Guerre from France.

4. The Rifle No. 1, Short Magazine Lee Enfield Mark III, adopted by the British Army in January 1907 and still in use into the post–World War II era.

5. The promotion problem before, during, and after World War I is analyzed in D.F. Bittner, *A Ghost of a General and the Royal Marine Officer Corps of 1914*, Royal Marine Historical Society Publication No. 6 (Portsmouth, 1983). Promotion to Major was based on seniority and vacancy, then by selection. The system also provided for non-permanent advancements (temporary, acting, and local) linked to an assignment, and possible advancement to the next higher grade upon retirement. Brevet promotions could also occur.

6. Captain William Patrick Arbuthnot, RMLI (1878–1949), commissioned in January 1897, promoted Lieutenant Colonel in March 1924, and advanced to Colonel on retirement in April 1928.

7. "Senior" is a relative term. Captain Arbuthnot would be considered "senior" only in the sense of years in grade, i.e., seven. *Lean's Navy List* of January 1911 (page 78A) lists Arbuthnot as 51 of 100 Captains of the Royal Marine Light Infantry.

8. Mylor: A town in Cornwall, on Mylor Creek, an outlet of Carrick Creek, located two miles north-northeast of Falmouth.

9. Sites all in Cornwall: Lizard is south-southwest from Falmouth, on the Lizard Peninsula, approximately 22 air miles from Falmouth. Helford is south-southwest from Falmouth, approximately four and a half sea miles from Falmouth to the entrance of Falmouth estuary—and became the Jerrams' final retirement home. Ruan Lanihorne is a village up the River Fal.

10. Jerram's promotion to Captain was dated 1 September 1912. In January 1912, he was the senior Lieutenant in the RMLI.

11. Headquarters of the Corps, located in The Admiralty, Whitehall, London. In 1912, it had three officers: The head of the Corps, the Deputy Adjutant General (a General Officer); the Assistant Adjutant General (a Lieutenant Colonel); and the Deputy Assistant Adjutant General (a Major), plus two quartermasters and three warrant officers.

12. HMS *Nile*—Twin screw battleship, 1st Class Armored (1888), of 11,940 tons and ten guns of 4-inch caliber or larger. This reference is unclear, as Jerram's Record of Service dates this duty as 1–5 March 1913—but all of it spent in the *Suffolk*.

13. HMS *Swiftsure*—Twin screw battleship of 11,800 tons (1903), with 4 10-inch and 14 7.5-inch guns.

14. *The Navy List* for July 1913 lists Major Hugh D.E. O'Sullivan, RMLI (1874–1958), as the "Major, RM," on *Swiftsure*, with a reporting date on board of 25 April 1913. Between 1912 and 1914, he served as senior Royal Marine officer, East Indies. Commissioned in September 1892, promoted Colonel Second Commandant in January 1924, retired in October 1926, and advanced to Major General in 1928. Awarded CBE (1919). O'Sullivan had extensive service in the Middle East, and was awarded two orders by the government of Egypt.

15. Lieutenant George H. Kendle, RMA (1885–1954), commissioned in January 1903, promoted

Major in January 1919, Brevet Lieutenant Colonel in April 1932, and retired in October 1932.

16. The text is as written by Jerram. In this case, he has misidentified the country for whom the two ships were built, and identified Germany as Britain's concern whereas in 1903 it was Russia. *Swiftsure* and *Triumph* also had 10-inch guns as their main armament, not 11-inch. *Triumph* was torpedoed and sunk off the Gallipoli peninsula in 1915. Both vessels were purchased from Chile in December 1903.

17. Probably Lieutenant C. Winthrop Swithinbank, RN.

18. HMS *Highflyer:* Twin screw Protected Cruiser (1898) of 5,600 tons, with 11 guns of 4-inch caliber or higher.

19. HMS *Exmouth:* Twin screw battleship (1901) of 14,000 tons, with 16 guns of 4-inch calibre or higher.

20. During the time Jerram was aboard *Exmouth*, she had two commanders. Thus, the reference may be to either or both Commander Lionel J.G. Anderson, RN, or Commander Walter E. Woodward, RN. In July 1913, Woodward replaced Anderson.

21. Captain Harold Frederick Harrison Strugnell, RMLI (1878–1919), commissioned in September 1900, promoted Captain in September 1911, and Major in June 1917. He died on 21 March 1919 on the Isle of Wight while still on active service.

22. The reference is probably to Captain Richard Noel White, RMLI (1878–1940). Commissioned in September 1897, promoted to Major in June 1916, and retired in August 1922.

23. On the cited locations, Saltash is on the River Tamar, northwest of Plymouth, with the River Lynher flowing to the west of it. A large bay separates Saltash and the peninsula upon which Torpoint is located at its tip. Depending upon the route, the march could have been 13 miles.

24. Morwenstow to Boscastle: Along the north Cornish coast, a distance of over 20 miles. Brown Willy is the highest point on Bodmin Moor, 1,375 feet; the moor itself runs 12 miles from north to south, and 11 miles east to west. According to legend, Sir Bedivere threw King Arthur's sword, Excalibur, into Dozmary Pool, at the command of the dying monarch.

25. For a fictional account of change ringing, see Dorothy L. Sayers, *The Nine Tailors: Change Rung on an Old Theme in Two Short Touches and Two Full Peals* (New York, 1934).

26. The company is now called Whitechapel Bell Foundry Ltd; the charges were just over 278 pounds. Jerram was listed as Chairman of the Church Bell Committee, his address as 51 Durnford Street, Stonehouse, Plymouth. Whitechapel Bell Foundry Ltd., letter to editor of 24 May 1994, with copy of ledger entry for "Talland Bells" dated 8 June 1914.

27. HMS *Eclipse:* Twin screw protected cruiser, 2nd Class (1894), of 5,600 tons, with 11 guns of 4.7-inch caliber or higher.

28. *The Navy Lists* for March to June 1914 show no Sub-Lieutenants, either RN or RNR, appointed to HMS *Eclipse*. The commanders of *AE1* and *AE2*, both sunk, were Royal Navy officers. The commander of *AE2* was Lieutenant, later Captain and DSO, Hew G.D. Stoker, RN (1885–1966); *The Navy List* for August 1914 notes by his name, "Lent for duty under Australian Government." (p. 124). Also, Stoker was promoted to Lieutenant, Royal Navy, on 31 December 1906. For a discussion of the operations of *AE2* and Stoker, see Victor Rudenno, *Gallipoli: Attack from the Sea* (New Haven, CT, 2008), 62–63 and 88–92; footnote 39 on page 300 addresses *AE1* and *AE2*'s movement to Australia with *Eclipse* and their Royal Navy officers, and British and Australian crews.

29. Lieutenant Albert Clarence St. Clair-Morford, RM (1893–1945), commissioned in January 1912, promoted to substantive Colonel Commandant in October 1941, and Temporary Brigadier in December 1939 and October 1941. Awarded the MC in 1916 for service in France and the CBE in 1941. While serving with the Royal Flying Corps, twice shot down within one week. During 1940 and 1941, a brigade commander in the Royal Marine Division and would have commanded the ground forces of various "Atlantic Islands" operations (the Azores, Canaries, Cape Verdes, and/or Madeira Islands) if contingency plans had been implemented.

30. Lieutenant John Andrew Bath, RM (1893–1929), commissioned in January 1912, and promoted to Captain in March 1917. Died on 26 July 1929 aboard HMS *Devonshire* in an accidental explosion in a gun turret. Awarded the DSC and the French Croix de Guerre for actions in Siberia in 1919.

31. General Sir Herbert Edward Blumberg (1869–1934), commissioned in February 1888, promoted General in January 1924, and retired in January 1926; created CB (1916) and KCB (1923), and received the Legion of Honour from France and the Order of the Redeemer from Greece. Between 30 November 1920 and 30 March 1924, served as the Adjutant General, Royal Marines. Also author of a history of the Corps in World War I: *Britain's Sea Soldiers: A Record of the Royal Marines during the War, 1914–1919* (Devonport, 1927).

32. HMS *Caesar:* Twin screw battleship (1896) of 14,900 tons and 16 guns of 4-inch caliber or higher.

33. Jerram has a "non-traditional" view on Churchill! Another perspective on the Churchill–Admiral Jerram relationship is preserved in the Admiral Jerram papers at the National Maritime Museum, Greenwich. In 1912, Churchill offered the then Rear Admiral Jerram the China Station, and then the more prestigious command of the Second Battle Squadron of the Home Fleet (of what would become the Grand Fleet in the First World War). Jerram replied to the latter offer by saying he could accept only if given the rank of Vice Admiral. Churchill then withdrew it, saying that officers of His Majesty's forces did not make conditions on their acceptance of assignments. Jerram then went to China for three years, after which he received command of the squadron and led it during the Battle of Jutland. Jerram stated he had to have Vice Admiral's pay in order to afford the expenses attendant to the command. National Maritime Museum Personal Papers Collection. Jerram Papers, JRM 16/1. Churchill letters dated 14 November, 5 December, and 19 December 1912, and rough drafts of two of Jerram's replies, no dates. This incident is not discussed, nor the correspondence reproduced, in Volume II, with its supporting documents volume, of the Randolph Churchill/Martin Gilbert multi-volume biography of Winston Churchill.

34. For a recent assessment of the implications for

Britain, a continental ground commitment, and the British Army (which would effect Jerram between 1915 and 1918), see Allan Mallinson, *1914: Fight the Good Fight—Britain, The Army, & the Coming of the First World War* (London, 2014).

Chapter 6

1. Chatham Division was disbanded after the World War II (1950) and its barracks complex, located outside the southern entrance to the dockyard, eventually demolished.

2. The Royal Naval Division, hastily raised, within three months fought at Antwerp, Ostende, and Dunkirk; later at Gallipoli; and, after that ill-fated campaign, on the Western Front. Its history was written by an officer who served with it: Douglas Jerrold, *The Royal Naval Division* (London, 1923). As Jerram indicates, in the operation in France some Royal Marines crossed the border into The Netherlands and were interned. A photo of the Non-Commissioned Officers and troops with a letter from one appeared in the Corps journal—with comment that the "Average Service 2 years 2 months," their age apparent in the picture. Morres served on the staff of the British Consul General of The Netherlands. "Prisoners of War Interned in Holland," *The Globe and Laurel*, Vol. XXV, No. 9, September 1914, 154–155; and "Biographical Notes. Major Eric Hody Mores, RMLI," *The Globe and Laurel*, Vol. XXVII, No. 10, October 1920, 133.

3. HMS *Euryalus*: One of six Cressy class vessels, completed in 1903, of 12,000 tons. Armament: two 9.2-inch guns, twelve 6-inch guns, twelve 12-pounders, and three 3-pounders; main batteries in turrets fore and aft, with main secondary armament enclosed along the port and starboard sides. Fred T. Jane, ed., *Jane's Fighting Ships, 1914*, 3rd ed. (London, 1914), 61.

4. Captain Eustace La Trobe Leatham, RN (1870–1935), eventually Vice Admiral, CB, plus awards from Belgium, France, Russia, and Japan. He assumed command on 1 August 1914.

5. Rear Admiral Arthur H. Christian, MVO (1863–1926), eventually Admiral, CB, MVO. His Southern Force also had two destroyer flotillas, one of ten submarines, and other attached ships.

6. The senior Marine in the squadron was Captain Harold Ozanne, RMLI (1879–1945), serving in HMS *Cressy*; the others, in order of seniority, were Captain Cuthbert Williams, RMLI (1881–1938), on HMS *Hogue*; Captain Clifford Field, RMLI (1882–1914), in HMS *Aboukir*, and Jerram in *Euryalus*.

7. The area off the German and Dutch coasts, from Heligoland, northwest of Cuxhaven, north of Wilhelmshaven, southwest past Emden/Borkum, to Bovard 14 Shoal off the western coast of The Netherlands. Why here? Exits existed where German vessels could enter the North Sea or English Channel; these areas also had extensive coastal defenses, thus precluding any British landings.

8. Harwich Force consisted of the 1st and 3rd Destroyer Flotillas, of 20 and 15 destroyers, respectively. If the German fleet challenged the Royal Navy in the North Sea, its task would have been to screen the Grand Fleet of Admiral Jellicoe.

9. HMS *Laurel* and HMS *Liberty* (1913), home ported at Chatham, were torpedo boat destroyers of 807 tons, with a speed of 21 knots, and armed with four 21-inch torpedoes and three 4-inch guns. *Lurcher*, Portsmouth based, was actually a special "I" Class vessel (1912) of 790 tons, with a speed of 32 knots, and armed with two 4-inch guns, two 12-pounders, and two 21-inch torpedoes.

10. The referenced officers: Commander Frank F. Rose, RN (1878–1955), eventually Vice Admiral and KCB, and Engineer Lieutenant Commander Edward H.T. Meeson, RN (1877–1916). Both received the DSO for this action, with Meeson specially promoted to Engineer Commander.

11. Jerram wrote *Bismarck*, but the ship was SMS *Mainz*, a German light cruiser (1909), 4362 tons, with a crew of 379, and twelve 4.1-inch guns, two 17.7-inch torpedoes, and 100 mines. The action is recounted in Sir Julian S. Corbett, *History of the Great War, Naval Operations: To the Battle of the Falklands, December 1914*. Vol. I (London, 1920), 118–119.

12. For an assessment of this disaster by Jerram's former commanding officer on *Suffolk* and echoing his, but from a different command perspective, see the comments of the then Rear Admiral Beatty to his wife in a letter from HMS *Lion* dated 19–13 September 1914. Ranft, ed., *The Beatty Papers, I*, 135–136.

13. This disaster occurred on 22 September 1914. It is discussed in Corbett, *History of the Great War, Naval Operations. Vol. I*, 171–177. For a recent analyses, see James Goldrick, *The King's Ships Were at Sea: The War in the North Sea, August 1914–February 1915* (Annapolis, 1984), 126–135. The obsolete cruisers were not the issue, but their crews. For a discussion of this and the why such a huge loss of life ensued, see Duncan Redford and Philip D. Grove, *The Royal Navy: A History since 1900* (London, 2014), 47–48; see also Nicholas Lambert, *The British Naval Staff in the First World War* (London, 2009), 110. The sinking sequence was *Aboukir*, *Hogue*, and *Cressy*; the loss of life: 1,459 officers and men, with only 60 officers and 777 men surviving. The submarine was the U-9 with only six torpedoes and a cruising range of just 1800 miles surfaced and 80 miles submerged. For contemporary accounts with photographs and drawings reflecting both analysis, unknowns, and wartime atmosphere, see H.W. Wilson and J.A. Hamilton, *The Great War: The Standard History of the All-Europe Conflict*, Vols. I and II (London, 1914 and 1915), 381, and 288–295 and 302–303, respectively); in this analysis, the obsolescence of the ships was noted (although built in 1900), i.e., not significant operational losses, whereas the loss of sailors was.

14. Jerram has misidentified the officer. The officers affected in sequence of sinkings were Field (*Aboukir*), Williams (*Hogue*) and then Ozanne (*Cressy*), with Field dying.

15. Western Patrol: Formed in August 1914, this was a combined Anglo-French patrol of four Royal Navy light cruisers and five armored cruisers, and two French light cruisers. It operated off the western entrance into the English Channel on a line between St. Alban's Head and Cherbourg, or east of a line between Portland and Cap de la Hague. Corbett, *Naval Operations, Vol. I*, 76.

16. Eventually Commander Alfred M. Williams, CBE, DSC, Royal Navy (1897–1985). Caerhays castle

is due west from Dodman Point, near Portholland on Veryan Bay, one half mile from the hamlet.

17. Unclear. Since 20 March 1913, the Commander-in-Chief, Plymouth, was Admiral Sir George LeClerc Egerton, KCB. *The Navy Lists* for August to October 1914 do not show a Midshipman Egerton serving in *Euryalus*; the only one by that name was the Honourable G.A. Egerton, serving in HMS *Implacable*.

18. Royal Naval Division: Raised by Churchill at the Admiralty in 1914, it originally could be considered a light infantry division without any organic fire support, i.e., artillery. Originally composed of one Royal Marine and two Royal Navy Brigades, it was later reorganized along Army lines and became the 63rd (Royal Naval) Division composed of 188th, 189th, and 190th Brigades. In the official history of the Division, Jerram is mentioned twice with both references to this appointment: Jerrold, *The Royal Naval Division,* 46 and 58.

19. Royal Hospital, Plymouth: The reference could be to Surgeon General William H. Norman, who assumed his post at the Royal Hospital, Plymouth, on 1 May 1914. There were too many (13) surgeons listed on the staff to identify the specific doctor who conducted the tests.

20. Brigadier Charles N. Trotman (1864–1929), commissioned in RMLI in September 1882, commander of the Royal Marine Brigade, retired as a full General with KCB in January 1923. Mentioned in despatches for Gallipoli in 1915 and France in 1916; also received the Legion of Honour and the Croix de Guerre from France.

21. Brigadier General Sir George Grey Aston, KCB (1861–1938), commissioned in the RMA in September 1879, first commander of the Royal Marine Brigade of the Royal Naval Division, promoted Major General in September 1917 on the day of his retirement. Wrote six books on strategy and defense policy, biographies of Nelson and Foch, a history of the Great War and another on the Secret Service, two on fishing, edited the 7th edition of Hamley's *Operations of War,* and penned a memoir: *Memories of a Marine: An Amphibiography* (London, 1919).

22. Invalided: Removed from active service for medical reasons.

23. Royal Naval Division: In 1914, the Corps had no permanent force to conduct amphibious operations, i.e., no organization, doctrine, or equipment. Britain's amphibious warfare capability consisted of raising ad hoc forces and landing them, ideally where the enemy wasn't! At this time, the Corps viewed its primary duty as service at sea with the Fleet—as Jerram makes all too clear.

24. Major General Sir Archibald Paris, KCB (1861–1937), commissioned in the RMA in September 1879; in 1914 a permanent Lieutenant Colonel, Brevet Colonel, and Temporary Brigadier General; promoted to Major General in October 1914 for command of the Royal Naval Division, and retired in June 1917 due to medical unfitness for further active service. Received the Croix de Guerre and Legion of Honour from France, and Order of Leopold from Belgium.

25. Commodore Oliver Backhouse, RN (1876–1943), eventually CB (1915) and Admiral (1934). Received the Legion of Honour and Croix de Guerre from France.

26. Eventually General Sir David Mercer, KCB (1864–1920), commissioned in the RMLI in February 1883, advanced to Temporary Brigadier in November 1914, and promoted to substantive rank of Major General on assuming the office of Adjutant General, Royal Marines in April 1916.

27. Sea Service: Jerram here addresses the traditional focus of his Corps by its assignment policies of officers during the war: Regulars with the Fleet, whilst the Royal Naval Division received temporary officers augmented by a few regulars. The Royal Marines thus viewed the major ground operations of The Great War as an aberration from the norm.

28. Temporary Officers: Officers commissioned for the duration of the war. They came from civilian life and could be assigned any duties, or men commissioned for service only with the Royal Naval Division. The planned accession of regular officers for 1914 proceeded, plus commissioning noncommissioned officers.

29. Major John A. Tupman, RMLI (1868–1938), commissioned in September 1888; promoted Major in July 1905; Paymaster at Deal in 1911; promoted Temporary Lieutenant Colonel in 1915, Brevet Lieutenant Colonel in 1916, and substantive Lieutenant Colonel in September 1918; and Colonel and retired in 1923. He succeeded Lieutenant Colonel Richard N. Bendyshe (1866–1915), who was killed at Gallipoli on 1 May 1915, as commander of the Deal Battalion. Jerrold, *The Royal Naval Division,* p. 119.

30. Lieutenant Colonel Cunliffe McNeile Parsons, RMLI (1865–1923), commissioned in February 1883, promoted Major General in January 1921, and retired for medical unfitness on 15 January 1923—and died six days later; made CB (1915), and Aide de Camp to the King (1919). Lieutenant Colonel Godfrey E. Matthews, CB, RMLI (1866–1917), commissioned in September 1884, promoted to Colonel Second Commandant in July 1915 and Temporary Brigadier in June 1916, and, whilst commanding 198 Infantry Brigade of the 66th Division (2nd/East Lancashire) Division, died of wounds received in action on 13 April 1917; awarded CMG (1915). Lieutenant Colonel Frank W. Luard, RMLI (1865–1915), commissioned in September 1884, promoted to Colonel Second Commandant in June 1915, and, whilst commanding the Portsmouth Battalion, killed in action at Gallipoli on 14 July 1915.

31. For accounts of this action, which can be considered either as a traditional "age of sail" operation or a precursor of the modern amphibious raid, see Robert Rhodes James, *Gallipoli* (London, 1965), 44–45; Alan Moorehead, *Gallipoli* (New York, 1956), 54–57; Jerrold, *The Royal Naval Division,* 63–65; and L.A. Carlyon, *Gallipoli* (London, 2003), 80–81.

32. Lieutenant John Frederick May, RM (1871–1915), in September 1914 commissioned from the ranks (Sergeant Major) after 24 years of service. Killed in action at Gallipoli on 25 April 1915.

33. Captain Reginald Dawson Hopcraft Lough, RMLI (1885–1958), commissioned in January 1903, promoted to Lieutenant General in August 1940, and retired in January 1941. Awarded DSO (1916) and OBE (1919), and the Croix de Guerre by France (1916).

34. Major Arthur Edward Bewes, RMLI (1871–1922), commissioned in September 1890; appointed Barracksmaster, Deal, and Lieutenant Colonel in Jan-

uary 1917; and retired in July 1920, due to medical unfitness from wounds received in action at Gallipoli.

35. 29th Division: A regular army division composed of 86, 87, and 88 Infantry Brigades. It landed at Gallipoli on 25 April 1915 and remained there until evacuated on the night of 7/8 January 1916.

36. Acting Lieutenant Charles Broadhurst Conybeare, RM (1896–1926), commissioned in October 1913 and promoted to Captain in October 1917. Participated in the raid on Zeebrugge in April 1918. Awarded the French (1920) and Belgian (1921) Croix de Guerre. Died of tuberculosis while on active service.

37. Acting Lieutenant Francis Cecil Law, RM (1895–1958), commissioned in October 1913, promoted to Major in January 1932, placed on half pay in October 1936, and retired in October 1938. Wounded at Gallipoli on 25 April 1915, and later awarded DSC (1916) and the French Croix de Guerre (1920).

38. DCM: The Distinguished Conduct Medal was awarded only to troops and noncommissioned officers for gallantry in the field. Jerram here addresses a perennial Corps issue: Lack of appropriate recognition in honors and awards.

Chapter 7

1. For a recent succinct overview of the origins and flawed execution of Gallipoli, see Alan Mallinson, "Welcome to hell—the Gallipoli campaign of 1915," *The Times*, 12 April 2015. This is part of a series titled "1914 The First World War 1918." Mallinson, a retired British Army colonel and military historian, stresses that the theatre and fighting in Gallipoli was worse than on the Western Front—and explains why.

2. For assessments by two of Jerram's Royal Marine peers who were there, see Donald F. Bittner, "Dreadful!!! Two Royal Marine Officers Views and Analyses of Gallipoli While There, March–August 1915," *Journal of the Society for Army Historical Research*, Vol. 83, No. 336, Winter 2005, 309–326.

3. The references are to General Sir Ian Hamilton, GCB, DSO (1853–1947), the land commander of the Gallipoli operation, and later KCMG; and to Major General A.C. Hunter-Weston, CB, DSO (1864–1940), commanding general of the 29th Division and later VIII Corps, later Lieutenant General, KCB. A succinct assessment of what later occurred, especially in June and July 1915, is in Peter Hart, *Gallipoli* (Oxford, 2009), 272–274.

4. Jerram cited the two books on Gallipoli as of when he wrote; he believed Robert Rhodes James had recounted the essence of what occurred there. Since then, more literature has appeared, e.g., Michael Hickey, *Gallipoli* (London, 1995) which gives appropriate attention to the Corps at Gallipoli and, for a transnational perspective, Tim Travers, *Gallipoli, 1915* (Stroud, Glous., 2001). For assessments primarily from the Ottoman perspective, see two recent studies by Edward J. Erickson: *Gallipoli: The Ottoman Campaign* (Barnsley, South Yorkshire, 2015); in his introduction, Erickson quotes historian George H. Casar that Gallipoli has produced "more books in the English speaking world" than any other campaign of the Great War (p. xi); he also divides the campaign into four distinct phases (p. xiv). In *Gallipoli: Command under Fire* (London, 2015), Erickson focuses on the command (and control) function and military effectiveness, and how the defenders responded to the various crises during the campaign. For a recent international perspective (minus the French), see Major General Julian Thompson, CB, OBE, Dr. Peter Pedersen, and Dr. Haluk Oral, *Gallipoli* (2015). Two useful references for Gallipoli with maps and commentary are Martin Gilbert, *Atlas of the First World War: The Complete History*, 2nd ed. (New York, 1994), 35, 38, and 39; and Tonie and Valmai Holt, *Major and Mrs. Holt's Guide to Gallipoli* (Barnsley, 2000).

5. The manuscript spelling is "Cole," but Jerram is referring to Lieutenant Colonel A.S. Koe, 1st Battalion, KOSB, who was killed on "Y" Beach on 25 April 1915. Koe's date of rank was 10 November 1913, while Matthews' Army date of rank was 16 April 1909 ... C. F. Aspinall-Oglander, *Military Operations: Gallipoli, I* (London, 1929), 202. See also Elaine McFarland, *"A Slashing Man of Action": The Life of Lieutenant General Sir Aylmer Hunter-Weston, MP* (Bern, 2014), 153-156.

6. Jerram generously understates a missed opportunity after the landing on "Y" Beach—and the consequences for ensued when the *River Clyde* beached and tried to land her troops at "V" Beach at Cape Helles. See the cited references for discussion of this.

7. Billy: A pot, kettle, square tin, or re-used tin in which water was boiled for tea and food was cooked.

8. Lance Corporal Walter R. Parker, VC, RMLI (1881–1936), Portsmouth Battalion, for gallantry at Gaba Tepe, 30 April 1915. See Matthew G. Little, "Lance Corporal Walter Richard Parker," *The Royal Marines & the Victoria Cross* (Southsea, 2002), 22–24.

9. Captain Edward Allen Smeathman Hatton, RMLI (1883–1915), commissioned in September 1901 and promoted Captain in September 1912. Killed in action at Anzac Beach on 29 April 1915.

10. Captain George Pinkard Lathbury, RMLI (1883–1957), commissioned in September 1902, promoted Major in September 1918, and retired in June 1920. Awarded the DSC, and Croix de Guerre from France, in 1916.

11. Reflective of this, Portsmouth Battalion officer casualties at Gallipoli were high. Of 49 Royal Marine officers killed at Gallipoli, 17 came from this battalion. Editor's compilation from diverse sources.

12. Major Harold Gage Bewes Armstrong, RMLI (1877–1915), commissioned in September 1896, promoted Major in August 1913, and killed in action on 5 May 1915 at "Quinn's Post" while with Portsmouth Battalion. References to Quinn's Post (also known as the Chessboard because of the network of trenches which evolved) and Courtenay's Post were to locations named after officers associated with their defense. See, for example, John Laffin, *Damn the Dardanelles! The Story of Gallipoli* (Sydney, 1980), 76 78, 80, 82, 110–111, and 119; and Peter Stanley, *Quinn's Post, Anzac, Gallipoli* (Crows Nest, NSW Australia, 2005), chaps. 2 and 3.

13. Lieutenant General Sir W.R. Birdwood, CB, CSI, KCMG, CIE, DSO (1865–1951), Commander of the Australian and New Zealand Army Corps; later Field Marshal, GCB, GCSI, GCMG, GCVO, First Baron of Anzac and Totnes.

14. The reference is to Major Hugh Quinn (1888–1915), 15th Australian Battalion, Australian Imperial Force, killed on 29 May 1915. Quinn did not receive the Victoria Cross, but was Mentioned in Despatches. In civilian life, he was an auditor and public accountant from Townsville, Queensland. C.E.W. Bean, *Official History of Australia in the War of 1914–18. Volume I. From the Outbreak of the War to the End of the First Phase of the Gallipoli Campaign, May 4, 1915* (Sydney, 1938), 579; and Stanley, *Quinn's Post, Anzac, Gallipoli*, 35.

15. Achi Baba, the dominating terrain overlooking the Cape Helles beaches and the British positions inland from them. All attacks to capture it failed after the landing force delayed in doing so after the landings on 25 April 1915. The Turkish defense of and attacks from it were continuous throughout the Gallipoli campaign.

16. The 42nd (East Lancashire) Division: A Territorial Army Division, composed of the 125th (Lancashire Fusiliers), 126th (East Lancashire), and 127th (Manchester) Brigades. Served at Gallipoli from February 1915 to January 1916.

17. Shrapnel: Jerram is technically correct, but artillery rounds since them have evolved to achieve the same effect, e.g., air bursts with various types of fuses to achieve this.

18. Major Maurice Christian Festing, RMLI (1879–1931), commissioned in September 1898 and promoted brevet Lieutenant Colonel in December 1922. Awarded the DSO (1918) and the French Croix de Guerre (1917). Transferred to the Royal Tank Corps in November 1923 and died in a British military hospital in Burma in the rank of Colonel whilst serving as chief of staff (GSO-1) of the 4th Indian Division. *The Army List, July 1931* (London, 1931), 78 and 157. For his career, with various overlappings with that of Lieutenant Colonel Jerram, see his detailed obituary: "Obituary. [Colonel Maurine C. Festing, DSO, psc]," *The Globe and Laurel*, Vol. XL, No. 1, January 1932, 28–29. He left Gallipoli suffering from dysentery. Festing was commissioned three years prior to Jerram (in 1898) but by the end of the First World War their duties, positions, and rank had closed that gap.

19. Brigade Major, or chief of staff. A brief description of the British staff system, and how Jerram served within it with the Army during the war, is in Allan Mallinson, *The Making of the British Army: From the English Civil War to the War on Terrorism* (London, 2009), 274–275; see also Mallinson, *1914: Fight the Good Fight*, 62–63.

20. The 52nd (Lowland) Division-A First Line Territorial Force Division, composed of the 155th (South Scottish), the 156th (Scottish Rifle), and the 157th (Highland Light Infantry) Brigades. Served at Gallipoli from June 1915 to January 1916.

21. This section of the manuscript reads August, an uncorrected error although the 52nd Division was also in a similar attack in August. The corrected month is in brackets.

22. Jerram assumed this position on 18 June 1915.

23. This attack occurred on 12 July 1915, and is described (with Jerram's point) by Hickey, *Gallipoli*, chap. 21, notably page 23. It continued the next day, with the decimation of the Chatham, Portsmouth, and Nelson Battalions of the Royal Naval Division. Both James and Travers vividly, succinctly, and critically describe the attacks and effect on both divisions: James, *Gallipoli*, pp. 231–232, and Travers, *Gallipoli*, 136–139.

24. Lieutenant General Hunter-Weston, who commanded the VIII Corps from 24 May to 17 July 1915. He was succeeded by Lieutenant General Francis John Davies, CB (1864–1948), eventually General (retired 1926), KCB, KCMG, KCVO. Hunter-Weston again commanded the Corps in France from 1916 to 1918.

25. Major Ernest Frederick Powys Sketchley, RMLI (1881–1916), commissioned in January 1900, promoted temporary Major in September 1914, awarded the DSO (1915) and died on 12 October 1916 of wounds received on the Somme.

26. DSO: Distinguished Service Order (DSO), second highest (next to the Victoria Cross) award for gallantry in action or exemplary leadership against an enemy.

27. ADC: Captain Charles T.J.G. Walmesby, RM, an officer with a temporary commission for service in the Royal Naval Division.

28. Lieutenant Colonel Edward George Evelegh, RMLI (1865–1915), commissioned in September 1885, promoted substantive Lieutenant Colonel in November 1910, and killed in action at Krithia, Gallipoli, on 13 July 1915.

29. Captain David J. Gowney, RM (1876–1936), commissioned from the ranks (with over 24 years' service) on 20 September 1914, promoted Major (1918), and retired in May 1926. Awarded the DSC and DSM.

30. Lieutenant Eric B.C. Dougherty, RM (1896–1915), commissioned in August 1914 and killed in action on 13 July 1915 at Gallipoli while serving with Portsmouth Battalion.

31. Lieutenant Commander Henry D. King, RNVR (1877–1930). Initially second in command of Drake (1st) Battalion of the 1st Brigade, Royal Naval Division. Eventually Commodore, and PC, CB, CBE, DSO, ADC, and Member of Parliament (1918–1930).

32. RASC: The Royal Army Service Corps dealt with transportation and supply. It assumed the form known by Jerram in 1885 as the Army Service Corps, and became the Royal Army Service Corps in 1918.

33. "W" Beach: One of the six original landing breaches at Cape Helles. It is located on the northwestern tip of the Gallipoli peninsula.

34. The references could be to either or both General Sir Charles C. Monro, CB, commander of Gallipoli and Salonika (later GCMG, GCB, GCSI, Bt.,) or to Lieutenant General Sir William R. Birdwood, former ANZAC Corps commander and in command at the peninsula itself; and Lieutenant General Davies as VIII Corps commander.

35. The *River Clyde* carried men of various regiments and beached at "V" Beach on 25 April 1915, at the southwestern tip of the Gallipoli peninsula at the entrance to the Dardanelles. The planned expeditious debarkation of troops failed disastrously due to Turkish machine guns emplaced above the beach which were ably and courageous manned.

36. HMS *Prince George:* A Majestic class battleship (1894) of 14,900 tons, with four 12-inch guns, twelve 6-inch guns, ten 12-pounders, and four 3-pounders.

37. A vague reference, possibly the *Britannic*, sister ship of the *Titanic*.

38. Lieutenant Colonel Edward James Stroud, RMLI (1867–1933), commissioned in November 1892, promoted Lieutenant General in January 1924, and retired in April 1925. Awarded CB (1922) and CMG (1916). Married in August 1918 the widow of Captain Herbert Claude Morton, RMLI (1880–1914), drowned on 26 November 1914 in the loss of HMS *Bulwark*. At the time of the evacuation, Stroud was the Commanding Officer, 2nd Brigade, Royal Naval Division; Jerram was still Brigade Major.

39. Rear Admiral John M. de Robeck (1862–1928), later Admiral of the Fleet, GCB, GCMG, GCVO, Bt.

Chapter 8

1. Many reference works are available for operations on the Western Front. In addition to the aforementioned Gilbert, *Atlas of the First World War: The Complete History*, two other valuable ones are: Arthur Banks, *A Military Atlas of the First World War* (Barnsley, South Yorkshire, 1994), and the more detailed Mark Adkin, *The Western Front Companion: The Complete Guide to How the Armies Fought for Four Devastating Years, 1914–1918* (London, 2013). Also, the Commonwealth War Graves Commission website (http://www.cwgc.org/) provides information on specific battlefield sites and cemeteries on the Western Front, including all of those mentioned by Jerram in his memoir.

2. The biographies of officers mentioned by Jerram indicate a high mortality rate. However, the Royal Marines assigned *most* of their regular officers at sea with the fleet, in other traditional duties, or, for a minority, on seconded assignments such as Jerram's subsequent postings in World War I. In reality, regular officer corps fatalities were so few that the perennial problem of promotion in the Corps was not affected by the war. For a discussion of this, see Donald F. Bittner, *A Ghost of a General and the R. M. Officer Corps of 1914. Royal Marines Historical Society Special Publication No. 6*. R. W. Walker, *To What End Did They Die? Officers Died at Gallipoli* (Worcester, 1985), lists 48 Royal Marine officers, of all types of commissions, units, and assignments, who died at Gallipoli; there were actually 49: Walker omitted Captain Guy S. Perkins (1886–1915), who died on 23 November 1915.

3. Although he provides no dates, Jerram must be referring to the period of 26–30 November 1915 which saw a combination of rain, gale force winds, snow, and three days of temperatures below freezing. For a vivid description, to include comments on open trenches and frostbite, see Jerrold, *Royal Naval Division*, 158.

4. Captain Ernest John Bocart Tagg, RMLI (1885–1947), commissioned in September 1904, advanced to temporary major in 1918, transferred in 1919 to the Durham Light Infantry, and eventually Colonel, King's Own Yorkshire Light Infantry. Awarded the OBE and DSO. Wounded in action at Gallipoli, June 1915.

5. Brigades: British Army First World War divisions had three infantry brigades. Brigade numbers generally indicated their parent division: Multiply the division number by three, with the resulting figure the number of the middle brigade, with the other two brigades numbered one above and one below it. Thus, for the 63rd (Royal Naval) Division: 63 × 3 = 189, hence 188th, 189th, and 190th Brigades.

6. MC: The Military Cross (MC) is a British gallantry award, ranking below the Victoria Cross (VC), Distinguished Service Order (DSO), and the Distinguished Service Cross (DSC). Captain St. Clair-Morford was then serving with 2/RMLI.

7. The Somme: Many parts of the Somme battlefield are well preserved with appropriate memorials and cemeteries, including the area around Beaumont Hamel. For a brief account of this battle, the state of the battlefield today, and guide to sites, see Tonie and Valmai Holt, *Major and Mrs. Holt's Guide to The Somme*, 6th ed., rev. (Barnsley, South Yorkshire, 2012). Many histories of The Somme have been written. A recent one, with an appendix listing the divisions, with their respective brigades and battalions which composed each, is Peter Hart, *The Somme: The Darkest Hour on the Western Front* (New York, 2008); the 63rd (Royal Naval) Division and its composition is on page 558.

8. The date of this incident was 12 October 1916. The records of service of both General Paris (ADM 196/61, p. 267) and Major Sketchley (ADM 196/63, p. 89) give this date, as do supporting documents attached to them. Jerrold, *The Royal Naval Division*, 186–187, erroneously dates this on 14 October 1916. Paris was placed on the retired list on 20 June 1917 as "unfit for further service owing to wounds." He assessed the raising and capability of the Royal Naval Division in "The Royal Naval Division, 1914–18," Royal Marines Museum, Eastney, Southsea, Portsmouth, Hampshire. (Archives 2/2/2.).

9. Major General Cameron Shute, CB, CMG (1866–1936), commanded from 14 October 1916 to 19 February 1917. Originally commissioned in the Welch Regiment, he later transferred to the Rifle Brigade, and retired in 1931 as General. Eventually KCB, KCMG. For a brief Corps commentary, see "The Royal Marines in the Great War, 1914 [sic]." *Globe and Laurel*, April 1920, Vol. XXVII, No. 4, 70. For an historian's assessment of the sour relationship between Shute and the 63rd (Royal Naval) Division, see Hart, *The Somme*, 503–508—and the ensuing battle (509–515).

10. Barnshute: In his views written decades later, Jerram reflects the views of the officers and troops of the division of 1916. Troops played upon their commander's name and nickname; for examples, Max Arthur, "That Shit Shute," *When This Bloody War Is Over: Soldiers Songs of the First World War* (London, 2001), 90; Arthur provides a succinct background on Shute's relations with the Royal Naval Division and the four stanzas of the song—a negative and dirty (in more ways than one) ditty about the disliked division commander. See also the four stanza poem by Captain A.P. Herbert of Hawke Battalion, quoted in Hart, *The Somme*, 506. Jerram is being discreet in not defining the meaning; he knew, as implied in his text.

11. Lieutenant Colonel Cecil Faber Aspinall-Oglander, CMG (1878–1959), of the Royal Munster Fusiliers; retired in 1920 as a Brigadier General, eventually CB, CMG, DSO. Also author of the British Army's official history of the Gallipoli campaign.

12. Lieutenant Colonel Alexander Richard Hamilton Hutchinson, CMG, RMLI (1871–1930), commissioned February 1889, eventually Adjutant General, Royal Marines (1924–27), promoted General June

1927, and retired April 1928. Awarded KCB (1927), CMG (1916), and DSO (1917).

13. Brigadier General the Honourable Charles John Sackville-West, CMG, psc (1870–1962), originally commissioned in the King's Royal Rifle Corps. Eventually Major General, KBE, CB, CMG.

14. Blumberg, *Britain's Sea Soldiers*, 317–336; see also Jerrold, *The Royal Naval Division*, chap. XI.

15. Brigadier General William C.G. Heneker, DSO (1867–1939). Originally commissioned in the Connaught Rangers, later transferred to the North Staffordshire Regiment, retiring in 1920 as a General. Eventually KCB, KCMG, DSO.

16. In the 1960s, Jerram and Major General J.L. Moulton, CB, DSO, OBE (1906–1993), engaged in an extensive correspondence on this issue, with Jerram raising the issue of correcting the record. Moulton's wise counsel was, after so many years, let the issue lie. Copies of correspondence in editor's possession.

17. The 37th Division was a New Army Division, originally numbered 44 but the designation was changed; it formed part of the 2nd New Army.

18. The British Army Staff College, Camberley, was located next to the Royal Military College (now Academy) Sandhurst, in Surrey, but the two entities were separate military commands.

19. Brigadier General Charles Edward Lawrie, CB, DSO (1864–1953). Originally commissioned in the Royal Artillery, retired as a Major General in 1920.

20. Various official documents give three dates for Jerram's secondment to the British Army: 21, 22, and 24 January 1917. The date in his official record of service is 21 January 1917.

21. 31st Division: A New Army Division, raised from Yorkshire and Lancashire. Originally numbered 38, but changed in 1915 to 31.

22. Major General Robert Wanless-O'Gowan, CB (and later CMG) (1864–1947). Originally commissioned in the Scottish Rifles, but later transferred to the East Lancashire Regiment.

23. For a detailed explanation of the British staff system by the end of the war, see Major G.R.N. Collins, *Military Organization and Administration* (London, 1918). A succinct assessment is in John A. English, *The Canadian Army and the Normandy Campaign: A Study of Failure in High Command* (New York, 1991), pp. 92–97.

24. Lieutenant Colonel Wilfred B. Spender (1876–1960), commissioned in the Royal Artillery in June 1897, promoted Captain in February 1902, retired in August 1913 over the Ulster question, and recalled to active service during the war. Eventually, KCB, CBE, DSO, and MC, and Permanent Secretary, Ministry of Finance and Head of Civil Service, Northern Ireland.

25. Captain John Howard Stafford, MC, Royal Engineers, commissioned in July 1910, and promoted Brevet Major in June 1919. (War Diary, 31st Division, February 1917. WO 95/2342.).

26. Much of the ensuing action of the 31st Division described by Jerram occurred in the Gommecourt area, eight miles north of Albert. The area is within The Somme battlefield.

27. At this time, 5th Army was composed of the following corps: II, V, VIII, X, XIII, Canadian, and I Anzac.

28. Hindenburg Line: German defensive line, about 100 miles in length, running in general from east of Arras through St. Quentin (significant to Jerram in 1918) to Rheims.

29. The 19th (Western) Division was part of the 2nd New Army, raised from Lancashire, Warwickshire, Gloucestershire, Staffordshire, Cheshire, and Wales.

30. The 58th (2nd/1st London) Division was a Second Line (or reserve) Territorial Force division.

31. The 46th (North Midland) Division was a First Line Territorial Force division; for further details, see chapter 9.

32. General Sir Hubert de la Poer Gough (1870–1963), General Officer Commanding, 5th Army, 1916–18. Originally commissioned in the 16th Lancers. Eventually GCB, GCMG, KCVO. At the time, the 31st Division was part of 5th Army, but soon was transferred to the 1st Army.

33. Vimy Ridge is considered the turning point in the evolution of the Canadian Army. For a history of the battle, see Brereton Greenhous and Stephen J. Harris, *Canada and the Battle of Vimy Ridge, 9–12 April, 1917* (Ottawa, 1992).

34. The Gavrelle village area is located approximately seven miles northeast of Arras.

35. Jerrold, *The Royal Naval Division*, chaps. XI to XIV, and Blumberg, *Britain's Sea Soldiers*, chap. 26.

36. The Oppy Wood area, located northeast of Arras, was part of the Hindenburg Line and thus heavily defended in every way.

37. The Royal Marines Museum is currently located in the former officers' mess of the now closed Royal Marine Barracks, Eastney, Southsea, Portsmouth, Hampshire. Now part of the National Museum of the Royal Navy, plans are to move the museum (to include its library and archives) to the dockyard, Portsmouth in 2019.

38. XIII Corps was commanded by Lieutenant General Sir Frederick W.N. McCracken, KCB, DSO (1859–1949), commissioned in the 49th Foot (later Royal Berkshire Regiment). It was composed of the 5th, 31st, and 63rd (Royal Naval) Divisions and was part of 1st Army.

39. All the armies on the Western Front established schools in the rear areas behind the front lines. For a fictional commentary on such schools, see Siegfried Sassoon, *The Complete Memoirs of George Sherston* (London, 1937), chap. I, "At the Army School" in "Memoirs of an Infantry Officer."

40. The implications are clear: Jerram desired instructors who had proved themselves in combat via leadership and courage under fire. With the high casualties amongst such leaders, this also ensured they survived both to teach younger officers and for service later in the war.

41. The 5th Division was originally a regular army division and part of the original British Expeditionary Force sent to France in 1914. Brigades were transferred into and from it.

42. Jerram addresses, and reflects upon here and later, the misunderstandings and poor communication between the line and headquarters staff. This type of Clausewitzian friction is inevitable, and good commanders and staff officers strive to overcome it.

43. Brigadier General Ian Stewart (1874–1941), DSO, later also CMG (1919). Originally commissioned in the Scottish Rifles, retired in 1921.

44. The reference is to the series of German offensives in the spring of 1918. After containing them, the Allies launched their own offensives which culminated in the Armistice of 11 November 1911. (See chapter 9).

45. Embusque: In the First World War, a term connotating avoiding dangerous duty, i.e., combat. For a discussion of this as it relates to British headquarters in World War I, see Tim Travers, *The Killing Ground: The British Army and the Experience of Modern Warfare, 1900–1918* (London, 1987), 105.

46. Actually the 56th (1st) London Division, a prewar 1st Line Territorial Force unit.

47. There are many accounts of the German offensives of 1918. A succinct assessment is in Hew Strachan, *The First World War* (New York, 2003), Chap. 9; Strachan also addresses German munitions production and quality of the Reich's shells.

48. XVII Corps was composed of the 25th, 46th, and 51st Divisions. It was commanded by Lieutenant General Sir Charles Fergusson, Bt. (1865–1951), originally commissioned in the Grenadier Guards, retired from the Army in 1922, and died in 1951; eventually GCB, GCMG, MVO, and DSO.

49. The 3rd and 4th Divisions were originally regular army divisions and part of the British Expeditionary Force of 1914. The 15th (Scottish) Division was part of the 2nd New Army.

Chapter 9

1. The 46th Division, a First Line Territorial Force Infantry Division, was comprised of the 137th (Staffordshire), 138th (Lincolnshire and Leicester), and 139th (Sherwood Forester) Brigades. Mobilized on 4 August 1914, in March 1915 it assembled in France—thus being the initial territorial division to arrive in an overseas theatre in the war. Major A.F. Becke, RFA (Ret.), *Order of Battle of Divisions. Part 2A. The Territorial Force Mounted Divisions and the 1st-Line Territorial Force Divisions (42–56)* (London, 1936), 61–67. The British Army was composed of four types of forces: Regulars, Reservists, Territorial Forces, and New Army; *Mallinson, 1914: Fight the Good Fight*, 78–91 and 515–516. See also K.W. Mitchinson, *The Territorial Force at War, 1914–1916* (London, 2014).

2. Jerram was now chief of staff of a division with a permanent rank of Major. The 46th Division's key commanders and staff officers are listed in Major R. E. Priestly, MC, RE, *Breaking the Hindenburg Line: The Story of the 46th (North Midland) Division* (London, 1919), Appendix V: Order of Battle, September 29th, 1918. Jerram is listed as GSO1 on page 180. The same information is in a new history of the division; Simon Peaple, *Mud, Blood and Determination: The History of the 46th (North Midlands) in the Great War* (Solihull, West Midlands, 2015), Appendix II.

3. Major General William Thwaites (1868–1947), originally commissioned in the Royal Artillery in February 1887, eventually General and made KCB and KCMG; commanded the division from 8 July 1916 to 2 September 1918.

4. Brigadier General John Vaughn Campbell (1876–1944), commissioned in the Coldstream Guards in September 1896, commanded his regiment (1923–27), and retired in 1933 as a Brigadier. Awarded the VC (1916), CMG (1918), and DSO (1900).

5. Brigadier General Frank George Mathias Rowley (1866–1949), commissioned in January 1886 in the Middlesex Regiment, and retired as a Brigadier. Awarded the CB (1919), CMG (1915), and DSO (1918).

6. Brigadier General John Harington (1873–1943), commissioned in the Rifle Brigade in April 1895, and wounded four times in World War I. Awarded the CB (1927), CMG (1919), and DSO (1915).

7. Brigadier General Sir Smith Hill Child, Bt. (1880–1958), commissioned in the Irish Guards and served in the Boer War. Eventually GCVO (1941), CB (1919), CMG (1918), and DSO (1916). Served in Parliament from 1918 to 1922.

8. Bruay, located approximately four miles (or six kilometers) southwest of Bethune and 16 miles (or 26 kilometers) northwest of Arras.

9. French Officer: Not identifiable in the War Diary of the 46th (North Midland) Division for 1918: TNA, WO 95/2665 and 2666; nor could the French military archives at Vincennes provide his name.

10. The Brigade Major and Staff Captain, respectively, were Captain Archie Cecil Thomas White, VC, MC (1891–1971), originally commissioned in the Yorkshire Regiment, with a later career in the Royal Army Education Corps and retired as a Colonel; and Captain I. Jackson, MC, East Yorkshire Regiment. Both were New Army officers.

11. Lieutenant Colonel Francis H. Dorling, DSO, Chief of Staff of the 46th Division from 13 October 1917 to 22 July 1918. Commissioned in September 1897, and later colonel (1930–1947) of the Manchester Regiment.

12. Portuguese: The reference is to the 2nd Portuguese Division serving with 1st Army, defeated near Estaires (approximately seven miles or 11 kilometers) west of Armentieres in the German offensive of April 1918. Portugal had two divisions serving on the Western Front. Their service is detailed in the military museum in Porto, Portugal.

13. Brevet Major William Neilson, DSO, commissioned in July 1915 as a Lieutenant in the Canadian 107th East Kootenay Regiment. He served as the GSO-2 of the 46th Division between 21 March and 25 August 1918, thence served in the Royal Canadian Regiment. Neilson signed orders and messages as "J. W. Neilson." (46th Division War Diaries, WO 95/2665 and 2666).

14. Lieutenant Colonel Isaac William Burns-Lindow, DSO (1868–1946), commissioned in January 1892, severely wounded in the Boer War, and retired from the 8th Hussars in 1904; in 1914, on retired pay and a Major in the South Irish Horse; promoted Lieutenant Colonel in 1917. Eventually High Sheriff of Cumberland and himself a Master of the Foxhounds, South Union.

15. Lieutenant Colonel William Humphrey May Freestun, DSO (1878–1964), commissioned in May 1889 in the Somerset Light Infantry, eventually, Colonel and CMG (1919). Retired, 1934, recalled for World War II (Commandant, P.O.W. Camp, 1939–42).

16. Corbie, just over nine miles or 15 kilometers east of Amiens.

17. St. Quentin is due east of Amiens, north of Soissons, and northwest of Reims. Travel time is about one hour.

18. The reference is to Lieutenant Colonel Charles

Louis Brooke, RMA (1868–1938), in 1918 the Deputy Assistant Adjutant General, Royal Marines. Commissioned in September 1885, promoted Lieutenant Colonel in September 1916, retired in May 1921 and promoted to Colonel. Made CB (1919). Brooke's career encompassed sea duty and administrative headquarters staff duty.

19. St. Pol-sur-Ternoise: Approximately 29 kilometers southwest of Bethune and 34 kilometers west-north-west of Arras.

20. Major General Sir Gerald Farrell Boyd, KCB, CMG, DSO, DCM (1877–1930). Boyd enlisted in the Devonshire Regiment in 1895 and received the DCM in the Boer War. Commissioned in 1900 in the East Yorkshire Regiment, later transferred to the Leinster Regiment and then the Royal Irish Regiment. During the First World War, served as Brigadier General, General Staff, 5th Army; Brigade Commander, 170th Infantry Brigade; and General Officer Commanding, 46th Division. Later, commanded the Dublin District, Ireland; Commandant, Indian Army Staff College, Quetta, 1923–27; and, from 1927 until his death in 1930, Military Secretary to the Secretary of State for War.

21. Jerram is addressing two traits of a good commander and leader: Set the proper example and keep the troops informed. In the 21st century, General Tony Zinni, USMC (Ret.) and General Peter Pace, USMC (Ret.) have addressed this key point in presentations to field grade officers of many countries and services.

22. For a complete summary of Neilson's career and glimpses into his post-war service, see Major R.C. Fetherstonhaugh, *The Royal Canadian Regiment, 1833–1933* (Fredericton, New Brunswick, 1936), 406–410, and 426.

23. Identified; full name and regiment withheld.

24. The reference is to Lieutenant Colonel Ralph Duckworth, DSO, commissioned in December 1899 in the South Staffordshire Regiment.

25. The reference is to either Major Kenneth Greenville Williams (1892–1972), originally commissioned in 1912 in the Northumberland Fusiliers, later Lieutenant-Colonel, OBE, the DAAG; or (temporary) Major H.N. Forbes, MC, DCM, commissioned in 1917 in the 5th (Royal Irish) Lancers, the DAQMG.

26. Studies have appeared (and still are) of the British approach to World War I. For example, Travers, *The Killing Ground*, and Tim Travers, "The Evolution of British Strategy and Tactics on the Western Front in 1918: GHQ, Manpower, and Technology," *The Journal of Military History*, April 1990, 173–200; Shelford Bidwell and Dominick Graham, *Fire-Power: British Army Weapons and Theories of War, 1901–1945* (London, 1982); and J.H. Johnson, *Stalemate: The Great Trench Warfare battles of 1915–1917* (London, 1995). See also the recent work of William Philpott, to include *Attrition: Fighting the First World War* (London, 2014), which challenges the concept of the return to mobile and open warfare in 1918, especially chap. 14, "Victory on All Fronts."

27. Pontruet: Less than two kilometers (or approximately 1.2 miles) southwest of Bellenglise.

28. The 1st Division, a regular Army division, served in France from August 1914 till 1918.

29. The reference is to the U.S. Army's II Corps, composed of the 27th and 30th Divisions. An American division was larger than those of the British, German, or French, or 28,000 as compared to 14,000, 13,000, and 12,000, respectively. II Corps was the only U.S. corps operating for a sustained period of time under British operational control, as A.E.F. policy was to employ its units as a separate American army, with most of it located in the area near Verdun (from where its St. Michiel and Meuse-Argonne offensives would be based).

30. The 32nd Division, a New Army Division, originally numbered 39 but later redesignated as the 32nd.

31. The terrain, German defenses, British preparations, and the ensuing operations are discussed in detail in Priestly, *Breaking the Hindenburg Line: The Story of the 46th (North Midland) Division*, especially Part I, "The Battle of Bellenglise, 29th September 1918." Priestly included maps plus photographs of the St. Quentin Canal, aerial photos of the defensive area, and pictures of the main commanders and junior personnel decorated for gallantry; the volume does not include a photograph of the division's Chief of Staff, i.e., Jerram. For a photograph of Brigadier Campbell addressing his troops of 137 Brigade from the Riqueval Bridge over the canal tunnel entrance, see Adkin, *The Western Front Companion*, 80. Some of the troops are still wearing life preservers.

32. In October 1918, a Territorial Division on the Western Front rated two artillery brigades, one machine gun battalion, and three field engineer companies. Each artillery brigade possessed thirty-six 18-pounders and twelve 4.5-inch howitzers; and the machine gun battalion had four companies, each with sixteen Vickers machine guns. In addition, the division had two medium trench mortar batteries, each possessing six 2-inch mortars. Becke, *Order of Battle of Divisions, Part 2A*, 151.

33. Jerram addressed the use of the term "if possible" in a fiery letter to the Corps' journal just prior to his death: "If Possible," *The Globe and Laurel*, Vol. LXXIV, No. 3, June 1966, 189.

34. Officially, the battle of the St. Quentin Canal, on the Hindenburg Line, lasted five days: 29 September to 2 October 1918. Tony Ball, "Battle and the British Army: A Comparative Study of Battle Duration," *Journal of the Society for Army Historical Research*, Vol. XCII, Summer, 2014, No. 370, 137.

35. The War Diary of the 46th Division, TNA, WO 95/2666. See also Priestly, *Breaking the Hindenburg Line: The History of the 46th (North Midland) Division*, chaps. I to III.

36. Gieves is the expensive, but high quality, naval tailor.

37. The issue of the life belts is discussed in Priestly, who identified the source of the idea as "some genius." *Breaking the Hindenburg Line: The History of the 46th (North Midland) Division*, 42.

38. This an instance where Jerram has a faulty memory. He has confused four officers: The GSO-2, Major Hay; the AAQMG, Lieutenant-Colonel Duckworth; the DAAG, Major Forbes; and the DAQMG, Major Williams.

39. A contemporary photograph of the canal with a brief commentary reads: "British troops at the St. Quentin Canal. This photograph indicates something of the formidable nature of the obstacle afforded by

the canal with its high steep banks. It was across this canal that the men of the glorious 46th Division were sent in lifebelts in that great attack toward St. Quentin on September 27th. Four days later the obstinately defended city of St. Quentin was captured." *The War Illustrated*, Vol. 9, No. 221, 9 November 1918, 193. The previous week, a more limited photograph appeared with succinct comments: "British and Australian soldiers at the entrance to the tunnel through which the St. Quentin Canal passes from Bellicourt. The ridge above the tunnel had been the scene of stubborn fighting." *The War Illustrated*, Vol. 9, No. 220, 2 November 1918, 182.

40. In 1918, the American Expeditionary Force (A.E.F.) generally lacked extensive combat experience, despite previous operations which have passed down into U.S. Army lore. Troops, staff officers, and commanders too often "learned by doing." Hence, their initial military efforts would be viewed critically by officers such as Jerram, who by now had experienced years of combat. For studies on the American effort in World War I, see Edward M. Coffman, *The War to End all Wars: The American Experience in World War I* (New York, 1968); Paul F. Braim, *The Test of Battle: The American Expeditionary Forces in the Meuse-Argonne Campaign* (Newark, 1987); David F. Trask, *The AEF and Coalition Warmaking 1917–1918* (Lawrence, KS, 1993); and Edward G. Lengel, *The Meuse-Argonne, 1918* (New York, 2008). Wilpott, in *Attrition*, has a balance perspective on the AEF.

41. A published press report of the time reported "the 46th (North Midland) Division alone captured 4,000 prisoners and some 40 guns." Note the division was clearly identified. "Hard Fighting on British Front. Gains at Cambrai and St. Quentin. Struggle for canal Tunnel." *The Times*, 1 October 1918. A chronology of events appeared shortly after the armistice: *The War Illustrated*, Vol. 9, No. 222, 16 November 1918, 224.

42. Lieutenant Colonel Bernard William Vann, VC, MC (with bar) (1887–1918), of The Sherwood Foresters (Nottinghamshire and Derbyshire Regiment), 8th Battalion Territorials. He was killed on 3 October 1918 at the battle of Ramicourt. For a photograph of Vann, see Priestly, *Breaking the Hindenburg Line: The History of the 46th (North Midland) Division*, 70. Vann is listed, with his biography, as an ordained priest in the pre-war Church of England directories, e.g., *The Clergy List, 1914* (London, 1914), 1104.

43. This operation is succinctly discussed, to include the details of the named 46th Division's operation, the physical challenge associated with it, the tactical perspective, the human element, and some unit friction, in Peter Hart, *1918: A Very British Victory* (London, 2009), 446–454.

44. The Croix de Guerre is both an individual and unit gallantry award. For individuals, the medal is a bronze Maltese cross with crossed swords; the First World War ribbon is green, with red borders and five vertical red stripes. For units, its emblem is a red and green fourragere worn on the left shoulder.

45. This is an example of emotional nationalistic perspectives. The ill-fated German offensives of 1918 stemmed from the growing Entente manpower advantage coupled with the psychological impact of U.S. entry into the war. These, coupled the Allied offensives commencing in July 1918, consumed the Reich's best troops and reserves in operations. Despite their rawness, the Allies wanted American troops—and in the crisis of that spring these were provided. By autumn the increased size of the A.E.F. resulted in the formation of the 1st, 2nd, and 3rd Armies. From the context of the memoir, Jerram must have encountered Americans who boasted that "we won the war"—and his emotional reaction is understandable. The comment about U.S. forces not being able to feed themselves is of interest, since the standards of American supply were considered excessive by the British and French.

46. IX Corps was raised in June 1915, served at Gallipoli and in Egypt, arrived on the Western Front in July 1916 and remained there until the end of the war. It consisted of the 1st, 6th, 32nd, and 46th Divisions.

47. Jerram must be referring to the Headquarters of all British forces in France. The GOC was Field Marshal Sir Douglas Haig. The irony about this observation: Haig was a cavalryman.

48. Jerram indirectly addresses an issue current scholarship is assessing: The issue of a "break-through" as opposed to a "break-in" against the German defenses in depth which been skillfully developed. There is no doubt the 46th Division achieved a "break-in," but associated with a "break-through" is the ability to exploit such an achievement. Priestly in his official history uses the term "break-through," but within the military and technological conditions of the First World War, did a real ability to exploit what was achieved really exist? See Priesty, *Breaking the Hindenburg Line: The History of the 46th (North Midland) Division*, 65 and 73.

49. Sequehart: A village approximately 4.9 miles (or eight kilometers) northeast of St. Quentin; Montbrehain: A village approximately 6.2 miles (or 10 kilometers) southwest of Bohain; and Ramicourt, a village approximately 19 miles (or 31 kilometers) south of Cambrai. Bellenglise is approximately 6.4 kilometers Or four miles) from Sequehart and 4.4 kilometers (or 2.8 miles) from Bellicourt.

50. The 5th Cavalry Brigade of the 2nd Cavalry Division, serving with 4th Army, consisted of the Scots Greys, the 12th Lancers, and 20th Hussars. Brigadier Neill W. Haig, CMG (1868–1926) commanded, later also CB.

51. The 6th Division, a regular Army division, moved to France in 1914 and remained there on the Western Front till 1918.

52. Eventually Brigadier Roy Jerram, DSO, MC (and U.S. Legion of Merit), Royal Tank Regiment (1895–1974), although originally commissioned in the Hampshire Regiment (1914). Eldest son of Admiral Sir Martyn Jerram, GCMG, KCB.

53. Bethell Force: A mixed force from IX and XIII Corps, formed on 9 October 1918 and broken up after the Armistice, it consisted of the 5th Cavalry Brigade, the South African Brigade, an armored car battalion, two RAF squadrons, and other detachments. Commanded by Major General Sir Keppel Bethell, KBE, CMG, CVO, DSO (1882–1947), originally commissioned in the 7th Hussars and later Military Attaché in Washington, 1919 to 1923. For a brief discussion of this and comments on the capability of the retreating Germans echoing those of Jerram, see The Marquess of Anglesey, *A History of the British Cavalry, 1816– 1919. Vol 8. The Western Front, 1915–1918; Epilogue,*

1919–1939 (London, 1997), 275–276; Angelsey used the official British history of the war in his work: J.E. Edmonds and R. Maxwell-Hyslop, *Military Operations France and Belgium, 1918*, V, 528, 533, and 534.

54. Jerram here addresses the issue of supplying rapidly advancing troops. Ironically, the British were experiencing the same problems the Germans had in their advance into France in 1914. Simply stated, although railroads could move supplies quickly to a railhead distribution point, the problem arose in distribution from there to the front line troops.

55. Often called "rapid fire," the "make or break" in marksmanship scores, especially with a bolt action rifle. In addition to speed, however, aimed shots were emphasized. The monetary references are to pay supplements for marksmanship proficiency.

56. Such an advance was substantial after almost four years of trench warfare, hence must be viewed within the context of World War I operations and not those of the Second World War.

57. General Sir Henry Seymour Rawlinson, GCB, GCSI, GCVO, KCB, KCMG, later Baron Trent of Dorset (1864–1925).

58. Lieutenant General Sir Brian Horrocks, KCB, KBE, DSO, MC (1896–1985), most noted for his command of XXX Corps in 1944–45. The book cited by Jerram is Horrocks' memoir, *A Full Life* (London, 1974); Horrocks also wrote, with Major General H.E. Essame and Eversley Belfield, *Corps Commander* (London, 1977).

59. King George V visited the 46th (North Midland) Division at Landrecis on 1 December 1918, and the next day toured the St. Quentin Canal battlefield area at Bellenglise.

60. Companion of the Most Distinguished Order of St. Michael and St. George (CMG), founded in 1818. Normally conferred on diplomats and members of the Foreign Service, as well as others who had performed valuable service to the Empire (and now Commonwealth).

Chapter 10

1. psc: "Passed Staff College," essential for Army staff appointments, and potential promotions and eventual command. The initials *psc* were placed at the end of an officer's name. For a discussion of the importance of this professional qualification in the Army (and in contrast to Jerram's Corps in his era), see Mallinson, *The Making of the British Army*, 215–216; see also 327–328.

2. One reason for this: At the time the Corps did not have permanent ground operational forces and a minimal ashore establish requiring many staff officers. It still viewed its primary mission as service with the fleet. Thus, few appointments existed for experienced staff officers.

3. For an assessment of Jerram's class, see Major R.N.C. Gossop, "A Vintage Year," *British Army Review*, No. 96, December 1990, 49–51.

4. Lieutenant General Sir Warren H. Anderson, KCB (1872–1930), Commandant, Staff College, Camberley, 1919–22.

5. Eventually Field Marshal the Viscount Gort, VC, GCB, CBE, DSO, MVO, MC (1886–1946). Commissioned in 1905 in the Grenadier Guards, later served as Commandant of the Staff College, Camberley, Chief of the Imperial General Staff (1937–39), commander of the British Expeditionary Force in France (1939–40), Commander-in-Chief, Gibraltar (1941–42), Governor and Commander-in-Chief, Malta (1942–44), and finally High Commissioner and Commander-in-Chief, Palestine (1944–45). Cyril Falls, rev. Brian Bond, "Vereker, John Standish Surtees Prendergast, Viscount Gort ... (1886–1946)," *Oxford Dictionary of National Biography*, Vol. 56 (Oxford, 2004), 317–320.

6. Eventually Field Marshal Sir John G. Dill, GCB, CMG, DSO (1881–1944). Originally commissioned in 1901 in the Prince of Wales's Leinster Regiment, later Chief of the Imperial General Staff (1940–41) and then head of the British Joint Staff Mission in Washington, D.C. (1941–44). On his death, the U.S. Congress approved his burial in Arlington National Cemetery, Virginia.

7. A Canadian officer, Lieutenant Colonel Ronald O. Alexander, DSO (1888–1949), Royal Canadian Regiment, later Major General, CB, DSO.

8. Whippet Tank: A British tank of the First World War, weighing 14 tons, with 14mm of armour, a speed of 8.3 miles per hour, a crew of three, and armed with four machine guns.

9. Drag Hunt: A substitute for a real "hunt": A horseman drags a bag of straw dipped in anise seed through an area. The dogs then follow the scent and the horsemen ride after them.

10. Throughout the 19th and 20th centuries, officers of the Corps were constantly concerned about financial matters. For a discussion of this, see Donald F. Bittner, "Shattered Images: Officers of Royal Marines, 1867–1913," *The Journal of Military History*, Vol. 59, No. 1, January 1995, pp. 27–51.

11. The Army requested synopses of Jerram's confidential reports. A copy this is in his official record of service.

12. HMS *Raleigh:* A Cavendish class cruiser, laid down in November 1916, commissioned in April 1921, and wrecked in August 1922. Main armament: seven 7.5-inch guns, six 12-pounders, four 3-inch anti-aircraft guns, four three-pounders, and six 21-inch torpedo tubes. Crew complement: 712.

13. Jerram does not explain why. Perhaps they were too much alike? In Festing's obituary, its writer assessed his deceased colleague with these words: "To have served with Festing, either in the field or at home, was an unforgettable experience. Rigid in his ideas as to what constituted good soldiering ... he was at heart the kindest and most genial of men, who could forgive anything except lack of keenness. Many Captains and Subalterns have been instructed by him, and the Corps, as is fitting, bears his stamp." "Obituary. Festing," *The Globe and Laurel*, January 1932, 29. The same could have been written about Lieutenant Colonel Jerram.

14. This comment is unclear. Of the recipients between 1914 and 1923, of the King George V Scholarship prize recipients who attended staff college, either the Army's at Camberley or the Navy's at Greenwich, only two transferred and both indeed achieved higher rank than Lieutenant Colonel: Festing (Colonel) and Harold C. Harrison (Brigadier). The other officers of the Corps who remained had varied career fates. See Appendix IX.

15. Lieutenant Colonel Guy Charles Williams, CMG, DSO, Royal Engineers (1881–1959), later General, KCB, CMG, DSO.

16. The quotation is from an extract from a final report retained in the Jerram folder in the officers' biographical file, Royal Marines Museum (ARCHIVES 9/2/J). The reference is to Admiral Sir John F. Parry, KCB, FRGS (1863–1926). However, despite Jerram's statement of Parry's official position, the Lord Lieutenant of Dorset during this period was Anthony Ashley-Cooper, 9th Earl of Shaftesbury, who held the office from 1916 to 1952. The obituary for Admiral Parry in *The Times* provided extensive details on his service which culminated as the Hydrographer of the Royal Navy, but provided none for his post retirement years. "Admiral Sir J.F. Parry. Services in the War," *The Times*, 23 April 1926.

17. Great Railway Strike: The reference is to the 1921 strike involving the miners, and railroad and transport workers. Also called "The Coal Strike" and, in Royal Marine records, "The Present Emergency."

18. 13 Royal Marine Battalion: An organized entity only during the crisis associated with the strike, after which it was disbanded. References to the 13th, and the 9th, 10th, 11th, and 12th RM Battalions, are rare. However, the journal of the Corps in June 1921 announced their formation, and printed the names of their commanding officers and adjutants. *The Globe and Laurel*, "List of Officers, R.M. called up for service during the present emergency," Vol. XXVIII, No. 6, June 1921, 87.

19. Lewis Gun: The primary British Army light machine gun of the First World War. Calibre .303, gas operated, automatic fire only; weight: 27 pounds; muzzle velocity: 2,440 feet per second. Drum magazine: 47 rounds per magazine.

20. Captain D. Hill, MC. No further information available.

21. The Commanding Officer was Lieutenant Colonel Percy Molloy, RMLI (1876–1973), commissioned February 1894, promoted Lieutenant General June 1930, and retired April 1931. Major Nutt retired in 1920 but was recalled for active service between April–June 1921.

22. North America and West Indies Station. In 1921 and 1922, it consisted of the 8th Light Cruiser Squadron (HMS *Raleigh* [flagship], HMS *Capetown*, HMS *Constance*, and HMS *Curlew*), plus two sloops, a depot ship, and, temporarily, one survey service ship. Its home base was the Bermuda dockyard.

23. Commander Ronald Mountstevens Fraser, DSO, RN (later Captain). In July 1922, Commander James W.S. Dorling (1889–1966, later Vice Admiral, CB) relieved Fraser.

24. Lieutenant Richard W. Spraggett, MC, RM (1894–1976), commissioned from the ranks of the Royal Warwickshire Regiment into the RMLI in November 1916, promoted Colonel June 1946, and retired 1949. Eventually CMG, CVO, and CBE. The manuscript erroneously reads "Captain," but Spraggett was not promoted to that rank till 1923.

25. All of these comments, along with both Jerram and Spraggett's afloat postings, address a significant issue: What, if any, was the role of Marines' afloat—and, by implication, that of the Corps in Britain's maritime establishment? Before, during, and after The Great War they were posted to and functioned on ship in traditional roles even as warfare had changed drastically from its age of sail character.

26. Sergeant Major: For both a humorous but also serious recounting of the functioning role of this important leader in a Royal Marine detachment aboard shop, see Jackstaff, "The Major," *The Globe and Laurel*, Vol. XXIV, No. 264, October, 1917, 183–184. In this instance, "The Major" within the detachment was the ranking Non-Commissioned officer in the detachment, called by that phrase regardless of his rank—usually a Colour Sergeant.

27. Warwick Camp: A training area, with rifle ranges, located on the south coast of Bermuda opposite the entrance to Chaplin Bay. Now the home of the Bermuda Regiment.

28. Captain, and Flag Captain and Chief of Staff to the Admiral, Captain Sir Arthur Bromley, CMG, RN (1876–1961), later Rear Admiral, KCMG, KCVO.

29. Cutter: A pulling boat which can also be sailed (one mast), usually with 12 oars, carried on cruisers and larger ships.

30. Jerram here penned a detailed account pertaining to the sheet anchor. Detailed and specialized, it has been edited out.

31. Pacific Base of the U.S. Marine Corps: Today, in addition to the Marine Corps Recruit Depot, San Diego, California, the U.S. Marine Corps presence in the state has risen to five major bases: The 1st Marine Division at Camp Pendleton; the 3rd Marine Corps Aircraft Wing at Marine Corps Air Station, Miramar; a combined arms training center at Marine Corps Base, 29 Palms; a logistics center at the Marine Corps Supply Center, Barstow; and the Winter Warfare and Mountain Leadership School at Pickle Meadows. There are also reserve ground and aviation units in the state.

32. "Dry": The reference is to Prohibition (1921–33), which made the production and sale of alcoholic beverages illegal in the United States. U.S. Navy vessels were already "dry" by General Order 99 of 1914.

33. Esquimalt: A town, with port and naval base, in British Columbia, a western suburb of Victoria on Vancouver Island.

34. Admiral Sir William C. Pakenham, KCB, KCMG, KCVO (1861–1933).

35. Hopalong Cassidy: The hero in a series of American boys' novels of the early 20th century by Clarence E. Mulford. These books formed the basis of 66 films between 1935 and 1946, and a television series in the 1950s, all starring William Boyd. "Johnny Nelson" was another name for the actor James or Jimmy Ellison, who played one of Hopalong Cassidy's sidekicks in eight of those films of the 1930s.

36. Quantico: Then called the Marine Barracks, Quantico, Virginia. It was established in 1917 as a major training and transshipment base for U.S. Marines heading for Europe in the First World War. Since 1920, the home of the professional military education system of the Marine Corps, and later doctrinal and equipment development. For an account of this visit to Quantico, see Jerram's report in *The Globe and Laurel*, Vol. XXIX, No. 9, September 1922, 140.

37. Jerram here used "division" in two ways, neither of which meant an operational combat "division": (1) In the Royal Marines sense, i.e., Marine Barracks,

Quantico, Virginia; and (2) the permanent standing East Coast Expeditionary Force (antecedent of the U.S. Marine Corps Fleet Marine Force, which was not founded until 1933), a shore based organization ready for operational deployment. The Royal Marines then had no such organization, hence his comment "green with envy."

38. Forteau: A small fishing village on the west shore of Forteau Bay, an inlet six miles long and four miles wide at the entrance of the Belle Isle Strait, southeastern Labrador. On the northeastern side of the entrance is Amour Point.

39. The date was 8 August 1922; the location: Amour Point in the Belle Isle Strait, Labrador. Jerram wrote a detailed account of the wreck in "Fleet Notes. The Wreck of HMS *Raleigh*," *The Globe and Laurel*, Vol. XXIX, No. 10, October 1922, 154–155.

40. Midshipman Edward M. Hutton, who entered service on 15 September 1921.

41. Carley Raft: A large lifesaving apparatus, constructed so that it floats on its bottom side. It may also automatically detach and float if a ship is sinking.

42. Commander Leslie C. Bott, RN.

43. Scraesdon Fort and Tregantle Ranges: Military complex in the Plymouth, Devon, area, west of the Tamar River, with the cited facilities located in Cornwall. The brick and masonry fort lies above the ranges.

44. Captain Archibald Maxwell Craig, RM (1895–1953), commissioned October 1912, promoted Major General October 1932, and retired June 1944. Received CB (1944) and OBE (1919).

45. Captain Leslie Hollis, RM (1897–1963) commissioned August 1914, and eventually General and Commandant General, Royal Marines, 1949–52, after serving before and during World War II within the Secretariat of the War Cabinet. Made KCB (1951) and KBE (1946); authored two memoirs: *One Marine's Tale* (London, 1956) and *War at the Top* (London, 1959).

46. Admiral Sir Richard F. Phillimore, KCB, KCMG, MVO (1864–1940). His command consisted of HMS *Impregnable* (an establishment of four ships); the Gunnery School; the Torpedo School; the Third Submarine Flotilla; a vessel for the Royal Naval College, Dartmouth; and three independent ships in Irish waters. Before World War I, as Flag Captain to the Commander-in-Chief, Portsmouth, he had proposed the creation of a permanently organized and operational ready force of Royal Marines, to include a "spearhead" brigade of a British Expeditionary Force for service in Europe, plus smaller units for the Mediterranean and China. The National Archives, ADM 116/999. Case 609. "Officers, Royal Marines and Engineers."

47. Amalgamated: Between 1862 and 1923, the Corps had separate Royal Marine Light Infantry (RMLI) and Royal Marine Artillery (RMA) branches. However, from 1912, newly commissioned officers entering the Corps were placed on one "Royal Marine list." Amalgamation occurred on 22 June 1923, primarily as a cost-efficiency measure. This, however, did little to address the central question of the proper role and function of the Corps.

48. Jerram's report was submitted in 1924 to the Madden Committee, established to study the Royal Marines. The National Archives, ADM 1/8664/134, "Functions and Training of Royal Marines (1923), 1924." For a discussion of this, see Donald F. Bittner, "Britannia's Sheathed Sword," *The Journal of Military History*, July 1991, 349–351.

49. The Mobile Naval Base Defence Organisation was a defensive force designed to defend a *temporary* advanced naval base. The defense of *permanent* naval bases was an Army responsibility.

50. "Our chief": Since 1825, the title of the head of the Corps had been Deputy Adjutant General, Royal Marines; it then changed to Adjutant General, Royal Marines (1916); General Officer Commanding, Royal Marines (1943); Commandant General, Royal Marines (1945); and Commandant General, Royal Marines and Commander, United Kingdom Amphibious Force, COMUKAMPHIBFOR (2002).

51. Jerram proposed eliminating three of the four existing divisions, i.e., historic age of sail locations by ports: The Royal Marine Artillery, Portsmouth (Eastney Barracks); and three Royal Marine Light Infantry: Portsmouth (Forton Barracks), Plymouth (Stonehouse Barracks), and Chatham (Melville Barracks). A base near a major training area and a recruit depot (in 1924, at Deal) would be retained. The implications appeared to be further reduced employment opportunities for senior officers.

52. Commandos: The British Army initially assumed this role after the fall of France in 1940. By 1945, the Royal Marines had raised nine commandos (40 to 48). This was a shift in policy from the creation and employment of a Royal Marine Division, which existed between 1940 and 1943, and the two Mobile Naval Base Defence Organisations. The new emphasis and capability would be on battalion sized amphibious assault forces, which could be and were (and one still is) organized into brigade formations.

53. Major (and Brevet Lieutenant Colonel) Robert Daly Ormsby (1879–1946), Deputy Assistant Adjutant General, Royal Marines. Commissioned (RMLI), January 1898; promoted Lieutenant General, September 1935, and retired August 1936. Awarded CBE (1924).

54. Admiral of the Fleet Sir Charles Edward Madden, Bt., GCB, GCVO, KCMG, LLD (1862–1935), President of the board studying the Royal Marines.

55. Two MNBDOs were raised. Jerram correctly addressed one aspect of the MNBDO: Diversion of manpower, as each had a strength approximating 7,000 officers and men. For interwar development, see Donald F. Bittner, "Marines and Amphibious Warfare, Parts I and II," *The Sheet Anchor: The Journal of the Royal Marines Historical Society*, Vol. XIV, No. 1, Summer 1989, 2–8, and Vol. XIV, No. 2, Autumn–Winter, 1989, 33–40; and Bittner, "Britannia's Sheathed Sword," *The Journal of Military History*, 353–357. A Mobile Naval Base Defence Organisation appears in former Royal Marine officer Evelyn Waugh's novel *The Sword of Honour Trilogy*, Volume II, *Officers and Gentlemen* (London, 1955).

56. Admiral Sir Rudolph W. Bentinck, KCMG, CB (1869–1947). He relieved Admiral Phillimore in October 1926.

57. This reference is probably to the Assistant Adjutant General. In 1926, Colonel Second Commandant Richard V.T. Ford (1878–1949), commissioned RMA in September 1896, promoted General October 1932, and served as Adjutant General, Royal Marines, between 1930–33. Appointed KCB (1933) and CBE (1919).

58. Either Captain Edmund M.C. Parker, RM (1895–1949), commissioned in October 1912, promoted Major June 1930, and retired April 1938; or Captain Albert Rendell, RM (1887–1970), commissioned October 1914 from the ranks, and promoted Major on the retired list in June 1932 after retiring in February. Rendell relieved Parker in October 1926.

59. HMS *Defiance*: The Torpedo School, located in Devonport, consisted of four 19th century vessels. The Captain and Commander: Captain Alexander R. Palmer, RN (later Rear Admiral, retired 1929), and Commander Sir Lionel A.D. Sturdee, Bt., RN (1884–1970), later Rear Admiral, CBE.

60. Colonel Commandant George James Herbert Mullins (1864–1943), commissioned RMLI in February 1889, promoted General in April 1928, and retired December 1928; awarded CB (1919).

61. The time sequence is unclear. Mullins' report on Jerram must have been at the end of the former's assignment during Jerram's posting as Instructor of Musketry and tour as Senior Marine on the staff of the Commander-in-Chief, Plymouth (the latter beginning in March 1926 and ending in January 1928). When he returned to Plymouth Division, the Colonel Commandant was Colonel Commandant Robert O. Paterson, OBE (1926–28) who was succeeded by Colonel Commandant George L. Raikes, CB, DSC, in April 1928. Paterson (1878–1941) was originally commissioned in the RMLI in September 1895 but transferred to the RMA in 1896, promoted General October 1930, and retired October 1931. Raikes (1876–1949) was commissioned in the RMA in September 1896, promoted Major General December 1929, and retired June 1930. Note that Raikes had been awarded the DSC.

62. Promotion to Major was by seniority and vacancy, but to grades above that by selection. Order in Council No. 62 of 29 November 1881. *The Orders in Council for the Regulation of the Naval Service, Vol. IV* (London, 1883), 115. However, examinations in various subjects had to be passed, with the results so noted in each officer's official record of service.

63. Helford: Five miles south-southwest of Falmouth, in Cornwall, located on the south side of the river of the same name, with the river emptying into Falmouth Bay.

64. Patrick William O'Hara Phibbs (1902–1975), commissioned (RM) in October 1920. Promoted Captain in 1931 and Brevet Major in 1940.

Chapter 11

1. Jerram's date of rank as a Lieutenant Colonel on the retired list: 30 October 1931. He retired as a Major on 18 January 1929. Advancement in rank upon, or after, retirement was not automatic.

2. Lieutenant General Sir Phillip Neame, VC, KBE, CB, DSO (1888–1978). Commissioned in the Royal Engineers, he was an instructor at the Staff College, Camberley, from 1919 to 1923.

3. The Corps' journal noted Jerram's return to active service: "Recalled for Active Service ... LtColonel C.F. Jerram, CMG, DSO (Ret'd), Ply. (at Deal), to serve in the rank of Major, 10-1-40." *The Globe and Laurel*, February 1940, Vol. XLVIII, No. 3, 96. Training for which he was responsible would soon shift from Hampshire to Devon.

4. The reference is to General Sir Alan George B. Bourne, KCB, DSO, MVO (1882–1967), Adjutant General, Royal Marines, from October 1939 to June 1943, and in 1940 the first Director of Combined Operations. Commissioned (RMA) September 1899, promoted General January 1942, and retired in June 1943.

5. WRNS: Women's Royal Naval Service. Then, as today, the Royal Marines have no women in their Corps. WRNS are assigned to them by the Royal Navy to perform various non-combat duties.

6. At a 50th anniversary dinner at the officers' mess at Eastney Barracks for a batch commissioned in 1941, officers trained by Jerram commented on this point, vividly recalling his approach and emphasis on "the principles of war"; Major Jack Alvey, RM (Ret.), interview with editor, 10 January 1991. At the 2014 annual meeting of the Friends of the Royal Marines Museum, another young officer trained by Jerram recalled his emphasis on discipline, standards, and training; Captain Allan H. Prebble, RM (Ret.) interview with editor, 19 March 2014. Prebble's date of rank as a Lieutenant was 1 January 1943, Alvey's 4 January 1943.

7. Mrs. Jerram health's slowly declined; she died in 1953.

8. "it was most badly needed": The reference is to the open French-Belgian border, which would be defended by entrenched British and French troops.

9. 10th Armoured Division: As written in the text. This reference is unclear. During the Second World War, Britain eventually raised 10 numbered armoured divisions plus the Guards Armoured Division, but not all served simultaneously nor all in the European theatre. (See Appendix X.) A 10th Armoured Division was indeed raised in the Middle East and was active from 1 June 1941 to 15 June 1944; it fought in North Arica. Lieut-Col. H.F. Joslen, *Orders of Battle, Second World War, 1939–1945*, I (London, 1960), 3–33. Jerram could also be referring to an armoured division's table of organization and equipment.

10. Gort was Chief of the Imperial General Staff (1937–39) before his appointment as Commander-in-Chief of the British Expeditionary Force. See J.R. Colville, *Man of Valour: Field Marshal Lord Gort, V.C.* (London, 1972), 79, 119, 128, and 145.

11. An interesting and shrewd assessment of Gort. The official British history of the operations in France in 1940 would seem to agree. For a balanced assessment of Gort and the challenges of the post he held and his strength and weaknesses as a commander and the multiple implications inherent in his position, see Major F.F. Ellis, CVO, CBE, DSO, MC, *The War in France and Flanders, 1939–1940* (London, 1953), 11–12, 20, and 321–324. Ellis also addresses the issues associated with British armoured divisions before and in the years 1939 and 1940. See also Colville, *Man of Valour*, 125–126, 130, 146, 190, and especially, 224–226—and ensuing chapters on Gort at Gibraltar and Malta.

12. Malta was awarded the George Cross during World War II for withstanding a long siege by German and Italian military forces. Lord Gort served as Governor and Commander-in-Chief, Malta, between 1942–44.

13. Marshal of France Ferdinand Foch (1851–1929), appointed Allied Commander-in-Chief on the Western Front in 1918.

14. This issue is addressed by David French, *Raising Churchill's Army: The British Army and the War against Germany, 1939–1945* (Oxford, 2001), especially chapters 1–3, with succinct discussion of Gort's actions on pages 44 and 46, and Dill's lament to what occurred on page 119.

15. Principles of War: Conceptually articulated by British Major General J.F.C. Fuller, based upon his studies of Napoleon and military history. Inculcated in American military officers, traditionally there are nine: Objective, Offensive, Mass, Maneuver, Economy of Force, Unity of Command, Security, Surprise, and Simplicity; to these have been added Restraint, Perseverance, and Legitimacy. *JP 3-0, Principles of Joint Operations* (11 August 2011), listed on page I-2 and discussed in Appendix A. The British ones are similar, but worded differently.

16. Lympstone: In Devon, near Dartmoor. Currently the Commando Training Centre, Royal Marines, where initial Marine training, both enlisted and officer, is conducted.

17. Jerram succinctly notes the coming and going of his staff; also included were the continually changes of Commanding Officers. All of this became duly noted in the notes for monthly contributions of the "R.M. Military School" which appeared under the monthly submission under that name in the Corps' journal, *The Globe and Laurel*, beginning in October 1941. As it stated, the school had three wings: Officers, Cadet, and NCOs. Jerram was clearly identified by name: "The Officers' Wing under Major C.F. Jerram, CMG, DSO," "R.M. Military School," *The Globe and Laurel*, October 1941, Vol. XIX, No. 10, 354. The journal noted that the "Officers wing, which used to be called the Military Course, joined the School recently," i.e., three courses were consolidated into one establishment.

18. Lieutenant John K. Gardiner, RM (1918–1997), commissioned in 1937, promoted Major on retirement in 1952, and awarded an OBE. In 1940, serving in HMS *Suffolk*. At his death, Major the Reverend J.K. Gardiner, OBE. "Old Comrades," *The Globe and Laurel*, September-October 1997, Vol. CV, No. 5, 339; and obituary, "Maj the Rev. J.K. Gardiner, OBE," *The Globe and Laurel*, November-December 1997, Vol. CV, No. 6, 410.

19. Thurlestone: A village in Devon, located near the River Avon and Bigbury Bay, with Plymouth/Devonport to the northwest and Dartmouth to the northeast.

20. The reference is to Mrs. Vera Laughton Mathews, MBE (1888–1959), later DBE. Director of the Women's Royal Naval Service, 1939–46.

21. The Corps library referenced by Jerram became the nucleus of the library at the Royal Marines Museum, Eastney, Hampshire.

22. Eventually Lieutenant General Sir Robert Sturges, KBE, DSO (1891–1970). Sturges commanded the British forces which occupied Iceland in 1940 and seized Madagascar in 1942, the Royal Marine Division between 1940 43, and then the Commando Group (1943–45). Commissioned (RM) in May 1912, promoted Lieutenant General June 1945, and retired June 1946.

23. The Royal Marine Division was a combat division. Raised in 1940, it was disbanded in 1943 when most of its combat troops were transformed into commandos and others became the nucleus of landing craft units.

24. Horses: For a comment on this during the war (and mentioning Jerram by name reference this and his students), see, "R.M. Military School," *The Globe and Laurel*, May 1942, Vol. L, No. 5, 109–110.

25. Riding is no longer a part of initial officer training, eliminated over four decades ago partly due to injuries.

26. The three separate service staff colleges (The Army Command and Staff College, Camberley; the Royal Naval Staff College, Greenwich; and the Royal Air Force Staff College, Bracknell) no longer exist. In 1998 they were amalgamated into one institution: The Joint Services Command and Staff College at Shrivenham, Near Swindon, Wiltshire.

27. General Sir Thomas Lionel Hunton, KCB, MVO, OBE (1885–1970), in office between 1943 and 1946. Commissioned (RMLI) in September 1903, promoted General in May 1945, and retired in June 1946.

28. Cury Hunt: On the website "Hunts in the South West," the area of Cornwall in which this Hunt is conducted is described as "bordered by the sea on three sides and lies mainly to the south of the Penzance, Helston, Falmouth road, being a Cornish bank and moorland country where a strong horse is required." http://www.countrysportssouthwest.co.uk/experienced/experienced-horse-rider/hunting/hunts-in-south-west-england/ (accessed 28 November 2014).

29. Porth Navas: A small village on an inlet on the north bank of the Helford River, opposite Helford.

30. Gweek: A small seaport in Cornwall at the head of the Helford River, seven miles west-southwest of Falmouth and west of Helford.

31. Penarvon: Presumably farms around or near Penarvon Cove, on the southern side of the Helford River and several hundred yards west of the village of Helford.

32. Jerram here addressed the issue of "preservation and conservation" versus development; over five decades after he penned his memoirs, still a controversial issue.

33. The celebration occurred on 23 July 1964. The text of Elizabeth II's speech is in the archives of the Royal Marines Museum, Eastney, Portsmouth, Hampshire, England. ARCHIVES 9/2/T. "Biographies. Royal Marine Officers. Sir N.H. Tailyour." The Queen concluded her remarks: "Today the Royal Marines provide a flexible and versatile amphibious force, for which there seems to be a continuous demand in a great number of places.... I am confident that as long as Britain needs to be defended and to play its part in preserving peace throughout the world, they will have an honoured place in the armed forces of the realm." For the printed text of the Queen's remarks, see *The Globe and Laurel*, Vol. LXXII, No. 6, October 1964, 314–315. These comments could have been said by Jerram in the 1920s, the Second World War, or in 1964. In 2014, the Corps celebrated its 350th anniversary—with similar activities occurring throughout Britain.

Appendix I

1. Basic career information on Lieutenant Colonel Jerram is from his official "Record of Service" (The National Archives, ADM 196/63, pp. 155 and 146). Unless otherwise cited, factual material in this essay

is from that source. *In this assessment, no quotations are used from Jerram's memoir.* All quotations by him are from other sources and are appropriately cited; documents in the Royal Marines Museum, Eastney, are identified by "ARCHIVES" followed by appropriate record group name, numbers, and letters.

2. Lieutenant Colonel C.F. Jerram, "If Possible," *The Globe and Laurel,* Vol. LXXIV, No. 3, June 1966, 189.

3. "Notes on Musketry for Company and Platoon Commanders," General Staff, XIII Corps, 22 July 1917, issued by C.F. Jerram. ARCHIVES 11/14/5(A); copy also in ARCHIVES 11/13/24(E).

4. "RMLI Detachment—HMS *Raleigh*," by Major C.F. Jerram, RMLI, 1 September 1922. ARCHIVES 11/14/5(D).

5. Jerram believed the Royal Marines were a regiment, *but still a maritime regiment.* See Jerram's piece "Not a Regiment?," *The Globe and Laurel,* Vol. LXXIV, No. 6, December 1966, 384. This hybrid status was reflected in two ways: Royal Marine officers were listed by rank and dates of rank in both the Army and Navy lists; and, in 1914, when on parade with the Army, Marines marched between the Princess Charlotte of Wales's (Royal Berkshire Regiment) and the Queen's Own (Royal West Kent Regiment).

6. This issue is assessed in Donald F. Bittner, "Britannia's Sheathed Sword: The Royal Marines and Amphibious Warfare in the Interwar Years—A Passive Response," *The Journal of Military History,* Vol. 55, No. 3, July 1991, 349–352. It was not new; see C.L., "Employment of the Marines," *The Royal Military Chronicle, or British Officers Monthly Register, Chronicle, & Military Mentor,* April 1811, 492–493. Reflective Marines by the late 19th century also addressed the subject. With the changes in naval warfare induced by new technology, altered skills needed for manning and fighting warships, changed recruiting patterns, and different types of Royal Navy officer and sailor, the traditional missions of the Corps at sea (i.e. security guards, manning guns, boarding parties, landing parties, and marksman in close combat) were gradually becoming a heritage of the past. For a late 19th century view, see Major W.H. Poyntz, *Per Mare Per Terram: Reminiscences of Thirty-Two Years Military, Naval, and Constabulary Service* (London, 1892), 49. Still, older views persisted into the 20th century, i.e., discipline aboard ships and suppression of mutiny; for an example as late as 1931, see Alan Coles, *Invergordon Scapegoat: The Betrayal of Admiral Tomkinson* (Stroud, Gloucestershire, 1993), ix, 121, 123, 128, 130, and 131.

7. Lieutenant Colonel Charles F. Jerram, "Some Reminences [sic] in the Corps of Royal Marines" (Unpublished Manuscript, n.d.), 3. ARCHIVES 2/7/1. Hereafter cited as Jerram, "Reminences." For a naval officer's account, see Admiral Sir R.H. Bacon, *The Life of Lord Fisher of Kilverstone.* Vol. I. (London, 1929), 105.

8. Jerram overrated what he saw in the U.S. Marine Corps Expeditionary Forces, although it was indeed a permanently organized ground force. What he conceptually envisioned would not occur in the United States until 7 December 1933 with the creation of the Fleet Marine Force placed under the operational command of the Commander-in-Chief, United States Fleet.

9. In 1923, the Royal Marine Light Infantry and Royal Marine Artillery merged into literally one corps of standard uniforms, seniority lists, pay, promotion, etc. With this, only three divisions, i.e., barracks, of Royal Marines remained: Plymouth, Eastney (east of Portsmouth), and Chatham. The Corps lost one: The RMLI barracks at Gosport (west of Portsmouth).

10. Major C.F. Jerram, CMG, DSO, Royal Marines, Memo for Madden Committee (No Title, No Date—but 1923–1924). The National Archives, Kew. ADM 1/8664/134.

11. With the fall of France, Britain through necessity had to develop an amphibious assault capability. Included were the raising of the commando forces, and by 1945 both the Corps and Army had such units. After that conflict, the Royal Marines assumed this role. Jerram believed the Royal Marine commandos reflected the original heritage of the maritime regiments raised in the 17th and 18th centuries rather than the Royal Marine Light Infantry of the 19th century. Lieutenant Colonel C.F. Jerram, "Our Forebears," *The Globe and Laurel,* Vol. LXXVI, No. 3, June 1968, 140.

12. Two Royal Marines served on the Madden Committee: Lieutenant General (later General) Sir Herbert E. Blumberg, KCB, and Colonel Commandant (later General, KCB) Alexander R.H. Hutchinson, CB, CMG, DSO. Blumberg served as Adjutant General of the Corps, and Hutchinson succeeded him. They did not torpedo his career, as Blumberg was a friend and Jerram had served under Hutchinson. Jerram in his papers did not identify the RMA officers and they are not identifiable in his official record of service.

13. G. Gidley Robinson letter to Mr. Charles Samuel Jerram dated 12 August 1895. ARCHIVES 11/12/16. "Letters, 1879–1897." For a picture and commentary on Hillside School, see http://www.andrewsgen.com/photo/godalming/frithhill_hillside01.htm (accessed 11 April 2015).

14. For an example of changes in child rearing and childhood between Jerram's youth and the contemporary era, especially societal and government views, see Donna St. George, "They want 'free range' kids, but not all do. Maryland couple face investigation after letting their kids walk alone," *The Washington Post,* 15 January 2015; and Donna St. George and Brigid Schultz, "A Free-range flap: Montgomery County agency's inquiry puts a spotlight on parenting style," *The Washington Post,* 18 January 2015. The incident produced many news reports and spirited commentaries, e.g., Petula Dvorak, "Parenting in an Age of Anxiety, The Line between protecting children, revving up the nanny state," *The Washington Post,* 16 January 2015; and Linda Chavez, "Don't be afraid to give kids independence: Letting children walk alone brings trouble in Maryland," *Fredericksburg Free Lance-Star,* 21 January 2015. In May resolution started to occur: Donna S. George, "'Free Range' family cleared in one neglect case," *The Washington Post,* 26 May 2015; and Editorial, "'Free range' parents cleared in one case: Good News for Parents," *Fredericksburg Free Lance-Star,* 6 June 2015. For examples of recent commentaries on these issues in 21st century Britain, see Janice Turner, "In this girls' world, boys are deviants," *The Times,* 29 January 2005; and Philip Johnston, "Taking risks is a healthy thing for children," *The Daily Telegraph,* 22 June 2008. With regard to modern

differing views on self-confidence, self-esteem, and potential ambition and associated failure, see the commentary in "Our Little Emperors: A backlash has begun against all-must have prizes culture that has turned children used to getting their own way," *The Sunday Times*, 29 June 2008; and Libby Purves, "However high you aim, try not to look down: Allowing children to risk failure is vital to their education...," *The Times*, 29 October 2012.

15. Jerram, "Reminences," 1. He later (3–5) addressed other financial matters pertaining to his early years in the Plymouth Division, including officers living on a minimal income, his uncle purchasing his uniforms (for 100 pounds, thus keeping him from debt), and the Admiralty requiring parents to give their newly commissioned sons an allowance of five pounds a month (which Jerram insisted be discontinued).

16. Jerram, "Reminences," 2.

17. "Division" meant barracks. In 1902, there were four: three Royal Marine Light Infantry (Plymouth, Portsmouth [Gosport], and Chatham), and one Royal Marine Artillery (Eastney, Portsmouth). In his history of the Corps, Major General Julian Thompson stated that each division had its own traditions and heritage, hence Marines developed an emotional "home" attachment to them similar to soldiers and their parent Army regiment. Major General Julian Thompson, *The Royal Marines: From Sea Soldiers to Special Force* (London, 2000), 16–17.

18. Unless otherwise cited, quotations from Confidential Reports are from two sources: Jerram's Record of Service, and a 1926 "Confidential and Other Special Reports of Service Prepared by the Royal Marines Headquarters for the War Office from 1901–1925"; this latter document is in Jerram's Record of Service. Naval reporting seniors provided a summary report on their subordinates in a document called a "Flimsy," including Royal Marine officers serving at sea or on naval staffs. Jerram saved his, and these are retained at the Royal Marines Museum: Officers Biographies, "Jerram, Charles Frederic." ARCHIVES 9/2/J. Material from this source hereafter cited via the document, followed by "Jerram," ARCHIVES 9/2/J.

19. Jerram, "Reminences," 6. Lieutenant Colonel Charles F. Jerram, "The Navy at the Beginning of the 20th Century," (Unpublished Manuscript, n.d.), 1–2. ARCHIVES 2/20/1. Hereafter cited as Jerram, "Navy."

20. *Who's Who, 1968–1969* (London, 1968), "Jerram, Lieut.-Col. Charles Frederic," 1609. Service with the future Admiral of the Fleet and Earl made a greater impression on Jerram than the reverse, as in published editions of Beatty's papers and biographies his command tour in HMS *Suffolk* is barely mentioned. As it was short, i.e., just over a year, and the editors and biographers illustrated his approach to training and hospitality via his first command as a Captain in HMS *Juno*, this is not surprising.

21. Jerram, "The Navy," 6.

22. Jerram, "The Navy," 8, 9, and 12.

23. Jerram. ARCHIVES 9/2/J. The reference is to Major Horace C. Evans, RMLI (1866–1950), commissioned on 1 September 1886, promoted Lieutenant Colonel in April 1912, and retired on 11 April 1918.

24. Jerram, "The Navy," 21–24.

25. ar Diary of Royal Marine Brigade, Dardanelles (copy), n.d., 116. Last entry, handwritten. ARCHIVES 11/13/24(A).

26. Various documents in Jerram's official record of service cite positions and dates for his staff appointments. A summary of his war service is in General Sir H.E. Blumberg, KCB, *Britain's Sea Soldiers: A Record of the Royal Marines during the War, 1914–1919* (Devonport, 1927), Appendix 2, 480.

27. Album (personal) entry dated 1 June 1915, p. 88. ARCHIVES 11/14/5(B).

28. The quotation is from Jerram's Record of Service.

29. Brigadier Charles Trotman letter to Mrs. C.F. Jerram, 20 March [1917]. ARCHIVES 11/13/24 (E).

30. Paris sent Jerram a handwritten summary, dated 25 March 1916: "An excellent officer, capable and reliable. More suited for General Staff than for A&Q work. I can recommend him for employment on General Staff or as Brigade Major." "Jerram," ARCHIVES 9/2/J.

31. Trotman sent a copy to Jerram. "Jerram," ARCHIVES 9/2/J. Also recorded in Adjutant General, Royal Marines: Précis for the War office of "Confidential or other Special Reports of Service," 1926.

32. Lieutenant Colonel C.F. Jerram letter to Major General J.L. Moulton, "RRJ's Gallipoli," no date but from subject and content written in the year of publication of Robert Rhodes James's *Gallipoli* (1965). Copy, editor's possession.

33. Adjutant General, Royal Marines: Précis for the War office of "Confidential or other Special Reports of Service," of Lieutenant Colonel C.F. Jerram, CMG, DSO, RM, 1926. Copy in Jerram's official record of service.

34. Jerram personal diary and scrapbook, entries for 14 April and 30 May 1918 (ARCHIVES 11/13/24(E)) and 9 October and 6 November 1918 (ARCHIVES 11/13/24(D)).

35. All five of the Mentioned in Despatches certificates awarded to Jerram are retained in the archives of the Royal Marines Museum (ARCHIVES 6/13/3.) In addition to the previously mentioned two, the other three are from Field Marshal Sir Douglas Haig.

36. *London Gazette*, 10 June 1919, p. 7508, and 21 July 1919. The Croix de Guerre citation reads: "Pendant les operations du 14 au 20 Octobre 1918, en liaison avec la 126o Division Francaise, qui ont ete couronnees de succes le Chef d'Etat-Major de la 46o Division britannique a fait assurer avec efficacite l'appui de la 126o D.I. par la cooperation de la 46o D.I. Britannique a sa gauche en prevoyant avec grande intelligence toutes mesures necessaires a cet effet." (Ordre No. 153, 22 Octobre 1918. Le General [Louis C.A.F.] Mathieu, Comdt 126 Division d'Infanterie). Copy in Jerram File, ARCHIVES 9/2/J.

37. Lieutenant Colonel C.F. Jerram to Corps Historian letter of 20 September 1968. "Jerram." ARCHIVES 9/2/J2.

38. Blumberg, *Britain's Sea Soldiers*, 480.

39. Jerram personal diary and scrapbook, 1 October 1918. ARCHIVES 11/13/24(E). In his history of World War I, Hew Strachan succinctly described this action, concluding, "The capture of the canal by the 46th Division was one of the great feats of arms of the war..." Hew Strachan, *The First World War* (New York, 2003), 319. This operation at the time received considerable publicity, to include his Division's achievements in the St. Quentin area; for example, see the

news reports, often general but with accompanying maps, in *The Times*, 10, 13, 17, 25, 26 (two), 27, and 30 September, and 1 (three), 2 (three), 3 (three), 4 (two), 5, 8 (three), and 10 October 1918. A little more detail is in one report dated 1 October 1918: "Hard Fighting on the British Front," in which the 46th (North Midland) Division was identified by name and its accomplishments noted.

40. Copies of the published order, report, and other communications pertaining to the St. Quentin operation are in Jerram's diaries and scrapbooks. ARCHIVES 11/13/24(D) and (E).

41. Personal and official (copy) war diaries, XIII Army Corps and 46th Division, 11 November and 10 November 1918, respectively. ARCHIVES 11/13/24 (D).

42. Jerram personal diary and scrapbook, 12 and 13 November 1918. ARCHIVES 11/13/24(E). (No entry for 11 November 1918).

43. Officers Recommended for Command and Staff Appointments, 46th Division: Major (T/Lt-Col.) C.F. Jerram, D.S.O., by Major General G.F. Boyd, December 1918. "Jerram," ARCHIVES 9/2/J.

44. "King George V Scholarships," Summary of, 1923. This file provides background information on the establishment of the fund and its evolution, plus the names of recipients from 1914 to 1923. Eleven officers are listed as having received the prize (after nominated by the head of the Royal Marines to the Trustees), with Jerram being the third/fourth—as an officer could hold in for two years (the second did, Captain Alan Bourne in 1914 and 1915—a future head of the Corps during World War II and was later important in Jerram's service in that conflict). Other recipients were Captain Dudley Aman, the first awardee in 1914 and later Baron Marley of Marley, a Labourite peer in the 1930s; Captain and Brevet Major Edward Bamford, awarded the Victorian Cross in the First World War; and Captain Eric Weston, who later commanded the Mobile Naval Base Defence Organisation I on Crete when the Germans invaded that island in May 1941. ARCHVES 9/2/-. "Young Officers Training." (See also Appendix IX.)

45. This was a requirement for the course; Confidential Third Army No. G.71132 of 10/12/18 in Jerram personal diary and scrapbook. ARCHIVES 11/13/24(E). For an analysis of the background and future of this class, see Major R.N.C. Mossop, "A Vintage Year," *British Army Review*, December 1990, 49–51. For an overview, albeit not objective, of the Staff College in the post–World War I era, see Brevet-Major A.R. Godwin Austen, *The Staff and the Staff College* (London, 1927), chap. X: "The Great War and After, 1914–1927"; Jerram's class of 1919 is discussed on pages 270–273.

46. *Owl Pie*, Camberley, Christmas, 1919, 45 (printed). *An Owl's Wife*, Xmas, 1919, "Mrs. Jerram," no page number. (Handwritten). Both formerly in the Library of the British Army Staff College, Camberley. Copies, editor's possession.

47. C. F. Jerram Photograph Album, "Emergency Battalion," pages 38–40. ARCHIVES 11/14/5 (D).

48. Lieutenant Colonel P. Molloy letter to Major C.F. Jerram, 7 June 1921. "Jerram," ARCHIVES 9/2/J.

49. Extract, Report of Admiral Sir John F. Parry, KCB, on forming a Citizen Guard in Dorset, October 1919. "Jerram," ARCHIVES 9/2/J.

50. Jerram, "The Navy," 25. For another perspective on the Royal Navy of this era, see Vice Admiral Sir Louis Le Bailly, KBE, CB *From Fisher to the Falklands* (London, 1991), chaps. 1 to 5.

51. *The Globe and Laurel*, Vol. XXIX, no. 6, June 1922, 89; No. 9, September 1922, 139–140; and No. 10, October 1922, 154–155.

52. C. F. Jerram Photograph Album, cutting: "Plymouth Division. Morning Orders," 14 September 1925, p. 83. ARCHIVES 11/14/5(D).

53. Adjutant General, Royal Marines: Précis for the War office of "Confidential or other Special Reports of Service," 1926.

54. Adjutant General, Royal Marines, to Lieutenant Colonel C.F. Jerram, CMG, DSO, RM: Orders to Active Duty, 1 January 1940. "Jerram," ARCHIVES 9/2/J.

55. The course for which Jerram was responsible was only one of several others at the Royal Marines Military School. Ironically, when he left it was commanded by one of his former subalterns, Major General A.C. St. Clair Morford, CBE, MC—who died within two months of Jerram's departure. For background, see "R.M. Military School," *The Globe and Laurel*, September 1944, Vol. LII, No. 9, p. 227; and "Obituary. Major General A.C. St. Clair-Morford, CBE, MC (Ret.), *The Globe and Laurel*, June 1945, Vol. LIII, No 6, 192.

56. Lieutenant Anthony Patrick Jerram, RM, date of rank of 22 January 1942; Chatham Division, serving with 46 Royal Marine Commando. *The Navy List*, June 1944, 1067. He was killed in action at Normandy on 11 June 1944. His death (with the names and ranks of many other Marines, including 30 other offices, covering half a page), was announced in *The Globe and Laurel*, October 1944, Vol. LII, No.11, 267. Lieutenant Jerram is buried at the Commonwealth War Graves cemetery in Bayeux, France. Lieutenant Colonel Jerram crossed the Channel and the Commanding Officer of 46 Commando took him over the ground in which the action occurred.

57. A description of his departures, and quite tumultuous one it must have been, is reported in "R/M/ Military School," *The Globe and Laurel*, May 1945, Vol. LIII, No. 5, 144–145.

58. General Sir T.L. Hunton letter to Lieutenant Colonel C.F. Jerram, 22 March 1945; and Major General Dallas Brooks letter to Lieutenant Colonel C.F. Jerram, 26 March 1945. "Jerram," ARCHIVES 9/2/J.

59. Lieutenant Colonel Charles E.C. Ransome, Major John J. Carter, Major Thomas A.H. Scott, Captain Bernard G. Tozer, and Captain Pater Harris letter to Lieutenant Colonel C.F. Jerram, of 3 April 1945. "Jerram." ARCHIVEs 9/2/J.

60. Royal Marines Association: A registered charity in the United Kingdom, its stated purpose "is to maintain and promote esprit de corps and comradeship amongst all Royal Marines and their families, past and present."

61. General obituary by Major General J.L. Moulton, CB, DSO, OBE, under "Old Comrades. Lt.-Col. C.F. Jerram, CMG, DSO, by J.L.M.," *The Globe and Laurel*, Vol. LXXVII, No. 2, April, 1969, 130.

62. "Old Comrades. Lt.-Col. C.F. Jerram, CMG, DSO. M.B. writes," *The Globe and Laurel*, Vol. LXXVII, No. 2, April, 1969, 130.

63. E. R. Roullier, "Lieutenant Colonel Jerram," *The Globe and Laurel*, Vol. LXXVII, No. 3, June 1969, 144.

Essay on Sources

In editing the memoir of Lieutenant Colonel Charles Frederic Jerram, CMG, DSO, Royal Marines, and in compiling the biographical overview of his life, diverse sources have been used. Jerram's official record of service (the National Archives, formerly the Public Record Office, ADM 196/63, pages 155 and 146) provides the *official* record of his career in the Royal Marines (minus confidential reports but with some excerpts). This contains detailed information on his professional life, both as recorded on its pages and in loose documents attached to them. The first numbered page is the original created when he entered the Corps, the second a continuation sheet pertaining to his later years. By 1901, an officer's record of service included such basic information as name, date and place of birth, chronological list of assignments ("Where Serving"), dates of promotion ("Dates of Commissions and Appointments"), father's "profession," date of marriage and name of wife, date and place of death, professional qualifications (under "Examinations" and "Special Attainments"), awards and orders ("Rewards and Distinctions"), professional schools, and other information.

"Records of Service," however, do not contain copies of "Confidential Reports," the latter which are closed to the public. Nonetheless, they may contain excerpts from them via two means: An extension of the "Where Serving" blocks with dates of reports, abbreviations for evaluations on "General Conduct, Ability, Professional Knowledge, Whether Temperate Habits, Special Knowledge or Acquirements, and Remarks"; and, under "Special Reports of Service," extracts might be recorded from reports or other official documents. Also, other official correspondence may also be in a "Record of Service."

However, the basic source for the memoir is Jerram's own manuscript (see Preface), retained by the Royal Marines Museum, Eastney, Portsmouth, Hampshire, (originally in ARCHIVES 9/2/J, now in ARCHIVES 11/13/206) and other Jerram personal papers spread throughout various record groups. In ARCHIVES 9/2/J, "Officers Biographies," the Jerram file contains various documents, including copies of "flimsies," i.e., brief evaluations of his performance of duty while at sea as part of various ships' companies; commendations pertaining to intelligence activities while in China; a copy of his performance evaluation by the commander of the Royal Naval Division, dated 25 March 1916; a typed copy of his Croix de Guerre citation awarded by the French Government during the First World War; a copy of the 46th Division commander's recommendation for a command and staff appointment; Rear Admiral Sir John F. Parry's commendation of 1919, written after an assignment to work on aide-to-the-civil-power in case of civil unrest; a copy of the orders of 1940 recalling Jerram to active service with the Corps in Second World War; and commendatory letters on his release from active duty in 1945. At one time there were other materials in this file, but these have been dispersed into other Jerram papers record groups in the archives of the Royal Marines Museum.

These include copies of official and personal war diaries from his service in World War I (ARCHIVES 11/13/24), extensive and detailed spread over five volumes. The personal ones include commentary, newspaper cuttings, and some photographs. Jerram also retained copies of the War Diary of the Royal Marine Brigade, Dardanelles, 1915–16, and a continuation of this brigade's service throughout 1916 in its various evolutions as part of the 63rd (Royal Naval) Division; a personal war diary when he served with the 31st Division, XIII Corps, and 46th Division in 1917 and 1918; and an extensive personal and candid handwritten diary, with newspaper cuttings, for the period from 9 April 1917 to early 1919.

Four separate albums are in ARCHIVES 11/14/5 which contain photographs, newspaper cuttings, personal memorabilia, and other items. These cover the prewar years from 1906 to 1914, postwar family pictures, materials pertaining to activity during the possible general strike of 1921 and his service on board HMS *Raleigh*, and a scrapbook of newspaper cuttings titled "Operations in the Dardanelles, 1914," although it covers the year 1915. In ARCHIVES 11/13/024 (G) is a personal diary for 1914 and early 1915; this contains his writings on the initial days of the war, the Royal Marine Brigade's commitment to Ostend; the loss of HMS *Aboukir*, HMS *Cressy*, and HMS *Hogue*; his illness of 1914, and then appointment as R.M. Brigade Captain, with its final entry dated 19 February 1915.

The Jerram papers also include four photograph albums (PHOTOGRAPH 13/11/89); these provide extensive coverage of his service in the Far East and other sea duty before World War I, the cruise of HMS *Raleigh* in North America in 1921 and 1922, and some personal events, including his wedding and family holidays. Significantly, there are few photographs from World War I in this collection.

Jerram also wrote many small pieces in the Corps' journal, *The Globe and Laurel*, and two long unpublished essays on the pre–Great War Royal Navy and Royal Marines. The latter are "The Navy at the Beginning of the 20th Century" (ARCHIVES 2/20/1) and "Some Reminences [sic] in the Corps of Royal Marines" (ARCHIVES 2/7/1; carbon copy in ARCHIVES 2/20/1). There were also materials pertaining to Jerram retained in the former library of the Army Staff College, Camberley. No material exists in his personal papers for his year of study at the Royal Naval College, Greenwich—although comments pertaining to his "batch," i.e., officers of the Royal Marine Light Infantry commissioned on 1 September 1901, are included in the annual report to the Admiralty of the Admiral President for 1902; this explains in general indirect verbiage why Jerram was not awarded the Sword of Honour when he completed the course. However, *The Navy Lists* in late 1902 and early 1903 reflected his higher order of merit standing at Greenwich by his moving up the seniority list because of his excellence at Greenwich—as noted in comparison with the initial standings of his batch in *The Navy List* of late 1901 (National Maritime Museum, Greenwich, NAI/3/29).

The Jerram papers, however, lack one major document important to both his career and views on a modern, capable, and relevant Corps: The paper he wrote and submitted to the Madden Committee (1923–24) which studied the role and mission of the Royal Marines. In his memoir, Jerram recounted exchanges he had with the committee but did not quote from his own paper. However, Jerram's submission, along with others, and the Madden Committee's terms of reference and its final report are retained in the National Archives, ADM 1/8664/134, "Functions and Training of Royal Marines, (1923) 1924." Jerram's paper is attached, but it has no title and no date.

Many other sources were consulted in preparing this memoir for publication. As needed, archival materials were consulted at the National Archives (formerly the Public

Record Office); Royal Marines Museum, Eastney; Naval Historical Branch, Portsmouth; National Maritime Museum, Greenwich; and the libraries and archives of the former Army Staff College, Camberley, and Royal Naval College, Greenwich. Citations note when such material has been used with appropriate locations and record group identification.

In additional to checking on aspects of Jerram's career, much of this context and identification material pertained to the identification of personnel, and the provision of biographical and professional details for individuals mentioned in the text. For Royal Marines, the basic source has been the Records of Service of Royal Marine officers retained at the National Archives, Kew, Richmond, Surrey. These are contained in eight ledger volumes, ADM 196/58 to ADM 196/65. Other sources of information on Royal Marine and Royal Naval officers were the official monthly Navy lists prepared by the Admiralty. These also included data on ships of the Royal Navy, the officers assigned to them and their respective assignments; requirements for obtaining a commission in the Royal Marines and Royal Navy; uniform regulations; and the various naval schools and their curricula and instructional staffs. For other Marine and naval information as needed, the similar quarterly, but privately published, Lean's *The Royal Navy List and Recorder* was used. Lean's included both officers on active service and those retired, plus an officers' biographical section titled "War and Meritorious Services" (prepared by each individual who voluntarily submitted his entry), plus lists with dates of rank, career promotions, assignments, and awards of medals and decorations; language qualifications; a summary of ships commissions; naval bibliography, etc.

Information on Army officers was also obtained from the official monthly and quarterly Army lists prepared by the War Office. Royal Marine officers were also included in these official Army lists. For Army and Marine officers, one other privately published reference was used: *Hart's Annual Army List, Special Reserve List, and Territorial Force List*. This data was supplemented, as needed, for officers and civilians by entries in *Who Was Who* or the annually produced *Who's Who*.

As appropriate, other sources for biographical background information were used. These included Burke's *A Genealogical and Heraldic History of the Landed Gentry of Great Britain & Ireland* and Burke's *Genealogical and Heraldic History of the Peerage, Baronetage, and Knightage*. For Church of England clerical information, the annual editions of *Crockford's Clerical Directory* were consulted. Requests for information on individuals was asked of and provided by the Foreign and Commonwealth Office, the Royal Navy Historical Branch, the Royal Marines Museum, and various Army (British and Canadian) regimental museums.

Information on various subjects has been provided for perspective or reference in the endnotes, as deemed appropriate. The sources for ships were the official monthly *Navy Lists*; the privately published Lean's *Royal Navy List and Recorder*; the annual editions of *Jane's Fighting Ships*; Conway's *All The World's Fighting Ships, 1860–1905* (1979) and Conway's *All The World's Fighting Ships, 1906–1921* (1985); *The Naval Annual, 1913* (1913, reprinted, 1970, edited by Viscount Hythe); and, for quick reference to individual vessels, Captain T. D. Manning, CBE, VRD, RNVR (Ret'd) and Commander C. F. Walker, RN (Ret'd), *British Warship Names* (1959), J. J. Colledge, *Ships of the Royal Navy, Vol. I*, (1987), and F. J. Dittmar & J. J. Colledge, *British Warships, 1914–1919* (1972). A further general reference was David A. Thomas, *A Companion to the Royal Navy* (1988).

Detailed information on World War I army formations was obtained from Major A. F. Becke's four-part order of battle series (The Army Council, G.H.Q.s, Armies, Corps, and Divisions), published by His Majesty's Stationery Office as part of the official History of the

Great War, and Ray Westlake's *Kitchener's Army* (1989). For background information on various Army regiments mentioned in the text, the principal references were J. M. Brereton's *A Guide to the Regiments and Corps of the British Army* (1985), Arthur Swinson's *A Register of the Regiments and Corps of the British Army* (1972), and David Ascoli's *A Companion to the British Army, 1660–1983* (1983).

Other sources were checked for different kinds of needed information. The following gazetteers and atlases were used to identify locations: Primarily *The Times Gazetteer of the World* (1895), but also *The Concise Oxford Dictionary of English Place-names*, 4th edition (1985), *The Columbia Lippincott Gazetteer of the World* (1952), *The Times Atlas of the World* (1980), and the websites of the British Commonwealth War Graves Commission (http://www.cwgc.org/), and official websites of towns and villages in France. Sources for naval and sailing terms were *A Naval Encyclopaedia: Comprising Dictionary of Nautical Words and Phrases*, etc. (1881); *Jackspeak: The Pusser's Rum Guide to Royal Navy Slanguage* (1989); Rene de Kerchove, *International Marine Dictionary*, 2nd Edition (1961); and Peter Kemp, *The Oxford Companion to Ships and the Sea* (1975). For First World War one sites and maps, Martin Gilbert, *Atlas of the First World War: The Complete History* (1994); Arthur Banks, *A Military Atlas of the First World War* (Barnsley, South Yorkshire, 1998); and Mark Adkin, *The Western Front Companion: The Complete Guide to How the Armies Fought for Four Devastating Years, 1914–1918* (London, 2013). Also, the Commonwealth War Graves Commission website (http://www.cwgc.org/), with reference to specific locations.

The Jerram memoir is by a Royal Marine and about his career in the Corps; therefore, certain histories were used as needed. The principal ones were: Colonel Cyril Field, RMLI, *Britain's Sea Soldiers: A History of the Royal Marines*, Vols. I and II (1924); Major General Sir H. E. Blumberg, KCB, *Britain's Sea Soldiers: A Record of the Royal Marines during the War, 1914–1919* (1927); James D. Ladd, *The Royal Marines, 1919–1980* (1980); Major General Julian Thompson, *The Royal Marines: From Sea Soldiers to Special Force* (2000); Richard Brooks, *The Royal Marines, 1664 to the Present* (2002); and Edward Fraser and L. G. Carr-Laughton, *The Royal Marine Artillery, 1804–1923*, Vols. I and II (1930).

With the centennial of the First World War, many histories of the lead-up to and what occurred in that conflict are appearing. This includes the Royal Navy—with much of the new literature challenging long help interpretations of that service. The volume of the results of this, and older, research is too much to list here. However, as appropriate, the content and course citations include references to appropriate material.

Lieutenant Colonel Jerram devoted much space in his memoir to the First World War. With the centennial of that conflict that is now upon us, a flood of literature has appeared on the causes of that cataclysmic event of the early 20th century, the opening campaigns, and ensuing ones and battles—so much so that all of this voluminous literature cannot be addressed. However, one of the best one volume overview histories of that conflict, for both general background and analysis, is Hew Strachan, *The First World War* (2003) and for the British Army in 1914, Allan Mallinson, *1914: Fight the Good Fight—Britain, The Army, & the Coming of the First World War* (2014). Gallipoli was a major event in Jerram's life and he devoted considerable attention to that ill-fated campaign; from his perspective, the standard detailed account of that operation from the "naval" ground operations perspective is Douglas Jerrold, *The Royal Naval Division* (1923). Also important for overview of it are Alan Moorehead, *Gallipoli* (1956); Michael Hickey, Gallipoli (1995); Tim Travers, *Gallipoli, 1915* (2001); L.A. Carlyon, *Gallipoli* (2003); Peter Hart, *Gallipoli* (2011); and many others appearing in bookstores. However, Jerram considered Robert Rhodes James, *Gallipoli* (1966), the best history then available of that operation. For all the major British campaigns and operations of that war, the battlefield guides by Major Tonie and Valmai Holt are invaluable.

With regard to the Western Front, the centennial of the Great War many new works have appeared and will continue to do so. These span the spectrum from the very tactical through the operational to the strategic levels of war. With respect to the operations in which Lieutenant Colonel Jerram was involved, appropriate literature has been cited in the notes. This includes the history of the 46th (North Midland) Division of which he was Chief of Staff (or as it was called then, General Staff Officer-1 or GSO[1]): Major R. E. Priestly, MC, RE, *Breaking the Hindenburg Line: The Story of the 46th (North Midland) Division* (1919) Jerram wrote from the tactical perspective and some of the new research and writing addressing the operations in which he served include Peter Hart, *The Somme: The Darkest Hours* on the Western Front (2008); William Philpott, *Three Armies on the Somme: The First Battle of the 20th Century* (2010). More recent works include Peter Simkins, *From the Somme to Victory: The British Army's Experiences on the Western Front, 1916-1918* (2014). With regard to the 46th (North Midland) Division, its operations are assessed with respect to what the British Army learned through four years of fighting in Simon Peaple, *Mud, Blood and Determination: The History of the 46th Division (North Midlands) in the Great War* (2015). Within the larger perspective of the Army Britain raised for The Great War, K. W. Mitchinson studied the Territorials in the first two years of the conflict in *The Territorial Force at War at War, 1914-1916* (2014). Biographies of individuals under whom Jerram served and on whom he had strong opinions are appearing; an assessment of the command situation on "Y" Beach at Gallipoli which he discussed is in Elaine McFarland, *A Slashing Man of Action: The Life of Lieutenant General Sir Aylmer Hunter-Weston, MP* (2015). Finally, as necessary various war diaries retained at the National Archives, Kew, were used, especially that of the 46th Division.

As needed, other sources were consulted, to include the journal of the Corps, *The Globe and Laurel*, regimental and division histories, World War I official and unofficial histories, official and unofficial casualty and awards books, railroad sources, and other references pertinent to the life and career of Lieutenant Colonel Jerram. These were used to prepare appropriate notes, or validate various passages in the manuscript. These and other sources not listed above, if appropriate, are cited in specific notes.

In summary, bringing Lieutenant Colonel Jerram "back to life" so he could "speak" to a 21st century reader about his life and perspectives of his world was more than simply finding a handwritten manuscript and typing a manuscript. Other sources were needed to ensure a proper context was provided, and details of his and other men's lives could be accurately recounted. Ultimately, I hope the reader has found this endeavor of value—as indeed has the editor!

Index

Aboukir 79, 80, 160, 171, 196*n*6, 196*n*13, 196*n*14, 214
AE1 74, 195*n*28
AE2 74, 195*n*28
Alexander, Maj. Gen. Ronald O. (Canada) 126 134, 205*n*7
Algerine 46, 193*n*12
Alvey, Maj. Jack (RM) 208*n*6
Aman, Maj. Dudley L. (RMA) 183, 212*n*44
Anderson, Lt. Gen. Warren H. (Army) 125, 126, 130, 205*n*4
ANZAC *see* Gallipoli
Arbuthnot, Col. William P. (RMLI) 70, 194*n*6
Armistice 1918 3, **122**, 123, 129, 162, 164, 182, 202*n*44, 204*n*41
armour divisions 145, 184–185, 208*n*9, 208*n*11
Armstrong, Maj. Harold G.B. (RMLI) 89, 198*n*12
Arras (France) 97, 100, 102, 104, 168, 201*n*28, 201*n*34, 201*n*36, 202*n*8, 203*n*19
Arrogant 192*n*5
artillery (army) 25, 28, 78, 87, 91, 93, 97, 99, 101, 108, 109, 116, 117, 118, 122, 126, 145, 148, 164, 172, 177, 188*n*25, 188*n*26, 189*n*1, 189*n*6, 197*n*18, 199*n*17, 201*n*19, 201*n*24, 203*n*32
Aspinall-Oglander, Brig. Gen. Cecil F. (Army) 98, 200*n*11
Aston, Maj. Gen. Sir George G. (RMA) 81, 197*n*21
Astraea 46, 47, **48**, **49**, 52, **53**, 54, 55, **57**, 58, 60, 61, 62, 64, 66, 67, 143, 159, 170, 171, 174, 193*n*3, 193*n*13, 194*n*43
Australians 74, 88, 89, 112, 114, 119, 120, 143, 160, 193*n*5, 195*n*28, 198*n*12, 198*n*13, 199*n*14, 204*n*39

Backhouse, Adm. Oliver (RN) 82, 197*n*25
Baldwin, Col. Frederick (RMLI) 26, 190*n*25
Ballantyne, Lt. Ernest O. (RN) 31, 191*n*46
Bamford, Maj. Edward (RMLI) 183, 212*n*44
Barker, Maj. Geoffrey (RMLI) 180
Barnshute (nickname) 98, 200*n*10
Bath, Capt. John A. (RM) 75, 82, 195*n*30
Beatty, Adm. of the Fleet David (RN) 33, 34, 35, 36, 124, 137, 157, 158, 170, 176, 191*n*3, 192*n*5, 192*n*8, 192*n*14, 196*n*12, 211*n*20
Bedford 58
Bellenglise (France) 114, **115**, **116**, 117, 118, 163, 164, 174, 203*n*27, 203*n*31, 204*n*49, 205*n*59
Bendyshe, Lt. Col. Richard N. (RMLI) 197*n*29
Bentinck, Adm. Rudolph W. (RN) 139, 207*n*56
Bermuda 131, 132, 189*n*7, 206*n*22
Bethell, Maj. Gen. Keith (Army) 204*n*53
Bethell's Force 122, 204*n*53
Bethune (France) **107**, 108, 202*n*8, 203*n*19
Bewes, Lt. Col. Arthur Edward (RMLI) 84, 85, 197*n*34
Birdwood, Field Marshal William R. (Army) 198*n*13, 199*n*34

Bismarck (German ship) 80, 196*n*11
Blumberg, Gen. Sir Herbert E. (RMLI) 75, 112, 137, **138**, 139, 140, 141, 142, 163, 195*n*31, 210*n*12, 211*n*26, 216
"Bobby" (also "Bobbie") (horse) 83, 91, 94, 109, 162
Bott, Commander Leslie C. (RN) 135, 207*n*42
Bourne, Gen. Sir Alan G. B. (RM) **145**, 183, 208*n*4, 212*n*44
Boxer Rebellion/War 21, 26, 45, 49, 55, 189*n*7, 189*n*8, 191*n*50, 192*n*8, 193*n*15
Boyd, Maj. Gen. Gerald Farrell (Army) 113, 114, 116, 118, 120, 121, 123, 124, 125, 128, 161, 165, 203*n*, 212*n*43
Boyd, William (actor) 206*n*35
Braemar Castle 83
Brewer, Maj. Herbert Reginald (RMLI) 180
Britannic 95, 199*n*37
Bromley, Rear Adm. Arthur (RN) 131, 133, 135, 206*n*28
Brooke, Col. Charles L. B. (RMA) 112, 203*n*18
Brooks, Gen. Dallas (RM) 168, 189*n*8, 212*n*58
Brough, Lt. Col. John B. (RMA) 189*n*6
Bruay (France) 109, 202*n*8
Bulwark 190*n*32, 200*n*38
Bunker Hill (Battle 1775) 27, 190*n*26
Burns-Lindow, Lt. Col. Isaac William (Army) 111, 114, 117, 120, 121, 202*n*14
Burton, Capt. Reginald E. G. (RMLI) 180

Bush, Rear Adm. James Tobin (RN) 16, 188*n*16

Cadmus 45, 193*n*12
Caesar 77, 95, 171, 174, 195*n*32
Camberley *see* Staff College, Camberley
Campbell, Brig. Gen. John Vaughn (Army) 109, 110, 202*n*4, 203*n*31
Cape Helles *see* Gallipoli
Capetown 134, 136
Cassidy, Hopalong 134, 206*n*35
casualties *see* killed and wounded; *also see under* Gallipoli; Jerram, Charles Federic; Western Front
cavalry 110, 113, 119, 120, 121, 122, 126, 133, 181*n*, 184, 185*n*, 188*n*25, 190*n*30, 204*n*47, 204*n*50, 204*n*53
Cawdor Castle 83
Centurion 191*n*50
Charterhouse (Surrey) 9, 11, 14, 18, 187*ch*1*n*3
Charybdis 67, 159, 171, 174, 193*n*13
Chatham Division (Barracks), Royal Marines 20, 23, 77, 78, 129, 158, 183, 190*n*28, 196*n*1, 207*n*51, 210*n*9, 211*n*17, 212*n*56
Cheesman, Lt. Col. Ernest G. (RMLI) 180
Child, Brig. Gen. Smith Hill (Army) 109, 202*n*7
Chinese Regiment 49, 193*n*15
Chobham (Surrey) 9, 127, 187*ch*1*n*1
Christian, Adm. Arthur H. (RN) 79, 80, 196*n*5
Churchill, Winston L.S. 5, 77, 79, 82, 91, 101, 137, 157, 188*n*23, 195*n*33, 197*n*18
Clio 45, 46, 58, 62, 174, 193*n*12
colours (unit) 26, 27, 29, 166, 191*n*35
Colquhoun, Maj. Robert C. (RMLI) 189*n*6
commandos 56, 87, 138, 148, 156, 177, 207*n*52, 209*n*16, 209*n*22, 209*n*23, 210*n*11, 212*n*56
Constance 206*n*22
Conybeare, Capt. Charles B. (RM) 85, 86, 198*n*36
Coode, Lt. Col. Cuthbert H. (RMLI) 183
Corrigon, Gordon (Historian) 1, 187*pref.n*2
Craig, Maj. Gen. Archibald M. (RM) 137, 207*n*44

crammer 19, 188*n*23
Cressy 79, 80, 160, 171, 196*n*6, 196*n*13, 196*n*14, 214
Croix de Guerre (France) 119, 163, 175, 194*n*3, 195*n*30, 197*n*20, 197*n*24, 197*n*25, 197*n*33, 198*n*36, 198*n*37, 198*ch*7*n*10, 199*n*18, 204*n*44, 211*n*36, 213
Curlew 206*n*22

Davidson, John W.O. (Diplomat) 56, 58, 193*n*22
Davidson, Mrs. (Widow–Landlady, Stonehouse) 72, 73
Davies, Gen. Francis John (Army) 199*n*24
Deal, Royal Marines Depot 20, 83, 138, 144, 167, 172, 207*n*51
Deed, Capt. John C. (RMLI) 35, 192*n*7
Defiance 141, 208*n*59
de Robeck, Adm. of the Fleet John (RN) 98, 200*n*39
Devonshire 195*n*30
Diana 192*n*5
Dill, Field Marshal John (Army) 126, 144, 157, 205*n*6, 209*n*14
Distinguished Conduct Medal (DCM) 86, 102, 113, 178, 198*n*38, 203*n*
Distinguished Service Cross (DSC) 178, 199*n*29, 200*n*6
Distinguished Service Medal (DSM) 178, 199*n*29
Distinguished Service Order (DSO) 108, 123, 124, 161, 175, 176, 178, 199*n*26, 200*n*6
Dixon, Maj. William (RMA) 43, 60, 193*n*29
Dodman (also "Deadman") Point (Cornwall) 18, 80, 188*n*20, 197*n*16
Dorling, Col. Francis H. (Army) 110, 202*n*11
Dorling, Vice Adm. James W. S. (RN) 206*n*23
Dougherty, Lt. Eric B. C. (RM) 93, 199*n*
Drag Hunt (Also Paper Hunt or Paper Chase) 126, 205*n*9; *see also* Paper Hunt
Drake 167, 172
Drake, Col. Henry D. (RMA) 23, 24, 189*n*6
Dreadnought 34, 40, 58, 68, 77, 158, 191*n*38, 191*n*49, 194*n*1
Drury, Lt. Col. William Price (RMLI) 53, 190*n*28, 192*n*2
Duckworth, Lt. Col. Ralph (Army) 203*n*4

Durst, Maj. Alan Lydiat (RMLI) 180
Dustan, Maj. John W. (RMLI) 32, 35, 36, **37**, 191*n*50

Eagles, Maj. Charles E. C. (RMLI) 180
Eastney Divsiion (Barracks), Royal Marines 20, 104, 153, 181*n*, 200*n*8, 201*n*37, 207*n*51, 208*n*6, 210*n*1, 211*n*17
Eclipse 74, 82, 171, 174, 195*n*27, 195*n*28
Ecoivres (France) 104, 106
Edward VII 24, 38, **57**, 63, **64**
Elizabeth II 151, 209*n*33
Embusque 106, 109, 114
Euryalus 77, 78, 79, 81, 91, 159, 160, 171, 174, 196*n*3, 197*n*17
Evans, Maj. Arthur Kelly (RMLI) 180
Evans, Maj. Horace Carlyon (RMLI) 159
Evelegh, Lt. Col. Edward G. (RMLI) 93, 199*n*28
Excellent 189*n*1
Exmouth 73, 74, 171, 195*n*19
Eyres, Adm. Cresswell J. (RN) 44, 193*n*7

Festing, Col. Maurice C. (RMLI) 91, 128, 183, 199*n*18, 205*n*13
Field, Capt. Clifford (RMLI) 79, 80, 196*n*6
Flimsy (Royal Navy office reports) 136, 211*n*18, 213
Flora 47, 52, 54, **60**, 62, **63**, 65, 159, 170, 171, 174, 189*n*2, 193*n*13, 194*n*41
Foch, Marshal Ferdinand (France) 112, 146, 197*n*21, 208*n*13
Forbes, Maj. H. N. (Army) 203*n*25
Ford, Gen. Richard V. T. (RMA) 207*n*57
Formidable 192*n*7
Forteau (on the St. Lawrence River) 134, 135, 136, 166, 172, 207*n*38
Forton Division (barracks) *see* Portsmouth Division (barracks), Royal Marines
46th Division Chap. 9, 102, 108, 147, 161, 162, 163, 164, 165, 172, 174, 202*n*31, 202*n*48, 202*ch*9*n*1, 202*ch*9*n*1, 202*ch*9*n*9, 202*ch*9*n*11, 202*ch*9*n*13, 203*n*20, 203*n*31, 203*n*35, 203*n*37, 204*n*39, 204*n*41, 204*n*42, 204*n*43,

204n46, 204n48, 205n59, 211–212n39, 212n41, 212n43, 213, 214, 217
"Foxtrot" (horse) 149, 150
Fraser, Capt. Ronald A. (RN) 130, 206n23
Freestun, Col. William H. M. (Army) 111, 114, 202n15
French 17, 21, 45, 46, 79, 90, 93, 94, 100, 106, 109, 112, 118, 119, 120, 121, 122, 162, 163, 182, 202n9, 203n29, 204n45
Fresnoy (France) 120, 163
Freyberg, Field Marshal Bernard (New Zealand) 99, 157
friction (Clausewitzian) 4, 54, 201n42, 204n43

Gallipoli 3, 87, 90, 91, 95, 97, 117, 141, 154, 156, 159, 160, 161, 162, 163, 164, 171, 180, 181, 195n16, 196n2, 197n20, 197n32, 198n34, 198n35, 198ch7n1, 198ch7n4, 199n15; Achi Baba 90, 91, 199n15; ANZAC 88, 89, 90, 94, 160, 174, 198n34, 201n27; Bulair 88; Cape Helles 83, 84, 86, 88, 90, 91, 160, 174, 198n11, 199n15; casualties 84, 85, 87, 88, 90, 94, 97, 100, 198n37; Chatham Battalion (RND) 83, 88, 89, 92, 93, 97, 199n23; Deal Battalion (RND) 83, 88, 197n29; demonstration 87, 88; Drake Battalion (RND) 93, 199n31; evacuation 94, 95, 97; Kum Kale 84, 160, 174; Nelson Battalion (RND) 92, 93, 94, 199n23; Plymouth Battalion (RND) 75, 83, 84, 88, 92, 93, 95, 97; Portsmouth Battalion (RND) 82, 83, 87, 88, 89, 92, 93, 94, 95, 97, 197n30, 198n11, 199n23; Royal Naval Division (RND) 78, 81, 82, 83, 86, 87, 88, 160, 198ch7n2, 199n23; trenches 84, 85, 89, 90, 91, 92, 93, 94, 95, 198n12, 200n3; "V" Beach 95, 198n6, 199n35; "W" Beach 94, 199n33; "Y" Beach 88, 198n5
Gardiner, Maj. (The Reverend) John K. (RM) 147, 209n18
Gavrelle (France) 103, 104, 105, 106, 201n34
George, David Lloyd (prime minister, UK) 3
George V 77, 165, 183,
187$pref.n$4, 205n59, 205ch10n14, 212n44
Germany and Germans 3, 50, 73, 78, 101, 103, 104, 105, 106, 112, 114, 120, 122, 123, 124, 126, 139, 145, 159, 164, 167, 182n, 187$pref.n$4, 189n1, 195n16, 202n44, 202n47, 204n45, 204n48, 204n53, 205n54, 212n44
Gibraltar 31, 33, 36, **37**, 44, 158, 205n5, 208n11
Gieve lifebelt (naval tailor) 117, 163, 164, 203n36
Globe and Laurel (journal of the Royal Marines) xii, 153, 166, 181, 183, 214, 217
Gloucester Castle 88
Glunicke, Maj. Gen. Robert C. A. (RMLI) 183
Godalming (Surrey) 9, 10 11, 13, 14, 157, 172, 210n13
Godfray, Maj. Alfred D. B. (RMA) 23, 24, 189n12
Gommecourt (France) 100, 102, 201n26
Gort, Field Marshal John (Army) 125, 127, 144, 146, 157, 183, 205n5, 208n10, 208n11, 208n12
Gosport *see* Portsmouth Division (barracks), Royal Marines
Gough, Gen. Hubert de la Poer (Army) 102, 201n32
Gowney, Maj. David J. (RM) 93, 199n5
Graham, Darcie (friend) 46, 58, **59**, 137
Grant, Engineer Capt. Henry W. (RN) 39, 192n14
Greenwich *see* Royal Naval College, Greenwich

Haig, Field Marshal Douglas (Army) 101, 161, 204n47, 211n35
Haig, Brig. Neill (Army) 119, 204n50
"Hairy" (horse) 125, 127
Hamilton, Gen. Ian (Army) 87, 91, 160, 198n3
Hammet, Read Adm. John L. (RN) **41**, 192n19
Hankey, Col. Maurice P. A. (RMA) 157 72
Hardy, Gen. Campbell (RM) **148**, 177
Harington, Brig. Gen. John (Army) 109, 202n6
Harrison, Brig. Harold C. (RMA) 183, 205n14

Hatton, Capt. Edward Allen S. (RMLI) 88, 180, 198n9
Hay, Maj. Stuart (Army) 113, 114, 117, 120, 203n23
Helford (Cornwall) 72, 142, 145, 149, **150**, 168, 173, 194n9, 208n63, 209n30
Heligoland Bight 79, 174, 196n7
Heneker, Gen. William C. G. (Army) 99, 201n15
Highflyer 73, 171, 174, 195n18
Hindenburg Line *see* Western Front
Hogue 29, 32, 43, 79, 80, 158, 160, 170, 171, 174, 191n38, 191n42, 192n4, 196n6, 196n13, 196n14, 214
Hollis, Gen. Leslie (RM) 137, 188n, 207n45
Home, Brig. Francis W. (RMLI) 28, 190n33
Hong Kong 43, 44, 45, 48, 49, **51**, 52, 53, 54, 56, 60, 62, 128, 183, 193n5
Horrocks, Lt. Gen. Brian (Army) 124, 205n58
Howe 190n32
hunt (paper/drag) 59, 122, 126, 205n9
Hunter-Weston, Lt. Gen. A. C. (Army) 87, 88, 92, 198n3
Hunton, Gen. Thomas L. (RM) 168, 209n27, 212n58
Hutchinson, Gen. Alexander R. H. (RMLI) 98, 100, 108, 140, **141**, 200n12, 210n12
Hutton, Midshipman Edward M. (RN) 134, 207n40
Hythe, Army School of Musketry 69, 159, 171, 174

Implacable 197n17
Impregnable (ex–*Howe*, ex–*Bulwark*) 28, 167, 172, 190n32, 207n46
Indian Army Staff College 203n20
infantry 19, 20, 22, 25, 42, 54, 69, 83, 88, 90, 109, 111, 117, 119, 121, 122, 137, 139, 156, 158, 181n, 182, 188n25, 197n18, 200n5, 207n51, 210n9, 211n17, 214
Irresistible 180

Jackson, Capt. I. (Army) 110, 202n10
James, Robert Rhodes (author) 87, 161, 197n31, 198n4, 211n32, 216
Japan/Japanese 3, 5, 33, 36, 40, 43, 47, 48, 49, 50, 51, 52, 58,

62, 137, 159, 187n4, 193n16, 193n25, 196n4
Jerram, Agnes Winifred (also Winnie; sister) 10, 11, 12, 27, 46, 124, 176
Jerram, Lt. Anthony Patrick (son and RM) 130, 145, 148, *149*, 167, 177, 212n56
Jerram, Catherine Florence (also Kitty and Posy; sister) 9, 11, 16, 17, 46, 81, 97, 124, 176
Jerram, Cecil Bertrand (brother) 11, 18, 61, 70, 124, 176, 188n7
Jerram, Charles (grandfather) 5, 16
Jerram, Lt. Col. Charles Frederic (RMLI) 5, 170–173, 174–175, 187pref.n6; appointments 20, 24, 29, 32, 43, 68, 77, 81, 91, 100, 104, 108, 124, 128, 137, 142, 144, 153, 158, 160, 162, 163, 165, 166, 167, 170–173, 174–174, 176, 199n22, 202n2; awards and decorations 174–175; bells 10, 74, 75, 123, 133, 167, 195n26; boating and sailing 16, 18, 28, 41, 44, 68, 72, 131, 132, 134, 135, 137, 142, 143, 149, 159, 167, 168; Britain (comments on) 9, 14, 31, 77, 142, 150, 151; candidness 138, 140, 141, 155, 156, 161, 167; casualties 84, 85, 87, 88, 90, 94, 97, 100, 103, 106, 116, 119, 198n5, 201n40, 217; childhood freedom 10, 11, 12, 16, 17, 18, 157; China (comments on) 45, 46, 47, 66, 67, 48, 52, 54, 61, 76, 67; Clifton House (school in Bristol) 19; command 2, 3, 22, 24, 29, 34, 55, 70, 73, 77, 80, 83, 87, 88, 92, 93, 96, 99, 100, 108, 118, 122, 123, 124, 125, 128, 137, 139, 142, 145, 153, 154, 156, 161, 163, 165, 166, 168, 195n20, 203n21, 205n1, 209n17; companion of St. Michael and St. George (CMG) 124, *127*, 163, 172, 175, 205n60; concussion 95; confidential (and other) reports 24, 65, 140, 141, 158, 159, 161, 165, 166, 167, 168, 190n18, 205n11, 206n36, 211n18, 212n40; Croix de Guerre (France) 119, 163, 172, 175, 204n44, 211n36, 213; daughter (infant death) 74; discipline 19, 23, 77, 88, 92, 130, 135, 139, 140, 153, 154, 155, 208n6, 210n6; Distinguished Service Order (DSO) 99, *108*, *123*, 124, 161, 171, 175, 199n18; "Doddites (school; also Hillside) 9, 13, 14, 15, 16, 157, 210n13; examinations (for military) 17, 19, 20, 158; family 5, 9, 11, 17, 70, 72, *75*, *76*, 81, 124, 125, 128, 130, 142, 145, 150, 157, 167, 168, 176, 177, 187ch1n3, 188n7, 214; Flimsy *65*, *136*, 211n18; Gen. (also Coal or Railroad) Strike of 1921 128, 129, 165, 166, 172, 180, 206n17, 214; ghosts, Plymouth 27, 28, 43; Hermitage (school, in Bath) 18, 19; "If Possible" orders 117, 154, 203n33, 210n2; intelligence work (China) 43, 55, 56, 57, 58, 159; Japanese (comments on) 49; Korea (comments on) 50, 51; leadership 4, 5, 118, 153, 199n26, 201n40; "Live Bait Squadron" 79, 80, 160; Madden Committee 4, 137, 138, 139, 154, 155, 156, 207n48, 210n10, 214; memorial service, Edward VII 64, 65, 66; memory 9, 10, 11, 24, 74, 83, 92, 203n38; Mentioned in Despatches *91*, *101*, 160, 163, 174, 175, 211n35; mess life 2, *25*, 26, 27, 43, 68, 69, 129, 130, 190n28; mobilization 77, 78, 79, 144, 160, 167; pay and expenses 20, 24, 25, 29, 53, 70, 71, 79, 125, 126, 142, 157, 158, 181n, 188n25, 189n1, 190n17; Pengwedhen, Helford (retirement home) 168, 173; promotion (Jerram's) 55, 70, 73, 81, 82, 138, 141, 142, 144, 158, 159, 161, 194n10, 208n61; Record of Service (official), 173n, 190n15, 194n12, 201n20, 205n11, 208n62, 209n1, 210n12, 211n18, 214; riding and horses 25, 26, 46, 58, 59, 76, 83, 91, 94, 98, 101, 109, 110, 117, 118, 119, 120, 121, 122, 125, 126, 127, 130, 131, 133, 137, 138, 148, 149, 150, 157, 162, 163, 164, 165, 167, 168, 189n1, 209n24; Royal Marines, reforms 4, 137, 138, 139, 154, 155, 156, 157, 207n47, 210n9, 214; Royal Naval College, Greenwich (education and training), 20, 21, 22, 23, 27, 69, 70, 145, 158; schooling (childhood) 11, 13, 14, 15, 18, 157, 187ch1n3, 210n13; Shanghai Fleet Reaction Plan 54, 55, 56; shooting and hunting 52, 53, 54, 61, 62, 63, 94, 133, 150, 163, 193n26; Talland, Cornwall 11, 12, 13, 19, 68, 70, 71, 74, 75, 80, 81, 142, 188n9, 195n26; tanks and armour 119, 120, 121, 122, 126, 133, 145, 146; 13 Royal Marine Battalion, 128, 129, 165, 166, 172, 206n18; traditions 3, 45, 18, 130, 154, 156, 166, 189n4, 195n33, 197n27, 211; training (officer) 2, 21, 22, 56, 75, 83, 104, 107, 108, 125, 126, 141, 144, 145, *146*, 147, 153, 158, 165, 168, 181n, 188n27, 190n27, 208n3, 209n25, 212n44; under enemy fire 85, 89, 94, 95, 99, 102, 104, 105, 106, 121, 160, 162; wife and marriage *71*, *72*, 73, 74, *76*, 77, 80, 81, 82, 123, 124, 125, 127, 137, 142, 143, 145, 149, 159, 165, 213; *see also* Companion of St. Michael and St. George (C<G); Croix de Guerre (France); and Distinguished Service Order (DSO); Jerram, Sibyl Victoria Greys O'Neill; promotions (Gen.); training (Gen.)
Jerram, Charles Samuel (father) 9, 10, 12, 13, 14, 16, 18, 19, 25, 71, 124, 127, 157, 176, 187ch1n3
Jerram, Helen Muriel (sister) 11, 27, 124, 176
Jerram, Jon (son and Army) 76, 130, 145, 177
Jerram, (Lowenna) Jennifer (daughter) *76*, 130, 145, 150, 177
Jerram, Maria Florence [Knight]—(mother) 9, 10, 11, 14, 15, 16, 17, 18, 70, 74, 176
Jerram, Martin Ralph Knight (brother) 11, 12, 13, 16, 17, 18, 19, 71, 84, 124, 157, 176, 188n7, 188n22
Jerram, Adm. Sir Martyn (uncle) 5, 18, 70, 77, 188n7, 188n21, 204n52
Jerram, (Rosemary) Morwenna

Index

(WRNS–daughter) *76*, 130, 145, *147*, 148, 177
Jerram, Rowland Christopher (brother) 11, 18, 61, 70, 124, 176, 188n7, 188n22, 193n33
Jerram, Brig. Roy Marty Jerram (cousin) 121, 188n, 204n
Jerram, Maj. Gen. Roy Martyn Jerram (cousin) 188n7
Jerram, Sibyl Victoria Greys O'Neill (wife) 19, 31, 70, *71*, 72, 73, 74, *76*, 77, 80, 81, 82, 123, 124, 125, *129*, 137, 142, 143, 145, 149, 159, 173
Jerrold, Douglas (Author) 196n2, 197n18, 197n29, 197n31, 200n3, 200n8, 201n35, 216
"Joe" (horse) 110, 121, 122
Juno 192n5, 211n20

Kendle, Lt. Col. George H. (RMA) 73, 194n15
Kent 58, 62, 194n35
Kiangtun (Chinese) 60, 61
Kiaochow (also Tsingtao, China) 3, 57, 58, 193n24
Kiddle, Adm. Edward B. (RN) 67, 194n43
killed and wounded 39, 42, 76, 88, 89, 91, 93, 97, 98, 99, 100, 104, 106, 118, 120, 149, 159, 167, 177, 180, 189n6, 197n29, 197n30, 197n32, 198n5, 198n9, 198n11, 198n12, 199n14, 199n28, 199n30, 200n, 204n42, 212n56
King, Commodore Henry D. (RN) 93, 199n31
King Alfred 43, 58, 61, 193n33
King George V Scholarships 165, 183, 205n14, 212n44
Knight, Charles (maternal "uncle") 70, 71
Knight, Edward (maternal grandfather) 9
Knight, Edward Frederick (maternal uncle) 10, 187ch1n4
Knight, Frederic (maternal cousin) 9, 17, 188n18
Knight family (maternal) 11, 17, 187ch1n2
Koe, Lt. Col. A. S. (Army) 88, 198n5
Korea 3, 48, 50, 63, 64, 159, 193n14, 194n39
Kum Kale, Turkey (Gallipoli) *see* Gallipoli

Lambton, Adm. Hedworth (RN) *see* Meux
Lancaster 32, 38, *40*, 191n51, 192n17
Lathbury, Maj. George P. (RMLI) 89, 198
Laurel 79, 80, 196n9
Law, Maj. Francis C. (RM) 85, 86, 198n37
Lawrance, Engineer Capt. William W. (RN) 39, 192n14
Lawrie, Maj. Gen. Charles Edward (Army) 100, 201n19
Learmont, Lt. J. (RA) 25, 26, 190n19
Leatham, Vice Adm. Eustace L. (RN) 78, 196n4
Lethbridge, Frank (Diplomat) 16, 17, 188n15
Liberty 79, 80, 196n9
Lion 124, 196n12
Lizard (Cornwall) 72, 80, 194n9
Loring, Vice Adm. Ernest (RN) 43, 44, 193n6
Lough, Lt. Gen. Reginald D. H. (RMLI) 84, 85, 86, 197n33
Lowther-Crofter, Vice Adm. Ernest G. (RN) 29, 33, 34, 191n40, 192n4
Luard, Col. Frank W. (RMLI) 83, 89, 93, 197n30
Lurcher 79, 80, 196n9

Mack Sennett Studio (California) 131
Madden, Adm. of the Fleet Charles E. (RN) 207n54
Madden Committee (on Royal Marines 1922) 4, 137, 138, 139, 154, 155, 156, 207n48, 210n10, 214
Mainz (German) 196n11
Malacca (British) 33
Malta 33, 38, 39, 40, *41*, 43, 44, 45, 83, 145, 180, 192n19, 205n5, 208n11
Mars 192n5
Marshman, Moore H. (RMLI) 29, 30, 191n39, 191n42
Marx, Adm. John L. (RN) 31, 32, 33, *37*, 191n47
Mathews, Mrs. Vera Laughton (RN—WRNS) 148, 209n20
Mathieu, Maj. Gen. Louis C. A. F. (France) 118, 163, 211n36
Matthews, Brig. Godfrey E. (RMLI) 83, 84, 85, 88, 197n30, 198n5
May, Rear Adm. Henry John (RN) 20, 23, 24, 189n2
May, 2nd Lt. Henry William Meads (Army) 20, 23, 24, 189n13
May, Lt. John (RM) 84, 197n32

McCracken, Lt. Gen. Frederick W. N. (Army) 105, 201n38
Meeson, Engineer Commander Edward H. T. (RN) 80, 196n10
Mercer, Gen. Sir David (RMLI) 82, 197n26
Meux, Adm. of the Fleet Hedworth (RN) 62, 194n34
Military Cross (MC) 98, 121, 124, 176, 189n13, 200n6
Milne, Sergeant Maj. (RMLI) 91
Mobile Naval Base Defence Organisation (Royal Marines) 137, 138, 139, 156, 207n49, 207n52, 207n55, 212n44
Molloy, Lt. Col. Percy (RMLI) 166, 206n21, 212n48
Monmouth 58, 191n49
Monro, Gen. Charles C. (Army) 199n34
Moorehead, Alan (author) 87, 197n31, 216
More-Molyneux, Adm. Robert Henry (RN) 20, 189n2
Morford, Brig. Albert Clarence (RM) *see* St. Clair-Morford, Brig. Albert Clarence (RM)
Morres, Maj. Elliott (RMLI) 26, 27, 78, 190n22, 190n29, 196n2
Morton, Capt. Herbert C. (RMLI) 200n38
Moulton, Maj. Gen. James L. (RM) 161, 189n9, 201n16, 211n32, 212n61
Mullins, Col. George J. H. (RMLI) 141, 208n60

Neame, Lt. Gen. Phillip (Army) 144, 208n2
Neilson, Maj. (J.) William (Canada) 111, 202n13, 203n14
New Zealand 88, 89, 114, 159, 160, 193n28, 198n13
Nicholas, Vice Adm. John (RN) 20, 189n2, 194n41
Nile 73, 170, 194n12
Nutt, Maj. Robert K.C. (RMLI) 24, 129, 190n16, 206n21

O'Neill, Carinna (sister-in-law) 127
O'Neill, Sibyl Victoria Greys (wife) *see* Jerram, Sibyl Victoria Greys
Oppy Wood (France) 103, 104, 106, 163, 201n36
Order of St. Michael and St. George 127, 163, 176, 178, 179, 205n60

Ormsby, Lt. Col. Robert D. (RMA) 138, 207*n*53
O'Sullivan, Maj. Gen. Hugh O. E. (RMLI) 73, 194*n*14
Owl Pie (Army Staff College Publication) 165, 212*n*46
An Owl's Wife (Army Staff College publication) 165, 212*n*46
Ozanne, Capt. Harold (RMLI) 79, 80, 196*n*6

Pakenham, Adm. William C. (RN) 133, 134, 206*n*34
Paper Hunt (or Paper Chase or Drag Hunt) 59, 122, 126, 193*n*26; *see also* Drag Hunt
Paris, Maj. Gen. Archibald (RMA) 82, 92, 93, 98, 161, 197*n*24, 200*n*8, 211*n*30
Parker, Maj. Edmund M. C. (RM) 208*n*58
Parker, Lance Corp. Walter R. (RMLI) 88, 198*n*8
Parry, Adm. John F. (RN) 128, 206*n*16, 212*n*49, 213
Parsons, Maj. Gen. Cunliffe Mc N. (RMLI) 83, 89, 93, 197*n*30
Paterson, Gen., Robert O. (RMLI>RMA) 208*n*61
Pekin (Chinese) 60
Pelly, Adm. Henry (RN) 189*n*2
Phibbs, Maj. Patrick W. O. (RM) 208*n*64
Phillimore, Adm. Richard F. (RN) 139, 140, 207*n*46
Pitcairn, Maj. John (Marines) 27, 190*n*27
Plymouth Division (Barracks), Royal Marines 20, 23, 24, 26, 27, 28, 68, 69, 77, 128, 137 139, 151, 158, 159, 165, 166, 167, 170, 171, 172, 190*n*21, 190*n*25, 208*n*61, 211*n*15, 212*n*52
Polperro, Cornwall 11, 12, 13, 28, 41, 142, 149, 188*n*20
Pommern (Finland) 143
Pontruet (France) 112, 114, 116, 118, 203*n*27
Port Arthur 51, 193*n*14
"Portland" (Horse) 59
Portsmouth Division (Barracks), Royal Marines 20, 207*n*51, 210*n*9, 211*n*17
Prebble, Capt. Allan Humphrey (RM) 208*n*6
Prince George 95, 199*n*36
principles of war 146, 208*n*6, 209*n*15
prize sword of honour (Royal Naval College, Greenwich)
23, 24, 183, 189*n*11, 190*n*15, 214
promotions (general) 20, 21, 22, 34, 113, 163, 167, 181*n*, 188*n*26, 189*n*10, 194*n*5, 200*n*2, 205*n*1, 208*n*62, 210*n*9, 213, 215
psc (Passed Staff College) 125, 128, 179, 189*n*14, 199*n*18, 201*n*13, 205*n*1

Quantico, Virginia (U.S. Marine Corps Barracks) *132*, *133*, 134, 156, 206*n*36, 207*n*37
Quinn, Maj. Hugh (Australia) 89, 90, 199*n*14
Quinn's Post (Gallipoli) 89, 198*n*12

Raikes, Maj. Gen. George L. (RMA) 208*n*61
Raleigh 30, 128, 130, *131*, 132, 133, *135*, 136, 154, 166, 172, 174, 205*n*12, 206*n*22, 207*n*39, 210*n*4, 214
Ramicourt (France) 119, 120, 163, 204*n*42
Rawlinson, Gen. Henry Seymour (Army) 123, 164, 205*n*57
Rees, Maj. Harold F. P. (RMLI) 180, 181
Regnicourt (France) 115, 120, 163
Rendell, Capt. Albert (RM) 208*n*58
Renown 39, 192*n*15
Riqueval (France) *112*, 114, 117, 162, 163, 203*n*31
Risk, Lt. Col. Charles E. (RMLI) 26, 181, 190*n*20
River Clyde (British) 95, 198*n*6, 199*n*35
Robert (Old, Menheniot Coachman) 13, 71
Rose, Vice Adm. Frank F. (RN) 80, 196*n*10
Rossignol Wood (France) 101, 102
Rowley, Brig. Gen. rank G. M. (Army) 109, 202*n*5
Royal Engineers (Gen.) 28, 111, 116, 117, 120, 188*n*25, 201*n*25, 206*n*15, 208*n*2
Royal Marine Artillery (also RMA) 19, 20, 21, 22, 23, 73, 83, 120, 137, 138, 144, 156, 179, 181*n*, 183*n*, 188*n*17, 188*n*23, 188*n*25, 188*n*26, 188*n*27, 189ch1*n*28, 189*n*1, 189*n*5, 189*n*11, 189*n*12, 189*n*14, 190*n*24, 193*n*29,
194*n*15, 197*n*21, 197*n*24, 203*n*18, 207*n*47, 207*n*57, 208ch10*n*61, 210*n*4, 211*n*17
Royal Marine Light Infantry (also RMLI) 19, 20, 21, 22, 25, 34, 35, 37, 57, 63, 73, 92, 95, 98, 158, 159, 170, 179, 180, 181*n*, 183, 188*n*26, 188*n*27, 189*n*1, 189*n*5, 189*n*6, 189*n*11, 190*n*16, 190*n*17, 190*n*20, 190*n*22, 190*n*23, 190*n*25, 190*n*29, 190*n*33, 191*n*39, 191*n*50, 192ch3*n*7, 192ch4*n*2, 194*n*3, 194*n*6, 194*n*10, 194*n*11, 195*n*21, 196*n*2, 196*n*6, 197*n*20, 197*n*26, 197*n*29, 197*n*30, 197*n*33, 197*n*34, 198*n*8, 198*n*9, 198*n*10, 198*n*12, 199*n*18, 199*n*25, 199*n*28, 200ch7*n*38, 200*n*4, 200*n*6, 200*n*12, 206*n*21, 206*n*24, 207*n*47, 207*n*53, 208*n*60, 208*n*61, 209*n*27, 210*n*4, 210*n*9
Royal Marines Military School (World War II) *146*, *147*, 167, 172, 209*n*17, 209*n*24, 212*n*55, 212*n*57
Royal Marines Officers Batches 19, 21, 24, 88, 153, 180–181, 181*n*, 188*n*27, 189*n*11, 208*n*6
Royal Marines, roles and duties 3, 4, 21, 22, 29, 30, 35, 43, 54, 55, 56, 68, 69, 73, 78, 83, 87, 130, 131, 137, 138, 154, 155, 156, 157, 200*n*2
Royal Military Academy, Woolwich 19, 20, 25, 26, 126, 158, 188*n*17, 188*n*25, 190*n*24
Royal Military College, Sandhurst 19, 20, 126, 158, 163, 181*n*, 188*n*17, 188*n*25, 201*n*18
Royal Naval College, Greenwich 20, *21*, *22*, 23, 24, 25, 126, 146, 158, 170, 181*n*, 183, 189*n*4, 190*n*15, 205*n*14, 214, 215
Royal Naval Division (63rd; also RND) 3, 75, 81, 82, 83, 87, 88, 97, 103, 159, 160, 161, 171, 179, 180, 196*n*2, 197*n*18, 197*n*21, 197*n*23, 197*n*24, 197*n*27, 197*n*29, 197*n*31, 199*n*23, 199*n*27, 199*n*31, 200ch7*n*38, 200*n*3, 200*n*5, 200*n*7, 200*n*8, 200*n*9, 200*n*10
Russo-Japanese War 33, 36, 38, 40, 45, 50, 51, *52*, 187*n*4, 193*n*16

Sackville-West, Maj. Gen. Charles John (Army) 98, 99, 201*n*13

Sah, Adm. (China) 66
St. Clair-Morford, Brig. Albert Clarence (RM) 75, 76, 98, 144, 195n29, 200n6, 212n55
St. Pol-sur-Ternoise (France) 113, 203n19
St. Quentin Canal (France) *see* Western Front
San Diego, California 132, 206n31
Sandhurst *see* Royal Military College, Sandhurst
Seath, Maj. Gen. Gordon H. (RMLI) 183
Seoul, Korea 50, 64, 194n39
Sequehart (France) 115, 119, 204n49
servant (officer's volunteer) 24, 26, 27, 28, 29, 30, 31, 35, 53, 63, 71, 81, 82, 89, 109, 125, 154, 191n44
Shanghai 45, 46, 47, 49, 52, 53, 54, 55, 57, 58, 59, 60, 61, 62, 66, 67, 137, 159, 193n11, 193n20, 193n23, 193n30
Shantung Peninsula (China) 3, 50, 51, 58, 193n14
Shewell, Maj. Arthur M. M. (RMLI) 181
ships (miscellaneous): *Bismarck* (German) 80, 196n11; *Braemar Castle* 83; *Britannic* 95, 199n37; *Cawdor Castle* 83; *Gloucester Castle* 88; *Kiangtun* (Chinese) 60, 61; *Mainz* (German) 196n11; *Malacca* (British) 33; *Pekin* (Chinese) 60; *Pommern* (Finland) 143; *River Clyde* (British) 95, 198n6, 199n35; *U-9* (German) 196n13
ships (Royal Navy): *Aboukir* 79, 80, 160, 171, 196n6, 196n13, 196n14, 214; *AE1* 74, 195n28; *AE2* 74, 195n28; *Algerine* 46, 193n12; *Arrogant* 192n5; *Astraea* 46, 47, **48**, **49**, 52, **53**, 54, 55, **57**, 58, 60, 61, 62, 64, 66, 67, 143, 159, 170, 171, 174, 193n3, 193n13, 194n43; *Bedford* 58; *Bulwark* 190n32, 200n38; *Cadmus* 45, 193n12; *Caesar* 77, 95, 171, 174, 195n32; *Capetown* 134, 136; *Centurion* 191n50; *Charybdis* 67, 159, 171, 174, 193n13; *Clio* 45, 46, 58, 62, 174, 193n12; *Constance* 206n22; *Cressy* 79, 80, 160, 171, 196n6, 196n13, 196n14, 214; *Curlew* 206n22; *Defiance* 141, 208n59; *Devonshire* 195n30;

Diana 192n5; *Drake* 167, 172; *Dreadnought* 34, 40, 58, 68, 77, 158, 191n38, 191n49, 194n1; *Eclipse* 74, 82, 171, 174, 195n27, 195n28; *Euryalus* 77, 78, 79, 81, 91, 159, 160, 171, 174, 196n3, 197n17; *Excellent* 189n1; *Exmouth* 73, 74, 171, 195n19; *Flora* 47, 52, 54, **60**, 62, **63**, 65, 159, 170, 171, 174, 189n2, 193n13, 194n41; *Formidable* 192n7; *Highflyer* 73, 171, 174, 195n18; *Hogue* 29, 32, 43, 79, 80, 158, 160, 170, 171, 174, 191n38, 191n42, 192n4, 196n6, 196n13, 196n14, 214; *Howe* 190n32; *Implacable* 197n17; *Impregnable* (ex–*Howe*, ex–*Bulwark*) 28, 167, 172, 190n32, 207n46; *Irresistible* 180; *Juno* 192n5, 211n20; *Kent* 58, 62, 194n35; *King Alfred* 43, 58, 61, 193n33; *Lancaster* 32, 38, **40**, 191n51, 192n17; *Laurel* 79, 80, 196n9; *Liberty* 79, 80, 196n9; *Lion* 124, 196n12; *Lurcher* 79, 80, 196n9; *Mars* 192n5; *Monmouth* 58, 191n49; *Nile* 73, 170, 194n12; *Prince George* 95, 199n36; *Raleigh* 30, 128, 130, **131**, 132, 133, **135**, 136, 154, 166, 172, 174, 205n12, 206n22, 207n39, 210n4, 214; *Renown* 39, 192n15; *Spartiate* 43, 170, 174, 193n4; *Suffolk* 32, **34**, **35**, 37, **38**, **40**, 41, 50, 73, 83, 138, 158, 170, 171, 174, 191n3, 192n4, 192n5, 192n7, 192n8, 192n17, 194n12, 196n12, 209n18, 211n20; *Swiftsure* 73, 159, 171, 174, 194n13, 194n14, 195n16; *Tamar* 159, 170, 193n5; *Triumph* 85, 195n16
shrapnel 84, 90, 105, 121, 199n17
Shute, Gen. Cameron (Army) 98, 99, 100, 200n9
Simmons, Capt. Percy (RMLI) 189n6
Sinclair, Maj. Robert (RMLI) 181
Sketches of the Royal Marine Barracks Stonehouse 129
Sketchley, Maj. Ernest F. P. (RMLI) 92, 98, 199n25, 200n8
Soochow Creek (Shanghai) 45, **55**, 56

Spartiate 43, 170, 174, 193n4
Spender, Lt. Col. Wilfred S. (Army) 100, 102, 110, 201n24
Spraggett, Col. Richard W. (RM) 130, 135, 136, 206n24
Staff College, Camberley (Army) 100, 124, 125, 127, 128, 130, 134, 141, 149, 154, 156, 162, 165, 166, 172, 174, 179, 183, 187n5, 201n18, 202n2, 205n4, 205n5, 208n2, 209n26, 212n45, 214, 215
staff system (British Army) 55, 81, 95, 97, 100, 105, 109, 110, 111, 112, 113, 114, 117, 120, 121, 154, 160, 161, 165, 166, 199n19, 201n23, 202n2, 205n1, 209n17
Stafford, Maj. John Howard (Army) 100, 201n25
Stewart, Brig. Gen. Ian (Army) 105, 201n43
Stonehouse Barracks, Royal Marines 20, **23**, **25**, 68, 74, **129**, **139**, 195n26, 207n51; *see also* Plymouth (Barracks) Division, Royal Marines
Stroud, Lt. Gen. Edward J. (RMLI) 95, 200n38
Strugnell, Maj. Harold F. W. (RMLI) 73, 74, 195n21
Sturges, Lt. Gen., Robert (RM) 148, 177, 209n22
Suffolk 32, **34**, **35**, 37, **38**, **40**, 41, 50, 73, 83, 138, 158, 170, 171, 174, 191n3, 192n4, 192n5, 192n7, 192n8, 192n17, 194n12, 196n12, 209n18, 211n20
"Surefoot" (also "Sugarfoot"; horse) 162
Swiftsure 73, 159, 171, 174, 194n13, 194n14, 195n16

Tagg, Ernest J. B. (RMLI) 97, 98, 200n4
Tamar 159, 170, 193n5
tanks (Also Royal Tank Corps or Regiment) 121, 126, 183, 199n18, 204n52, 205n8
31st Division Chap. 8, 106, 110, 162, 171, 174, 201n21, 214
Thompson, Maj. Gen. Julian (RM) x, 198n4, 211n17, 216
Thwaites, Gen. William (Army) 109, 110, 113, 128, 202n3
training (general) 2, 20, 50, 54, 75, 82, 83, 110, 111, 138, 140, 154, 155, 156, 181n, 189n4, 194n2, 206n27, 206n31,

206n36, 207n48, 207n51, 209n25, 214
trenches 51, 190n26, 208n8; *see also* Gallipoli and Western Front
Triumph 85, 195n16
Trotman, Gen. Sir Charles N. (RMLI) 81, **82**, 83, 89, 92, 93, 95, 97, 98, 160, 161, 197n20, 211n29, 211n31
Tupman, Col. John A. (RMLI) 83, 197n29

U-9 (German) 196n13
United States 2, 131, 156, 166, 182, 192n1, 206n32, 210n8
United States Marine Corps 132, 133, 134, 206n31, 206n36, 207n37, 210n8

Vann, Lt. Col. Bernard William (Army) 118, 120, 204n42
Victoria (Queen) 19
Victoria Cross (VC) 85, 88, 99, 110, 179, 183, 198n8, 199n14, 199n26, 200n6
Vimy Ridge 103, 105, 108, 201n33
Vladivostok 48, 51

Wace, Maj. Stephen A. (RMA) 19, 189n28
Walmesby, Capt. Charles T. J. P. (RM) 93, 199n27
Wanless-O'Gowan, Maj. Gen. Robert (Army) 101, 201n22
Wei-hai-Wei (China) 48, 49, **50**, **58**, **61**, 64, **65**, 143, 193n14
Welch, Lt. Col. Alfred Davis (RMLI) 181
Weller, Lt. Col. Bernard (RMLI) 68, 69, 81, 82, 93, 194n3
Western Front 3, 97, 101, 107, 123, 160, 161, 162, 171, 172, 182, 196n2, 198n1, 200n1, 201n39, 202n12, 203n26, 203n32, 204n46, 204n51, 208n13, 217; Armistice Day 122, 123, 164; casualties 103, 106, 116, 119; embusque 106, 109, 114; Hindenburg Line 101, 105, 112, 114, 117, 118, 123, 145, 163, 164, 201n28, 201n36, 202n2, 203n31, 203n34, 203n35, 203n37, 204n42, 204n48; open warfare (also mobile operations) 111, 114, 119, 120, 122, 123, 162, 203n26; Portuguese Divisions 110, 182, 202n12; Royal Engineers (also Sappers) 108, 111, 112, 116, 117, 120, 137, 206n15; Royal Naval Division 97, 103; St. Quentin (Canal) **111**, **112**, 114, **115**, **116**, 117, 118, 120, 123, 163, 164, 201n28, 202n17, 203n31, 203n34, 203n39, 204n39, 205n59, 211n39; Sambre Canal 121, 123; Somme 98, 103, 160, 200n7, 200n9, 200n10, 201n26; trenches, 97, 98, 102, 103, 104, 105, 110, 113, 114, 115, 116, 118, 163, 203n32, 205n56
Weston, Lt. Gen. Eric C. (RMA) 183, 212n44
White, Col. Archie C.T. (Army) 110, 202n10
White, Maj. Richard N. (RMLI) 73, 74, 195n22
Whitechapel Bell Foundry 74, 195n26
Wilhelm II **37**, 158, 159, 187n4
Williams, Commander Alfred M. (RN) 80, 196n16

Williams, Capt. Cuthbert (RMLI) 79, 80, 196n6
Williams, Gen. Guy C.W. (RE) 166, 206n15
Williams, Maj. Kenneth Grenville (Army) 203n25
Willow Pattern Tea House (Shanghai) 46, **47**
Wilson, Adm. of the Fleet Arthur K. (RN) 30, 191n41
Wilson, Col. Leslie Orme (RMLI) 157
wireless (radio/telegraphy) 9, 28, 31, 62, 79, 80, 117, 158, 160, 170, 180, 190–191n33, 192n5
Woolwich *see* Royal Military Academy, Woolwich
Woolwich Division (Barracks), Royal Marines 26, 190n
Worth, Engineer Commander Frederick (RN) 31, 191n24
wounded (in action) 75, 76, 80, 90, 91, 93, 97, 99, 100, 102, 117, 120, 124, 176, 181, 198n37, 200n4, 200n8, 202n6, 202n14
Wright, "Shiner" (Royal Marine servant) 31, **53**, 63, 71, 82, 191n45
WRNS (Women Royal Naval Service) 144, 147, 148, 177, 179, 208n5

XIII Corps Chap. 8, 104, 109, 126, 154, 162, 171, 174, 201n38, 204n53, 210n3, 212n41, 214

Zeebrugge 1918 Raid on (Royal Marines) 156, 163, 166, 180, 194n3, 198n36

www.ingramcontent.com/pod-product-compliance
Ingram Content Group UK Ltd.
Pitfield, Milton Keynes, MK11 3LW, UK
UKHW050531150426
5217IPUK00026B/1888